50% OFF ACCUPLACER Prep Course

Dear Customer,

We consider it an honor and a privilege that you chose our ACCUPLACER Study Guide. As a way of showing our appreciation and to help us better serve you, we have partnered with Mometrix Test Prep to offer you **50% off their online ACCUPLACER Test Prep Course.** Many ACCUPLACER courses are needlessly expensive and don't deliver enough value. With their course, you get access to the best ACCUPLACER prep material, and you only pay half price.

Mometrix has structured their online course to perfectly complement your printed study guide. The ACCUPLACER Online Course contains **in-depth lessons** that cover all the most important topics, **200+ video reviews** that explain difficult concepts, over **850+ practice questions** to ensure you feel prepared, and more than **500+ flashcards** so you can study on the go.

Online ACCUPLACER Test Prep Course

Topics Include:

- Reading
  - Information and Ideas
  - Rhetoric
  - Vocabulary
- Writing
  - Foundations of Grammar
  - Word Usage and Confusion
  - Punctuation
- Mathematics
  - Arithmetic
  - Quantitative Reasoning, Algebra, and Statistics
  - Advanced Algebra and Functions

Course Features:

- ACCUPLACER Study Guide
  - Get content that complements our best-selling study guide.
- Full-Length Practice Tests
  - With over 850 practice questions, you can test yourself again and again.
- Mobile Friendly
  - If you need to study on the go, the course is easily accessible from your mobile device.
- ACCUPLACER Flashcards
  - Their course includes a flashcard mode consisting of over 200 content cards to help you study.

To receive this discount, visit their website at mometrix.com/university/accuplacer or simply scan this QR code with your smartphone. At the checkout page, enter the discount code: **TPBACCU50**

If you have any questions or concerns, please contact Mometrix at support@mometrix.com

SCAN HERE

FREE Test Taking Tips Video/DVD Offer

To better serve you, we created videos covering test taking tips that we want to give you for FREE. **These videos cover world-class tips that will help you succeed on your test.**

We just ask that you send us feedback about this product. Please let us know what you thought about it—whether good, bad, or indifferent.

To get your **FREE videos**, you can use the QR code below or email freevideos@studyguideteam.com with "Free Videos" in the subject line and the following information in the body of the email:

    a. The title of your product

    b. Your product rating on a scale of 1-5, with 5 being the highest

    c. Your feedback about the product

If you have any questions or concerns, please don't hesitate to contact us at info@studyguideteam.com.

Thank you!

Interested in buying more than 10 copies of our product? Contact us about bulk discounts:
bulkorders@studyguideteam.com

ISBN 13: 9781637756355

Table of Contents

Welcome

Dear Reader,

Welcome to your new Test Prep Books study guide! We are pleased that you chose us to help you prepare for your exam. There are many study options to choose from, and we appreciate you choosing us. Studying can be a daunting task, but we have designed a smart, effective study guide to help prepare you for what lies ahead.

Whether you're a parent helping your child learn and grow, a high school student working hard to get into your dream college, or a nursing student studying for a complex exam, we want to help give you the tools you need to succeed. We hope this study guide gives you the skills and the confidence to thrive, and we can't thank you enough for allowing us to be part of your journey.

In an effort to continue to improve our products, we welcome feedback from our customers. We look forward to hearing from you. Suggestions, success stories, and criticisms can all be communicated by emailing us at info@studyguideteam.com.

Sincerely,
Test Prep Books Team

FREE Videos/DVD OFFER

Doing well on your exam requires both knowing the test content and understanding how to use that knowledge to do well on the test. We offer completely FREE test taking tip videos. **These videos cover world-class tips that you can use to succeed on your test.**

To get your **FREE videos**, you can use the QR code below or email freevideos@studyguideteam.com with "Free Videos" in the subject line and the following information in the body of the email:

   a. The title of your product
   b. Your product rating on a scale of 1-5, with 5 being the highest
   c. Your feedback about the product

If you have any questions or concerns, please don't hesitate to contact us at info@studyguideteam.com.

Quick Overview

As you draw closer to taking your exam, effective preparation becomes more and more important. Thankfully, you have this study guide to help you get ready. Use this guide to help keep your studying on track and refer to it often.

This study guide contains several key sections that will help you be successful on your exam. The guide contains tips for what you should do the night before and the day of the test. Also included are test-taking tips. Knowing the right information is not always enough. Many well-prepared test takers struggle with exams. These tips will help equip you to accurately read, assess, and answer test questions.

A large part of the guide is devoted to showing you what content to expect on the exam and to helping you better understand that content. In this guide are practice test questions so that you can see how well you have grasped the content. Then, answer explanations are provided so that you can understand why you missed certain questions.

Don't try to cram the night before you take your exam. This is not a wise strategy for a few reasons. First, your retention of the information will be low. Your time would be better used by reviewing information you already know rather than trying to learn a lot of new information. Second, you will likely become stressed as you try to gain a large amount of knowledge in a short amount of time. Third, you will be depriving yourself of sleep. So be sure to go to bed at a reasonable time the night before. Being well-rested helps you focus and remain calm.

Be sure to eat a substantial breakfast the morning of the exam. If you are taking the exam in the afternoon, be sure to have a good lunch as well. Being hungry is distracting and can make it difficult to focus. You have hopefully spent lots of time preparing for the exam. Don't let an empty stomach get in the way of success!

When travelling to the testing center, leave earlier than needed. That way, you have a buffer in case you experience any delays. This will help you remain calm and will keep you from missing your appointment time at the testing center.

Be sure to pace yourself during the exam. Don't try to rush through the exam. There is no need to risk performing poorly on the exam just so you can leave the testing center early. Allow yourself to use all of the allotted time if needed.

Remain positive while taking the exam even if you feel like you are performing poorly. Thinking about the content you should have mastered will not help you perform better on the exam.

Once the exam is complete, take some time to relax. Even if you feel that you need to take the exam again, you will be well served by some down time before you begin studying again. It's often easier to convince yourself to study if you know that it will come with a reward!

Test-Taking Strategies

1. Predicting the Answer

When you feel confident in your preparation for a multiple-choice test, try predicting the answer before reading the answer choices. This is especially useful on questions that test objective factual knowledge. By predicting the answer before reading the available choices, you eliminate the possibility that you will be distracted or led astray by an incorrect answer choice. You will feel more confident in your selection if you read the question, predict the answer, and then find your prediction among the answer choices. After using this strategy, be sure to still read all of the answer choices carefully and completely. If you feel unprepared, you should not attempt to predict the answers. This would be a waste of time and an opportunity for your mind to wander in the wrong direction.

2. Reading the Whole Question

Too often, test takers scan a multiple-choice question, recognize a few familiar words, and immediately jump to the answer choices. Test authors are aware of this common impatience, and they will sometimes prey upon it. For instance, a test author might subtly turn the question into a negative, or he or she might redirect the focus of the question right at the end. The only way to avoid falling into these traps is to read the entirety of the question carefully before reading the answer choices.

3. Looking for Wrong Answers

Long and complicated multiple-choice questions can be intimidating. One way to simplify a difficult multiple-choice question is to eliminate all of the answer choices that are clearly wrong. In most sets of answers, there will be at least one selection that can be dismissed right away. If the test is administered on paper, the test taker could draw a line through it to indicate that it may be ignored; otherwise, the test taker will have to perform this operation mentally or on scratch paper. In either case, once the obviously incorrect answers have been eliminated, the remaining choices may be considered. Sometimes identifying the clearly wrong answers will give the test taker some information about the correct answer. For instance, if one of the remaining answer choices is a direct opposite of one of the eliminated answer choices, it may well be the correct answer. The opposite of obviously wrong is obviously right! Of course, this is not always the case. Some answers are obviously incorrect simply because they are irrelevant to the question being asked. Still, identifying and eliminating some incorrect answer choices is a good way to simplify a multiple-choice question.

4. Don't Overanalyze

Anxious test takers often overanalyze questions. When you are nervous, your brain will often run wild, causing you to make associations and discover clues that don't actually exist. If you feel that this may be a problem for you, do whatever you can to slow down during the test. Try taking a deep breath or counting to ten. As you read and consider the question, restrict yourself to the particular words used by the author. Avoid thought tangents about what the author *really* meant, or what he or she was *trying* to say. The only things that matter on a multiple-choice test are the words that are actually in the question. You must avoid reading too much into a multiple-choice question, or supposing that the writer meant something other than what he or she wrote.

5. No Need for Panic

It is wise to learn as many strategies as possible before taking a multiple-choice test, but it is likely that you will come across a few questions for which you simply don't know the answer. In this situation, avoid panicking. Because

3

most multiple-choice tests include dozens of questions, the relative value of a single wrong answer is small. As much as possible, you should compartmentalize each question on a multiple-choice test. In other words, you should not allow your feelings about one question to affect your success on the others. When you find a question that you either don't understand or don't know how to answer, just take a deep breath and do your best. Read the entire question slowly and carefully. Try rephrasing the question a couple of different ways. Then, read all of the answer choices carefully. After eliminating obviously wrong answers, make a selection and move on to the next question.

6. Confusing Answer Choices

When working on a difficult multiple-choice question, there may be a tendency to focus on the answer choices that are the easiest to understand. Many people, whether consciously or not, gravitate to the answer choices that require the least concentration, knowledge, and memory. This is a mistake. When you come across an answer choice that is confusing, you should give it extra attention. A question might be confusing because you do not know the subject matter to which it refers. If this is the case, don't eliminate the answer before you have affirmatively

settled on another. When you come across an answer choice of this type, set it aside as you look at the remaining choices. If you can confidently assert that one of the other choices is correct, you can leave the confusing answer aside. Otherwise, you will need to take a moment to try to better understand the confusing answer choice. Rephrasing is one way to tease out the sense of a confusing answer choice.

7. Your First Instinct

Many people struggle with multiple-choice tests because they overthink the questions. If you have studied sufficiently for the test, you should be prepared to trust your first instinct once you have carefully and completely read the question and all of the answer choices. There is a great deal of research suggesting that the mind can come to the correct conclusion very quickly once it has obtained all of the relevant information. At times, it may seem to you as if your intuition is working faster even than your reasoning mind. This may in fact be true. The knowledge you obtain while studying may be retrieved from your subconscious before you have a chance to work out the associations that support it. Verify your instinct by working out the reasons that it should be trusted.

8. Key Words

Many test takers struggle with multiple-choice questions because they have poor reading comprehension skills. Quickly reading and understanding a multiple-choice question requires a mixture of skill and experience. To help with this, try jotting down a few key words and phrases on a piece of scrap paper. Doing this concentrates the process of reading and forces the mind to weigh the relative importance of the question's parts. In selecting words and phrases to write down, the test taker thinks about the question more deeply and carefully. This is especially true for multiple-choice questions that are preceded by a long prompt.

4

9. Subtle Negatives

One of the oldest tricks in the multiple-choice test writer's book is to subtly reverse the meaning of a question with a word like *not* or *except*. If you are not paying attention to each word in the question, you can easily be led astray by this trick. For instance, a common question format is, "Which of the following is...?" Obviously, if the question instead is, "Which of the following is not...?," then the answer will be quite different. Even worse, the test makers are aware of the potential for this mistake and will include one answer choice that would be correct if the question were not negated or reversed. A test taker who misses the reversal will find what he or she believes to be a correct answer and will be so confident that he or she will fail to reread the question and discover the original error. The only way to avoid this is to practice a wide variety of multiple-choice questions and to pay close attention to each and every word.

10. Reading Every Answer Choice

It may seem obvious, but you should always read every one of the answer choices! Too many test takers fall into the habit of scanning the question and assuming that they understand the question because they recognize a few key words. From there, they pick the first answer choice that answers the question they believe they have read. Test takers who read all of the answer choices might discover that one of the latter answer choices is actually *more* correct. Moreover, reading all of the answer choices can remind you of facts related to the question that can help you arrive at the correct answer. Sometimes, a misstatement or incorrect detail in one of the latter answer choices will trigger your memory of the subject and will enable you to find the right answer. Failing to read all of the answer choices is like not reading all of the items on a restaurant menu: you might miss out on the perfect choice.

11. Spot the Hedges

One of the keys to success on multiple-choice tests is paying close attention to every word. This is never truer than with words like *almost*, *most*, *some*, and *sometimes*. These words are called "hedges" because they indicate that a statement is not totally true or not true in every place and time. An absolute statement will contain no hedges, but in many subjects, the answers are not always straightforward or absolute. There are always exceptions to the rules in these subjects. For this reason, you should favor those multiple-choice questions that contain hedging language.

The presence of qualifying words indicates that the author is taking special care with his or her words, which is certainly important when composing the right answer. After all, there are many ways to be wrong, but there is only one way to be right! For this reason, it is wise to avoid answers that are absolute when taking a multiple-choice test. An absolute answer is one that says things are either all one way or all another. They often include words like *every*, *always*, *best*, and *never*. If you are taking a multiple-choice test in a subject that doesn't lend itself to absolute answers, be on your guard if you see any of these words.

12. Long Answers

In many subject areas, the answers are not simple. As already mentioned, the right answer often requires hedges. Another common feature of the answers to a complex or subjective question are qualifying clauses, which are groups of words that subtly modify the meaning of the sentence. If the question or answer choice describes a rule to which there are exceptions or the subject matter is complicated, ambiguous, or confusing, the correct answer will require many words in order to be expressed clearly and accurately. In essence, you should not be deterred by answer choices that seem excessively long. Oftentimes, the author of the text will not be able to write the correct answer without offering some qualifications and

modifications. Your job is to read the answer choices thoroughly and completely and to select the one that most

5

accurately and precisely answers the question.

13. Restating to Understand

Sometimes, a question on a multiple-choice test is difficult not because of what it asks but because of how it is written. If this is the case, restate the question or answer choice in different words. This process serves a couple of important purposes. First, it forces you to concentrate on the core of the question. In order to rephrase the question accurately, you have to understand it well. Rephrasing the question will concentrate your mind on the key words and ideas. Second, it will present the information to your mind in a fresh way. This process may trigger your memory and render some useful scrap of information picked up while studying.

14. True Statements

Sometimes an answer choice will be true in itself, but it does not answer the question. This is one of the main reasons why it is essential to read the question carefully and completely before proceeding to the answer choices. Too often, test takers skip ahead to the answer choices and look for true statements. Having found one of these, they are content to select it without reference to the question above. The savvy test taker will always read the entire question before turning to the answer choices. Then, having settled on a correct answer choice, he or she will refer to the original question and ensure that the selected answer is relevant. The mistake of choosing a correct-but-irrelevant answer choice is especially common on questions related to specific pieces of objective knowledge.

15. No Patterns

One of the more dangerous ideas that circulates about multiple-choice tests is that the correct answers tend to fall into patterns. These erroneous ideas range from a belief that B and C are the most common right answers, to the idea that an unprepared test-taker should answer "A-B-A-C-A-D-A-B-A." It cannot be emphasized enough that pattern-seeking of this type is exactly the WRONG way to approach a multiple-choice test. To begin with, it is highly unlikely that the test maker will plot the correct answers according to some predetermined pattern. The questions are scrambled and delivered in a random order. Furthermore, even if the test maker was following a pattern in the assignation of correct answers, there is no reason why the test taker would know which pattern he or she was using. Any attempt to discern a pattern in the answer choices is a waste of time and a distraction from the real work of taking the test. A test taker would be much better served by extra preparation before the test than by reliance on a pattern in the answers.

Introduction to the ACCUPLACER Exam

Function of the Test

ACCUPLACER is an adaptive, computerized test offered by the College Board and used by some colleges and high schools to determine placement of students in programs appropriate to the students' skill level. The test is offered nation-wide, at any college or high school that chooses to use it. Test-takers are almost always students of schools that use the ACCUPLACER in their course selection and placement efforts. Schools can also use the ACCUPLACER to assess students' skill levels and identify specific areas in which the students need improvement. Scores are generally used only by the college or high school the student is already attending for placement and instruction at that school.

According to the College Board, more than 1,500 secondary and post-secondary institutions are currently using the ACCUPLACER. Over 7.5 million ACCUPLACER tests are administered in a typical year. The College Board recommends that ACCUPLACER scores be used in conjunction with other variables including high school GPA, the number of years a student has taken coursework in a particular subject area, other test scores such as the SAT or ACT, as well as non-cognitive information such as motivation, family support, and time management skills, in order to place students in courses of appropriate difficulty.

Test Administration

ACCUPLACER is offered by computer, usually by the school that wants to use its results, whenever a student makes an appointment with the school to take it. In cases where a student is not able to take the test at the student's school, arrangements can sometimes be made to take the test at a more convenient location on another school's campus.

Fees for taking the ACCUPLACER vary from school to school. Students sometimes do not pay a fee at all; rather, the school pays the College Board for the right to administer the test and then students take it for free. Students may retake the ACCUPLACER at the discretion of the school administering the test and using its results. Students with documented disabilities can make arrangements, through the test center offering the ACCUPLACER, to take the test with appropriate accommodations, including the potential availability of a written version of the test.

Test Format

The core of the ACCUPLACER is five multiple-choice subject area tests: Arithmetic; Quantitative Reasoning, Algebra, and Statistics; Advanced Algebra and Functions, Reading, and Writing. The Writing test has twenty-five questions. It contains one literary passage with five associated questions, and four informational passages that each have five associated questions. A college may ask a student to test in any or all of the five subject areas, depending on the student's and the school's needs. There is also a sixth section, called the WritePlacer, in which students must write a brief essay. Finally, there are four multiple-choice ESL sections of the ACCUPLACER, which schools may ask students, for whom English is a second language, to take.

The multiple-choice sections of the ACCUPLACER are administered by computer. There is no time-limit, so test takers should feel free to work at their own pace. A typical test section might take around 30 minutes to complete. The test is adaptive, meaning it adjusts the difficulty of each question based on the student's success on the previous questions. The more questions a test-taker gets right, the harder succeeding questions will be and vice-versa. This allows the test to more readily determine test-takers' ability levels without wasting time on questions far above or far below what the test-takers can answer.

Section	Questions	Description
Arithmetic	20	Basic arithmetic and problem solving
Quantitative Reasoning, Algebra, and Statistics	20	Basic algebra, geometry, probability, statistics
Advanced Algebra and Functions	20	Advanced algebra, functions, trigonometry
Reading	20	Information and ideas, rhetoric, synthesis, vocabulary
Writing	25	Expression of ideas, standard English conventions
WritePlacer	1 essay	Effective written communication
ESL- Language Use	20	English grammar
ESL- Listening	20	Understanding spoken English communication
ESL- Reading Skills	20	Comprehension of short written English passages
ESL- Sentence Meaning	20	Understanding the meaning of English sentences

Scoring

The ACCUPLACER subject area tests are scored on a scale from 20 to 120. Schools are free to use the scores for placement as they see fit, given that the difficulty of coursework varies from school to school. A typical community college might separate scores into tiered groups from 50 to 75, from 75 to 99, and from 100 to 120. Scores are typically generated instantly by the computer, but may not be available from the school administering the test until the school has had a chance to review the scores and use them for placement purposes.

Recent Developments

In September 2016, the College Board made "next-generation" ACCUPLACER tests available to schools. Schools have the option of administering the next-generation tests or the older tests, but not both. The new next-generation tests include redesigned reading, writing, and math content, intended to more effectively help schools place students in classes that match their skill level.

Study Prep Plan for the ACCUPLACER Exam

1   **Schedule -** Use one of our study schedules below or come up with one of your own.

2   **Relax -** Test anxiety can hurt even the best students. There are many ways to reduce stress. Find the one that works best for you.

3   **Execute -** Once you have a good plan in place, be sure to stick to it.

One Week Study Schedule		
	Day 1	Arithmetic
	Day 2	Quantitative Reasoning, Algebra, and Statistics
	Day 3	Advanced Algebra and Functions
	Day 4	Reading Test
	Day 5	Writing
	Day 6	Practice Test #1
	Day 7	Take Your Exam!

Two Week Study Schedule			
Day 1	Arithmetic	Day 8	Reading Test
Day 2	Percent	Day 9	Synthesis
Day 3	Quantitative Reasoning, Algebra, and Statistics	Day 10	Writing
Day 4	Linear Equations	Day 11	Punctuation
Day 5	Geometry Concepts	Day 12	Practice Test #1
Day 6	Advanced Algebra and Functions	Day 13	Practice Tests #2 & #3
Day 7	Radical and Rational Equations	Day 14	Take Your Exam!

9

This material is provided for exam preparation purposes only and does not indicate an endorsement of any specific scientific, political, or religious point of view. © TPB Publishing. You have been licensed one copy of this document for personal use only. Any other reproduction or redistribution is strictly prohibited. All rights reserved.

	One Month Study Schedule				
Day 1	Arithmetic	Day 11	Right Triangles: Pythagorean Theorem...	Day 21	Vocabulary
Day 2	Fraction Operations	Day 12	Advanced Algebra and Functions	Day 22	Writing
Day 3	Number Comparison and Equivalents	Day 13	Linear Applications and Graphs	Day 23	Effective Language Use
Day 4	Quantitative Reasoning, Algebra...	Day 14	Quadratics	Day 24	Usage
Day 5	Analyzing Proportional Relationships...	Day 15	Radical and Rational Equations	Day 25	Punctuation
Day 6	Linear Equations	Day 16	Trigonometry	Day 26	Appositive Phrases
Day 7	Linear Applications and Graphs	Day 17	Reading Test	Day 27	Practice Test #1
Day 8	Descriptive Statistics	Day 18	Rhetoric	Day 28	Practice Tests #2 & #3
Day 9	Perimeter and Area	Day 19	Analyzing the Structure of a Text	Day 29	Practice Tests #4 - #6
Day 10	Plane Geometry	Day 20	Synthesis	Day 30	Take Your Exam!

Build your own prep plan by visiting:

testprepbooks.com/prep

As you study for your test, we'd like to take the opportunity to remind you that you are capable of great things! With the right tools and dedication, you truly can do anything you set your mind to. The fact that you are holding this book right now shows how committed you are. In case no one has told you lately, you've got this! Our intention behind including this coloring page is to give you the chance to take some time to engage your creative side when you need a little brain-break from studying. As a company, we want to encourage people like you to achieve their dreams by providing good quality study materials for the tests and certifications that improve careers and change lives. As individuals, many of us have taken such tests in our careers, and we know how challenging this process can be. While we can't come alongside you and cheer you on personally, we can offer you the space to recall your purpose, reconnect with your passion, and refresh your brain through an artistic practice. We wish you every success, and happy studying!

Bonus Content

We host multiple bonus items online, including all 6 practice tests in digital format. Scan the QR code or go to this link to access this content:

testprepbooks.com/bonus/accuplacer

The first time you access the tests, you will need to register as a "new user" and verify your email address.

If you have any issues, please email support@testprepbooks.com.

Arithmetic

Whole Number Operations

Addition

Addition is the combination of two numbers so their quantities are added together cumulatively. The sign for an addition operation is the + symbol. For example, 9 + 6 = 15. The 9 and 6 combine to achieve a cumulative value, called a **sum**.

Addition holds the commutative property, which means that the order of the numbers in an addition equation can be switched without altering the result. The formula for the commutative property is a + b = b + a. The following examples can demonstrate how the commutative property works:

$$7 = 3 + 4 = 4 + 3 = 7$$

$$20 = 12 + 8 = 8 + 12 = 20$$

Addition also holds the **associative property**, which means that the grouping of numbers does not matter in an addition problem. In other words, the presence or absence of parentheses is irrelevant. The formula for the associative property is (a + b) + c = a + (b + c). Here are some examples of the associative property at work:

$$30 = (6 + 14) + 10 = 6 + (14 + 10) = 30$$

$$35 = 8 + (2 + 25) = (8 + 2) + 25 = 35$$

Subtraction

Subtraction is taking away one number from another, so their quantities are reduced. The sign designating a subtraction operation is the − symbol, and the result is called the **difference.** For example,

$$9 - 6 = 3$$

The number *6* detracts from the number *9* to reach the difference *3*.

Unlike addition, subtraction follows neither the commutative nor associative properties. The order and grouping in subtraction impact the result.

$$15 = 22 - 7 \neq 7 - 22 = -15$$

$$3 = (10 - 5) - 2 \neq 10 - (5 - 2) = 7$$

When working through subtraction problems involving larger numbers, it's necessary to regroup the numbers. The following practice problem uses regrouping:

$$\begin{array}{r} 3\ 2\ 5 \\ -\ 7\ 7 \\ \hline \end{array}$$

Here, it is clear that the ones and tens columns for 77 are greater than the ones and tens columns for 325. To subtract this number, one needs to borrow from the tens and hundreds columns. When borrowing from a column, subtracting 1 from the lender column will add 10 to the borrower column:

$$
\begin{array}{r}
3\text{-}1 \quad 10\text{+}2\text{-}1 \quad 10\text{+}5 \qquad\qquad 2 \quad 11 \quad 15 \\
-\qquad\qquad 7 \qquad\quad 7 \quad = \quad -\qquad 7 \quad 7 \\
\hline
\qquad\qquad\qquad\qquad\qquad\qquad\qquad 2 \quad 4 \quad 8
\end{array}
$$

After ensuring that each digit in the top row is greater than the digit in the corresponding bottom row, subtraction can proceed as normal, and the answer is found to be 248.

Multiplication

Multiplication involves adding together multiple copies of a number. It is indicated by an × symbol or a number immediately outside of a parenthesis. For example:

$$5(8 - 2)$$

The two numbers being multiplied together are called **factors**, and their result is called a **product**. For example,
$$9 \times 6 = 54$$

This can be shown alternatively by expansion of either the 9 or the 6:

$$9 \times 6 = 9 + 9 + 9 + 9 + 9 + 9 = 54$$

$$9 \times 6 = 6 + 6 + 6 + 6 + 6 + 6 + 6 + 6 + 6 = 54$$

Like addition, multiplication holds the commutative and associative properties:

$$115 = 23 \times 5 = 5 \times 23 = 115$$

$$84 = 3 \times (7 \times 4) = (3 \times 7) \times 4 = 84$$

Multiplication also follows the **distributive property**, which allows the multiplication to be distributed through parentheses. The formula for distribution is:

$$a \times (b + c) = ab + ac$$

This is clear after the examples:

$$45 = 5 \times 9 = 5(3 + 6) = (5 \times 3) + (5 \times 6) = 15 + 30 = 45$$

$$20 = 4 \times 5 = 4(10 - 5) = (4 \times 10) - (4 \times 5) = 40 - 20 = 20$$

Multiplication becomes slightly more complicated when multiplying numbers with decimals. The easiest way to answer these problems is to ignore the decimals and multiply as if they were whole numbers. After multiplying the factors, a decimal gets placed in the product. The placement of the decimal is determined by taking the cumulative number of decimal places in the factors.

For example:

$$
\begin{array}{ccc}
\begin{array}{r} 0.7 \\ \times\,3 \\ \hline 2.1 \end{array} &
\begin{array}{r} 2.6 \\ \times\ 4.2 \\ \hline 10.92 \end{array} &
\begin{array}{r} 1.5 \\ \times\,6.4 \\ \hline 9.60 \end{array}
\end{array}
$$

14

Starting with the first example, the first step is to ignore the decimal and multiply the numbers as though they were whole numbers, which results in a product of 21. The next step is to count the number of digits that follow a decimal (one, in this case). Finally, the decimal place gets moved that many positions to the left, because the factors have only one decimal place. The second example works the same way, except that there are two total decimal places in the factors, so the product's decimal is moved two places over. In the third example, the decimal should be moved over two digits, but the digit zero is no longer needed, so it is erased, and the final answer is 9.6.

Division

Division and multiplication are inverses of each other in the same way that addition and subtraction are opposites. The signs designating the division operation are the ÷ and / symbols. In division, the second number divides into the first.

The number before the division sign is called the **dividend** or, if expressed as a fraction, the **numerator.** For example, in $a \div b$, a is the dividend, while in $\frac{a}{b}$, a is the numerator.

The number after the division sign is called the **divisor** or, if expressed as a fraction, the **denominator.** For example, in $a \div b$, b is the divisor, while in $\frac{a}{b}$, b is the denominator.

Like subtraction, division doesn't follow the commutative property, as it matters which number comes before the division sign, and division doesn't follow the associative or distributive properties for the same reason. For example:

$$\frac{3}{2} = 9 \div 6 \neq 6 \div 9 = \frac{2}{3}$$

$$2 = 10 \div 5 = (30 \div 3) \div 5 \neq 30 \div (3 \div 5) = 30 \div \frac{3}{5} = 50$$

$$25 = 20 + 5 = (40 \div 2) + (40 \div 8) \neq 40 \div (2 + 8) = 40 \div 10 = 4$$

If a divisor doesn't divide into a dividend evenly, whatever is left over is termed the **remainder**. The remainder can be further divided out into decimal form by using long division; however, this doesn't always give a **quotient** with a finite number of decimal places, so the remainder can also be expressed as a fraction over the original divisor.

Division with decimals is similar to multiplication with decimals in that when dividing a decimal by a whole number, one should ignore the decimal and divide as if it was a whole number.

Upon finding the answer, or quotient, the decimal point is inserted at the decimal place equal to that in the dividend.

$$15.75 \div 3 = 5.25$$

When the divisor is a decimal number, both the divisor and dividend get multiplied by 10. This process is repeated until the divisor is a whole number, then one needs to complete the division operation as described above.

$$17.5 \div 2.5 = 175 \div 25 = 7$$

Order of Operations

When solving equations with multiple operations, special rules apply. These rules are known as the **Order of Operations**. The order is as follows: Parentheses, Exponents, Multiplication and Division from left to right, and Addition and Subtraction from left to right. A popular mnemonic device to help remember the order is Please Excuse My Dear Aunt Sally (PEMDAS).

Evaluate the following two problems to understand the Order of Operations:

1) $4 + (3 \times 2)^2 \div 4$

      First, solve the operation within the parentheses: $4 + 6^2 \div 4$.
      Second, solve the exponent: $4 + 36 \div 4$.
      Third, solve the division operation: $4 + 9$.
      Fourth, finish the operation with addition for the answer, 13.

2) $2 \times (6 + 3) \div (2 + 1)^2$

      $2 \times 9 \div (3)^2$
      $2 \times 9 \div 9$
      $18 \div 9$
      2

Estimation and Rounding

Estimation is finding a value that is close to a solution but is not the exact answer. For example, if there are values in the thousands to be multiplied, then each value can be estimated to the nearest thousand and the calculation performed. This value provides an approximate solution that can be determined very quickly.

When estimating, it's often convenient to **round** a number, which means to give an approximate figure to make it easier to compare amounts or perform mental math. Round up when the digit is 5 or more. The digit used to determine the rounding, and all subsequent digits, become 0, and the selected place value is increased by 1. Here are some examples:

      75 rounded to the nearest ten is 80
      380 rounded to the nearest hundred is 400
      22.697 rounded to the nearest hundredth is 22.70

Round down when rounding on any digit that is below 5. The rounded digit, and all subsequent digits, becomes 0, and the preceding digit stays the same. Here are some examples:

      92 rounded to the nearest ten is 90
      839 rounded to the nearest hundred is 800
      22.643 rounded to the nearest hundredth is 22.64

In a cause/efThe same estimation strategies and techniques used when working with standard math problems can be employed when working with real-life situations. Estimation is frequently used in calculations involving money, such as for determining if one has enough money for a purchase, how much one needs to save weekly to buy a desired product, or how much a restaurant bill will sum to.

Applying Operations to Real-World Contexts

Addition and subtraction are **inverse operations**. Adding a number and then subtracting the same number will cancel each other out, resulting in the original number, and vice versa. For example,

$$8 + 7 - 7 = 8 \text{ and } 137 - 100 + 100 = 137$$

Similarly, multiplication and division are inverse operations. Therefore, multiplying by a number and then dividing by the same number results in the original number, and vice versa. For example,

$$8 \times 2 \div 2 = 8 \text{ and } 12 \div 4 \times 4 = 12$$

Inverse operations are used to work backwards to solve problems. In the case that 7 and a number add to 18, the inverse operation of subtraction is used to find the unknown value:

$$18 - 7 = 11$$

If a school's entire 4th grade was divided evenly into 3 classes each with 22 students, the inverse operation of multiplication is used to determine the total students in the grade:

$$22 \times 3 = 66$$

Additional scenarios involving inverse operations are included in the tables below.

There are a variety of real-world situations in which one or more of the operators is used to solve a problem. The tables below display the most common scenarios.

Addition & Subtraction

	Unknown Result	Unknown Change	Unknown Start
Adding to	5 students were in class. 4 more students arrived. How many students are in class? $5 + 4 =?$	8 students were in class. More students arrived late. There are now 18 students in class. How many students arrived late? $8+? = 18$ Solved by inverse operations $18 - 8 =?$	Some students were in class early. 11 more students arrived. There are now 17 students in class. How many students were in class early? $? +11 = 17$ Solved by inverse operations $17 - 11 =?$
Taking from	15 students were in class. 5 students left class. How many students are in class now? $15 - 5 =?$	12 students were in class. Some students left class. There are now 8 students in class. How many students left class? $12-? = 8$ Solved by inverse operations $8+? = 12 \rightarrow 12 - 8 =?$	Some students were in class. 3 students left class. Then there were 13 students in class. How many students were in class before? $? -3 = 13$ Solved by inverse operations $13 + 3 =?$

17

	Unknown Total	Unknown Addends (Both)	Unknown Addends (One)
Putting together/ taking apart	The homework assignment is 10 addition problems and 8 subtraction problems. How many problems are in the homework assignment? $$10+8=?$$	Bobby has $9. How much can Bobby spend on candy and how much can Bobby spend on toys? $$9=?+?$$	Bobby has 12 pairs of pants. 5 pairs of pants are shorts, and the rest are long. How many pairs of long pants does he have? $$12=5+?$$ Solved by inverse operations $12-5=?$

	Unknown Difference	Unknown Larger Value	Unknown Smaller Value
Comparing	Bobby has 5 toys. Tommy has 8 toys. How many more toys does Tommy have than Bobby? $$5+?=8$$ Solved by inverse operations $8-5=?$ Bobby has $6. Tommy has $10. How many fewer dollars does Bobby have than Tommy? $$10-6=?$$	Tommy has 2 more toys than Bobby. Bobby has 4 toys. How many toys does Tommy have? $$2+4=?$$ Bobby has 3 fewer dollars than Tommy. Bobby has $8. How many dollars does Tommy have? $$?-3=8$$ Solved by inverse operations $8+3=?$	Tommy has 6 more toys than Bobby. Tommy has 10 toys. How many toys does Bobby have? $$?+6=10$$ Solved by inverse operations $10-6=?$ Bobby has $5 less than Tommy. Tommy has $9. How many dollars does Bobby have? $$9-5=?$$

Multiplication and Division

	Unknown Product	Unknown Group Size	Unknown Number of Groups
Equal groups	There are 5 students, and each student has 4 pieces of candy. How many pieces of candy are there in all? $$5\times4=?$$	14 pieces of candy are shared equally by 7 students. How many pieces of candy does each student have? $$7\times?=14$$ Solved by inverse operations $14\div7=?$	If 18 pieces of candy are to be given out 3 to each student, how many students will get candy? $$?\times3=18$$ Solved by inverse operations $18\div3=?$

18

	Unknown Product	Unknown Factor	Unknown Factor
Arrays	There are 5 rows of students with 3 students in each row. How many students are there? $5 \times 3 = ?$	If 16 students are arranged into 4 equal rows, how many students will be in each row? $4 \times ? = 16$ Solved by inverse operations $16 \div 4 = ?$	If 24 students are arranged into an array with 6 columns, how many rows are there? $? \times 6 = 24$ Solved by inverse operations $24 \div 6 = ?$

	Larger Unknown	Smaller Unknown	Multiplier Unknown
Comparing	A small popcorn costs $1.50. A large popcorn costs 3 times as much as a small popcorn. How much does a large popcorn cost? $1.50 \times 3 = ?$	A large soda costs $6 and that is 2 times as much as a small soda costs. How much does a small soda cost? $2 \times ? = 6$ Solved by inverse operations $6 \div 2 = ?$	A large pretzel costs $3 and a small pretzel costs $2. How many times as much does the large pretzel cost as the small pretzel? $? \times 2 = 3$ Solved by inverse operations $3 \div 2 = ?$

Fraction Operations

A **fraction** is a part of something that is whole. Items such as apples can be cut into parts to help visualize fractions. If an apple is cut into 2 equal parts, each part represents ½ of the apple. If each half is cut into two parts, the apple now is cut into quarters. Each piece now represents ¼ of the apple. In this example, each part is equal because they all have the same size. Geometric shapes, such as circles and squares, can also be utilized to help visualize the idea of fractions. For example, a circle can be drawn and divided into 6 equal parts:

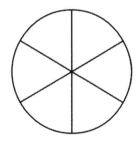

Shading can be used to represent parts of the circle that can be translated into fractions. The top of the fraction, the **numerator**, can represent how many segments are shaded. The bottom of the fraction, the **denominator**, can represent the number of segments that the circle is broken into. A pie is a good analogy to use in this example. If one piece of the circle is shaded, or one piece of pie is cut out, $1/_6$ of the object is being referred to. An apple, a pie, or a circle can be utilized in order to compare simple fractions. For example, showing that ½ is larger than ¼ and that ¼ is smaller than $1/_3$ can be accomplished through shading. A **unit fraction** is a fraction in which the numerator is 1, and the denominator is a positive whole number. It represents one part of a whole—one piece of pie.

19

Imagine that an apple pie has been baked for a holiday party, and the full pie has eight slices. After the party, there are five slices left. How could the amount of the pie that remains be expressed as a fraction? The numerator is 5 since there are 5 pieces left, and the denominator is 8 since there were eight total slices in the whole pie. Thus, expressed as a fraction, the leftover pie totals $\frac{5}{8}$ of the original amount.

Fractions come in three different varieties: proper fractions, improper fractions, and mixed numbers. **Proper fractions** have a numerator less than the denominator, such as $\frac{3}{8}$, but **improper fractions** have a numerator greater than the denominator, such as $\frac{7}{2}$. **Mixed numbers** combine a whole number with a proper fraction, such as $3\frac{1}{2}$. Any mixed number can be written as an improper fraction by multiplying the integer by the denominator, adding the product to the value of the numerator, and dividing the sum by the original denominator. For example:

$$3\frac{1}{2} = \frac{3 \times 2 + 1}{2} = \frac{7}{2}$$

Whole numbers can also be converted into fractions by placing the whole number as the numerator and making the denominator 1. For example, $3 = \frac{3}{1}$.

The bar in a fraction represents division. Therefore $^6/_5$ is the same as $6 \div 5$. In order to rewrite it as a mixed number, division is performed to obtain $6 \div 5 = 1\,R1$. The remainder is then converted into fraction form. The actual remainder becomes the numerator of a fraction, and the divisor becomes the denominator. Therefore $1\,R1$ is written as $1\frac{1}{5}$, a mixed number. A mixed number can also decompose into the addition of a whole number and a fraction. For example,

$$1\frac{1}{5} = 1 + \frac{1}{5} \text{ and } 4\frac{5}{6} = 4 + \frac{1}{6} + \frac{1}{6} + \frac{1}{6} + \frac{1}{6} + \frac{1}{6}$$

Every fraction can be built from a combination of unit fractions.

One of the most fundamental concepts of fractions is their ability to be manipulated by multiplication or division. This is possible since $\frac{n}{n} = 1$ for any non-zero integer. As a result, multiplying or dividing by $\frac{n}{n}$ will not alter the original fraction since any number multiplied or divided by 1 doesn't change the value of that number. Fractions of the same value are known as equivalent fractions. For example, $\frac{2}{8}, \frac{25}{100}$, and $\frac{40}{160}$ are equivalent, as they all equal $\frac{1}{4}$.

Like fractions, or **equivalent fractions**, are the terms used to describe these fractions that are made up of different numbers but represent the same quantity. For example, the given fractions are $^4/_8$ and $^3/_6$. If a pie was cut into 8 pieces and 4 pieces were removed, half of the pie would remain. Also, if a pie was split into 6 pieces and 3 pieces were eaten, half of the pie would also remain. Therefore, both of the fractions represent half of a pie. These two fractions are referred to as like fractions. **Unlike fractions** are fractions that are different and cannot be thought of as representing equal quantities. When working with fractions in mathematical expressions, like fractions should be simplified. Both $^4/_8$ and $^3/_6$ can be simplified into $^1/_2$.

Comparing fractions can be completed through the use of a number line. For example, if $^3/_5$ and $^6/_{10}$ need to be compared, each fraction should be plotted on a number line. To plot $^3/_5$, the area from 0 to 1 should be broken into 5 equal segments, and the fraction represents 3 of them. To plot $^6/_{10}$, the area from 0 to 1 should be broken into 10 equal segments, and the fraction represents 6 of them.

It can be seen that $\frac{3}{5} = \frac{6}{10}$

Like fractions are plotted at the same point on a number line. Unit fractions can also be used to compare fractions. For example, if it is known that:

$$\frac{4}{5} > \frac{1}{2} \ and \ \frac{1}{2} > \frac{4}{10}$$

then it is also known that

$$\frac{4}{5} > \frac{4}{10}$$

Also, converting improper fractions to mixed numbers can be helpful in comparing fractions because the whole number portion of the number is more visible.

Adding and subtracting mixed numbers and fractions can be completed by decomposing fractions into a sum of whole numbers and unit fractions. For example, the given problem is

$$5\frac{3}{7} + 2\frac{1}{7}$$

Decomposing into

$$5 + \frac{1}{7} + \frac{1}{7} + \frac{1}{7} + 2 + \frac{1}{7}$$

This shows that the whole numbers can be added separately from the unit fractions. The answer is:

$$5 + 2 + \frac{1}{7} + \frac{1}{7} + \frac{1}{7} + \frac{1}{7} = 7 + \frac{4}{7} = 7\frac{4}{7}$$

Although many equivalent fractions exist, they are easier to compare and interpret when reduced or simplified. The numerator and denominator of a simple fraction will have no factors in common other than 1. When reducing or simplifying fractions, divide the numerator and denominator by the greatest common factor. A simple strategy is to divide the numerator and denominator by low numbers, like 2, 3, or 5 until arriving at a simple fraction, but the same thing could be achieved by determining the greatest common factor for both the numerator and denominator and dividing each by it. Using the first method is preferable when both the numerator and denominator are even, end in 5, or are obviously a multiple of another number. However, if no numbers seem to work, it will be necessary to factor the numerator and denominator to find the GCF. For example:

1) Simplify the fraction $\frac{6}{8}$:

Dividing the numerator and denominator by 2 results in $\frac{3}{4}$, which is a simple fraction.

2) Simplify the fraction $\frac{12}{36}$:

Dividing the numerator and denominator by 2 leaves $\frac{6}{18}$. This isn't a simple fraction, as both the numerator and denominator have factors in common. Diving each by 3 results in $\frac{2}{6}$, but this can be further simplified by dividing by 2 to get $\frac{1}{3}$. This is the simplest fraction, as the numerator is 1. In cases like this, multiple division operations can be avoided by determining the greatest common factor between the numerator and denominator.

3) Simplify the fraction $\frac{18}{54}$ by dividing by the greatest common factor:

First, determine the factors for the numerator and denominator. The factors of 18 are 1, 2, 3, 6, 9, and 18. The factors of 54 are 1, 2, 3, 6, 9, 18, 27, and 54. Thus, the greatest common factor is 18. Dividing both the numerator and denominator by 18 leaves $\frac{1}{3}$, which is the simplest fraction. This method takes slightly more work, but it definitely arrives at the simplest fraction.

Adding and Subtracting Fractions

Adding and subtracting fractions that have the same denominators involves adding or subtracting the numerators. The denominator will stay the same. Therefore, the decomposition process can be made simpler, and the fractions do not have to be broken into unit fractions.

For example, the given problem is:

$$4\frac{7}{8} - 2\frac{6}{8}$$

The answer is found by adding the answers to both

$$4 - 2 \text{ and } \frac{7}{8} - \frac{6}{8}$$

$$2 + \frac{1}{8} = 2\frac{1}{8}$$

A common mistake would be to add the denominators so that

$$\frac{1}{4} + \frac{1}{4} = \frac{1}{8} \text{ or } \frac{2}{8}$$

However, conceptually, it is known that two quarters make a half, so neither one of these are correct.

"If two fractions have different denominators, equivalent fractions must be used to add or subtract them. The fractions must be converted into fractions that have common denominators. A **least common denominator** or the product of the two denominators can be used as the common denominator. For example, in the problem $\frac{5}{6} + \frac{2}{3}$, either 6, which is the least common denominator, or 18, which is the product of the denominators, can be used. In order to use 6, $\frac{2}{3}$ must be converted to sixths. A number line can be used to show the equivalent fraction is $\frac{4}{6}$. What happens is that $\frac{2}{3}$ is multiplied by a fractional form of 1 to obtain a denominator of 6. Hence:

$$\frac{2}{3} \times \frac{2}{2} = \frac{4}{6}$$

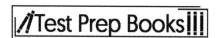

Therefore, the problem is now $\frac{5}{6} + \frac{4}{6} = \frac{9}{6}$, which can be simplified into $\frac{3}{2}$. In order to use 18, both fractions must be converted into having 18 as their denominator. $\frac{5}{6}$ would have to be multiplied by $\frac{3}{3}$, and $\frac{2}{3}$ would need to be multiplied by $\frac{6}{6}$. The addition problem would be $\frac{15}{18} + \frac{12}{18} = \frac{27}{18}$, which reduces into $\frac{3}{2}$.

It is always possible to find a common denominator by multiplying the denominators. However, when the denominators are large numbers, this method is unwieldy, especially if the answer must be provided in its simplest form. Thus, it's beneficial to find the least common denominator of the fractions—the least common denominator is incidentally also the least common multiple.

"In order to use 18, both fractions must be converted into having 18 as their denominator. $\frac{5}{6}$ would have to be multiplied times $\frac{3}{3}$, and $\frac{2}{3}$ would need to be multiplied times $\frac{6}{6}$. The addition problem would be:

$$\frac{15}{18} + \frac{12}{18} = \frac{27}{18}$$

This reduces into $\frac{3}{2}$.

It is always possible to find a common denominator by multiplying the denominators. However, when the denominators are large numbers, this method is unwieldy, especially if the answer must be provided in its simplest form. Thus, it's beneficial to find the **least common denominator** of the fractions—the least common denominator is incidentally also the **least common multiple**.

Once equivalent fractions have been found with common denominators, simply add or subtract the numerators to arrive at the answer:

1) $\frac{1}{2} + \frac{3}{4} = \frac{2}{4} + \frac{3}{4} = \frac{5}{4}$

2) $\frac{3}{12} + \frac{11}{20} = \frac{15}{60} + \frac{33}{60} = \frac{48}{60} = \frac{4}{5}$

3) $\frac{7}{9} - \frac{4}{15} = \frac{35}{45} - \frac{12}{45} = \frac{23}{45}$

4) $\frac{5}{6} - \frac{7}{18} = \frac{15}{18} - \frac{7}{18} = \frac{8}{18} = \frac{4}{9}$

Multiplying and Dividing Fractions

Of the four basic operations that can be performed on fractions, the one that involves the least amount of work is multiplication. To multiply two fractions, simply multiply the numerators together, multiply the denominators together, and place the products of each as a fraction. Whole numbers and mixed numbers can also be expressed as a fraction, as described above, to multiply with a fraction.

Because multiplication is commutative, multiplying a fraction times a whole number is the same as multiplying a whole number times a fraction. The problem involves adding a fraction a specific number of times. The problem $3 \times \frac{1}{4}$ can be translated into adding the unit fraction 3 times:

$$\frac{1}{4} + \frac{1}{4} + \frac{1}{4} = \frac{3}{4}$$

In the problem $4 \times \frac{2}{5}$, the fraction can be decomposed into $\frac{1}{5} + \frac{1}{5}$ and then added 4 times to obtain $\frac{8}{5}$. Also, both of these answers can be found by just multiplying the whole number times the numerator of the fraction being multiplied.

23

The whole numbers can be written in fraction form as:

$$\frac{3}{1} \times \frac{1}{4} = \frac{3}{4}$$

$$\frac{4}{1} \times \frac{2}{5} = \frac{8}{5}$$

Multiplying a fraction times a fraction involves multiplying the numerators together separately and the denominators together separately. For example,

$$\frac{3}{8} \times \frac{2}{3} = \frac{3 \times 2}{8 \times 3} = \frac{6}{24}$$

This can then be reduced to $\frac{1}{4}$.

Dividing a fraction by a fraction is actually a multiplication problem. It involves flipping the divisor and then multiplying normally. For example,

$$\frac{22}{5} \div \frac{1}{2} = \frac{22}{5} \times \frac{2}{1} = \frac{44}{5}$$

The same procedure can be implemented for division problems involving fractions and whole numbers. The whole number can be rewritten as a fraction over a denominator of 1, and then division can be completed.

A common denominator approach can also be used in dividing fractions. Considering the same problem, $\frac{22}{5} \div \frac{1}{2}$, a common denominator between the two fractions is 10. $\frac{22}{5}$ would be rewritten as:

$$\frac{22}{5} \times \frac{2}{2} = \frac{44}{10}$$

$\frac{1}{2}$ would be rewritten as:

$$\frac{1}{2} \times \frac{5}{5} = \frac{5}{10}$$

Dividing both numbers straight across results in:

$$\frac{44}{10} \div \frac{5}{10} = \frac{44/5}{10/10} = \frac{44/5}{1} = 44/5$$

Many real-world problems will involve the use of fractions. Key words include actual fraction values, such as half, quarter, third, fourth, etc. The best approach to solving word problems involving fractions is to draw a picture or diagram that represents the scenario being discussed, while deciding which type of operation is necessary in order to solve the problem. A phrase such as "one fourth of 60 pounds of coal" creates a scenario in which multiplication should be used, and the mathematical form of the phrase is $\frac{1}{4} \times 60$.

Decimal Operations

The **decimal system** is a way of writing out numbers that uses ten different numerals: 0, 1, 2, 3, 4, 5, 6, 7, 8, and 9. This is also called a "base ten" or "base 10" system. Other bases are also used. For example, computers work with a base of 2. This means they only use the numerals 0 and 1.

The **decimal place** denotes how far to the right of the decimal point a numeral is. The first digit to the right of the decimal point is in the **tenths** place. The next is the **hundredths**. The third is the *thousandths*.

So, 3.142 has a 1 in the tenths place, a 4 in the hundredths place, and a 2 in the thousandths place.

The **decimal point** is a period used to separate the *ones* place from the *tenths* place when writing out a number as a decimal.

A **decimal number** is a number written out with a decimal point instead of as a fraction, for example, 1.25 instead of $\frac{5}{4}$. Depending on the situation, it can sometimes be easier to work with fractions and sometimes easier to work with decimal numbers.

A decimal number is **terminating** if it stops at some point. It is called **repeating** if it never stops but repeats over and over. It is important to note that every rational number can be written as a terminating decimal or as a repeating decimal.

Addition with Decimals

To add decimal numbers, each number needs to be lined up by the decimal point in vertical columns. For each number being added, the zeros to the right of the last number need to be filled in so that each of the numbers has the same number of places to the right of the decimal. Then, the columns can be added together. Here is an example of 2.45 + 1.3 + 8.891 written in column form:

$$2.450$$

$$1.300$$

$$+\ 8.891$$

Zeros have been added in the columns so that each number has the same number of places to the right of the decimal.

Added together, the correct answer is 12.641:

$$2.450$$

$$1.300$$

$$+\ 8.891$$

$$12.641$$

Subtraction with Decimals

Subtracting decimal numbers is the same process as adding decimals. Here is 7.89 − 4.235 written in column form:

$$7.890$$

$$-\ 4.235$$

$$3.655$$

A zero has been added in the column so that each number has the same number of places to the right of the decimal.

25

Multiplication with Decimals

The simplest way to multiply decimals is to calculate the product as if the decimals are not there, then count the number of decimal places in the original problem. Use that total to place the decimal the same number of places over in your answer, counting from right to left. For example, 0.5×1.25 can be rewritten and multiplied as 5×125, which equals 625. Then the decimal is added three places from the right for .625.

The final answer will have the same number of decimal *points* as the total number of decimal *places* in the problem. The first number has one decimal place, and the second number has two decimal places. Therefore, the final answer will contain three decimal places:

$$0.5 \times 1.25 = 0.625$$

Division with Decimals

Dividing a decimal by a whole number entails using long division first by ignoring the decimal point. Then, the decimal point is moved the number of places given in the problem.

For example, $6.8 \div 4$ can be rewritten as $68 \div 4$, which is 17. There is one non-zero integer to the right of the decimal point, so the final solution would have one decimal place to the right of the solution. In this case, the solution is 1.7.

Dividing a decimal by another decimal requires changing the divisor to a whole number by moving its decimal point. The decimal place of the dividend should be moved by the same number of places as the divisor. Then, the problem is the same as dividing a decimal by a whole number.

For example, $5.72 \div 1.1$ has a divisor with one decimal point in the denominator. The expression can be rewritten as $57.2 \div 11$ by moving each number one decimal place to the right to eliminate the decimal. The long division can be completed as $572 \div 11$ with a result of 52. Since there is one non-zero integer to the right of the decimal point in the problem, the final solution is 5.2.

In another example, $8 \div 0.16$ has a divisor with two decimal points in the denominator. The expression can be rewritten as $800 \div 16$ by moving each number two decimal places to the right to eliminate the decimal in the divisor. The long division can be completed with a result of 50.

Estimation and Rounding with Decimals

Prior to performing operations and calculating the answer to a problem involving addition, subtraction, multiplication, or division, it is helpful to estimate the result. Doing so will enable the test taker to determine whether their computed answer is logical within the context of a given problem and prevent careless errors. For example, it is unfortunately common under the pressure of a testing situation for test takers to inadvertently perform the incorrect operation or make a simple calculation error on an otherwise easy math problem. By quickly estimating the answer by eyeballing the numbers, rounding if needed, and performing some simple mental math, test takers can establish an approximate expected outcome before calculating the specific answer. The derived result after computation can then be evaluated by its nearness to the expected answer. This is performed by approximating given values to perform mental math. Numbers should be rounded to the nearest value possible to check the initial results.

As mentioned, sometimes when performing operations such as multiplying numbers, the result can be estimated by rounding. For example, to estimate the value of 11.2×2.01, each number can be rounded to the nearest integer. This will yield a result of 22.

Rounding numbers helps with estimation because it changes the given number to a simpler, although less accurate, number than the exact given number. Rounding allows for easier calculations, which estimate the results of using the exact given number. The accuracy of the estimate and ease of use depends on the place value to which the number is rounded. First, the place value is specified. Then, the digit to its right is looked at. For example, if rounding to the nearest hundreds place, the digit in the tens place is used. If it is a zero, one, 2, 3, or 4, the digit being rounded to is left alone. If it is a 5, 6, 7, 8 or 9, the digit being rounded to is increased by one. All other digits before the decimal point are then changed to zeros, and the digits in decimal places are dropped. If a decimal place is being rounded to, all digits that come after are just dropped.

For example, if 845,231.45 was to be rounded to the nearest thousands place, the answer would be 845,000. The 5 would remain the same due to the 2 in the hundreds place. Also, if 4.567 were to be rounded to the nearest tenths place, the answer would be 4.6. The 5 increased to 6 due to the 6 in the hundredths place, and the rest of the decimal is dropped.

Percent

Percent Problems

Think of percentages as fractions with a denominator of 100. In fact, percentage means "per hundred." The basic percent equation is the following:

$$\frac{is}{of} = \frac{\%}{100}$$

The placement of numbers in the equation depends on what the question asks.

Example 1
Find 40% of 80.

Basically, the problem is asking, "What is 40% of 80?" The 40% is the percent, and 80 is the number to find the percent "of." The equation is:

$$\frac{x}{80} = \frac{40}{100}$$

After cross-multiplying, the problem becomes:

$$100x = 80(40)$$

Solving for *x* produces the answer: $x = 32$.

Example 2
What percent of 100 is 20?

20 fills in the "is" portion, while 100 fills in the "of." The question asks for the percent, so that will be x, the unknown. The following equation is set up:

$$\frac{20}{100} = \frac{x}{100}$$

Cross-multiplying yields the equation:

$$100x = 20(100)$$

27

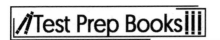

Solving for x gives the answer: 20%.

Example 3
30% of what number is 30?

The following equation uses the clues and numbers in the problem:

$$\frac{30}{x} = \frac{30}{100}$$

Cross-multiplying results in the equation:

$$30(100) = 30x$$

Solving for x gives the answer: $x = 100$.

Relationships in Numerical Data

In some cases, it is useful to compare numerical data and determine the relationship between values. One of the best ways to mathematically compare two values is to compute the percentage difference between the two values. For example, consider a given music shop that had a net profit of $120,000 in the first year of operation and $185,000 over the second year. Rather than simply finding the net difference between the two years (using subtraction), the business owner may want to know by what percentage his profit increased; in other words, how much his profit in the second year increased relative to his first year. In such cases, the percentage change is desired. The following sections provide some guidance for this process.

Percent Increase/Decrease
Problems dealing with percentages may involve an original value, a change in that value, and a percentage change. A problem will provide two pieces of information and ask to find the third. To do so, this formula is used:

$$\frac{change}{original\ value} \times 100 = percent\ change$$

Here's a sample problem:

> Attendance at a baseball stadium has dropped 16% from last year. Last year's average attendance was 40,000. What is this year's average attendance?

Using the formula and information, the change is unknown (x), the original value is 40,000, and the percent change is 16%. The formula can be written as:

$$\frac{x}{40,000} \times 100 = 16$$

When solving for x, it is determined the change was 6,400. The problem asked for this year's average attendance, so to calculate, the change (6,400) is subtracted from last year's attendance (40,000) to determine this year's average attendance is 33,600.

28

Percent More Than/Less Than

Percentage problems may give a value and what percent that given value is more than or less than an original unknown value. Here's a sample problem:

> A store advertises that all its merchandise has been reduced by 25%. The new price of a pair of shoes is $60. What was the original price?

This problem can be solved by writing a proportion. Two ratios should be written comparing the cost and the percent of the original cost. The new cost is 75% of the original cost (100% - 25%); and the original cost is 100% of the original cost. The unknown original cost can be represented by x. The proportion would be set up as:

$$\frac{60}{75} = \frac{x}{100}$$

Solving the proportion, it is determined the original cost was $80.

Real-World Rate, Percent, and Measurement Problems

A **ratio** compares the size of one group to the size of another. For example, there may be a room with 4 tables and 24 chairs. The ratio of tables to chairs is 4: 24. Such ratios behave like fractions in that both sides of the ratio by the same number can be multiplied or divided. Thus, the ratio 4:24 is the same as the ratio 2:12 and 1:6.

One quantity is **proportional** to another quantity if the first quantity is always some multiple of the second. For instance, the distance travelled in five hours is always five times to the speed as travelled. The distance is proportional to speed in this case.

One quantity is **inversely proportional** to another quantity if the first quantity is equal to some number divided by the second quantity. The time it takes to travel one hundred miles will be given by 100 divided by the speed travelled. The time is inversely proportional to the speed.

When dealing with word problems, there is no fixed series of steps to follow, but there are some general guidelines to use. It is important that the quantity to be found is identified. Then, it can be determined how the given values can be used and manipulated to find the final answer.

Example 1

Jana wants to travel to visit Alice, who lives one hundred and fifty miles away. If she can drive at fifty miles per hour, how long will her trip take?

The quantity to find is the *time* of the trip. The time of a trip is given by the distance to travel divided by the speed to be traveled. The problem determines that the distance is one hundred and fifty miles, while the speed is fifty miles per hour. Thus, 150 divided by 50 is:

$$150 \div 50 = 3$$

Because *miles* and *miles per hour* are the units being divided, the miles cancel out. The result is 3 hours.

Example 2

Bob had $20 and Tom had $4. After selling 4 ice cream cones to Bob, Tom has as much money as Bob. The cost of an ice cream cone is an unknown quantity and can be represented by a variable (x).

The amount of money Bob has after his purchase is four times the cost of an ice cream cone subtracted from his original

$$\$20 \rightarrow 20 - 4x$$

The amount of money Tom has after his sale is four times the cost of an ice cream cone added to his original

$$\$4 \rightarrow 4x + 4$$

After the sale, the amount of money that Bob and Tom have is equal

$$\rightarrow 20 - 4x = 4x + 4$$

Solving for x yields $x = 2$.

Number Comparison and Equivalents

The Position of Numbers Relative to Each Other

Place Value of a Digit

Numbers count in groups of 10. That number is the same throughout the set of natural numbers and whole numbers. It is referred to as working within a base 10 numeration system. Only the numbers from zero to 9 are used to represent any number. The foundation for doing this involves **place value**. Numbers are written side by side. This is to show the amount in each place value.

For place value, let's look at how the number 10 is different from zero to 9. It has two digits instead of just one. The one is in the tens' place, and the zero is in the ones' place. Therefore, there is one group of tens and zero ones. 11 has one 10 and one 1. The introduction of numbers from 11 to 19 should be the next step. Each value within this range of numbers consists of one group of 10 and a specific number of leftover ones. Counting by tens can be practiced once the tens column is understood. This process consists of increasing the number in the tens place by one. For example, counting by 10 starting at 17 would result in the next four values being 27, 37, 47, and 57.

A place value chart can be used for understanding and learning about numbers that have more digits. Here is an example of a place value chart:

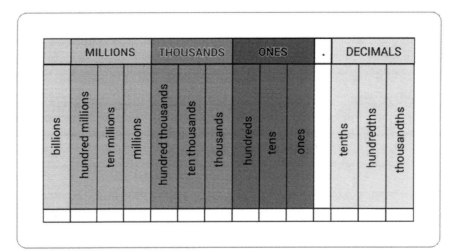

In the number 1,234, there are 4 ones and 3 tens. The 2 is in the hundreds' place, and the one is in the thousands' place. Note that each group of three digits is separated by a comma. The 2 has a value that is 10 times greater than the 3. Every place to the left has a value 10 times greater than the place to its right. Also, each group of three digits is also known as a *period*. 234 is in the ones' period.

30

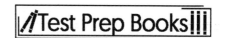

The number 1,234 can be written out as *one-thousand, two hundred thirty-four*. The process of writing out numbers is known as the *decimal system*. It is also based on groups of 10. The place value chart is a helpful tool in using this system. In order to write out a number, it always starts with the digit(s) in the highest period. For example, in the number 23,815,467, the 23 is in highest place and is in the millions' period. The number is read *twenty-three million, eight hundred fifteen thousand, four hundred sixty-seven*. Each period is written separately through the use of commas. Also, no "ands" are used within the number. Another way to think about the number 23,815,467 is through the use of an addition problem. For example:

$$23,815,467 = 20,000,000 + 3,000,000 + 800,000 + 10,000 + 5,000 + 400 + 60 + 7$$

This expression is known as *expanded form*. The actual number 23,815,467 is known as being in **standard form**.

In order to compare whole numbers with many digits, place value can be used. In each number to be compared, it is necessary to find the highest place value in which the numbers differ and to compare the value within that place value. For example, $4,523,345 < 4,532,456$ because of the values in the ten thousands place. A similar process can be used for decimals. However, number lines can also be used. Tick marks can be placed within two whole numbers on the number line that represent tenths, hundredths, etc. Each number being compared can then be plotted. The value farthest to the right on the number line is the largest.

Comparing, Classifying, and Ordering Real Numbers

Rational numbers are any number that can be written as a fraction or ratio. Within the set of rational numbers, several subsets exist that are referenced throughout the mathematics topics. **Counting numbers** are the first numbers learned as a child. Counting numbers consist of 1,2,3,4, and so on. **Whole numbers** include all counting numbers and zero (0,1,2,3,4,…). **Integers** include counting numbers, their opposites, and zero (…,-3,-2,-1,0,1,2,3,…). **Rational numbers** are inclusive of integers, fractions, and decimals that terminate, or end (1.7, 0.04213) or repeat $(0.136\overline{5})$.

A **number line** typically consists of integers (…3,2,1,0,-1,-2,-3…), and is used to visually represent the value of a rational number. Each rational number has a distinct position on the line determined by comparing its value with the displayed values on the line. For example, if plotting −1.5 on the number line below, it is necessary to recognize that the value of −1.5 is .5 less than −1 and .5 greater than −2. Therefore, −1.5 is plotted halfway between −1 and −2.

The number system that is used consists of only ten different digits or characters. However, this system is used to represent an infinite number of values. As mentioned, the **place value system** makes this infinite number of values possible. The position in which a digit is written corresponds to a given value. Starting from the decimal point (which is implied, if not physically present), each subsequent place value to the left represents a value greater than the one before it. Conversely, starting from the decimal point, each subsequent place value to the right represents a value less than the one before it.

In accordance with the **base-10 system**, the value of a digit increases by a factor of ten each place it moves to the left. For example, consider the number 7. Moving the digit one place to the left (70), increases its value by a factor of 10:

$$7 \times 10 = 70$$

Moving the digit two places to the left (700) increases its value by a factor of 10 twice:

$$7 \times 10 \times 10 = 700$$

31

Moving the digit three places to the left (7,000) increases its value by a factor of 10 three times:

$$7 \times 10 \times 10 \times 10 = 7,000$$

Conversely, the value of a digit decreases by a factor of ten each place it moves to the right. (Note that multiplying by $\frac{1}{10}$ is equivalent to dividing by 10). For example, consider the number 40. Moving the digit one place to the right (4) decreases its value by a factor of 10:

$$40 \div 10 = 4$$

Moving the digit two places to the right (0.4), decreases its value by a factor of 10 twice:

$$40 \div 10 \div 10 = 0.4 \text{ or } 40 \times \frac{1}{10} \times \frac{1}{10} = 0.4$$

Moving the digit three places to the right (0.04) decreases its value by a factor of 10 three times:

$$40 \div 10 \div 10 \div 10 = 0.04 \text{ or } 40 \times \frac{1}{10} \times \frac{1}{10} \times \frac{1}{10} = 0.04$$

Ordering Numbers

A common question type asks to order rational numbers from least to greatest or greatest to least. The numbers will come in a variety of formats, including decimals, percentages, roots, fractions, and whole numbers. These questions test for knowledge of different types of numbers and the ability to determine their respective values.

Before discussing ordering all numbers, let's start with decimals.

To compare decimals and order them by their value, utilize a method similar to that of ordering large numbers.

The main difference is where the comparison will start. Assuming that any numbers to left of the decimal point are equal, the next numbers to be compared are those immediately to the right of the decimal point. If those are equal, then move on to compare the values in the next decimal place to the right.

For example:

Which number is greater, 12.35 or 12.38?

Check that the values to the left of the decimal point are equal:

$$12 = 12$$

Next, compare the values of the decimal place to the right of the decimal:

$$12.3 = 12.3$$

Those are also equal in value.

Finally, compare the value of the numbers in the next decimal place to the right on both numbers:

$$12.3\mathbf{5} \text{ and } 12.3\mathbf{8}$$

Here the 5 is less than the 8, so the final way to express this inequality is:

$$12.35 < 12.38$$

32

Comparing decimals is regularly exemplified with money because the "cents" portion of money ends in the hundredths place. When paying for gasoline or meals in restaurants, and even in bank accounts, if enough errors are made when calculating numbers to the hundredths place, they can add up to dollars and larger amounts of money over time.

Now that decimal ordering has been explained, let's expand and consider all real numbers. Whether the question asks to order the numbers from greatest to least or least to greatest, the crux of the question is the same—convert the numbers into a common format. Generally, it's easiest to write the numbers as whole numbers and decimals so they can be placed on a number line. Follow these examples to understand this strategy.

1) Order the following rational numbers from greatest to least:

$$\sqrt{36}, 0.65, 78\%, \frac{3}{4}, 7, 90\%, \frac{5}{2}$$

Of the seven numbers, the whole number (7) and decimal (0.65) are already in an accessible form, so concentrate on the other five.

First, the square root of 36 equals 6. (If the test asks for the root of a non-perfect root, determine which two whole numbers the root lies between.) Next, convert the percentages to decimals. A percentage means "per hundred," so this conversion requires moving the decimal point two places to the left, leaving 0.78 and 0.9.

Lastly, evaluate the fractions:

$$\frac{3}{4} = \frac{75}{100} = 0.75 \, ; \frac{5}{2} = 2\frac{1}{2} = 2.5$$

Now, the only step left is to list the numbers in the request order:

$$7, \sqrt{36}, \frac{5}{2}, 90\%, 78\%, \frac{3}{4}, 0.65$$

2) Order the following rational numbers from least to greatest:

$$2.5, \sqrt{9}, -10.5, 0.853, 175\%, \sqrt{4}, \frac{4}{5}$$

$$\sqrt{9} = 3$$

$$175\% = 1.75$$

$$\sqrt{4} = 2$$

$$\frac{4}{5} = 0.8$$

From least to greatest, the answer is:

$$-10.5, \frac{4}{5}, 0.853, 175\%, \sqrt{4}, 2.5, \sqrt{9}$$

Expressing Numeric Relationships

If a question asks to give words to a mathematical expression and says "equals," then an = sign must be included in the answer. Similarly, "less than or equal to" is expressed by the inequality symbol ≤, and "greater than or equal" to is expressed as ≥. Furthermore, "less than" is represented by <, and "greater than" is expressed by >.

Equations use the equals sign because the numeric expressions on either side of the symbol (=) are equivalent. In contrast, inequalities compare values or expressions that are unequal. Although not always true, linear equations that include a variable often have just one value for the variable that makes the statement true. Linear inequalities generally have an infinite number of values that make the statement true.

Inequalities are a concise mathematical way to express the relationship between unequal values. More specifically, they describe in what way the values are unequal. A value could be greater than (>); less than (<); greater than or equal to (≥); or less than or equal to (≤) another value. The statement "five times a number added to forty is more than sixty-five" can be expressed as:

$$5x + 40 > 65$$

Common words and phrases that express inequalities are:

Symbol	Phrase
<	is under, is below, smaller than, beneath
>	is above, is over, bigger than, exceeds
≤	no more than, at most, maximum
≥	no less than, at least, minimum

Conversions

Decimals and Percentages
Since a percentage is based on "per hundred," decimals and percentages can be converted by multiplying or dividing by 100. Practically speaking, this always amounts to moving the decimal point two places to the right or left, depending on the conversion. To convert a percentage to a decimal, move the decimal point two places to the left and remove the % sign. To convert a decimal to a percentage, move the decimal point two places to the right and add a % sign.

Here are some examples:

$$65\% = 0.65$$
$$0.33 = 33\%$$
$$0.215 = 21.5\%$$
$$99.99\% = 0.9999$$
$$500\% = 5.00$$
$$7.55 = 755\%$$

Fractions and Percentages
Remember that a percentage is a number per one hundred. So, a percentage can be converted to a fraction by making the number in the percentage the numerator and putting 100 as the denominator:

$$43\% = \frac{43}{100}$$

$$97\% = \frac{97}{100}$$

Note that the percent symbol (%) kind of looks like a 0, a 1, and another 0. So think of a percentage like 54% as 54 over 100.

To convert a fraction to a percent, follow the same logic. If the fraction happens to have 100 in the denominator, you're in luck. Just take the numerator and add a percent symbol:

$$\frac{28}{100} = 28\%$$

Otherwise, divide the numerator by the denominator to get a decimal:

$$\frac{9}{12} = 0.75$$

Then convert the decimal to a percentage:

$$0.75 = 75\%$$

Another option is to make the denominator equal to 100. Be sure to multiply the numerator and the denominator by the same number. For example:

$$\frac{3}{20} \times \frac{5}{5} = \frac{15}{100}$$

$$\frac{15}{100} = 15\%$$

Changing Fractions to Decimals

To change a fraction into a decimal, divide the denominator into the numerator until there are no remainders. There may be repeating decimals, so rounding is often acceptable. A straight line above the repeating portion denotes that the decimal repeats.

Example: Express 4/5 as a decimal.

Set up the division problem.

$$5\overline{)4}$$

5 does not go into 4, so place the decimal and add a zero.

$$5\overline{)4.0}$$

5 goes into 40 eight times. There is no remainder.

$$\begin{array}{r} 0.8 \\ 5\overline{)4.0} \\ -\underline{4.0} \\ 0 \end{array}$$

The solution is 0.8.

Example: Express 33 1/3 as a decimal.

Since the whole portion of the number is known, set it aside to calculate the decimal from the fraction portion.

Set up the division problem.

$$3\overline{)1}$$

3 does not go into 1, so place the decimal and add zeros. 3 goes into 10 three times.

$$\begin{array}{r} 0.3 \\ 3\overline{)1.0} \end{array}$$

This will repeat with a remainder of 1.

$$\begin{array}{r} 0.333 \\ 3\overline{)1.000} \\ -9 \\ \hline 10 \\ -9 \\ \hline 10 \end{array}$$

So, we will place a line over the 3 to denote the repetition. The solution is written $0.\overline{3}$.

Changing Decimals to Fractions

To change decimals to fractions, place the decimal portion of the number, the numerator, over the respective place value, the denominator, then reduce, if possible.

Example: Express 0.25 as a fraction.

This is read as twenty-five hundredths, so put 25 over 100. Then reduce to find the solution.

$$\frac{25}{100} = \frac{1}{4}$$

Example: Express 0.455 as a fraction

This is read as four hundred fifty-five thousandths, so put 455 over 1000. Then reduce to find the solution.

$$\frac{455}{1000} = \frac{91}{200}$$

There are two types of problems that commonly involve percentages. The first is to calculate some percentage of a given quantity, where you convert the percentage to a decimal, and multiply the quantity by that decimal. Secondly, you are given a quantity and told it is a fixed percent of an unknown quantity. In this case, convert to a decimal, then divide the given quantity by that decimal.

Example: What is 30% of 760?

Convert the percent into a useable number. "Of" means to multiply.

$$30\% = 0.30$$

Set up the problem based on the givens, and solve.

$$0.30 \times 760 = 228$$

Example: 8.4 is 20% of what number?

Convert the percent into a useable number.

$$20\% = 0.20$$

The given number is a percent of the answer needed, so divide the given number by this decimal rather than multiplying it.

$$\frac{8.4}{0.20} = 42$$

Distribution of a Quantity into its Fractional Parts

A quantity may be broken into its fractional parts. For example, a toy box holds three types of toys for kids. $\frac{1}{3}$ of the toys are Type A and $\frac{1}{4}$ of the toys are Type B. With that information, how many Type C toys are there?

First, the sum of Type A and Type B must be determined by finding a common denominator to add the fractions. The lowest common multiple is 12, so that is what will be used. The sum is:

$$\frac{1}{3} + \frac{1}{4} = \frac{4}{12} + \frac{3}{12} = \frac{7}{12}$$

This value is subtracted from 1 to find the number of Type C toys. The value is subtracted from 1 because 1 represents a whole. The calculation is:

$$1 - \frac{7}{12} = \frac{12}{12} - \frac{7}{12} = \frac{5}{12}$$

This means that $\frac{5}{12}$ of the toys are Type C. To check the answer, add all fractions together, and the result should be 1.

Practice Quiz

1. Which of the following numbers has the greatest value?
   - a. 1.43785
   - b. 1.07548
   - c. 1.43592
   - d. 0.89409

2. After a 30% discount, Frank purchased a new refrigerator for $660. How much did he save from the original price?
   - a. $282.86
   - b. $212.50
   - c. $105.75
   - d. $200

3. A school has 15 teachers and 20 teaching assistants. They have 200 students. What is the ratio of faculty to students?
   - a. $3:20$
   - b. $4:17$
   - c. $3:2$
   - d. $7:40$

4. Express the solution to the following problem in decimal form:
$$\frac{3}{5} \times \frac{7}{10} \div \frac{1}{2}$$
   - a. 0.042
   - b. 84%
   - c. 0.84
   - d. 0.42

5. If Sarah reads at an average rate of 21 pages in four nights, how long will it take her to read 140 pages?
   - a. 6 nights
   - b. 26 nights
   - c. 8 nights
   - d. 27 nights

See answers on the next page.

38

Answer Explanations

1. A: Compare each number after the decimal point to figure out which overall number is greatest. In Choices *A* (1.43785) and *C* (1.43592), both have the same tenths place (4) and hundredths place (3). However, the thousandths place is greater in Choice *A* (7), so *A* has the greatest value overall.

2. A: Since $660 is the price *after* a 30% discount, $660 represents 70% of the original price. To determine the original price, set up a proportion with the ratio of the sale price (660) to original price (unknown) equal to the ratio of sale percentage (where x represents the unknown original price):

$$\frac{660}{x} = \frac{70}{100}$$

To solve a proportion, cross multiply the numerators and denominators and set the products equal to each other:
$$(660)(100) = (70)(x)$$

Multiplying each side results in the equation:

$$66,000 = 70x$$

To solve for x, divide both sides by 70:

$$\frac{66,000}{70} = \frac{70x}{70}$$

$$x = 942.86$$

Remember that x represents the original price. Subtracting the sale price from the original price ($942.86 - $660) indicates that Frank saved $282.86.

3. D: The total faculty is:

$$15 + 20 = 35$$

So, the ratio is $35 : 200$. Then, divide both of these numbers by 5, since 5 is a common factor to both, with a result of $7 : 40$.

4. C: The first step in solving this problem is expressing the result in fraction form. Multiplication and division are typically performed in order from left to right but they can be performed in any order. For this problem, let's start with the division operation between the last two fractions. When dividing one fraction by another, invert or flip the second fraction and then multiply the numerators and denominators.

$$\frac{7}{10} \times \frac{2}{1} = \frac{14}{10}$$

Next, multiply the first fraction by this value:

$$\frac{3}{5} \times \frac{14}{10} = \frac{42}{50}$$

In this instance, to find the decimal form, we can multiply the numerator and denominator by 2 to get 100 in the denominator.

$$\frac{42}{50} \times \frac{2}{2} = \frac{84}{100}$$

In decimal form, this would be expressed as 0.84.

5. D: This problem can be solved by setting up a proportion involving the given information and the unknown value. The proportion is:

$$\frac{21 \text{ pages}}{4 \text{ nights}} = \frac{140 \text{ pages}}{x \text{ nights}}$$

We can cross-multiply to get:

$$21x = 4 \times 140$$

Solving this, we find:

$$x = 26.67$$

Since this is not an integer, we round up to 27 nights. 26 nights would not give Sarah enough time.

Quantitative Reasoning, Algebra, and Statistics

Rational Numbers

All real numbers can be separated into two groups: rational and irrational numbers. **Rational numbers** are any numbers that can be written as a fraction, such as $\frac{1}{3}, \frac{7}{4}$, and −25. Alternatively, **irrational numbers** are those that cannot be written as a fraction, such as numbers with never-ending, non-repeating decimal values. Many irrational numbers result from taking roots, such as $\sqrt{2}$ or $\sqrt{3}$. An irrational number may be written as:

$$34.5684952...$$

The ellipsis (...) represents the line of numbers after the decimal that does not repeat and is never-ending.

When rational and irrational numbers interact, there are different types of number outcomes. For example, when adding or multiplying two rational numbers, the result is a rational number. No matter what two fractions are added or multiplied together, the result can always be written as a fraction. The following expression shows two rational numbers multiplied together:

$$\frac{3}{8} \times \frac{4}{7} = \frac{12}{56}$$

The product of these two fractions is another fraction that can be simplified to $\frac{3}{14}$.

As another interaction, rational numbers added to irrational numbers will always result in irrational numbers. No part of any fraction can be added to a never-ending, non-repeating decimal to make a rational number. The same result is true when multiplying a rational and irrational number. Taking a fractional part of a never-ending, non-repeating decimal will always result in another never-ending, non-repeating decimal. An example of the product of rational and irrational numbers is shown in the following expression: $2 \times \sqrt{7}$.

The last type of interaction concerns two irrational numbers, where the sum or product may be rational or irrational depending on the numbers being used. The following expression shows a rational sum from two irrational numbers:
$$\sqrt{3} + \left(6 - \sqrt{3}\right) = 6$$

The product of two irrational numbers can be rational or irrational. A rational result can be seen in the following expression:

$$\sqrt{2} \times \sqrt{8} = \sqrt{2 \times 8} = \sqrt{16} = 4$$

An irrational result can be seen in the following:

$$\sqrt{3} \times \sqrt{2} = \sqrt{6}$$

Structure of the Number System

The mathematical number system is made up of two general types of numbers: real and complex. **Real numbers** are both irrational and rational numbers. **Complex numbers** are those composed of both a real number and an imaginary one. Imaginary numbers are the result of taking the square root of −1, and $\sqrt{-1} = i$.

The real number system is often explained using a Venn diagram similar to the one below. After a number has been labeled as a real number, further classification occurs when considering the other groups in this diagram. If a number is a never-ending, non-repeating decimal, it falls in the irrational category. Otherwise, it is rational. More information on these types of numbers is provided in the previous section. Furthermore, if a number does not have a fractional part, it is classified as an integer, such as –2, 75, or zero. Whole numbers are an even smaller group that only includes positive integers and zero. The last group of natural numbers is made up of only positive integers, such as 2, 56, or 12.

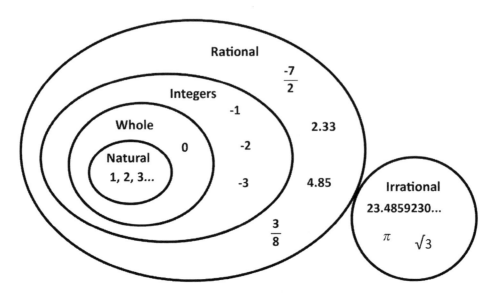

Real numbers can be compared and ordered using the number line. If a number falls to the left on the real number line, it is less than a number on the right. For example, $-2 < 5$ because -2 falls to the left of zero, and 5 falls to the right. Numbers to the left of zero are negative while those to the right are positive.

Complex numbers are made up of the sum of a real number and an imaginary number. Some examples of complex numbers include $6 + 2i$, $5 - 7i$, and $-3 + 12i$. Adding and subtracting complex numbers is similar to collecting like terms. The real numbers are added together, and the imaginary numbers are added together. For example, if the problem asks to simplify the expression:

$$6 + 2i - 3 + 7i$$

The 6 and (-3) are combined to make 3, and the $2i$ and $7i$ combine to make $9i$. Multiplying and dividing complex numbers is similar to working with exponents. One rule to remember when multiplying is that:

$$i \times i = -1$$

For example, if a problem asks to simplify the expression:

$$4i(3 + 7i)$$

The $4i$ should be distributed throughout the 3 and the $7i$. This leaves the final expression $12i - 28$. The 28 is negative because $i \times i$ results in a negative number. The last type of operation to consider with complex numbers is the conjugate. The **conjugate** of a complex number is a technique used to change the complex number into a real number. For example, the conjugate of $4 - 3i$ is $4 + 3i$. Multiplying $(4 - 3i)(4 + 3i)$ results in:

$$16 + 12i - 12i + 9$$

$$16 + 9 = 25$$

42

The order of operations—PEMDAS—simplifies longer expressions with real or imaginary numbers. Each operation is listed in the order of how they should be completed in a problem containing more than one operation. Parenthesis can also mean grouping symbols, such as brackets and absolute value. Then, exponents are calculated. Multiplication and division should be completed from left to right, and addition and subtraction should be completed from left to right.

Simplification of another type of expression occurs when radicals are involved. Root is another word for radical. For example, the following expression is a radical that can be simplified: $\sqrt{24x^2}$. First, the number must be factored out to the highest perfect square. Any perfect square can be taken out of a radical. Twenty-four can be factored into 4 and 6, and 4 can be taken out of the radical. $\sqrt{4} = 2$ can be taken out, and 6 stays underneath. If $x > 0$, x can be taken out of the radical because it is a perfect square. The simplified radical is $2x\sqrt{6}$. An approximation can be found using a calculator.

There are also properties of numbers that are true for certain operations. The **commutative** property allows the order of the terms in an expression to change while keeping the same final answer. Both addition and multiplication can be completed in any order and still obtain the same result. However, order does matter in subtraction and division. The **associative** property allows any terms to be "associated" by parenthesis and retain the same final answer. For example:

$$(4 + 3) + 5 = 4 + (3 + 5)$$

Both addition and multiplication are associative; however, subtraction and division do not hold this property. The **distributive** property states that:

$$a(b + c) = ab + ac$$

It is a property that involves both addition and multiplication, and the a is distributed onto each term inside the parentheses.

Absolute Value

The distance that a number is from zero is called its **absolute value**. For example, both 3 and −3 are three spaces from zero. Thus, both −3 and 3 have an absolute value of 3 since they're both three spaces away from zero.

An absolute number is written by placing | | around the number. So, |3| and |−3| both equal 3, as that's their common absolute value.

Ratio and Proportional Relationships

Ratios and Proportional Relationships

Ratios are used to show the relationship between two quantities. The ratio of oranges to apples in the grocery store may be 3 to 2. That means that for every 3 oranges, there are 2 apples. This comparison can be expanded to represent the actual number of oranges and apples, such as 36 oranges to 24 apples. Another example may be the number of boys to girls in a math class. If the ratio of boys to girls is given as 2 to 5, that means there are 2 boys to every 5 girls in the class. Ratios can also be compared if the units in each ratio are the same. The ratio of boys to girls in the math class can be compared to the ratio of boys to girls in a science class by stating which ratio is higher and which is lower.

Rates are used to compare two quantities with different units. **Unit rates** are the simplest form of rate. With unit rates, the denominator in the comparison of two units is one. For example, if someone can type at a rate of 1000 words in 5 minutes, then their unit rate for typing is $\frac{1000}{5} = 200$ words in one minute or 200 words per minute. Any rate can be converted into a unit rate by dividing to make the denominator one. 1000 words in 5 minutes has been converted into the unit rate of 200 words per minute.

Ratios and rates can be used together to convert rates into different units. For example, if someone is driving 50 kilometers per hour, that rate can be converted into miles per hour by using a ratio known as the **conversion factor**. Since the given value contains kilometers and the final answer needs to be in miles, the ratio relating miles to kilometers needs to be used. There are 0.62 miles in 1 kilometer. This, written as a ratio and in fraction form, is:

$$\frac{0.62 \text{ miles}}{1 \text{ km}}$$

To convert 50km/hour into miles per hour, the following conversion needs to be set up:

$$\frac{50 \text{ km}}{\text{hour}} \times \frac{0.62 \text{ miles}}{1 \text{ km}} = 31 \text{ miles per hour}$$

The ratio between two similar geometric figures is called the **scale factor**. For example, a problem may depict two similar triangles, A and B. The scale factor from the smaller triangle A to the larger triangle B is given as 2 because the length of the corresponding side of the larger triangle, 16, is twice the corresponding side on the smaller triangle, 8. This scale factor can also be used to find the value of a missing side, x, in triangle A. Since the scale factor from the smaller triangle (A) to larger one (B) is 2, the larger corresponding side in triangle B (given as 25) can be divided by 2 to find the missing side in A ($x = 12.5$). The scale factor can also be represented in the equation $2A = B$ because two times the lengths of A gives the corresponding lengths of B. This is the idea behind similar triangles.

Unit Rate

Unit rate word problems will ask to calculate the rate or quantity of something in a different value. For example, a problem might say that a car drove a certain number of miles in a certain number of minutes and then ask how many miles per hour the car was traveling. These questions involve solving proportions. Consider the following examples:

1) Alexandra made $96 during the first 3 hours of her shift as a temporary worker at a law office. She will continue to earn money at this rate until she finishes in 5 more hours. How much does Alexandra make per hour? How much will Alexandra have made at the end of the day?

This problem can be solved in two ways. The first is to set up a proportion, as the rate of pay is constant. The second is to determine her hourly rate, multiply the 5 hours by that rate, and then add the $96.

To set up a proportion, put the money already earned over the hours already worked on one side of an equation. The other side has x over 8 hours (the total hours worked in the day). It looks like this:

$$\frac{96}{3} = \frac{x}{8}$$

Now, cross-multiply to get:

$$768 = 3x$$

To get x, divide by 3, which leaves $x = 256$. Alternatively, as x is the numerator of one of the proportions, multiplying by its denominator will reduce the solution by one step. Thus, Alexandra will make $256 at the end of the day. To calculate her hourly rate, divide the total by 8, giving $32 per hour.

Alternatively, it is possible to figure out the hourly rate by dividing $96 by 3 hours to get $32 per hour. Now her total pay can be figured by multiplying $32 per hour by 8 hours, which comes out to $256.

2) Jonathan is reading a novel. So far, he has read 215 of the 335 total pages. It takes Jonathan 25 minutes to read 10 pages, and the rate is constant. How long does it take Jonathan to read one page? How much longer will it take him to finish the novel? Express the answer in time.

To calculate how long it takes Jonathan to read one page, divide the 25 minutes by 10 pages to determine the page per minute rate. Thus, it takes 2.5 minutes to read one page.

Jonathan must read 120 more pages to complete the novel. (This is calculated by subtracting the pages already read from the total.) Now, multiply his rate per page by the number of pages. Thus,

$$120 \times 2.5 = 300$$

Expressed in time, 300 minutes is equal to 5 hours.

3) At a hotel, $\frac{4}{5}$ of the 120 rooms are booked for Saturday. On Sunday, $\frac{3}{4}$ of the rooms are booked. On which day are more of the rooms booked, and by how many more?

The first step is to calculate the number of rooms booked for each day. Do this by multiplying the fraction of the rooms booked by the total number of rooms.

$$\text{Saturday:} \frac{4}{5} \times 120 = \frac{4}{5} \times \frac{120}{1} = \frac{480}{5} = 96 \text{ rooms}$$

$$\text{Sunday:} \frac{3}{4} \times 120 = \frac{3}{4} \times \frac{120}{1} = \frac{360}{4} = 90 \text{ rooms}$$

Thus, more rooms were booked on Saturday by 6 rooms.

4) In a veterinary hospital, the veterinarian-to-pet ratio is 1:9. The ratio is always constant. If there are 45 pets in the hospital, how many veterinarians are currently in the veterinary hospital?

Set up a proportion to solve for the number of veterinarians:

$$\frac{1}{9} = \frac{x}{45}$$

Cross-multiplying results in:

$$9x = 45$$

There are 5 veterinarians currently in the veterinary hospital.

Alternatively, as there are always 9 times as many pets as veterinarians, it is possible to divide the number of pets (45) by 9. This also arrives at the correct answer of 5 veterinarians.

5) At a general practice law firm, 30% of the lawyers work solely on tort cases. If 9 lawyers work solely on tort cases, how many lawyers work at the firm?

First, solve for the total number of lawyers working at the firm, which will be represented here with x. The problem states that 9 lawyers work solely on torts cases, and they make up 30% of the total lawyers at the firm. Thus, 30% multiplied by the total, x, will equal 9. Written as equation, this is:

$$30\% \times x = 9$$

It's easier to deal with the equation after converting the percentage to a decimal, leaving $0.3x = 9$. Thus,

$$x = \frac{9}{0.3} = 30$$

There are 30 lawyers working at the firm.

6) Xavier was hospitalized with pneumonia. He was originally given 35mg of antibiotics. Later, after his condition continued to worsen, Xavier's dosage was increased to 60mg. What was the percent increase of the antibiotics? Round the percentage to the nearest tenth.

An increase or decrease in percentage can be calculated by dividing the difference in amounts by the original amount and multiplying by 100. Written as an equation, the formula is:

$$\frac{new\ quantity - old\ quantity}{old\ quantity} \times 100$$

Here, the question states that the dosage was increased from 35mg to 60mg, so these are plugged into the formula to find the percentage increase.

$$\frac{60 - 35}{35} \times 100 = \frac{25}{35} \times 100 = 0.7142 \times 100 = 71.4\%$$

Analyzing Proportional Relationships and Using Them to Solve Real-World Problems

Much like a scale factor can be written using an equation like $2A = B$, a **relationship** is represented by the equation $Y = kX$. X and Y are proportional because as values of X increase, the values of Y also increase. A relationship that is inversely proportional can be represented by the equation $Y = \frac{k}{X}$, where the value of Y decreases as the value of x increases and vice versa.

Proportional reasoning can be used to solve problems involving ratios, percentages, and averages. Ratios can be used in setting up proportions and solving them to find unknowns. For example, if a student completes an average of 10 pages of math homework in 3 nights, how long would it take the student to complete 22 pages? Both ratios can be written as fractions. The second ratio would contain the unknown.

The following proportion represents this problem, where x is the unknown number of nights:

$$\frac{10\ pages}{3\ nights} = \frac{22\ pages}{x\ nights}$$

Solving this proportion entails cross-multiplying and results in the following equation:

$$10x = 22 \times 3$$

Simplifying and solving for x results in the exact solution: $x = 6.6\ nights$. The result would be rounded up to 7 because the homework would actually be completed on the 7th night.

The following problem uses ratios involving percentages:

If 20% of the class is girls and 30 students are in the class, how many girls are in the class?

["

To solve for x, the fractions must be cross multiplied:

$$(75\%x = 90\% \times 25\%)$$

To make things easier, let's convert the percentages to decimals:

$$(0.9 \times 0.25 = 0.225 = 0.75x)$$

To get rid of x's coefficient, each side must be divided by that same coefficient to get the answer:

$$x = 0.3$$

The question could ask for the answer as a percentage or fraction in lowest terms, which are 30% and $\frac{3}{10}$, respectively.

2) $\frac{x}{12} = \frac{30}{96}$

Cross-multiply: $96x = 30 \times 12$

Multiply: $96x = 360$

Divide: $x = 360 \div 96$

Answer: $x = 3.75$

3) $\frac{0.5}{3} = \frac{x}{6}$

Cross-multiply: $3x = 0.5 \times 6$

Multiply: $3x = 3$

Divide: $x = 3 \div 3$

Answer: $x = 1$

You may have noticed there's a faster way to arrive at the answer. If there is an obvious operation being performed on the proportion, the same operation can be used on the other side of the proportion to solve for x. For example, in the first practice problem, 75% became 25% when divided by 3, and upon doing the same to 90%, the correct answer of 30% would have been found with much less legwork. However, these questions aren't always so intuitive, so it's a good idea to work through the steps, even if the answer seems apparent from the outset.

Exponents

Radicals and Exponents

Exponents are used in mathematics to express a number or variable multiplied by itself a certain number of times. For example, x^3 means x is multiplied by itself three times. In this expression, x is called the **base**, and 3 is the **exponent**. Exponents can be used in more complex problems when they contain fractions and negative numbers.

Fractional exponents can be explained by looking first at the inverse of exponents, which are **roots**. Given the expression x^2, the square root can be taken, $\sqrt{x^2}$, cancelling out the 2 and leaving x by itself, if x is positive. Cancellation occurs because $\sqrt{x}$ can be written with exponents, instead of roots, as $x^{\frac{1}{2}}$. The numerator of 1 is the exponent, and the denominator of 2 is called the root (which is why it's referred to as **square root**). Taking the square root of x^2 is the same as raising it to the $\frac{1}{2}$ power. Written out in mathematical form, it takes the following progression:

$$\sqrt{x^2} = (x^2)^{\frac{1}{2}} = x$$

From properties of exponents,

$$2 \times \frac{1}{2} = 1$$

1 is the actual exponent of x. Another example can be seen with $x^{\frac{4}{7}}$. The variable x, raised to four-sevenths, is equal to the seventh root of x to the fourth power: $\sqrt[7]{x^4}$. In general,

$$x^{\frac{1}{n}} = \sqrt[n]{x} \text{ and } x^{\frac{m}{n}} = \sqrt[n]{x^m}$$

Negative exponents also involve fractions. Whereas y^3 can also be rewritten as $\frac{y^3}{1}$, y^{-3} can be rewritten as $\frac{1}{y^3}$. A negative exponent means the exponential expression must be moved to the opposite spot in a fraction to make the exponent positive. If the negative appears in the numerator, it moves to the denominator. If the negative appears in the denominator, it is moved to the numerator. In general, $a^{-n} = \frac{1}{a^n}$, and a^{-n} and a^n are reciprocals.

Take, for example, the following expression:

$$\frac{a^{-4}b^2}{c^{-5}}$$

Since a is raised to the negative fourth power, it can be moved to the denominator. Since c is raised to the negative fifth power, it can be moved to the numerator. The b variable is raised to the positive second power, so it does not move.

The simplified expression is as follows:

$$\frac{b^2c^5}{a^4}$$

In mathematical expressions containing exponents and other operations, the order of operations must be followed. PEMDAS states that exponents are calculated after any parenthesis and grouping symbols, but before any multiplication, division, addition, and subtraction.

There are a few rules for working with exponents. For any numbers a, b, m, n, the following hold true:

$$a^1 = a$$

$$1^a = 1$$

$$a^0 = 1$$

$$a^m \times a^n = a^{m+n}$$

$$a^m \div a^n = a^{m-n}$$

$$(a^m)^n = a^{m \times n}$$

$$(a \times b)^m = a^m \times b^m$$

$$(a \div b)^m = a^m \div b^m$$

Any number, including a fraction, can be an exponent. The same rules apply.

Manipulating Roots and Exponents

A **root** is a different way to write an exponent when the exponent is the reciprocal of a whole number. We use the **radical** symbol to write this in the following way:

$$\sqrt[n]{a} = a^{\frac{1}{n}}$$

This quantity is called the n-*th root* of a. The n is called the **index** of the radical.

Note that if the n-th root of a is multiplied by itself n times, the result will just be a. If no number n is written by the radical, it is assumed that n is 2:

$$\sqrt{5} = 5^{\frac{1}{2}}$$

The special case of the 2nd root is called the **square root**, and the third root is called the **cube root**.

A **perfect square** is a whole number that is the square of another whole number. For example, sixteen and 64 are perfect squares because 16 is the square of 4, and 64 is the square of 8.

Scientific Notation

Scientific notation is the conversion of extremely small or large numbers into a format that is easier to comprehend and manipulate. It changes the number into three separate parts: a mathematical sign $(+/-)$, a digit term (known as a **significand**), and an exponential term.

$$Scientific\ notation = (+ \text{ or } -)\ significand \times exponential\ term$$

To put a number into scientific notation, one should use the following steps:

- Move the decimal point to after the first non-zero number to find the digit number.
- Count how many places the decimal point was moved in step 1.
- Determine if the exponent is positive or negative.

- Create an exponential term using the information from steps 2 and 3.
- Combine the digit term and exponential term to get scientific notation.

For example, to put 0.0000098 into scientific notation, the decimal should be moved so that it lies between the last two numbers: 000009.8. This creates the digit number:

$$9.8$$

Next, the number of places that the decimal point moved is determined; to get between the 9 and the 8, the decimal was moved six places to the right. It may be helpful to remember that a decimal moved to the right creates a negative exponent, and a decimal moved to the left creates a positive exponent. Because the decimal was moved six places to the right, the exponent is negative.

Now, the exponential term can be created by using the base 10 (this is *always* the base in scientific notation) and the number of places moved as the exponent, in this case 10^{-6}.

Finally, the digit term and the exponential term can be combined as a product. Therefore, the scientific notation for the number 0.0000098 is:

$$9.8 \times 10^{-6}$$

Algebraic Expressions

Algebraic Expressions

Algebraic expressions look similar to equations, but they do not include the equal sign. Algebraic expressions are comprised of numbers, variables, and mathematical operations. Some examples of algebraic expressions are $8x + 7y - 12z$, $3a^2$, and $5x^3 - 4y^4$.

Algebraic expressions consist of variables, numbers, and operations. A **term** of an expression is any combination of numbers and/or variables, and terms are separated by addition and subtraction. For example, the expression:

$$5x^2 - 3xy + 4 - 2$$

This expression consists of 4 terms: $5x^2$, $-3xy$, $4y$, and -2. Note that each term includes its given sign (+ or −). The **variable** part of a term is a letter that represents an unknown quantity. The coefficient of a term is the number by which the variable is multiplied. For the term $4y$, the variable is y and the coefficient is 4. Terms are identified by the power (or exponent) of its variable.

A number without a variable is referred to as a **constant**. If the variable is to the first power (x^1 or simply x), it is referred to as a **linear** term. A term with a variable to the second power (x^2) is **quadratic** and a term to the third power (x^3) is **cubic**. Consider the expression:

$$x^3 + 3x - 1$$

The constant is −1. The linear term is $3x$. There is no quadratic term. The cubic term is x^3.

An algebraic expression can also be classified by how many terms exist in the expression. Any like terms should be combined before classifying. A **monomial** is an expression consisting of only one term. Examples of monomials are: 17, $2x$, and $-5ab^2$. A **binomial** is an expression consisting of two terms separated by addition or subtraction. Examples include $2x - 4$ and $-3y^2 + 2y$. A **trinomial** consists of 3 terms. For example,

$$5x^2 - 2x + 1$$

51

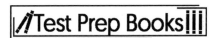

This is a trinomial.

Algebraic expressions and equations can be used to represent real-life situations and model the behavior of different variables. For example, $2x + 5$ could represent the cost to play games at an arcade. In this case, 5 represents the price of admission to the arcade and 2 represents the cost of each game played. To calculate the total cost, use the number of games played for x, multiply it by 2, and add 5.

Adding and Subtracting Linear Algebraic Expressions

An algebraic expression is simplified by combining like terms. A term is a number, variable, or product of a number, and variables separated by addition and subtraction. For the algebraic expression:

$$3x^2 - 4x + 5 - 5x^2 + x - 3$$

The terms are $3x^2$, $-4x$, 5, $-5x^2$, x, and -3. **Like terms** have the same variables raised to the same powers (exponents). The like terms for the previous example are $3x^2$ and $-5x^2$, $-4x$ and x, 5 and -3. To combine like terms, the coefficients (numerical factor of the term including sign) are added, and the variables and their powers are kept the same. Note that if a coefficient is not written, it is an implied coefficient of 1 ($x = 1x$). The previous example will simplify to:

$$-2x^2 - 3x + 2$$

When adding or subtracting algebraic expressions, each expression is written in parenthesis. The negative sign is distributed when necessary, and like terms are combined. Consider the following:

$$add\ 2a + 5b - 2\ to\ a - 2b + 8c - 4$$

The sum is set as follows:

$$(a - 2b + 8c - 4) + (2a + 5b - 2)$$

In front of each set of parentheses is an implied positive one, which, when distributed, does not change any of the terms. Therefore, the parentheses are dropped and like terms are combined:

$$a - 2b + 8c - 4 + 2a + 5b - 2$$

$$3a + 3b + 8c - 6$$

Consider the following problem:

$$Subtract\ 2a + 5b - 2\ from\ a - 2b + 8c - 4$$

The difference is set as follows:

$$(a - 2b + 8c - 4) - (2a + 5b - 2)$$

The implied one in front of the first set of parentheses will not change those four terms. However, distributing the implied -1 in front of the second set of parentheses will change the sign of each of those three terms:
$$a - 2b + 8c - 4 - 2a - 5b + 2$$

Combining like terms yields the simplified expression:

$$-a - 7b + 8c - 2$$

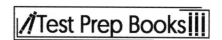

Multiplying Algebraic Expressions

The **distributive property** states that multiplying a sum (or difference) by a number produces the same result as multiplying each value in the sum (or difference) by the number and adding (or subtracting) the products. Using mathematical symbols, the distributive property states:

$$a(b + c) = ab + ac$$

The expression $4(3 + 2)$ is simplified using the order of operations. Simplifying inside the parenthesis first produces 4×5, which equals 20. The expression $4(3 + 2)$ can also be simplified using the distributive property:

$$4(3 + 2)$$

$$4 \times 3 + 4 \times 2$$

$$12 + 8$$

$$20$$

Consider the following example:

$$4(3x - 2)$$

The expression cannot be simplified inside the parenthesis because $3x$ and -2 are not like terms, and therefore cannot be combined. However, the expression can be simplified by using the distributive property and multiplying each term inside of the parenthesis by the term outside of the parenthesis: $12x - 8$. The resulting equivalent expression contains no like terms, so it cannot be further simplified.

Consider the expression:

$$(3x + 2y + 1) - (5x - 3) + 2(3y + 4)$$

Again, there are no like terms, but the distributive property is used to simplify the expression. Note there is an implied one in front of the first set of parentheses and an implied -1 in front of the second set of parentheses. Distributing the one, -1, and 2 produces:

$$1(3x) + 1(2y) + 1(1) - 1(5x) - 1(-3) + 2(3y) + 2(4)$$

$$3x + 2y + 1 - 5x + 3 + 6y + 8$$

This expression contains like terms that are combined to produce the simplified expression:

$$-2x + 8y + 12$$

Algebraic expressions are tested to be equivalent by choosing values for the variables and evaluating both expressions. For example, $4(3x - 2)$ and $12x - 8$ are tested by substituting 3 for the variable x and calculating to determine if equivalent values result.

Evaluating Algebraic Expressions

To evaluate the expression, the given values for the variables are substituted (or replaced) and the expression is simplified using the order of operations. Parenthesis should be used when substituting. Consider the following: Evaluate $a - 2b + ab$ for $a = 3$ and $b = -1$.

To evaluate, any variable a is replaced with 3 and any variable b with -1, producing:

$$(3) - 2(-1) + (3)(-1)$$

Next, the order of operations is used to calculate the value of the expression, which is 2.

Here's another example. Evaluate the following equation when $a = 3$ and $b = -1$:

$$a - 2b + ab$$

To evaluate an expression, the given values should be substituted for the variables and simplified using the order of operations. In this case:

$$(3) - 2(-1) + (3)(-1)$$

Parentheses are used when substituting.

Given an algebraic expression, students may be asked to simplify the expression. For example:

$$\text{Simplify } 5x^2 - 10x + 2 - 8x^2 + x - 1.$$

Simplifying algebraic expressions requires combining like terms. A term is a number, variable, or product of a number and variables separated by addition and subtraction. The terms in the above expression are: $5x^2$, $-10x$, 2, $-8x^2$, x, and -1. Like terms have the same variables raised to the same powers (exponents). To combine like terms, the coefficients (numerical factor of the term including sign) are added, while the variables and their powers are kept the same. The example above simplifies to:

$$-3x^2 - 9x + 1$$

Let's try two more.

Evaluate $\frac{1}{2}x^2 - 3, x = 4$.

The first step is to substitute in 4 for x in the expression:

$$\frac{1}{2}(4)^2 - 3$$

Then, the order of operations is used to simplify.

The exponent comes first, $\frac{1}{2}(16) - 3$, then the multiplication $8 - 3$, and then, after subtraction, the solution is 5.

Evaluate $4|5 - x| + 2y, x = 4, y = -3$.

The first step is to substitute 4 in for x and -3 in for y in the expression:

$$4|5 - 4| + 2(-3)$$

Then, the absolute value expression is simplified, which is:

$$|5 - 4| = |1| = 1$$

The expression is $4(1) + 2(-3)$ which can be simplified using the order of operations.

First is the multiplication, $4 + (-6)$; then addition yields an answer of -2.

54

Creating Algebraic Expressions

A linear expression is a statement about an unknown quantity expressed in mathematical symbols. The statement "five times a number added to forty" can be expressed as $5x + 40$. A linear equation is a statement in which two expressions (at least one containing a variable) are equal to each other. The statement "five times a number added to forty is equal to ten" can be expressed as:

$$5x + 40 = 10$$

Real world scenarios can also be expressed mathematically. Suppose a job pays its employees $300 per week and $40 for each sale made. The weekly pay is represented by the expression $40x + 300$ where x is the number of sales made during the week.

Consider the following scenario: Bob had $20 and Tom had $4. After selling 4 ice cream cones to Bob, Tom has as much money as Bob. The cost of an ice cream cone is an unknown quantity and can be represented by a variable (x). The amount of money Bob has after his purchase is four times the cost of an ice cream cone subtracted from his original $20 → $20 - 4x$. The amount of money Tom has after his sale is four times the cost of an ice cream cone added to his original $4 → $4x + 4$. After the sale, the amount of money that Bob and Tom have is equal:

$$→ 20 - 4x = 4x + 4$$

When expressing a verbal or written statement mathematically, it is key to understand words or phrases that can be represented with symbols. The following are examples:

Symbol	Phrase
$+$	added to, increased by, sum of, more than
$-$	decreased by, difference between, less than, take away
x	multiplied by, 3 (4, 5...) times as large, product of
$\div$	divided by, quotient of, half (third, etc.) of
$=$	is, the same as, results in, as much as
$x, t, n, etc.$	a number, unknown quantity, value of

Linear Equations

One-Variable Linear Equations and Inequalities

Linear equations and linear inequalities are both comparisons of two algebraic expressions. However, unlike equations in which the expressions are equal, linear inequalities compare expressions that may be unequal. Linear equations typically have one value for the variable that makes the statement true. Linear inequalities generally have an infinite number of values that make the statement true.

When solving a linear equation, the desired result requires determining a numerical value for the unknown variable. If given a linear equation involving addition, subtraction, multiplication, or division, working backwards isolates the variable. Addition and subtraction are inverse operations, as are multiplication and division. Therefore, they can be used to cancel each other out.

For example, solve $4(t - 2) + 2t - 4 = 2(9 - 2t)$

Distributing: $4t - 8 + 2t - 4 = 18 - 4t$

Combining like terms: $6t - 12 = 18 - 4t$

Adding $4t$ to each side to move the variable: $10t - 12 = 18$

Adding 12 to each side to isolate the variable: $10t = 30$

Dividing each side by 10 to isolate the variable: $t = 3$

The answer can be checked by substituting the value for the variable into the original equation, ensuring that both sides calculate to be equal.

Linear inequalities express the relationship between unequal values. More specifically, they describe in what way the values are unequal. A value can be greater than (>), less than (<), greater than or equal to (≥), or less than or equal to (≤) another value.

$$5x + 40 > 65$$

This is read as *five times a number added to forty is greater than sixty-five.*

When solving a linear inequality, the solution is the set of all numbers that make the statement true.

$$x + 2 \geq 6$$

The above inequality has a solution set of 4 and every number greater than 4 (4.01; 5; 12; 107; etc.). Adding 2 to 4 or any number greater than 4 results in a value that is greater than or equal to 6. Therefore, $x \geq 4$ is the solution set.

To algebraically solve a linear inequality, follow the same steps as those for solving a linear equation. The inequality symbol stays the same for all operations *except* when multiplying or dividing by a negative number. If multiplying or dividing by a negative number while solving an inequality, the relationship reverses (the sign flips). In other words, > switches to < and vice versa. Multiplying or dividing by a positive number does not change the relationship, so the sign stays the same. An example is shown below.

Solve $-2x - 8 \leq 22$ for the value of x.

Add 8 to both sides to isolate the variable:

$$-2x \leq 30$$

Divide both sides by –2 to solve for x:
$$x \geq -15$$

Solutions of a linear equation or a linear inequality are the values of the variable that make a statement true. In the case of a linear equation, the solution set (list of all possible solutions) typically consists of a single numerical value. To find the solution, the equation is solved by isolating the variable. For example, solving the equation $3x - 7 = -13$ produces the solution $x = -2$. The only value for x which produces a true statement is -2. This can be checked by substituting -2 into the original equation to check that both sides are equal. In this case,
$$3(-2) - 7 = -13 \rightarrow -13 = -13$$

Therefore, -2 is a solution.

Although linear equations generally have one solution, this is not always the case. If there is no value for the variable that makes the statement true, there is no solution to the equation. Consider the equation:

$$x + 3 = x - 1$$

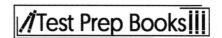

There is no value for *x* in which adding 3 to the value produces the same result as subtracting one from the value. Conversely, if any value for the variable makes a true statement, the equation has an infinite number of solutions. Consider the equation:

$$3x + 6 = 3(x + 2)$$

Any number substituted for *x* will result in a true statement (both sides of the equation are equal).

By manipulating equations like the two above, the variable of the equation will cancel out completely. If the remaining constants express a true statement (ex. $6 = 6$), then all real numbers are solutions to the equation. If the constants left express a false statement (ex. $3 = -1$), then no solution exists for the equation.

Solving a linear inequality requires all values that make the statement true to be determined. For example,
$$3x - 7 \geq -13$$

This produces the solution $x \geq -2$. This means that −2 and any number greater than −2 produces a true statement. Solution sets for linear inequalities will often be displayed using a number line. If a value is included in the set ($\geq$ or $\leq$), a shaded dot is placed on that value and an arrow extending in the direction of the solutions. For a variable > or $\geq$ a number, the arrow will point right on a number line, the direction where the numbers increase. If a variable is < or $\leq$ a number, the arrow will point left on a number line, which is the direction where the numbers decrease. If the value is not included in the set (> or <), an open (unshaded) circle on that value is used with an arrow in the appropriate direction.

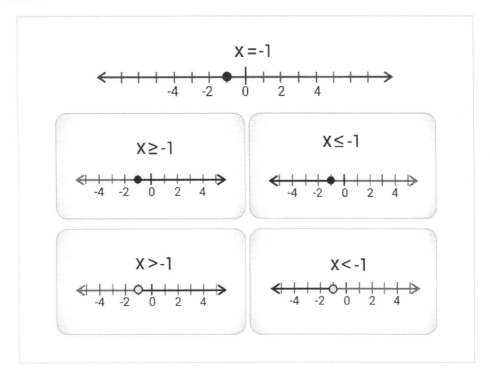

Similar to linear equations, a linear inequality may have a solution set consisting of all real numbers or can contain no solution. When solved algebraically, a linear inequality in which the variable cancels out and results in a true statement (ex. $7 \geq 2$) has a solution set of all real numbers. A linear inequality in which the variable cancels out and results in a false statement (ex. $7 \leq 2$) has no solution.

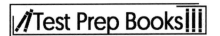

Linear Inequalities in One Variable

Linear inequalities and linear equations are both comparisons of two algebraic expressions. However, unlike equations in which the expressions are equal to each other, **linear inequalities** compare expressions that are unequal. Linear equations typically have one value for the variable that makes the statement true. Linear inequalities generally have an infinite number of values that make the statement true.

Linear inequalities are a concise mathematical way to express the relationship between unequal values. More specifically, they describe in what way the values are unequal. A value could be greater than ($>$); less than ($<$); greater than or equal to ($\geq$); or less than or equal to ($\leq$) another value. The statement "five times a number added to forty is more than sixty-five" can be expressed as:

$$5x + 40 > 65$$

Common words and phrases that express inequalities are:

Symbol	Phrase
$<$	is under, is below, smaller than, beneath
$>$	is above, is over, bigger than, exceeds
$\leq$	no more than, at most, maximum
$\geq$	no less than, at least, minimum

Solving Linear Inequalities

When solving a linear inequality, the solution is the set of all numbers that makes the statement true.

$$x + 2 \geq 6$$

The above inequality has a solution set of 4 and every number greater than 4 (4.0001, 5, 12, 107, etc.). Adding 2 to 4 or any number greater than 4 would result in a value that is greater than or equal to 6. Therefore, $x \geq 4$ would be the solution set.

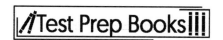

Solution sets for linear inequalities often will be displayed using a number line. If a value is included in the set ($\geq$ or $\leq$), there is a shaded dot placed on that value and an arrow extending in the direction of the solutions. For a variable $>$ or $\geq$ a number, the arrow would point right on the number line (the direction where the numbers increase); and if a variable is $<$ or $\leq$ a number, the arrow would point left (where the numbers decrease). If the value is not included in the set ($>$ or $<$), an open circle on that value would be used with an arrow in the appropriate direction.

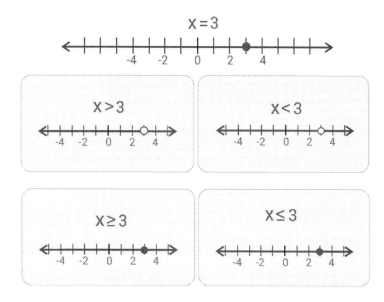

Students may be asked to write a linear inequality given a graph of its solution set. To do so, they should identify whether the value is included (shaded dot or open circle) and the direction in which the arrow is pointing.

In order to algebraically solve a linear inequality, the same steps should be followed as in solving a linear equation. The inequality symbol stays the same for all operations EXCEPT when multiplying or dividing by a negative number. If multiplying or dividing by a negative number while solving an inequality, the relationship reverses (the sign flips). Multiplying or dividing by a positive does not change the relationship, so the sign stays the same. In other words, $>$ switches to $<$ and vice versa. An example is shown below.

Solve $-2(x + 4) \leq 22$ for the value of x.

First, distribute -2 to the binomial by multiplying:

$$-2x - 8 \leq 22$$

Next, add 8 to both sides to isolate the variable:

$$-2x \leq 30$$

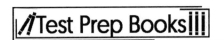

Divide both sides by −2 to solve for x:

$$x \geq -15$$

Systems of Two Linear Equations in Two Variables

A system of two linear equations in two variables is a set of equations that use the same variables, usually x and y. Here's a sample problem:

> An Internet provider charges an installation fee and a monthly charge. It advertises that two months of its offering costs $100 and six months costs $200. Find the monthly charge and the installation fee.

The two unknown quantities (variables) are the monthly charge and the installation fee. There are two different statements given relating the variables: two months added to the installation fee is $100; and six months added to the installation fee is $200. Using the variable x as the monthly charge and y as the installation fee, the statements can be written as the following:

$$2x + y = 100$$

$$6x + y = 200$$

These two equations taken together form a system modeling the given scenario.

Systems of Linear Inequalities in Two Variables

A system of linear inequalities consists of two linear inequalities making comparisons between two variables. Students may be given a scenario and asked to express it as a system of inequalities:

> A consumer study calls for at least 60 adult participants. It cannot use more than 25 men. Express these constraints as a system of inequalities.

This can be modeled by the system: $x + y \geq 60$; $x \leq 25$, where x represents the number of men and y represents the number of women. A solution to the system is an ordered pair that makes both inequalities true when substituting the values for x and y.

Linear Applications and Graphs

Linear Models and Relationships

Linear relationships describe the way two quantities change with respect to each other. The relationship is defined as linear because a line is produced if all the sets of corresponding values are graphed on a coordinate grid. When expressing the linear relationship as an equation, the equation is often written in the form $y = mx + b$ (slope-intercept form) where m and b are numerical values and x and y are variables. For example:

$$y = 5x + 10$$

Given a linear equation and the value of either variable (x or y), the value of the other variable can be determined.

Suppose a teacher is grading a test containing 20 questions with 5 points given for each correct answer, adding a curve of 10 points to each test. This linear relationship can be expressed as the equation:

$$y = 5x + 10$$

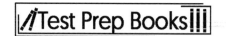

Where x represents the number of correct answers and y represents the test score. To determine the score of a test with a given number of correct answers, the number of correct answers is substituted into the equation for x and evaluated. For example, for 10 correct answers, 10 is substituted for x:

$$y = 5(10) + 10 \rightarrow y = 60$$

Therefore, 10 correct answers will result in a score of 60. The number of correct answers needed to obtain a certain score can also be determined. To determine the number of correct answers needed to score a 90, 90 is substituted for y in the equation (y represents the test score) and solved:

$$90 = 5x + 10 \rightarrow 80 = 5x \rightarrow 16 = x$$

Therefore, 16 correct answers are needed to score a 90.

Linear relationships may be represented by a table of 2 corresponding values. Certain tables may determine the relationship between the values and predict other corresponding sets. Consider the table below, which displays the money in a checking account that charges a monthly fee:

Month	0	1	2	3	4
Balance	$210	$195	$180	$165	$150

An examination of the values reveals that the account loses $15 every month (the month increases by one and the balance decreases by 15). This information can be used to predict future values. To determine what the value will be in month 6, the pattern can be continued, and it can be concluded that the balance will be $120. To determine which month the balance will be $0, $210 is divided by $15 (since the balance decreases $15 every month), resulting in month 14.

Similar to a table, a graph can display corresponding values of a linear relationship.

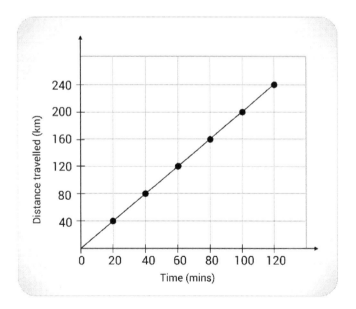

The graph above represents the relationship between distance traveled and time. To find the distance traveled in 80 minutes, the mark for 80 minutes is located at the bottom of the graph. By following this mark directly up on the graph, the corresponding point for 80 minutes is directly across from the 160-kilometer mark. This information indicates that the distance travelled in 80 minutes is 160 kilometers. To predict information not displayed on the

61

graph, the way in which the variables change with respect to one another is determined. In this case, distance increases by 40 kilometers as time increases by 20 minutes. This information can be used to continue the data in the graph or convert the values to a table.

Identifying Variables for Linear Models

The first step to writing a linear model is to identify what the variables represent. A **variable** represents an unknown quantity, and in the case of a linear equation, a specific relationship exists between the two variables (usually x and y). Within a given scenario, the variables are the two quantities that are changing. The variable x is considered the independent variable and represents the inputs of a function. The variable y is considered the dependent variable and represents the outputs of a function. For example, if a scenario describes distance traveled and time traveled, distance would be represented by y and time represented by x. The distance traveled depends on the time spent traveling (time is independent). If a scenario describes the cost of a cab ride and the distance traveled, the cost would be represented by y and the distance represented by x. The cost of a cab ride depends on the distance traveled.

Identifying the Slope and Y-Intercept for Linear Models

The **slope of the graph of a line** represents the rate of change between the variables of an equation. In the context of a real-world scenario, the slope will tell the way in which the unknown quantities (variables) change with respect to each other. A scenario involving distance and time might state that someone is traveling at a rate of 45 miles per hour. The slope of the linear model would be 45. A scenario involving the cost of a cab ride and distance traveled might state that the person is charged $3 for each mile. The slope of the linear model would be 3.

The **y-intercept of a linear function** is the value of y when $x = 0$ (the point where the line intercepts the y-axis on the graph of the equation). It is sometimes helpful to think of this as a "starting point" for a linear function. Suppose for the scenario about the cab ride that the person is told that the cab company charges a flat fee of $5 plus $3 for each mile. Before traveling any distance ($x = 0$), the cost is $5. The y-intercept for the linear model would be 5.

Identifying Ordered Pairs for Linear Models

A linear equation with two variables can be written given a point (ordered pair) and the slope or given two points on a line. An ordered pair gives a set of corresponding values for the two variables (x and y). As an example, for a scenario involving distance and time, it is given that the person traveled 112.5 miles in 2 ½ hours. Knowing that x represents time and y represents distance, this information can be written as the ordered pair (2.5, 112.5).

Linear Functions Model a Linear Relationship Between Two Quantities

Linear relationships between two quantities can be expressed in two ways: function notation or as a linear equation with two variables. The relationship is referred to as linear because its graph is represented by a line. For a relationship to be linear, both variables must be raised to the first power only.

Function/Linear Equation Notation

A **relation** is a set of input and output values that can be written as ordered pairs. A function is a relation in which each input is paired with exactly one output. The domain of a function consists of all inputs, and the range consists of all outputs. Graphing the ordered pairs of a linear function produces a straight line. An example of a function would be:

$$f(x) = 4x + 4$$

The equation is read as "f of x is equal to four times x plus four." In this example, the input would be x and the output would be $f(x)$. Ordered pairs would be represented as $(x, f(x))$. To find the output for an input value of 3, 3 would be substituted for x into the function as follows:

$$f(3) = 4(3) + 4$$

This results in $f(3) = 16$. Therefore, the ordered pair $(3, f(3)) = (3, 16)$. Note $f(x)$ is a function of x denoted by f. Functions of x could be named $g(x)$, read "g of x"; $p(x)$, read "p of x"; etc.

A linear function could also be written in the form of an equation with two variables. Typically, the variable x represents the inputs and the variable y represents the outputs. The variable x is considered the independent variable and y the dependent variable. The above function would be written as:

$$y = 4x + 4$$

Ordered pairs are written in the form (x, y).

Writing Linear Equations in Two Variables

When writing linear equations in two variables, the process depends on the information given. Questions will typically provide the slope of the line and its y-intercept, an ordered pair and the slope, or two ordered pairs.

Linear equations are commonly written in slope-intercept form, $y = mx + b$, where m represents the slope of the line and b represents the y-intercept. The slope is the rate of change between the variables, usually expressed as a whole number or fraction. The y-intercept is the value of y when $x = 0$ (the point where the line intercepts the y-axis on a graph). Given the slope and y-intercept of a line, the values are substituted for m and b into the equation. A line with a slope of $\frac{1}{2}$ and y-intercept of -2 would have an equation:

$$y = \frac{1}{2}x - 2$$

The point-slope form of a line, $y - y_1 = m(x - x_1)$, is used to write an equation when given an ordered pair (point on the equation's graph) for the function and its rate of change (slope of the line). The values for the slope, m, and the point (x_1, y_1) are substituted into the point-slope form to obtain the equation of the line. A line with a slope of 3 and an ordered pair $(4, -2)$ would have an equation:

$$y - (-2) = 3(x - 4)$$

If a question specifies that the equation be written in slope-intercept form, the equation should be manipulated to isolate y:

Solve: $y - (-2) = 3(x - 4)$

Distribute: $y + 2 = 3x - 12$

Subtract 2 from both sides: $y = 3x - 14$

Given two ordered pairs for a function, (x_1, y_1) and (x_2, y_2), it is possible to determine the rate of change between the variables (slope of the line). To calculate the slope of the line, m, the values for the ordered pairs should be substituted into the formula:

$$m = \frac{y_2 - y_1}{x_2 - x_1}$$

The expression is substituted to obtain a whole number or fraction for the slope. Once the slope is calculated, the slope and either of the ordered pairs should be substituted into the point-slope form to obtain the equation of the line.

Graphing a System of Two Linear Equations in Two Variables

A solution for a system of equations is an ordered pair that makes both equations true. One method for solving a system of equations is to graph both lines on a coordinate plane. If the lines intersect, the point of intersection is the solution to the system. Every point on a line represents an ordered pair that makes its equation true. The ordered pair represented by this point of intersection lies on both lines and therefore makes both equations true. This ordered pair should be checked by substituting its values into both of the original equations of the system. Note that given a system of equations and an ordered pair, the ordered pair can be determined to be a solution or not by checking it in both equations.

If, when graphed, the lines representing the equations of a system do not intersect, then the two lines are parallel to each other or they are the same exact line. Parallel lines extend in the same direction without ever meeting. A system consisting of parallel lines has no solution. If the equations for a system represent the same exact line, then every point on the line is a solution to the system. In this case, there would be an infinite number of solutions. A system consisting of intersecting lines is referred to as independent; a system consisting of parallel lines is referred to as inconsistent; and a system consisting of coinciding lines is referred to as dependent.

Parallel Lines	Intersecting Lines	Coincident Lines
Inconsistent	Independent	Dependent

Graphing Solution Sets for Linear Inequalities in Two Variables

A graph of the solution set for a linear inequality shows the ordered pairs that make the statement true. The graph consists of a boundary line dividing the coordinate plane and shading on one side of the boundary. The boundary line should be graphed just as a linear equation would be graphed. If the inequality symbol is $>$ or $<$, a dashed line can be used to indicate that the line is not part of the solution set. If the inequality symbol is $\geq$ or $\leq$, a solid line can be used to indicate that the boundary line is included in the solution set. An ordered pair (x, y) on either side of the line should be chosen to test in the inequality statement. Substituting the values for x and y results in a true statement. For example:

$$15(3) + 25(2) > 90$$

The ordered pair and all others on that side of the boundary line are part of the solution set. To indicate this, that region of the graph should be shaded. If substituting the ordered pair results in a false statement, the ordered pair and all others on that side are not part of the solution set.

Therefore, the other region of the graph contains the solutions and should be shaded.

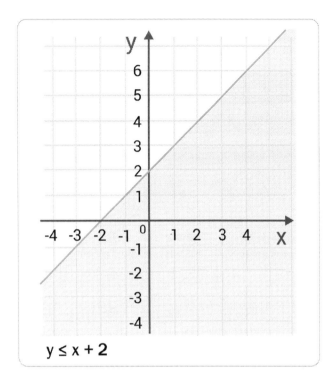

$$y \leq x + 2$$

A question may simply ask whether a given ordered pair is a solution to a given inequality. To determine this, the values should be substituted for the ordered pair into the inequality. If the result is a true statement, the ordered pair is a solution; if the result is a false statement, the ordered pair is not a solution.

Probability Sets

Chance Processes and Probability Models

Counting Techniques

There are many counting techniques that can help solve problems involving counting possibilities. For example, the **Addition Principle** states that if there are m choices from Group 1 and n choices from Group 2, then $n + m$ is the total number of choices possible from Groups 1 and 2. For this to be true, the groups can't have any choices in common. The **Multiplication Principle** states that if Process 1 can be completed n ways and Process 2 can be completed m ways, the total number of ways to complete both Process 1 and Process 2 is $n \times m$. For this rule to be used, both processes must be independent of each other. Counting techniques also involve permutations. A **permutation** is an arrangement of elements in a set for which order must be considered. For example, if three letters from the alphabet are chosen, ABC and BAC are two different permutations. The multiplication rule can be used to determine the total number of possibilities. If each letter can't be selected twice, the total number of possibilities is:

$$26 \times 25 \times 24 = 15,600$$

A formula can also be used to calculate this total. In general, the notation $P(n, r)$ represents the number of ways to arrange r objects from a set of n and, the formula is:

$$P(n, r) = \frac{n!}{(n-r)!}$$

In the previous example:

$$P(26, 3) = \frac{26!}{23!} = 15,600$$

Contrasting permutations, a **combination** is an arrangement of elements in which order doesn't matter. In this case, ABC and BAC are the same combination. In the previous scenario, there are six permutations that represent each single combination. Therefore, the total number of possible combinations is:
$$15,600 \div 6 = 2,600$$

In general, $C(n, r)$ represents the total number of combinations of n items selected r at a time where order doesn't matter. Another way to represent the combinations of r items selected out of a set of n items is $\binom{n}{r}$. The formula for select combinations of items is:

$$\binom{n}{r} = C(n, r) = \frac{n!}{(n-r)! \, r!}$$

Therefore, the following relationship exists between permutations and combinations:

$$C(n, r) = \frac{P(n, r)}{r!} = \frac{P(n, r)}{P(r, r)}$$

Fundamental Counting Principle

The **fundamental counting principle** that if there are m potential ways an event can occur, and n potential ways a second event can occur, then there are $m \times n$ potential ways both events can occur. For example, there are two events that can occur after flipping a coin and six events that can occur after rolling a die, so there are $2 \times 6 = 12$ total possible event scenarios if both are done simultaneously. This principle can be used to find probabilities involving finite sample spaces and independent trials because it calculates the total number of possible outcomes. For this principle to work, the events must be independent of each other.

Independence and Conditional Probability

Sample Subsets

A sample can be broken up into subsets that are smaller parts of the whole. For example, consider a sample population of females. The sample can be divided into smaller subsets based on the characteristics of each female. There can be a group of females with brown hair and a group of females that wear glasses. There also can be a group of females that have brown hair *and* wear glasses. This "and" relates to the **intersection** of the two separate groups of brunettes and those with glasses. Every female in that intersection group has both characteristics. Similarly, there also can be a group of females that either have brown hair *or* wear glasses. The "or" relates to the union of the two separate groups of brunettes and glasses. Every female in this group has at least one of the characteristics. Finally, the group of females who do not wear glasses can be discussed. This "not" relates to the **complement** of the glass-wearing group. No one in the complement has glasses. **Venn diagrams** are useful in highlighting these ideas. When discussing statistical experiments, this idea can also relate to events instead of characteristics.

Verifying Independent Events

Two events aren't always independent. For example, females with glasses and brown hair aren't independent characteristics. There definitely can be overlap because people with brown hair can wear glasses. Also, two events that exist at the same time don't have to have a relationship. For example, even if everyone in a given sample is wearing glasses, the characteristics aren't related. In this case, the probability of a brunette wearing glasses is equal to the probability of a person being a brunette multiplied by the probability of a person wearing glasses. This mathematical test of $P(A \cap B) = P(A)P(B)$ verifies that two events are independent.

Conditional Probability

Conditional probability is the probability that event A will happen given that event B has already occurred. An example of this is calculating the probability that a person will eat dessert once they have eaten dinner. This is different than calculating the probability of a person just eating dessert. The formula for the conditional probability of event A occurring given B is:

$$P(A|B) = \frac{P(A \text{ and } B)}{P(B)}$$

It's defined as the probability of both A and B occurring divided by the probability of event B occurring. If A and B are independent, then the probability of both A and B occurring is equal to $P(A)P(B)$, so $P(A|B)$ reduces to just $P(A)$. This means that A and B have no relationship, and the probability of A occurring is the same as the conditional probability of A occurring given B. Similarly, if A and B are independent:

$$P(B|A) = \frac{P(B \text{ and } A)}{P(A)} = P(B)$$

Independent Versus Related Events

To summarize, conditional probability is the probability that an event occurs given that another event has happened. If the two events are related, the probability that the second event will occur changes if the other event has happened. However, if the two events aren't related and are therefore independent, the first event to occur won't impact the probability of the second event occurring.

Measuring Probabilities with Two-Way Frequency Tables

When measuring event probabilities, two-way frequency tables can be used to report the raw data and then used to calculate probabilities. If the frequency tables are translated into relative frequency tables, the probabilities presented in the table can be plugged directly into the formulas for conditional probabilities. By plugging in the correct frequencies, the data from the table can be used to determine if events are independent or dependent.

Differing Probabilities

The probability that event A occurs differs from the probability that event A occurs given B. When working within a given model, it's important to note the difference. $P(A|B)$ is determined using the formula:

$$P(A|B) = \frac{P(A \text{ and } B)}{P(B)}$$

This represents the total number of A's outcomes left that could occur after B occurs. $P(A)$ can be calculated without any regard for B. For example, the probability of a student finding a parking spot on a busy campus is different once class is in session.

The Addition Rule

The probability of event A or B occurring isn't equal to the sum of each individual probability. The probability that both events can occur at the same time must be subtracted from this total. This idea is shown in the **addition rule**:

$$P(A \text{ or } B) = P(A) + P(B) - P(A \text{ and } B)$$

The addition rule is another way to determine the probability of compound events that aren't mutually exclusive. If the events are mutually exclusive, the probability of both A and B occurring at the same time is 0.

Computing Probabilities

Simple and Compound Events

A **simple event** consists of only one outcome. The most popular simple event is flipping a coin, which results in either heads or tails. A **compound event** results in more than one outcome and consists of more than one simple event. An example of a compound event is flipping a coin while tossing a die. The result is either heads or tails on the coin and a number from one to six on the die. The probability of a simple event is calculated by dividing the number of possible outcomes by the total number of outcomes. Therefore, the probability of obtaining heads on a coin is $\frac{1}{2}$, and the probability of rolling a 6 on a die is $\frac{1}{6}$. The probability of compound events is calculated using the basic idea of the probability of simple events. If the two events are independent, the probability of one outcome is equal to the product of the probabilities of each simple event. For example, the probability of obtaining heads on a coin and rolling a 6 is equal to:

$$\frac{1}{2} \times \frac{1}{6} = \frac{1}{12}$$

The probability of either A or B occurring is equal to the sum of the probabilities minus the probability that both A and B will occur. Therefore, the probability of obtaining either heads on a coin or rolling a 6 on a die is:

$$\frac{1}{2} + \frac{1}{6} - \frac{1}{12} = \frac{7}{12}$$

The two events aren't mutually exclusive because they can happen at the same time. If two events are mutually exclusive, and the probability of both events occurring at the same time is zero, the probability of event A or B occurring equals the sum of both probabilities. An example of calculating the probability of two mutually exclusive events is determining the probability of pulling a king or a queen from a deck of cards. The two events cannot occur at the same time.

Uniform and Non-Uniform Probability Models

A **uniform probability model** is one where each outcome has an equal chance of occurring, such as the probabilities of rolling each side of a die. A **non-uniform probability model** is one where each result has a different chance of taking place. In a uniform probability model, the conditional probability formulas for $P(B|A)$ and $P(A|B)$ can be multiplied by their respective denominators to obtain two formulas for $P(A \text{ and } B)$. Therefore, the multiplication rule is derived as:

$$P(A \text{ and } B) = P(A)P(B|A) = P(B)P(A|B)$$

In a model, if the probability of either individual event is known and the corresponding conditional probability is known, the multiplication rule allows the probability of the joint occurrence of A and B to be calculated.

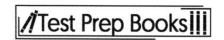

Descriptive Statistics

Basic Statistics

The field of statistics describes relationships between quantities that are related, but not necessarily in a deterministic manner. For example, a graduating student's salary will often be higher when the student graduates with a higher GPA, but this is not always the case. Likewise, people who smoke tobacco are more likely to develop lung cancer, but, in fact, it is possible for non-smokers to develop the disease as well. **Statistics** describes these kinds of situations, where the likelihood of some outcome depends on the starting data.

Descriptive statistics involves analyzing a collection of data to describe its broad properties such average (or mean), what percent of the data falls within a given range, and other such properties. An example of this would be taking all of the test scores from a given class and calculating the average test score. **Inferential statistics** attempts to use data about a subset of some population to make inferences about the rest of the population. An example of this would be taking a collection of students who received tutoring and comparing their results to a collection of students who did not receive tutoring, then using that comparison to try to predict whether the tutoring program in question is beneficial.

To be sure that inferences have a high probability of being true for the whole population, the subset that is analyzed needs to resemble a miniature version of the population as closely as possible. For this reason, statisticians like to choose random samples from the population to study, rather than picking a specific group of people based on some similarity. For example, studying the incomes of people who live in Portland does not reveal anything useful about the incomes of people who live in Tallahassee.

A statistical question is answered by collecting data with variability. Data consists of facts and/or statistics (numbers), and variability refers to a tendency to shift or change. Data is a broad term, inclusive of things like height, favorite color, name, salary, temperature, gas mileage, and language. Questions requiring data as an answer are not necessarily statistical questions. If there is no variability in the data, then the question is not statistical in nature. Consider the following examples: what is Mary's favorite color? How much money does your mother make? What was the highest temperature last week? How many miles did your car get on its last tank of gas? How much taller than Bob is Ed?

None of the above are statistical questions because each case lacks variability in the data needed to answer the question. The questions on favorite color, salary, and gas mileage each require a single piece of data, whether a fact or statistic. Therefore, variability is absent. Although the temperature question requires multiple pieces of data (the high temperature for each day), a single, distinct number is the answer. The height question requires two pieces of data, Bob's height and Ed's height, but no difference in variability exists between those two values. Therefore, this is not a statistical question. Statistical questions typically require calculations with data.

Consider the following statistical questions:

How many miles per gallon of gas does the 2016 Honda Civic get? To answer this question, data must be collected. This data should include miles driven and gallons used. Different cars, different drivers, and different driving conditions will produce different results. Therefore, variability exists in the data. To answer the question, the mean (average) value could be determined.

Are American men taller than German men? To answer this question, data must be collected. This data should include the heights of American men and the heights of German men. All American men are not the same height and all German men are not the same height. Some American men are taller than some German men and some German men are taller than some American men. Therefore, variability exists in the data. To answer the question, the median values for each group could be determined and compared.

The following are more examples of statistical questions: What proportion of 4th graders have a favorite color of blue? How much money do teachers make? Is it colder in Boston or Chicago?

An **experiment** is the method by which a hypothesis is tested using a controlled process called the scientific method. A cause and the effect of that cause are measured, and the hypothesis is accepted or rejected. Experiments are usually completed in a controlled environment where the results of a control population are compared to the results of a test population. The groups are selected using a randomization process in which each group has a representative mix of the population being tested. Finally, an **observational study** is similar to an experiment. However, this design is used when circumstances prevent or do not allow for a designated control group and experimental group (e.g., lack of funding or unrealistic expectations). Instead, existing control and test populations must be used, so this method has a lack of randomization.

Statistics involves making decisions and predictions about larger data sets based on smaller data sets. Basically, the information from one part or subset can help predict what happens in the entire data set or population at large. The entire process involves guessing, and the predictions and decisions may not be 100 percent correct all of the time; however, there is some truth to these predictions, and the decisions do have mathematical support. The smaller data set is called a **sample** and the larger data set (in which the decision is being made) is called a **population**. A **random sample** is used as the sample, which is an unbiased collection of data points that represents the population as well as it can. There are many methods of forming a random sample, and all adhere to the fact that every potential data point has a predetermined probability of being chosen.

Describing Distributions

Mean, Median, and Mode
The center of a set of data (statistical values) can be represented by its mean, median, or mode. These are sometimes referred to as measures of central tendency.

Mean
The first property that can be defined for this set of data is the **mean**. This is the same as the average. To find the mean, add up all the data points, then divide by the total number of data points. For example, suppose that in a class of 10 students, the scores on a test were 50, 60, 65, 65, 75, 80, 85, 85, 90, 100. Therefore, the average test score will be:

$$\frac{50 + 60 + 65 + 65 + 75 + 80 + 85 + 85 + 90 + 100}{10} = 75.5$$

The mean is a useful number if the distribution of data is normal (more on this later), which roughly means that the frequency of different outcomes has a single peak and is roughly equally distributed on both sides of that peak. However, it is less useful in some cases where the data might be split or where there are some outliers. **Outliers** are data points that are far from the rest of the data. For example, suppose there are 10 executives and 90 employees at a company. The executives make $1000 per hour, and the employees make $10 per hour.

Therefore, the average pay rate will be:

$$\frac{\$1000 \times 10 + \$10 \times 90}{100} = \$109 \text{ per hour}$$

In this case, this average is not very descriptive since it's not close to the actual pay of the executives *or* the employees.

Median

Another useful measurement is the **median**. In a data set, the median is the point in the middle. The middle refers to the point where half the data comes before it and half comes after, when the data is recorded in numerical order. For instance, these are the speeds of the fastball of a pitcher during the last inning that he pitched (in order from least to greatest):

$$90, 92, 93, 93, 95, 96, 97, 97, 97$$

There are nine total numbers, so the middle or *median* number is the 5th one, which is 95.

In cases where the number of data points is an even number, then the average of the two middle points is taken. In the previous example of test scores, the two middle points are 75 and 80. Since there is no single point, the average of these two scores needs to be found. The average is:

$$\frac{75 + 80}{2} = 77.5$$

The median is generally a good value to use if there are a few outliers in the data. It prevents those outliers from affecting the "middle" value as much as when using the mean.

Since an outlier is a data point that is far from most of the other data points in a data set, this means an outlier also is any point that is far from the median of the data set. The outliers can have a substantial effect on the mean of a data set, but they usually do not change the median or mode, or do not change them by a large quantity. For example, consider the data set (3, 5, 6, 6, 6, 8). This has a median of 6 and a mode of 6, with a mean of $\frac{34}{6} \approx 5.67$. Now, suppose a new data point of 1000 is added so that the data set is now (3, 5, 6, 6, 6, 8, 1000). The median and mode, which are both still 6, remain unchanged. However, the average is now $\frac{1034}{7}$, which is approximately 147.7. In this case, the median and mode will be better descriptions for most of the data points.

Outliers in a given data set are sometimes the result of an error by the experimenter, but oftentimes, they are perfectly valid data points that must be taken into consideration.

Mode

One additional measure to define for X is the **mode**. This is the data point that appears most frequently. If two or more data points all tie for the most frequent appearance, then each of them is considered a mode. In the case of the test scores, where the numbers were 50, 60, 65, 65, 75, 80, 85, 85, 90, 100, there are two modes: 65 and 85.

Quartiles and Percentiles

The **first quartile** of a set of data X refers to the largest value from the first ¼ of the data points. In practice, there are sometimes slightly different definitions that can be used, such as the median of the first half of the data points (excluding the median itself if there are an odd number of data points). The term also has a slightly different use: when it is said that a data point lies *in the first quartile*, it means it is less than or equal to the median of the first half of the data points. Conversely, if it lies *at* the first quartile, then it is equal to the first quartile.

When it is said that a data point lies in the **second quartile**, it means it is between the first quartile and the median.

The **third quartile** refers to data that lies between ½ and ¾ of the way through the data set. Again, there are various methods for defining this precisely, but the simplest way is to include all of the data that lie between the median and the median of the top half of the data.

Data that lies in the **fourth quartile** refers to all of the data above the third quartile.

Percentiles may be defined in a similar manner to quartiles. Generally, this is defined in the following manner:

If a data point lies in the nth **percentile**, this means it lies in the range of the first $n\%$ of the data.

If a data point lies at the nth **percentile**, then it means that $n\%$ of the data lies below this data point.

Standard Deviation

Given a data set X consisting of data points $(x_1, x_2, x_3, \ldots x_n)$, the **variance** of X is defined to be:

$$\frac{\sum_{i=1}^{n}(x_i - \bar{X})^2}{n}$$

This means that the variance of X is the average of the squares of the differences between each data point and the mean of X.

Given a data set X consisting of data points $(x_1, x_2, x_3, \ldots x_n)$, the **standard deviation** of X is defined to be:

$$s_x = \sqrt{\frac{\sum_{i=1}^{n}(x_i - \bar{X})^2}{n}}$$

In other words, the standard deviation is the square root of the variance.

Both the variance and the standard deviation are measures of how much the data tend to be spread out. When the standard deviation is low, the data points are mostly clustered around the mean. When the standard deviation is high, this generally indicates that the data are quite spread out, or else that there are a few substantial outliers.

As a simple example, compute the standard deviation for the data set (1, 3, 3, 5). First, compute the mean, which will be:

$$\frac{1+3+3+5}{4} = \frac{12}{4} = 3$$

Now, find the variance of X with the formula:

$$\sum_{i=1}^{4}(x_i - \bar{X})^2 = (1-3)^2 + (3-3)^2 + (3-3)^2 + (5-3)^2$$

$$-2^2 + 0^2 + 0^2 + 2^2 = 8$$

Therefore, the variance is $\frac{8}{4} = 2$. Taking the square root, the standard deviation will be $\sqrt{2}$.

Note that the standard deviation only depends upon the mean, not upon the median or mode(s). Generally, if there are multiple modes that are far apart from one another, the standard deviation will be high. A high standard deviation does not always mean there are multiple modes, however.

Describing a Set of Data

A set of data can be described in terms of its center, spread, shape and any unusual features. The center of a data set can be measured by its mean, median, or mode. The spread of a data set refers to how far the data points are from the center (mean or median). A data set with all its data points clustered around the center will have a small spread. A data set covering a wide range of values will have a large spread.

When a data set is displayed as a graph like the one below, the shape indicates if a sample is normally distributed, symmetrical, or has measures of skewness. When graphed, a data set with a normal distribution will resemble a bell curve.

If the data set is symmetrical, each half of the graph when divided at the center is a mirror image of the other. If the graph has fewer data points to the right, the data is skewed right. If it has fewer data points to the left, the data is skewed left.

 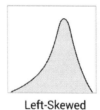

Right-Skewed   Symmetric   Left-Skewed

A description of a data set should include any unusual features such as gaps or outliers. A gap is a span within the range of the data set containing no data points. An outlier is a data point with a value either extremely large or extremely small when compared to the other values in the set.

The graphs above can be referred to as **unimodal** since they all have a single peak. In contrast, a bimodal graph has two peaks.

Geometry Concepts

Properties of Polygons and Circles

A **polygon** is a closed two-dimensional figure consisting of three or more sides. Polygons can be either convex or concave. A polygon that has interior angles all measuring less than 180° is **convex**. A **concave** polygon has one or more interior angles measuring greater than 180°. Examples are shown below.

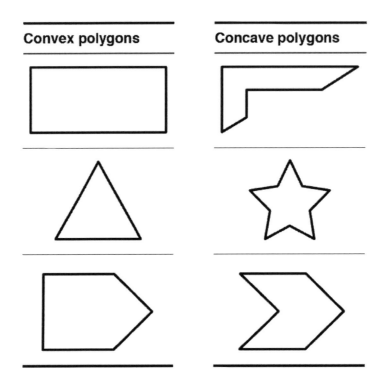

Polygons can be classified by the number of sides (also equal to the number of angles) they have. The following are the names of polygons with a given number of sides or angles:

# of Sides	Name of Polygon
3	Triangle
4	Quadrilateral
5	Pentagon
6	Hexagon
7	Septagon (or heptagon)
8	Octagon
9	Nonagon
10	Decagon

Equiangular polygons are polygons in which the measure of every interior angle is the same. The sides of equilateral polygons are always the same length. If a polygon is both equiangular and equilateral, the polygon is defined as a **regular polygon**. Examples are shown below.

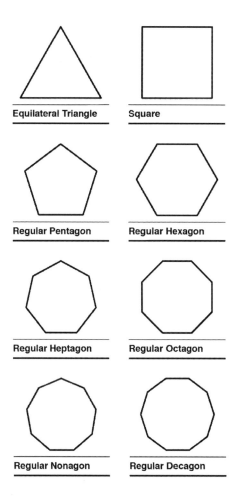

Triangles can be further classified by their sides and angles. A triangle with its largest angle measuring 90° is a **right triangle**.

Right triangle

75

A triangle with the largest angle less than 90° is an **acute triangle**. A triangle with the largest angle greater than 90° is an **obtuse triangle**.

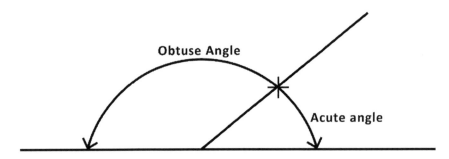

A triangle consisting of two equal sides and two equal angles is an **isosceles triangle**. A triangle with three equal sides and three equal angles is an **equilateral triangle**. A triangle with no equal sides or angles is a **scalene triangle**.

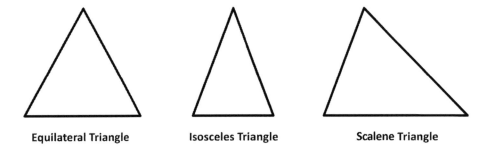

Quadrilaterals can be further classified according to their sides and angles. A quadrilateral with exactly one pair of parallel sides is called a **trapezoid**. A quadrilateral that shows both pairs of opposite sides parallel is a **parallelogram**. Parallelograms include rhombuses, rectangles, and squares.

A **rhombus** has four equal sides. A **rectangle** has four equal angles (90° each). A **square** has four 90° angles and four equal sides. Therefore, a square is both a rhombus and a rectangle.

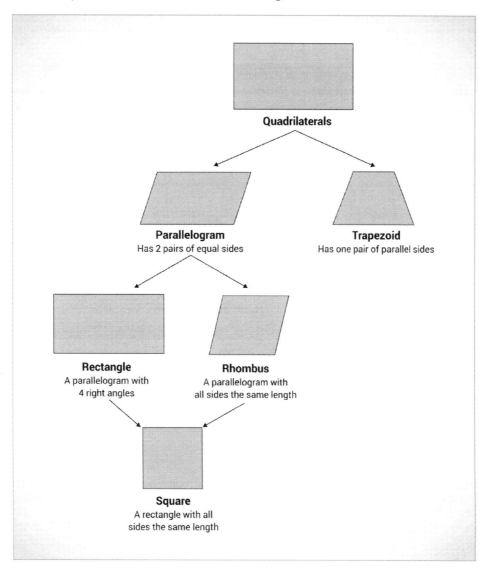

There are many key facts related to geometry that are applicable. The sum of the measures of the angles of a triangle are 180°, and for a quadrilateral, the sum is 360°. Rectangles and squares each have four right angles. A **right angle** has a measure of 90°.

Lines and Angles

In geometry, a **line** connects two points, has no thickness, and extends indefinitely in both directions beyond each point. If the length is finite, it's known as a **line segment** and has two **endpoints**. A **ray** is the straight portion of a line that has one endpoint and extends indefinitely in the other direction. An **angle** is formed when two rays begin at the same endpoint and extend indefinitely. The endpoint of an angle is called a **vertex**. **Adjacent angles** are two side-by-side angles formed from the same ray that have the same endpoint.

Angles are measured in **degrees** or **radians**, which is a measure of **rotation**. A **full rotation** equals 360 degrees or 2π radians, which represents a circle. Half a rotation equals 180 degrees or π radians and represents a half-circle. Angle measurement is additive. When an angle is broken into two non-overlapping angles, the total measure of the larger angle equals the sum of the two smaller angles. Lines are **coplanar** if they're located in the same plane. Two lines are **parallel** if they are coplanar, extend in the same direction, and never cross. If lines do cross, they're labeled as **intersecting lines** because they "intersect" at one point. If they intersect at more than one point, they're the same line. **Perpendicular lines** are coplanar lines that form a right angle at their point of intersection.

Two lines are parallel if they have the same slope and different intercept. Two lines are perpendicular if the product of their slope equals −1. Parallel lines never intersect unless they are the same line, and perpendicular lines intersect at a right angle. If two lines aren't parallel, they must intersect at one point. Determining equations of lines based on properties of parallel and perpendicular lines appears in word problems. To find an equation of a line, both the slope and a point the line goes through are necessary.

Therefore, if an equation of a line is needed that's parallel to a given line and runs through a specified point, the slope of the given line and the point are plugged into the point-slope form of an equation of a line. Secondly, if an equation of a line is needed that's perpendicular to a given line running through a specified point, the negative reciprocal of the slope of the given line and the point are plugged into the point-slope form. Also, if the point of intersection of two lines is known, that point will be used to solve the set of equations. Therefore, to solve a system of equations, the point of intersection must be found. If a set of two equations with two unknown variables has no solution, the lines are parallel.

Classification of Angles

An **angle** consists of two rays that have a common endpoint. This common endpoint is called the **vertex** of the angle. The two rays can be called sides of the angle. The angle below has a vertex at point B and the sides consist of ray BA and ray BC. An angle can be named in three ways:

1. Using the vertex and a point from each side, with the vertex letter in the middle.
2. Using only the vertex. This can only be used if it is the only angle with that vertex.
3. Using a number that is written inside the angle.

The angle below can be written $\angle ABC$ (read angle ABC), $\angle CBA$, $\angle B$, or $\angle 1$.

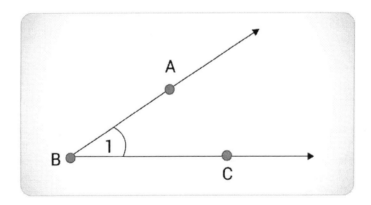

Quantitative Reasoning, Algebra, and Statistics

An angle divides a plane, or flat surface, into three parts: the angle itself, the interior (inside) of the angle, and the exterior (outside) of the angle. The figure below shows point *M* on the interior of the angle and point *N* on the exterior of the angle.

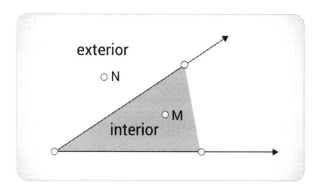

Angles can be measured in units called degrees, with the symbol °. The degree measure of an angle is between 0° and 180° and can be obtained by using a protractor.

A straight angle (or simply a line) measures exactly 180°. A right angle's sides meet at the vertex to create a square corner. A right angle measures exactly 90° and is typically indicated by a box drawn in the interior of the angle. An acute angle has an interior that is narrower than a right angle. The measure of an acute angle is any value less than 90° and greater than 0°. For example, 89.9°, 47°, 12°, and 1°. An obtuse angle has an interior that is wider than a right angle. The measure of an obtuse angle is any value greater than 90° but less than 180°. For example, 90.1°, 110°, 150°, and 179.9°.

79

Perimeter and Area

Perimeter is the measurement of a distance around something or the sum of all sides of a polygon. Think of perimeter as the length of the boundary, like a fence. In contrast, **area** is the space occupied by a defined enclosure, like a field enclosed by a fence.

When thinking about perimeter, think about walking around the outside of something. When thinking about area, think about the amount of space or **surface area** something takes up.

Square

The perimeter of a square is measured by adding together all of the sides. Since a square has four equal sides, its perimeter can be calculated by multiplying the length of one side by 4. Thus, the formula is $P = 4 \times s$, where s equals one side. For example, the following square has side lengths of 5 meters:

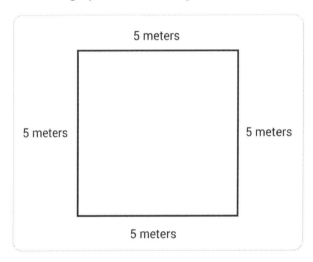

The perimeter is 20 meters because 4 times 5 is 20.

The area of a square is the length of a side squared. For example, if a side of a square is 7 centimeters, then the area is 49 square centimeters. The formula for this example is:

$$A = s^2 = 7^2 = 49 \text{ square centimeters}$$

An example is if the rectangle has a length of 6 inches and a width of 7 inches, then the area is 42 square inches:
$$A = lw = 6(7) = 42 \text{ square inches}$$

Rectangle

Like a square, a rectangle's perimeter is measured by adding together all of the sides. But as the sides are unequal, the formula is different. A rectangle has equal values for its lengths (long sides) and equal values for its widths (short sides), so the perimeter formula for a rectangle is:

$$P = l + l + w + w = 2l + 2w$$

l equals length
w equals width

The area is found by multiplying the length by the width, so the formula is $A = l \times w$.

For example, if the length of a rectangle is 10 inches and the width 8 inches, then the perimeter is 36 inches because:
$$P = 2l + 2w = 2(10) + 2(8) = 20 + 16 = 36 \text{ inches}$$

Triangle

A triangle's perimeter is measured by adding together the three sides, so the formula is $P = a + b + c$, where a, b, and c are the values of the three sides. The area is the product of one-half the base and height so the formula is:
$$A = \frac{1}{2} \times b \times h$$

It can be simplified to:
$$A = \frac{bh}{2}$$

The base is the bottom of the triangle, and the height is the distance from the base to the peak. If a problem asks to calculate the area of a triangle, it will provide the base and height.

For example, if the base of the triangle is 2 feet and the height 4 feet, then the area is 4 square feet. The following equation shows the formula used to calculate the area of the triangle:
$$A = \frac{1}{2} \text{bh} = \frac{1}{2}(2)(4) = 4 \text{ square feet}$$

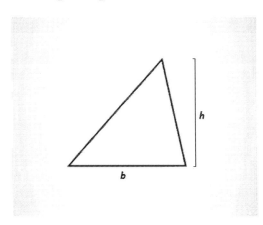

Circle

A circle's perimeter—also known as its circumference—is measured by multiplying the diameter by π.

Diameter is the straight line measured from a point on one side of the circle to a point directly across on the opposite side of the circle.

π is referred to as pi and is equal to 3.14 (with rounding).

So, the formula is $\pi \times d$.

This is sometimes expressed by the formula:
$$C = 2 \times \pi \times r$$

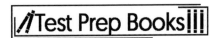

The variable r is the radius of the circle. These formulas are equivalent, as the radius equals half of the diameter.

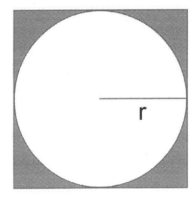

The area of a circle is calculated through the formula:

$$A = \pi \times r^2$$

The test will indicate either to leave the answer with π attached or to calculate to the nearest decimal place, which means multiplying by 3.14 for π.

The **arc of a circle** is the distance between two points on the circle. The length of the arc of a circle in terms of **degrees** is easily determined if the value of the central angle is known. The length of the arc is simply the value of the central angle. In this example, the length of the arc of the circle in degrees is 75°.

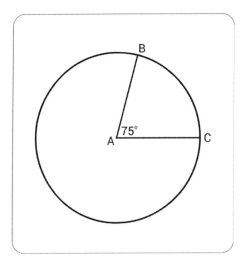

To determine the length of the arc of a circle in distance, the values for both the central angle and the radius must be known. This formula is:

$$\frac{central\ angle}{360°} = \frac{arc\ length}{2\pi r}$$

The equation is simplified by cross-multiplying to solve for the arc length.

In the following example, to solve for arc length, substitute the values of the central angle (75°) and the radius (10 inches) into the equation above.

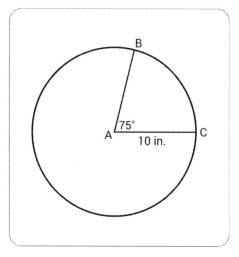

$$\frac{75°}{360°} = \frac{arc\ length}{2(3.14)(10\ in.)}$$

To solve the equation, first cross-multiply: $4{,}710 = 360 \times arc\ length$. Next, divide each side of the equation by 360. The result of the formula is that the arc length is 13.1 (rounded).

Irregular Shapes

The perimeter of an irregular polygon is found by adding the lengths of all of the sides. In cases where all of the sides are given, this will be very straightforward, as it will simply involve finding the sum of the provided lengths. Other times, a side length may be missing and must be determined before the perimeter can be calculated. Consider the example below:

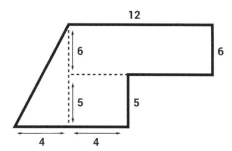

All of the side lengths are provided except for the angled side on the left. Test takers should notice that this is the hypotenuse of a right triangle. The other two sides of the triangle are provided (the base is 4 and the height is $6 + 5 = 11$). The Pythagorean Theorem can be used to find the length of the hypotenuse, remembering that:
$$a^2 + b^2 = c^2$$

Substituting the side values provided yields:

$$(4)^2 + (11)^2 = c2$$

83

Therefore:

$$c = \sqrt{16 + 121} = 11.7$$

Finally, the perimeter can be found by adding this new side length with the other provided lengths to get the total length around the figure:

$$4 + 4 + 5 + 8 + 6 + 12 + 11.7 = 50.7$$

Although units are not provided in this figure, remember that reporting units with a measurement is important.

The area of an irregular polygon is found by decomposing, or breaking apart, the figure into smaller shapes. When the area of the smaller shapes is determined, these areas are added together to produce the total area of the area of the original figure. Consider the same example provided before:

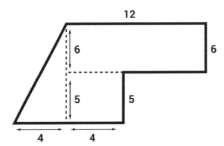

The irregular polygon is decomposed into two rectangles and a triangle. The area of the large rectangle is 72 square units:

$$A = l \times w \rightarrow A = 12 \times 6$$

The area of the small rectangle is 20 square units:

$$A = 4 \times 5$$

The area of the triangle is 22 square units:

$$A = \frac{1}{2} \times b \times h \rightarrow A = \frac{1}{2} \times 4 \times 11$$

The sum of the areas of these figures produces the total area of the original polygon:

$$A = 72 + 20 + 22 \rightarrow A = 114 \text{ square units}$$

Volume and Surface Area of Three-Dimensional Shapes

Geometry in three dimensions is similar to geometry in two dimensions. The main new feature is that three points now define a unique plane that passes through each of them. Three-dimensional objects can be made by putting together two-dimensional figures in different surfaces. Below, some of the possible three-dimensional figures will be provided, along with formulas for their volumes and surface areas.

Volume is the measurement of how much space an object occupies, like how much space is in the cube. Volume questions will ask how much of something is needed to completely fill the object. The most common surface area and volume questions deal with spheres, cubes, and rectangular prisms.

Surface area of a three-dimensional figure refers to the number of square units needed to cover the entire surface of the figure. This concept is similar to using wrapping paper to completely cover the outside of a box. For example, if a triangular pyramid has a surface area of 17 square inches (written 17 in^2), it will take 17 squares, each with sides one inch in length, to cover the entire surface of the pyramid. Surface area is also measured in square units.

A **rectangular prism** is a box whose sides are all rectangles meeting at 90° angles. Such a box has three dimensions: length, width, and height. If the length is x, the width is y, and the height is z, then the volume is given by $V = xyz$.

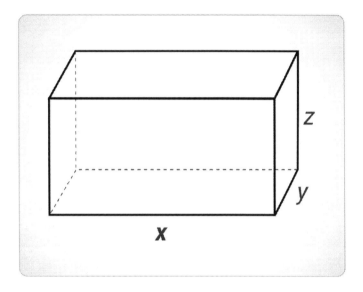

The surface area will be given by computing the surface area of each rectangle and adding them together. There is a total of six rectangles. Two of them have sides of length x and y, two have sides of length y and z, and two have sides of length x and z. Therefore, the total surface area will be given by:

$$SA = 2xy + 2yz + 2xz$$

A **cube** is a special type of rectangular solid in which its length, width, and height are the same. If this length is s, then the formula for the volume of a cube is:

$$V = s \times s \times s$$

The surface area of a cube is $SA = 6s^2$.

A **rectangular pyramid** is a figure with a rectangular base and four triangular sides that meet at a single vertex. If the rectangle has sides of length x and y, then the volume will be given by:

$$V = \frac{1}{3}xyh$$

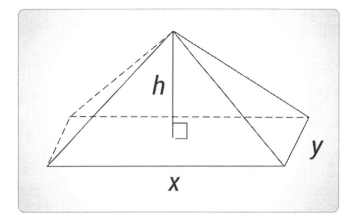

Many three-dimensional figures (solid figures) can be represented by nets consisting of rectangles and triangles. The surface area of such solids can be determined by adding the areas of each of its faces and bases. Finding the surface area using this method requires calculating the areas of rectangles and triangles. To find the area (A) of a rectangle, the length (l) is multiplied by the width:

$$(w) \rightarrow A = l \times w$$

The area of a rectangle with a length of 8cm and a width of 4 cm is calculated:

$$A = (8 \text{ cm}) \times (4 \text{ cm}) \rightarrow A = 32 \text{ cm}^2$$

To calculate the area (A) of a triangle, the product of $\frac{1}{2}$, the base (b), and the height (h) is found:

$$A = \frac{1}{2} \times b \times h$$

Note that the height of a triangle is measured from the base to the vertex opposite of it forming a right angle with the base. The area of a triangle with a base of 11 cm and a height of 6 cm is calculated:

$$A = \frac{1}{2} \times (11 \text{ cm}) \times (6 \text{ cm})$$

$$A = 33 \text{ cm}^2$$

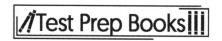

Consider the following triangular prism, which is represented by a net consisting of two triangles and three rectangles.

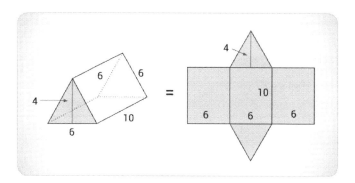

The surface area of the prism can be determined by adding the areas of each of its faces and bases. The surface area (*SA*) = area of triangle + area of triangle + area of rectangle + area of rectangle + area of rectangle.

$$SA = \left(\frac{1}{2} \times b \times h\right) + \left(\frac{1}{2} \times b \times h\right) + (l \times w) + (l \times w) + (l \times w)$$

$$SA = \left(\frac{1}{2} \times 6 \times 4\right) + \left(\frac{1}{2} \times 6 \times 4\right) + (6 \times 10) + (6 \times 10) + (6 \times 10)$$

$$SA = (12) + (12) + (60) + (60) + (60)$$

$$SA = 204 \text{ square units}$$

A **sphere** is a set of points all of which are equidistant from some central point. It is like a circle, but in three dimensions. The volume of a sphere of radius *r* is given by:

$$V = \frac{4}{3}\pi r^3$$

The surface area is given by $A = 4\pi r^2$.

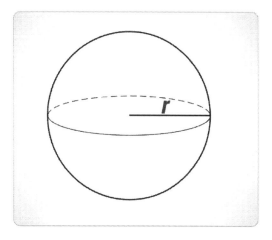

The volume of a **cylinder** is then found by adding a third dimension onto the circle. Volume of a cylinder is calculated by multiplying the area of the base (which is a circle) by the height of the cylinder. Doing so results in the equation $V = \pi r^2 h$. The volume of a **cone** is $\frac{1}{3}$ of the volume of a cylinder. Therefore, the formula for the volume of a cone is:

$$\frac{1}{3}\pi r^2 h$$

Plane Geometry

Algebraic equations can be used to describe geometric figures in the plane. The method for doing so is to use the **Cartesian coordinate plane**. The idea behind these Cartesian coordinates (named for mathematician and philosopher Descartes) is that from a specific point on the plane, known as the **origin**, one can specify any other point by saying *how far to the right or left* and *how far up or down*.

The plane is covered with a grid. The two directions, right to left and bottom to top, are called **axes** (singular **axis**). When working with x- and y-variables, the x-variable corresponds to the right and left axis, and the y-variable corresponds to the up and down axis.

Any point on the grid is found by specifying how far to travel from the center along the x-axis and how far to travel along the y-axis. The ordered pair can be written as (x, y). A positive x-value means go to the right on the x-axis, while a negative x value means to go to the left. A positive y-value means to go up, while a negative value means to go down. Several points are shown as examples in the figure.

Cartesian Coordinate Plane

The coordinate plane can be divided into four **quadrants**. The upper-right part of the plane is called the first quadrant, where both x and y are positive. The second quadrant is the upper-left, where x is negative but y is positive. The third quadrant is the lower left, where both x and y are negative. Finally, the fourth quadrant is in the lower right, where x is positive but y is negative. These quadrants are often written with Roman numerals:

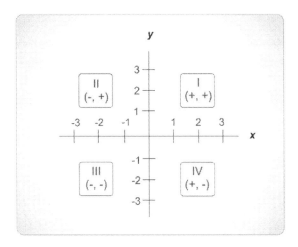

In addition to graphing individual points as shown above, the graph lines and curves in the plane can be graphed corresponding to equations. In general, if there is some equation involving x and y, then the graph of that equation consists of all the points (x, y) in the Cartesian coordinate plane, which satisfy this equation.

Given the equation $y = x + 2$, the point $(0, 2)$ is in the graph, since $2 = 0 + 2$ is a true equation. However, the point $(1, 4)$ will *not* be in the graph, because $4 = 1 + 2$ is false.

Proving Theorems with Coordinates

Many important formulas and equations exist in geometry that use coordinates. The distance between two points (x_1, y_1) and (x_2, y_2) is:

$$d = \sqrt{(x_2 - x_1)^2 + (y_2 - y_1)^2}$$

The slope of the line containing the same two points is:

$$m = \frac{y_2 - y_1}{x_2 - x_1}$$

Also, the midpoint of the line segment with endpoints (x_1, y_1) and (x_2, y_2) is:

$$M = \left(\frac{x_1 + x_2}{2}, \frac{y_1 + y_2}{2} \right)$$

The equations of a circle, parabola, ellipse, and hyperbola can also be used to prove theorems algebraically. Knowing when to use which formula or equation is extremely important, and knowing which formula applies to which property of a given geometric shape is an integral part of the process. In some cases, there are a number of ways to prove a theorem; however, only one way is required.

Formulas for Ratios

If a line segment with endpoints (x_1, y_1) and (x_2, y_2) is partitioned into two equal parts, the formula for midpoint is used. Recall this formula is:

$$M = \left(\frac{x_1 + x_2}{2}, \frac{y_1 + y_2}{2}\right)$$

The ratio of line segments is 1:1. However, if the ratio needs to be anything other than 1:1, a different formula must be used. Consider a ratio that is $a:b$. This means the desired point that partitions the line segment is $\frac{a}{a+b}$ of the way from (x_1, y_1) to (x_2, y_2). The actual formula for the coordinate is:

$$\left(\frac{bx_1 + ax_2}{a + b}, \frac{by_1 + ay_2}{a + b}\right)$$

Computing Side Length, Perimeter, and Area

The side lengths of each shape can be found by plugging the endpoints into the distance formula:

$$d = \sqrt{(x_2 - x_1)^2 + (y_2 - y_1)^2}$$

between two ordered pairs (x_1, y_1) and (x_2, y_2). The distance formula is derived from the Pythagorean theorem. Once the side lengths are found, they can be added together to obtain the perimeter of the given polygon. Simplifications can be made for specific shapes such as squares and equilateral triangles. For example, one side length can be multiplied by 4 to obtain the perimeter of a square. Also, one side length can be multiplied by 3 to obtain the perimeter of an equilateral triangle. A similar technique can be used to calculate areas. For polygons, both side length and height can be found by using the same distance formula. Depending on the shape, areas of triangles and quadrilaterals are straightforward through the use of:

$$A = \frac{1}{2}bh \text{ or } A = bh$$

To find the area of other polygons, their shapes can be partitioned into rectangles and triangles. The areas of these simpler shapes can be calculated and then added together to find the total area of the polygon.

Transformations

Given a figure drawn on a plane, many changes can be made to that figure, including rotation, translation, and reflection. **Rotations** turn the figure about a point, **translations** slide the figure, and **reflections** flip the figure over a specified line. When performing these transformations, the original figure is called the **pre-image**, and the figure after transformation is called the **image**.

More specifically, **translation** means that all points in the figure are moved in the same direction by the same distance. In other words, the figure is slid in some fixed direction. Of course, while the entire figure is slid by the same distance, this does not change any of the measurements of the figures involved. The result will have the same distances and angles as the original figure.

In terms of Cartesian coordinates, a translation means a shift of each of the original points (x, y) by a fixed amount in the x and y directions, to become $(x + a, y + b)$.

Another procedure that can be performed is called **reflection**. To do this, a line in the plane is specified, called the **line of reflection**. Then, take each point and flip it over the line so that it is the same distance from the line but on the opposite side of it. This does not change any of the distances or angles involved, but it does reverse the order in which everything appears.

To reflect something over the x-axis, the points (x, y) are sent to $(x, -y)$. To reflect something over the y-axis, the points (x, y) are sent to the points $(-x, y)$. Flipping over other lines is not something easy to express in Cartesian coordinates. However, by drawing the figure and the line of reflection, the distance to the line and the original points can be used to find the reflected figure.

Example: Reflect this triangle with vertices (-1, 0), (2, 1), and (2, 0) over the y-axis. The pre-image is shown below.

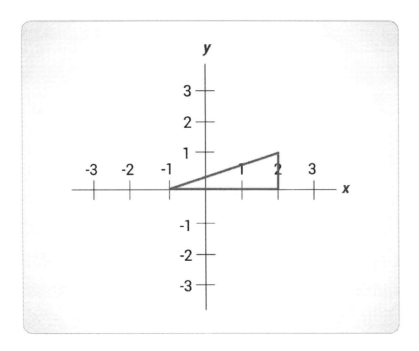

To do this, flip the x values of the points involved to the negatives of themselves, while keeping the y values the same. The image is shown here.

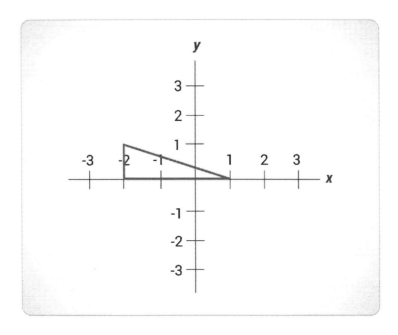

The new vertices will be (1, 0), (-2, 1), and (-2, 0).

Another procedure that does not change the distances and angles in a figure is **rotation**. In this procedure, pick a center point, then rotate every vertex along a circle around that point by the same angle. This procedure is also not easy to express in Cartesian coordinates, and this is not a requirement on this test. However, as with reflections, it's helpful to draw the figures and see what the result of the rotation would look like. This transformation can be performed using a compass and protractor.

Each one of these transformations can be performed on the coordinate plane without changes to the original dimensions or angles.

If two figures in the plane involve the same distances and angles, they are called **congruent figures**. In other words, two figures are congruent when they go from one form to another through reflection, rotation, and translation, or a combination of these.

Remember that rotation and translation will give back a new figure that is identical to the original figure, but reflection will give back a mirror image of it.

To recognize that a figure has undergone a rotation, check to see that the figure has not been changed into a mirror image, but that its orientation has changed (that is, whether the parts of the figure now form different angles with the x- and y-axes).

To recognize that a figure has undergone a translation, check to see that the figure has not been changed into a mirror image, and that the orientation remains the same.

To recognize that a figure has undergone a reflection, check to see that the new figure is a mirror image of the old figure.

Keep in mind that sometimes a combination of translations, reflections, and rotations may be performed on a figure.

Dilation
A **dilation** is a transformation that preserves angles, but not distances. This can be thought of as stretching or shrinking a figure. If a dilation makes figures larger, it is called an **enlargement**. If a dilation makes figures smaller, it is called a **reduction**. The easiest example is to dilate around the origin. In this case, multiply the x- and y-coordinates by a **scale factor**, k, sending points (x, y) to (kx, ky).

As an example, draw a dilation of the following triangle, whose vertices will be the points $(-1, 0)$, $(1, 0)$, and $(1, 1)$.

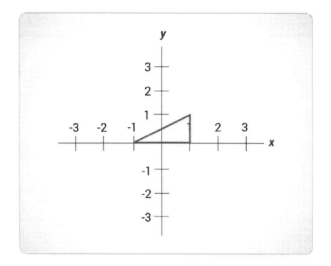

For this problem, dilate by a scale factor of 2, so the new vertices will be $(-2, 0)$, $(2, 0)$, and $(2, 2)$.

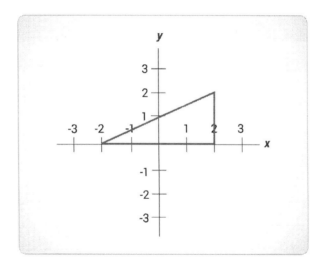

Note that after a dilation, the distances between the vertices of the figure will have changed, but the angles remain the same. The two figures that are obtained by dilation, along with possibly translation, rotation, and reflection, are all *similar* to one another. Another way to think of this is that similar figures have the same number of vertices and edges, and their angles are all the same. Similar figures have the same basic shape but are different in size.

Symmetry

Using the types of transformations above, if an object can undergo these changes and not appear to have changed, then the figure is symmetrical. If an object can be split in half by a line and flipped over that line to lie directly on top of itself, it is said to have **line symmetry**. An example of both types of figures is seen below.

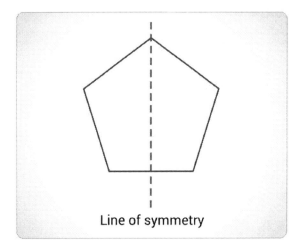

Line of symmetry

If an object can be rotated about its center to any degree smaller than 360, and it lies directly on top of itself, the object is said to have **rotational symmetry**. An example of this type of symmetry is shown below. The pentagon has an order of 5.

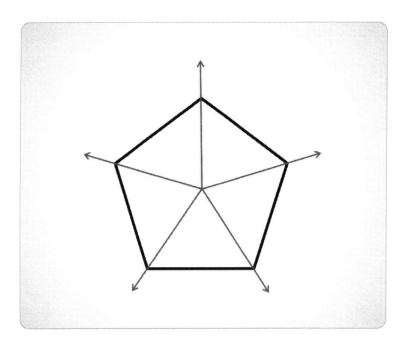

The rotational symmetry lines in the figure above can be used to find the angles formed at the center of the pentagon. Knowing that all of the angles together form a full circle, at 360 degrees, the figure can be split into 5 angles equally. By dividing the 360° by 5, each angle is 72°.

Given the length of one side of the figure, the perimeter of the pentagon can also be found using rotational symmetry. If one side length was 3 cm, that side length can be rotated onto each other side length four times. This

94

would give a total of 5 side lengths equal to 3 cm. To find the perimeter, or distance around the figure, multiply 3 by 5. The perimeter of the figure would be 15 cm.

If a line cannot be drawn anywhere on the object to flip the figure onto itself or rotated less than or equal to 180 degrees to lay on top of itself, the object is asymmetrical. Examples of these types of figures are shown below.

Symmetric   Asymmetric

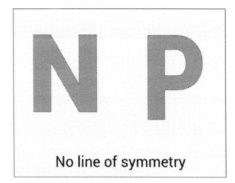

No line of symmetry

Right Triangles: Pythagorean Theorem and Trigonometric Ratio

The value of a missing side of a right triangle may be determined two ways. The first way is to apply the Pythagorean Theorem, and the second way is to apply Trigonometric Ratios. The Pythagorean Theorem states that for every right triangle, the square of the length of the hypotenuse is equal to the sum of the squares of the lengths of the remaining two sides. The hypotenuse is the longest side of a right triangle and is also the side opposite the right angle.

According to the diagram, $a^2 + b^2 = c^2$, where c represents the hypotenuse, and a and b represent the lengths of the remaining two sides of the right triangle.

The Pythagorean Theorem may be applied a multitude of ways. For example, a person wishes to build a garden in the shape of a rectangle, having the dimensions of 5 feet by 8 feet. The garden's design includes a diagonal board to separate various types of plants. The Pythagorean Theorem can be used to determine the length of the diagonal board.

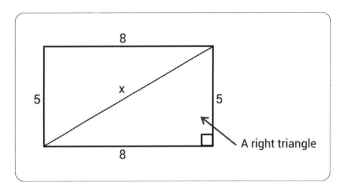

A right triangle

$$a^2 + b^2 = c^2$$

$$5^2 + 8^2 = c^2$$

$$25 + 64 = c^2$$

$$c = \sqrt{89}$$

$$c = 9.43$$

To solve for unknown sides of a right triangle using trigonometric ratios, the sine, cosine, and tangent are required.

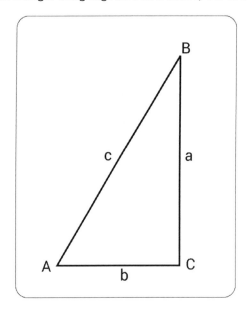

In the image above, angles are denoted by capital letters, and sides are denoted by lowercase letters. When examining angle A, b is the adjacent side, a is the opposite side, and c is the hypotenuse side. The various ratios of the lengths of the sides of the right triangle are used to find the sine, cosine, and tangent of angle A.

Thus, $\sin(A) = \frac{opposite}{hypotenuse}$, $\cos(A) = \frac{adjacent}{hypotenuse}$, and $\tan(A) = \frac{opposite}{adjacent}$. After substituting variables for the sides of the right triangle, $sin(A) = \frac{a}{c}$, $cos(A) = \frac{b}{c}$, and $tan(A) = \frac{a}{b}$.

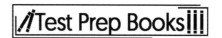

As a real-world example, the height of a tree can be discovered by using the information above. Surveying equipment can determine the tree's angle of inclination is 55.3 degrees, and the distance from the tree is 10 feet.

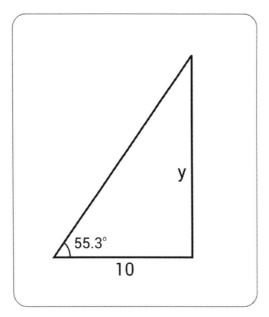

To find the height of the tree, substitute the known values into the trigonometric ratio of tangent:

$$\tan(55.3) = \frac{y}{10}$$

$$10 \times \tan(55.3) = y$$

$$10 \times 1.44418 = y$$

$$y = 14.4418$$

Similarity, Congruence, and Triangles

Triangles are similar if they have the same shape, the same angle measurements, and their sides are proportional to one another. Triangles are congruent if the angles of the triangles are equal in measurement and the sides of the triangles are equal in measurement.

There are five ways to show that a triangle is congruent.

- SSS (Side-Side-Side Postulate): When all three corresponding sides are equal in length, then the two triangles are congruent.

- SAS (Side-Angle-Side Postulate): If a pair of corresponding sides and the angle in between those two sides are equal, then the two triangles are congruent.

- ASA (Angle-Side-Angle Postulate): If a pair of corresponding angles are equal and the side within those angles are equal, then the two triangles are equal.

- AAS (Angle-Angle-Side Postulate): When a pair of corresponding angles for two triangles and a non-included side are equal, then the two triangles are congruent.

- HL (Hypotenuse-Leg Theorem): If two right triangles have the same hypotenuse length, and one of the other sides are also the same length, then the two triangles are congruent.

If two triangles are discovered to be similar or congruent, this information can assist in determining unknown parts of triangles, such as missing angles and sides.

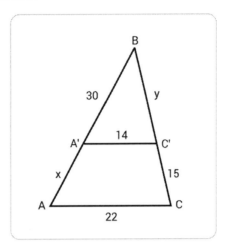

In the triangle shown above, AC and A'C' are parallel lines. Therefore, BA is a transversal that intersects the two parallel lines. The corresponding angles BA'C' and BAC are congruent. In a similar way, BC is also a transversal. Therefore, angle BC'A' and BCA are congruent. If two triangles have two congruent angles, the triangles are similar. If the triangles are similar, their corresponding sides are proportional.

Therefore, the following equation is established:

$$\frac{30 + x}{30} = \frac{22}{14} = \frac{y + 15}{y}$$

$$\frac{30 + x}{30} = \frac{22}{14}$$

$$x = 17.1$$

$$\frac{22}{14} = \frac{y + 15}{y}$$

$$y = 26.25$$

The example below involves the question of congruent triangles. The first step is to examine whether the triangles are congruent. If the triangles are congruent, then the measure of a missing angle can be found.

98

The above diagram provides values for angle measurements and side lengths in triangles *CAB* and *CDB*. Note that side *CA* is 3.2 and side *DB* is 3.2. Side *CD* is 4 and side *AB* is 4. Furthermore, line *CB* is congruent to itself by the reflexive property. Therefore, the two triangles are congruent by SSS (Side-Side-Side). Because the two triangles are congruent, all of the corresponding parts of the triangles are also congruent. Therefore, angle *x* is congruent to the inside of the angle for which a measurement is not provided in Triangle *CAB*. Thus,

$$115° + 32° = 147°$$

A triangle measures 180°, therefore:

$$180° - 147° = 33°$$

Angle $x = 33°$, because the two triangles are reversed.

Complementary Angle Theorem

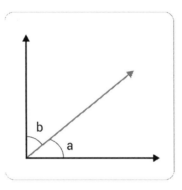

Two angles are complementary if the sum of the two angles equals 90°.

In the above diagram:

$$Angle\ a + Angle\ b = 90°$$

Therefore, the two angles are complementary. Certain trigonometric rules are also associated with complementary angles.

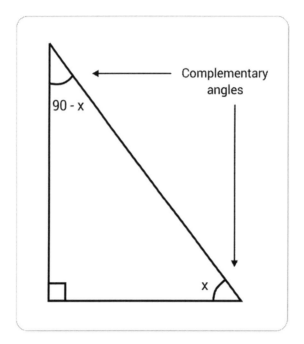

In the diagram above of a right triangle, if Angle A and Angle C are determined to be complementary angles, then certain relationships can be stated between the trigonometry of those angles.

$$sin(90° - x) = cos\ x$$

$$cos(90° - x) = sin\ x$$

For example, the sine of 80 degrees equals the cosine of $(90° - 80°)$, which is the cos $(10°)$.

This is true because the sine of an angle in a right triangle is equal to the cosine of its complement. Sine is known as the conjunction of cosine, and cosine is known as the conjunction of sine.

Examples:

1. $cos5° = sin\ x°$?
2. $sin(90° - x) = ?\ sin(90° - x) =?$

For problem number 1, the student should remember that:

$$sin(90° - x) = cos\ x$$

Cos5° would be the same as $sin(90 - 5)°$. Therefore, $cos5° = sin85°$.

For problem number 2, the student would use the same fact that $sin(90° - x)° = cos\ x$.

An *acute angle* is an angle that is less than 90°. If Angle *A* and Angle *B* are acute angles of a right triangle, then $sinA = cosB$. Therefore, the sine of any acute angle in a right triangle is equal to the cosine of its complement, and the cosine of any acute angle is equal to the sine of its complement.

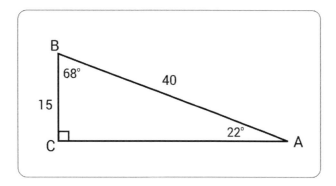

The example above is a right triangle. If only the value of angle *BAC* (which is 22°) was provided, the student would be able to figure out the value for angle *CBA* (68°) by knowing that a triangle is made up of 180°:

$$180° - 90° - 22° = 68°$$

From the information given about acute angles on the previous page, the following statement is true:

$$Sine(angle\ BAC) = \frac{15}{40}, \text{ which is equivalent to the } Cos(angle\ CBA) = \frac{15}{40}$$

Circles on the Coordinate Plane

If a circle is placed on the coordinate plane with the center of the circle at the origin (0,0), then point (x, y) is a point on the circle. Furthermore, the line extending from the center to point (x, y) is the radius, or r. By applying the Pythagorean Theorem,

$$a^2 + b^2 = c^2$$

It can be stated that:

$$x^2 + y^2 = r^2$$

However, the center of the circle does not always need to be on the origin of the coordinate plane.

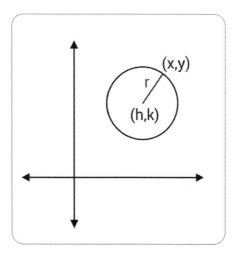

101

In the diagram above, the center of the circle is noted by (h, k). By applying the distance formula, the equation becomes:

$$r = \sqrt{(x-h)^2 + (y-k)^2}$$

When squaring both sides of the equation, the result is the standard form of a circle with the center (h, k) and radius r. Namely,

$$r^2 = (x-h)^2 + (y-k)^2$$

In this equation, $r = radius$ and $center = (h, k)$. The following examples may be solved by using this information:

Example: Graph the equation $-x^2 + y^2 = 25$

To graph this equation, first note that the center of the circle is (0,0). The radius is the positive square root of 25 or 5.

Example: Find the equation for the circle below.

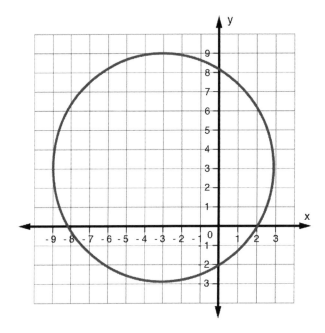

To find the equation for the circle, note that its center is not zero. Therefore, to find the circle's center, draw vertical and horizontal diameters to examine where they intersect. The center is located at point: $(-3, 3)$. Next, count the number of spaces from the center to the outside of the circle. This number is 6. Therefore, 6 is the radius. Finally, plug in the numbers that are known into the standard equation for a circle:

$$36 = \left(x - (-3)\right)^2 + (y - 3)^2$$

or

$$36 = (x + 3)^2 + (y - 3)^2$$

It is possible to determine whether a point lies on a circle or not within the coordinate plane. For example, a circle has a center of $(2, -5)$, and a radius of 6 centimeters. The first step is to apply the equation of a circle, which is:

$$r^2 = (x - h)^2 + (y - k)^2$$

102

Here $r = radius$ and the $center = (h, k)$. Next, substitute the numbers for the center point and the number for the radius. This action simplifies the equation to:

$$36 = (x - 2)^2 + (y + 5)^2$$

Note that the radius of 6 was squared to get 36.

To prove that the point $(2, -1)$ lies on the circle, apply the equation of the circle that was just used and input the values of $(2, -1)$ for x and y in the equation.

$$36 = (x - 2)^2 + (y + 5)^2$$

$$36 = (2 - 2)^2 + (1 + 5)^2$$

$$36 = (0)^2 + (6)^2$$

$$36 = 36$$

Because the left side of the equation equals the right side of the equation, point $(2, 1)$ lies on the given circle.

Practice Quiz

1. The graph of which function has an x-intercept of -2?
    a. $y = 2x - 3$
    b. $y = 4x + 2$
    c. $y = x^2 + 5x + 6$
    d. $y = 2x^2 + 3x - 1$

2. The table below displays the number of three-year-olds at Kids First Daycare who are potty-trained and those who still wear diapers.

	Potty-trained	Wear diapers	
Boys	26	22	48
Girls	34	18	52
	60	40	

What is the probability of a three-year-old girl from the school being potty-trained?
    a. 52%
    b. 34%
    c. 65%
    d. 57%

3. What is the volume of a cylinder, in terms of π, with a radius of 5 inches and a height of 10 inches?
    a. $250\pi\ in^3$
    b. $50\pi\ in^3$
    c. $100\pi\ in^3$
    d. $200\pi\ in^3$

4. What is the function that forms an equivalent graph to $y = \cos(x)$?
    a. $y = \tan(x)$
    b. $y = \csc(x)$
    c. $y = \sin\left(x + \frac{\pi}{2}\right)$
    d. $y = \sin\left(x - \frac{\pi}{2}\right)$

5. A rectangle was formed out of pipe cleaner. Its length was $\frac{1}{2}$ foot and its width was $\frac{11}{2}$ inches. What is its area in square inches?
    a. $\frac{11}{4}$ inches^2
    b. $\frac{11}{2}$ inches^2
    c. 22 inches^2
    d. 33 inches^2

See answers on the next page.

Answer Explanations

1. C: An x-intercept is the point where the graph crosses the x-axis. At this point, the value of y is 0. To determine if an equation has an x-intercept of –2, substitute –2 for x, and calculate the value of y. If the value of –2 for x corresponds with a y-value of 0, then the equation has an x-intercept of –2. The only answer choice that produces this result is Choice C.

$$0 = (-2)^2 + 5(-2) + 6$$

2. C: There are 34 girls who are potty-trained out of a total of 52 girls:

$$34 \div 52 = 0.65 = 65\%$$

3. A: The volume of a cylinder is $\pi r^2 h$. Plugging in the given values yields:

$$\pi \times (5 \text{ in})^2 \times 10 \text{ in} = 250\pi \text{ in}^3$$

Choice B is not the correct answer because that is $5^2 \times 2\pi$. Choice C is not the correct answer since that is $10 \times 10\pi$. Choice D is not the correct answer because that is $10^2 \times 2\pi$.

4. C: Graphing the function $y = \cos(x)$ shows that the curve starts at $(0, 1)$, has an amplitude of 2, and a period of 2π. This same curve can be constructed using the sine graph, by shifting the graph to the left $\frac{\pi}{2}$ units. This equation is in the form:

$$y = \sin\left(x + \frac{\pi}{2}\right)$$

5. D: Recall the formula for area of a rectangle, area = length × width. The answer must be in square inches, so all values must be converted to inches. Half of a foot is equal to 6 inches. Therefore, the area of the rectangle is equal to:

$$6 \text{ in} \times \frac{11}{2} \text{ in} = \frac{66}{2} \text{ in}^2 = 33 \text{ in}^2$$

Advanced Algebra and Functions

Linear Equations

Solving Linear Equations

When asked to solve a linear equation, it requires determining a numerical value for the unknown variable. Given a linear equation involving addition, subtraction, multiplication, and division, isolation of the variable is done by working backward. Addition and subtraction are inverse operations, as are multiplication and division; therefore, they can be used to cancel each other out.

The first steps to solving linear equations are to distribute if necessary and combine any like terms that are on the same side of the equation. Sides of an equation are separated by an $=$ sign. Next, the equation should be manipulated to get the variable on one side. Whatever is done to one side of an equation, must be done to the other side to remain equal. Then, the variable should be isolated by using inverse operations to undo the order of operations backward. Undo addition and subtraction, then undo multiplication and division.

Algebraically Solving Linear Equations (or Inequalities) in One Variable

Linear equations in one variable and linear inequalities in one variable can be solved following similar processes. Although they typically have one solution, a linear equation can have no solution or can have a solution set of all real numbers. Solution sets for linear inequalities typically consist of an infinite number of values either greater or less than a given value (where the given value may or may not be included in the set). However, a linear inequality can have no solution or can have a solution set consisting of all real numbers.

Linear Equations in One Variable – Special Cases

Solving a linear equation produces a value for the variable that makes the algebraic statement true. If there is no value for the variable that would make the statement true, there is no solution to the equation. Here's a sample equation: $x + 3 = x - 1$. There is no value for x in which adding 3 to the value would produce the same result as subtracting 1 from that value. Conversely, if any value for the variable would make a true statement, the equation has an infinite number of solutions. Here's another sample equation:

$$3x + 6 = 3(x + 2)$$

Any real number substituted for x would result in a true statement (both sides of the equation are equal).

By manipulating equations similar to the two above, the variable of the equation will cancel out completely. If the constants that are left express a true statement (ex., $6 = 6$), then all real numbers are solutions to the equation. If the constants left express a false statement (ex., $3 = -1$), then there is no solution to the equation.

A question on this material may present a linear equation with an unknown value for either a constant or a coefficient of the variable and ask to determine the value that produces an equation with no solution or infinite solutions. For example:

$3x + 7 = 3x + 10 + n$; Find the value of n that would create an equation with an infinite number of solutions for the variable x.

To solve this problem, the equation should be manipulated so the variable x will cancel. To do this, $3x$ should be subtracted from both sides, which would leave:

$$7 = 10 + n$$

106

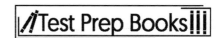

By subtracting 10 on both sides, it is determined that $n = -3$. Therefore, a value of -3 for n would result in an equation with a solution set of all real numbers.

If the same problem asked for the equation to have no solution, the value of n would be all real numbers except -3.

Linear Inequalities in One Variable – Special Cases

A linear inequality can have a solution set consisting of all real numbers or can contain no solution. When solved algebraically, a linear inequality in which the variable cancels out and results in a true statement (ex., $7 \geq 2$) has a solution set of all real numbers. A linear inequality in which the variable cancels out and results in a false statement (ex., $7 \leq 2$) has no solution.

Compound Inequalities

A compound inequality is a pair of inequalities joined by *and* or *or*. Given a compound inequality, to determine its solution set, both inequalities should be solved for the given variable. The solution set for a compound inequality containing *and* consists of all the values for the variable that make both inequalities true. If solving the compound inequality results in $x > -9$ and $x \leq 6$, the solution set would consist of all values between -2 and 3, including 3. This may also be written as follows: $-9 < x \leq 6$. Due to the graphs of their solution sets (shown below), compound inequalities such as these are referred to as conjunctions.

If there are no values that would make both inequalities of a compound inequality containing *and* true, then there is no solution. An example would be $x > 2$ and $x \leq 0$.

The solution set for a compound inequality containing *or* consists of all the values for the variable that make at least one of the inequalities true. The solution set for the compound inequality $x \leq -2$ or $x > 1$ consists of all values less than 2, 6, and all values greater than 6. Due to the graphs of their solution sets (shown below), compound inequalities such as these are referred to as disjunctions.

If the two inequalities for a compound inequality containing *or* "overlap," then the solution set contains all real numbers. An example would be $x > 2$ or $x < 7$. Any number would make at least one of these true.

Solving Systems of Two Linear Equations in Two Variables

A system of two linear equations in two variables is a set of equations that use the same variables (typically x and y). A solution to the system is an ordered pair that makes both equations true. One method for solving a system is by graphing. This method, however, is not always practical. Students may not have graph paper; or the solution may not consist of integers, making it difficult to identify the exact point of intersection on a graph. There are two methods for solving systems of equations algebraically: substitution and elimination. The method used will depend on the characteristics of the equations in the system.

Solving Systems of Equations with the Substitution Method

If one of the equations in a system has an isolated variable ($x =$ or $y =$) or a variable that can be easily isolated, the substitution method can be used. Here's a sample system:

$$x + 3y = 7 \text{ and } 2x - 4y = 24$$

The first equation can easily be solved for *x*. By subtracting 3y on both sides, the resulting equation is:

$$x = 7 - 3y$$

When one equation is solved for a variable, the expression that it is equal can be substituted into the other equation. For this example, $(7 - 3y)$ would be substituted for *x* into the second equation as follows:

$$2(7 - 3y) + 4y = 24$$

Solving this equation results in $y = -5$. Once the value for one variable is known, this value should be substituted into either of the original equations to determine the value of the other variable. For the example, −5 would be substituted for *y* in either of the original equations. Substituting into the first equation results in,

$$x + 3(-5) = 7$$

The solution is $x = 22$. The solution to a system is an ordered pair, so the solution to the example is written as $(22, 7)$. The solution can be checked by substituting it into both equations of the system to ensure it results in two true statements.

Solving Systems of Equations with the Elimination Method

The elimination method for solving a system of equations involves canceling out (or eliminating) one of the variables. This method is typically used when both equations of a system are written in standard form:

$$Ax + By = C$$

An example is:

$$2x + 3y = 12 \text{ and } 5x - y = 13$$

To perform the elimination method, the equations in the system should be arranged vertically to be added together and then one or both of the equations should be multiplied so that one variable will be eliminated when the two are added. Opposites will cancel each other when added together. For example, 8x and −8x will cancel each other when added. For the example above, writing the system vertically helps identify that the bottom equation should be multiplied by 3 to eliminate the variable *y*.

$$2x + 3y = 12 \quad \rightarrow \quad 2x + 3y = 12$$

$$3(5x - y = 13) \quad \rightarrow \quad 15x - 3y = 39$$

Adding the two equations together vertically results in $17x = 51$. Solving yields $x = 3$. Once the value for one variable is known, it can be substituted into either of the original equations to determine the value of the other variable. Once this is obtained, the solution can be written as an ordered pair (x, y) and checked in both equations of the system. In this example, the solution is $(3, 2)$.

Systems of Equations with No Solution or an Infinite Number of Solutions

A system of equations can have one solution, no solution, or an infinite number of solutions. If, while solving a system algebraically, both variables cancel out, then the system has either no solution or has an infinite number of solutions. If the remaining constants result in a true statement (ex., $7 = 7$), then there is an infinite number of solutions. This would indicate coinciding lines. If the remaining constants result in a false statement, then there is no solution to the system. This would indicate parallel lines.

Linear Applications and Graphs

Linear Growth and Decay

As mentioned, a linear equation can be written in the form $y = mx + b$, where x represents the inputs, y represents the outputs, b represents the y-intercept for the graph, and m represents the slope of the line. The y-intercept is the value of y when $x = 0$ and can be thought of as the "starting point." The slope is the rate of change between the variables x and y. A positive slope represents growth, and a negative slope represents decay. Given a table of values for inputs (x) and outputs (y), a linear function would model the relationship if: x and y change at a constant rate per unit interval—for every two inputs a given distance apart, the distance between their corresponding outputs is constant. Here are some sample ordered pairs:

x	0	1	2	3
y	-7	-4	-1	2

For every 1 unit increase in x, y increases by 3 units. Therefore, the change is constant and thus represents linear growth.

Given a scenario involving growth or decay, determining if there is a constant rate of change between inputs (x) and outputs (y) will identify if a linear model is appropriate. A scenario involving distance and time might state that someone is traveling at a rate of 45 miles per hour. For every hour traveled (input), the distance traveled (output) increases by 45 miles. This is a constant rate of change.

Graphing Linear Equations

The simplest equations to graph are the equations whose graphs are lines, called **linear equations**. Every linear equation can be rewritten algebraically so that it looks like:

$$Ax + By = C$$

First, the ratio of the change in the y-coordinate to the change in the x-coordinate is constant for any two distinct points on the line. In any pair of points on a line, two points, (x_1, y_1) and (x_2, y_2)—where $x_1 \neq x_2$—the ratio:

$$\frac{y_2 - y_1}{x_2 - x_1}$$

This will always be the same, even if another pair of points is used.

The following ratio is called the *slope* of the line and is often denoted with the letter m.

$$\frac{y_2 - y_1}{x_2 - x_1}$$

If the slope is **positive**, then the line goes upward when moving to the right. If the slope is **negative**, then it moves downward when moving to the right. If the slope is 0, then the line is **horizontal**, and the y coordinate is constant along the entire line. For lines where the x-coordinate is constant along the entire line, the slope is not defined, and these lines are called **vertical** lines.

The y coordinate of the point where the line touches the y-axis is called the y-**intercept** of the line. It is often denoted by the letter b, used in the form of the linear equation $y = mx + b$. The x coordinate of the point where the line touches the x-axis is called the x-**intercept**. It is also called the *zero* of the line.

Suppose two lines have slopes m_1 and m_2. If the slopes are equal, $m_1 = m_2$, then the lines are **parallel**. Parallel lines never meet one another.

If the below is true then the lines are called **perpendicular** or **orthogonal**.

$$m_1 = -\frac{1}{m_2}$$

Their slopes can also be called opposite reciprocals of each other.

There are several convenient ways to write down linear equations. The common forms are listed here:

- **Standard Form**: $Ax + By = C$, where the slope is given by $\frac{-A}{B}$, and the y-intercept is given by $\frac{C}{B}$.
- **Slope-Intercept Form**: $y = mx + b$, where the slope is m, and the y-intercept is b.
- **Point-Slope Form**: $y - y_1 = m(x - x_1)$, where m is the slope, and (x_1, y_1) is any point on the line.
- **Two-Point Form**: $\frac{y-y_1}{x-x_1} = \frac{y_2-y_1}{x_2-x_1}$, where (x_1, y_1), and (x_2, y_2) are any two distinct points on the line.
- **Intercept Form**: $\frac{x}{x_1} + \frac{y}{y_1} = 1$, where x_1 is the x-intercept, and y_1 is the y-intercept.

Depending upon the given information, different forms of the linear equation can be easier to write down than others. When given two points, the two-point form is easy to write down. If the slope and a single point is known, the point-slope form is easiest to start with. In general, which form to start with depends upon the given information.

Graphing a Line in Slope-Intercept Form

When an equation is written in slope-intercept form, $y = mx + b$, m represents the slope of the line and b represents the y-intercept. The y-intercept is the value of y when $x = 0$ and the point at which the graph of the line crosses the y-axis. The slope is the rate of change between the variables, expressed as a fraction. The fraction expresses the change in y compared to the change in x. If the slope is an integer, it should be written as a fraction with a denominator of 1. For example, 5 would be written as 5/1.

To graph a line given an equation in slope-intercept form, the y-intercept should first be plotted. For example:

$$y = -\frac{2}{3}x + 7$$

To graph the above expression, the y-intercept of 7 would be plotted on the y-axis (vertical axis) at the point $(0, 7)$. Next, the slope would be used to determine a second point for the line. Note that all that is necessary to graph a line is two points on that line. The slope will indicate how to get from one point on the line to another. The slope expresses vertical change (y) compared to horizontal change (x) and therefore is sometimes referred to as $\frac{rise}{run}$. The numerator indicates the change in the y-value (move up for positive integers and move down for negative integers), and the denominator indicates the change in the x-value. For the previous example, using the slope of $-\frac{2}{3}$, from the first point at the y-intercept, the second point should be found by counting down 2 and to the right 3. This point would be located at $(3, 5)$.

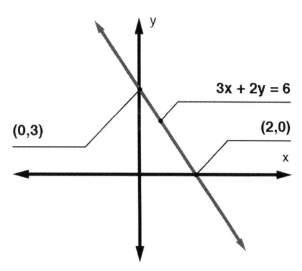

T - chart

x	y
0	3
2	0

Intercepts

x - intercept : (2,0)

y - intercept : (0,3)

$3x + 2y = 6$

(0,3)

(2,0)

Graphing a Line in Standard Form

It is easy to identify the x- and y-intercepts for the graph of the line when an equation is written in standard form:

$$Ax + By = C$$

Just as the y-intercept is the point at which the line intercepts the y-axis, the x-intercept is the point at which the line intercepts the x-axis. At the y-intercept, $x = 0$; and at the x-intercept, $y = 0$. Given an equation in standard form, $x = 0$ should be used to find the y-intercept.

Likewise, $y = 0$ should be used to find the x-intercept. For example,

$$3x + 2y = 6$$

To graph, change 0 for y. This results in:

$$3x + 2(0) = 6$$

Solving for y yields $x = 2$; therefore, an ordered pair for the line is $(2, 0)$. Substituting 0 for x results in:

$$3(0) + 2y = 6$$

Solving for y yields $y = 3$; therefore, an ordered pair for the line is $(0, 3)$. The two ordered pairs (the x- and y-intercepts) can be plotted and a straight line through them can be constructed.

Writing the Equation of a Line Given its Graph

Given the graph of a line, its equation can be written in two ways. If the y-intercept is easily identified (is an integer), it and another point can be used to determine the slope. When determining $\frac{change\ in\ y}{change\ in\ x}$ from one point to another on the graph, the distance for $\frac{rise}{run}$ is being figured. The equation should be written in slope-intercept form, $y = mx + b$, with m representing the slope and b representing the y-intercept.

The equation of a line can also be written by identifying two points on the graph of the line. To do so, the slope is calculated and then the values are substituted for the slope and either of the ordered pairs into the point-slope form of an equation.

Vertical, Horizontal, Parallel, and Perpendicular Lines

For a vertical line, the value of x remains constant (for all ordered pairs (x, y) on the line, the value of x is the same); therefore, the equations for all vertical lines are written in the form $x = number$. For example, a vertical line that crosses the x-axis at −2 would have an equation of $x = -2$. For a horizontal line, the value of y remains constant; therefore, the equations for all horizontal lines are written in the form $y = number$.

Parallel lines extend in the same exact direction without ever meeting. Their equations have the same slopes and different y-intercepts. For example, given a line with an equation of $y = -3x + 2$, a parallel line would have a slope of −3 and a y-intercept of any value other than 2. Perpendicular lines intersect to form a right angle. Their equations have slopes that are opposite reciprocal (the sign is changed and the fraction is flipped; for example, $-\frac{2}{3}$ and $\frac{3}{2}$) and y-intercepts that may or may not be the same. For example, given a line with an equation of:

$$y = \frac{1}{2}x + 7$$

A perpendicular line would have a slope of $-\frac{2}{1}$ and any value for its y-intercept.

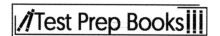

Graphing Solution Sets for Systems of Linear Inequalities in Two Variables

The solution set for a system of inequalities is the region of a graph consisting of ordered pairs that make both inequalities true. To graph the solution set, each linear inequality should first be graphed with appropriate shading. The region of the graph should be identified where the shading for the two inequalities overlaps. This region contains the solution set for the system.

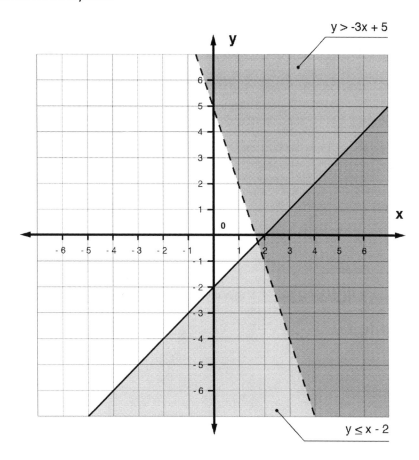

An ordered pair from the region of solutions can be selected to test in the system of inequalities.

Just as with manipulating linear inequalities in one variable, if dividing by a negative number in working with a linear inequality in two variables, the relationship reverses and the inequality sign should be flipped.

Factoring

Factors for polynomials are similar to factors for integers—they are numbers, variables, or polynomials that, when multiplied together, give a product equal to the polynomial in question. One polynomial is a factor of a second polynomial if the second polynomial can be obtained from the first by multiplying by a third polynomial.

$$6x^6 + 13x^4 + 6x^2$$

The above equation can be obtained by multiplying together:

$$(3x^4 + 2x^2)(2x^2 + 3)$$

This means $2x^2 + 3$ and $3x^4 + 2x^2$ are factors of:

$$6x^6 + 13x^4 + 6x^2$$

In general, finding the factors of a polynomial can be tricky. However, there are a few types of polynomials that can be factored in a straightforward way.

If a certain monomial is in each term of a polynomial, it can be factored out. There are several common forms polynomials take, which if you recognize, you can solve. The first example is a perfect square trinomial. To factor this polynomial, first expand the middle term of the expression:

$$x^2 + 2xy + y^2$$

$$x^2 + xy + xy + y^2$$

Factor out a common term in each half of the expression (in this case x from the left and y from the right):

$$x(x + y) + y(x + y)$$

Then the same can be done again, treating $(x + y)$ as the common factor:

$$(x + y)(x + y) = (x + y)^2$$

Therefore, the formula for this polynomial is:

$$x^2 + 2xy + y^2 = (x + y)^2$$

Next is another example of a perfect square trinomial. The process is the similar, but notice the difference in sign:

$$x^2 - 2xy + y^2$$

$$x^2 - xy - xy + y^2$$

Factor out the common term on each side:

$$x(x - y) - y(x - y)$$

Factoring out the common term again:

$$(x - y)(x - y) = (x - y)^2$$

Thus:

$$x^2 - 2xy + y^2 = (x - y)^2$$

The next is known as a difference of squares. This process is effectively the reverse of binomial multiplication:

$$x^2 - y^2$$

$$x^2 - xy + xy - y^2$$

$$x(x - y) + y(x - y)$$

$$(x + y)(x - y)$$

Therefore:

$$x^2 - y^2 = (x + y)(x - y)$$

The following two polynomials are known as the sum or difference of cubes. These are special polynomials that take the form of $x^3 + y^3$ or $x^3 - y^3$. The following formula factors the sum of cubes:

$$x^3 + y^3 = (x + y)(x^2 - xy + y^2)$$

Next is the difference of cubes, but note the change in sign. The formulas for both are similar, but the order of signs for factoring the sum or difference of cubes can be remembered by using the acronym SOAP, which stands for "same, opposite, always positive." The first sign is the same as the sign in the first expression, the second is opposite, and the third is always positive. The next formula factors the difference of cubes:

$$x^3 - y^3 = (x - y)(x^2 + xy + y^2)$$

The following two examples are expansions of cubed binomials. Similarly, these polynomials always follow a pattern:

$$x^3 + 3x^2y + 3xy^2 + y^3 = (x + y)^3$$

$$x^3 - 3x^2y + 3xy^2 - y^3 = (x - y)^3$$

These rules can be used in many combinations with one another. For example, the expression $3x^3 - 24$ has a common factor of 3, which becomes:

$$3(x^3 - 8)$$

A difference of cubes still remains which can then be factored out:

$$3(x - 2)(x^2 + 2x + 4)$$

There are no other terms to be pulled out, so this expression is completely factored.

When factoring polynomials, a good strategy is to multiply the factors to check the result. Let's try another example:

$$4x^3 + 16x^2$$

Both sides of the expression can be divided by 4, and both contain x^2, because $4x^3$ can be thought of as $4x^2(x)$, so the common term can simply be factored out:

$$4x^2(x + 4)$$

It sometimes can be necessary to rewrite the polynomial in some clever way before applying the above rules. Consider the problem of factoring $x^4 - 1$. This does not immediately look like any of the previous polynomials. However, it's possible to think of this polynomial as:

$$x^4 - 1 = (x^2)^2 - (1^2)^2$$

Now, it can be treated as a difference of squares to simplify this:

$$(x^2)^2 - (1^2)^2$$

$$(x^2)^2 - x^2 1^2 + x^2 1^2 - (1^2)^2$$

$$x^2(x^2 - 1^2) + 1^2(x^2 - 1^2)$$

$$(x^2 + 1^2)(x^2 - 1^2)$$

$$(x^2 + 1)(x^2 - 1)$$

Factoring an Algebraic Expression

There are many different ways to write algebraic expressions and equations that are equivalent to each other. Converting expressions from standard form to factored form and vice versa are skills commonly used in advanced mathematics. Standard form of an expression arranges terms with variables powers in descending order (highest exponent to lowest and then constants). Factored form displays an expression as the product of its factors (what can be multiplied to produce the expression).

Converting Standard Form to Factored Form

To factor an expression, a greatest common factor needs to be factored out first. Then, if possible, the remaining expression needs to be factored into the product of binomials. A binomial is an expression with two terms.

Greatest Common Factor

The greatest common factor (GCF) of a monomial (one term) consists of the largest number that divides evenly into all coefficients (number part of a term), and if all terms contain the same variable, the variable with the lowest exponent. The GCF of the following equation would be $3x^2$:

$$3x^4 - 9x^3 + 12x^2$$

To write the factored expression, every term needs to be divided by the GCF, then the product of the resulting quotient and the GCF (using parentheses to show multiplication) should be written. For the previous example, the factored expression would be:

$$3x^2(x^2 - 3x + 4)$$

Factoring $Ax^2 + Bx + C$ When $A = 1$

To factor a quadratic expression in standard form when the value of a is not equal to 1, the factors that multiply to equal the value of $a \times c$ should be found and then added to equal the value of b. Next, the expression splitting the bx term should be rewritten using those factors. Instead of three terms, there will now be four. Then the first two terms should be factored using GCF, and a common binomial should be factored from the last two terms. The factored form will be: (common binomial) (2 terms out of binomials). In the sample expression $2x^2 + 11x + 12$, the value of $a \times c$ (or 2×12) equals 24.

Two factors that multiply to 24 and added together to yield b (11) are 8 and 3. The bx term ($11x$) can be rewritten by splitting it into the factors:

$$2x^2 + 8x + 3x + 12$$

A GCF from the first two terms can be factored as:

$$2x(x + 4) + 3x + 12$$

A common binomial from the last two terms can then be factored as

$$2(x + 4) + 3(x + 4)$$

The factored form can be written as a product of binomials: $(x + 4)(2x + 3)$.

Converting Factored Form to Standard Form

To convert an expression from factored form to standard form, the factors are multiplied.

116

Quadratics

Quadratic Equations

A **quadratic equation** can be written in the form:

$$y = ax^2 + bx + c$$

The u-shaped graph of a quadratic function is called a **parabola**. The graph can either open up or open down (upside down u). The graph is symmetric about a vertical line, called the axis of symmetry. Corresponding points on the parabola are directly across from each other (same y-value) and are the same distance from the axis of symmetry (on either side). The axis of symmetry intersects the parabola at its vertex. The y-value of the vertex represents the minimum or maximum value of the function. If the graph opens up, the value of a in its equation is positive, and the vertex represents the minimum of the function.

If the graph opens down, the value of a in its equation is negative, and the vertex represents the maximum of the function.

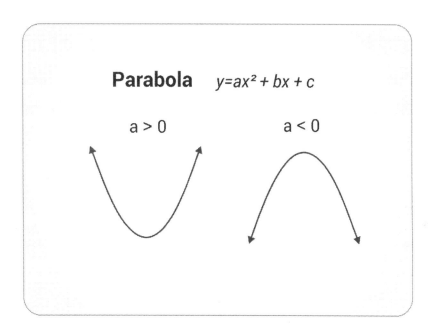

For a quadratic equation where the value of a is positive, as the inputs increase, the outputs increase until a certain value (maximum of the function) is reached. As inputs increase past the value that corresponds with the maximum output, the relationship reverses, and the outputs decrease. For a quadratic equation where a is negative, as the inputs increase, the outputs (1) decrease, (2) reach a maximum, and (3) then increase.

Consider a ball thrown straight up into the air. As time passes, the height of the ball increases until it reaches its maximum height. After reaching the maximum height, as time increases, the height of the ball decreases (it is falling toward the ground). This relationship can be expressed as a quadratic function where time is the input (x) and the height of the ball is the output (y).

To write a quadratic equation that models a real-life scenario, the following is needed: its vertex and any other ordered pair; or any three ordered pairs for the function. Given three ordered pairs, they should be substituted into the general form:

$$y = ax^2 + bx + c$$

This creates a system of three equations. For example, given the ordered pairs $(2, 3)$, $(3, 13)$, and $(4, 29)$, it yields:

$$3 = a(2)2 + b(2) + c \rightarrow 4a + 2b + c = 3$$

$$13 = a(3)2 + b(3) + c \rightarrow 9a + 3b + c = 13$$

$$29 = a(4)2 + b(4) + c \rightarrow 16a + 24b + c = 29$$

The values for a, b, and c in the system can be found and substituted into the general form to write the equation of the function. In this case, the equation is:

$$y = 3x^2 - 5x + 1$$

Given a curve of best-fit that models a quadratic relationship, the equation of the parabola can be written by identifying the vertex of the parabola and another point on the graph. The values for the vertex (h, k) and the point (x, y) should be substituted into the vertex form of a quadratic function to determine the value of a:

$$y = a(x - h)^2 + k$$

To write the equation of a quadratic model with a vertex of $(4, 7)$ and containing the point $(8, 3)$, the values for h, k, x, and y should be substituted into the vertex form of a quadratic equation, resulting in:

$$3 = a(8 - 4)^2 + 7$$

Solving for a, yields $a = -\frac{1}{4}$. Therefore, the equation can be written as:

$$y = -\frac{1}{4}(x - 4)^2 + 7$$

The vertex form can be manipulated in order to write the quadratic equation in standard form.

Solving a Quadratic Equation

A quadratic equation is one in which the highest exponent of the variable is 2. A quadratic equation can have two, one, or zero real solutions. Depending on its structure, a quadratic equation can be solved by (1) factoring, (2) taking square roots, or (3) using the quadratic formula.

Solving Quadratic Equations by Factoring

To solve a quadratic equation by factoring, the equation should first be manipulated to set the quadratic expression equal to zero. Next, the quadratic expression should be factored using the appropriate method(s). Then each factor should be set equal to zero. If two factors multiply to equal zero, then one or both factors must equal zero. Finally, each equation should be solved. Here's a sample:

$$x^2 - 10 = 3x - 6$$

The expression should be set equal to zero:

$$x^2 - 3x - 4 = 0$$

The expression should be factored:

$$(x - 4)(x + 1) = 0$$

Each factor should be set equal to zero:

$$x - 4 = 0; x + 1 = 0$$

Solving yields $x = 4$ or $x = -1$.

Solving Quadratic Equations by Taking Square Roots

If a quadratic equation does not have a linear term (variable to the first power), it can be solved by taking square roots. This means x^2 needs to be isolated and then the square root of both sides of the equation should be isolated. There will be two solutions because square roots can be positive or negative. $\sqrt{4} = 2$ or -2, because $2 \times 2 = 4$ and $-2 \times -2 = 4$.

Here's a sample equation:

$$3x^2 - 12 = 0$$

Isolating x^2 yields $x^2 = 4$. The square root of both sides is then solved: $x = 2$ or -2.

The Quadratic Formula

When a quadratic expression cannot be factored or is difficult to factor, the quadratic formula can be used to solve the equation. To do so, the equation must be in the form:

$$ax^2 + bx + c = 0$$

The quadratic formula is:

$$x = \frac{-b \pm \sqrt{b^2 - 4ac}}{2a}$$

(The $\pm$ symbol indicates that two calculations are necessary, one using $+$ and one using $-$.) Here's a sample equation:

$$3x^2 - 2x = 3x + 2$$

First, the quadratic expression should be set equal to zero:

$$3x^2 - 5x - 2 = 0$$

Then the values are substituted for a (3), b (-5), and c (-2) into the formula:

$$x = \frac{-(-5) \pm \sqrt{(-5)^2 - 4(3)(-2)}}{2(3)}$$

Simplification yields:

$$x = \frac{5 \pm \sqrt{49}}{6} \to x = \frac{5 \pm 7}{6}$$

Calculating two values for x using $+$ and $-$ yields:

$$x = \frac{5 + 7}{6} ; x = \frac{5 - 7}{6}$$

Simplification yields:

$$x = 2 \ or -\frac{1}{3}$$

119

Just as with any equation, solutions should be checked by substituting the value into the original equation.

Solving a System of One Linear Equation and One Quadratic Equation

A system of equations consists of two variables in two equations. A solution to the system is an ordered pair (x, y) that makes both equations true. When displayed graphically, a solution to a system is a point of intersection between the graphs of the equations. When a system consists of one linear equation and one quadratic equation, there may be one, two, or no solutions. If the line and parabola intersect at two points, there are two solutions to the system; if they intersect at one point, there is one solution; if they do not intersect, there is no solution.

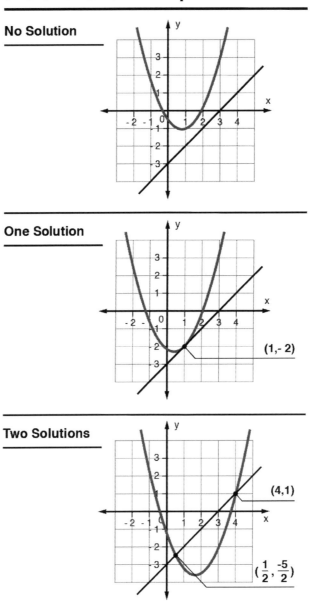

Systems with One Linear Equation and One Quadratic Equation

No Solution

One Solution

(1,- 2)

Two Solutions

(4,1)

$(\frac{1}{2}, \frac{-5}{2})$

120

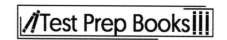

One method for solving a system of one linear equation and one quadratic equation is to graph both functions and identify point(s) of intersection. This, however, is not always practical. Graph paper may not be available, or the intersection points may not be easily identified. Solving the system algebraically involves using the substitution method. Consider the following system:

$$y = x^2 + 9x + 11 \text{ and } y = 2x - 1$$

The equivalent value of y should be substituted from the linear equation $(2x - 1)$ into the quadratic equation. The resulting equation is:

$$2x - 1 = x^2 + 9x + 11$$

Next, this quadratic equation should be solved using the appropriate method: factoring, taking square roots, or using the quadratic formula. Solving this quadratic equation by factoring results in $x = -4$ or $x = -3$. Next, the corresponding y-values should be found by substituting the x-values into the original linear equation:

$$y = 2(-4) - 1; y = 2(-3) - 1$$

The solutions should be written as ordered pairs: $(-4, -9)$ and $(-3, -7)$. Finally, the possible solutions should be checked by substituting each into both of the original equations. In this case, both solutions "check out."

Functions

A **function** is defined as a relationship between inputs and outputs where there is only one output value for a given input. As an example, the following function is in function notation:

$$f(x) = 3x - 4$$

The $f(x)$ represents the output value for an input of x. If $x = 2$, the equation becomes:

$$f(2) = 3(2) - 4 = 6 - 4 = 2$$

The input of 2 yields an output of 2, forming the ordered pair $(2, 2)$. The following set of ordered pairs corresponds to the given function: $(2, 2)$, $(0, -4)$, and $(-2, -10)$. The set of all possible inputs of a function is its **domain**, and all possible outputs is called the **range**. By definition, each member of the domain is paired with only one member of the range.

Functions can also be defined recursively. In this form, they are not defined explicitly in terms of variables. Instead, they are defined using previously-evaluated function outputs, starting with either $f(0)$ or $f(1)$. An example of a recursively-defined function is:

$$f(1) = 2$$

$$f(n) = 2f(n - 1) + 2n$$

$$n > 1$$

The domain of this function is the set of all integers.

Creating Functions Using Function Notation

A **function** is defined as a relationship between inputs and outputs where there is only one output value for a given input. As an example, the following function is in function notation:

$$f(x) = 3x - 4$$

The $f(x)$ represents the output value for an input of x. If $x = 2$, the equation becomes:

$$f(2) = 3(2) - 4 = 6 - 4 = 2$$

The input of 2 yields an output of 2, forming the ordered pair $(2, 2)$. The following set of ordered pairs corresponds to the given function:

$$(2, 2), (0, -4), (-2, -10)$$

The set of all possible inputs of a function is its **domain**, and all possible outputs is called the **range**. By definition, each member of the domain is paired with only one member of the range.

Functions can also be defined recursively. In this form, they are not defined explicitly in terms of variables. Instead, they are defined using previously-evaluated function outputs, starting with either $f(0)$ or $f(1)$. An example of a recursively-defined function is:

$$f(1) = 2, f(n) = 2f(n - 1) + 2n, n > 1$$

The domain of this function is the set of all integers.

A function $f(x)$ is a mathematical object which takes one number, x, as an input and gives a number in return. The input is called the **independent variable**. If the variable is set equal to the output, as in $y = f(x)$, then this is called the **dependent variable**. To indicate the dependent value a function, y, gives for a specific independent variable, x, the notation $y = f(x)$ is used.

The **domain** of a function is the set of values that the independent variable is allowed to take. Unless otherwise specified, the domain is any value for which the function is well defined. The **range** of the function is the set of possible outputs for the function.

In many cases, a function can be defined by giving an equation. For instance, $f(x) = x^2$ indicates that given a value for x, the output of f is found by squaring x.

Not all equations in x and y can be written in the form $y = f(x)$. An equation can be written in such a form if it satisfies the **vertical line test**: no vertical line meets the graph of the equation at more than a single point. In this case, y is said to be a *function of x*. If a vertical line meets the graph in two places, then this equation cannot be written in the form $y = f(x)$.

The graph of a function $f(x)$ is the graph of the equation $y = f(x)$. Thus, it is the set of all pairs (x, y) where $y = f(x)$. In other words, it is all pairs $(x, f(x))$. The x-intercepts are called the **zeros** of the function. The y-intercept is given by $f(0)$.

If, for a given function f, the only way to get $f(a) = f(b)$ is for $a = b$, then f is *one-to-one*. Often, even if a function is not one-to-one on its entire domain, it is one-to-one by considering a restricted portion of the domain.

A function $f(x) = k$ for some number k is called a **constant function**. The graph of a constant function is a horizontal line.

The function $f(x) = x$ is called the **identity function**. The graph of the identity function is the diagonal line pointing to the upper right at 45 degrees, $y = x$.

A function is called **monotone** if it is either always increasing or always decreasing. For example, the functions $f(x) = 3x$ and $f(x) = -x^5$ are monotone.

An **even function** looks the same when flipped over the y-axis: $f(x) = f(-x)$. The following image shows a graphic representation of an even function.

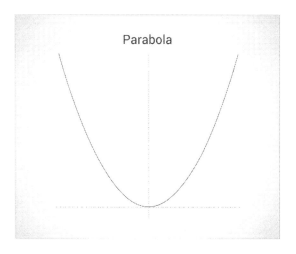

An **odd function** looks the same when flipped over the y-axis and then flipped over the x-axis: $f(x) = -f(-x)$. The following image shows an example of an odd function.

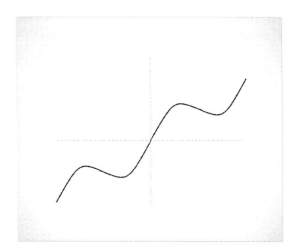

Domain and Range

The domain and range of a function can be found visually by its plot on the coordinate plane. In the function:
$$f(x) = x^2 - 3$$

The domain is all real numbers because the parabola stretches as far left and as far right as it can go, with no restrictions. This means that any input value from the real number system will yield an answer in the real number system. For the range, the inequality $y \geq -3$ would be used to describe the possible output values because the parabola has a minimum at $y = -3$. This means there will not be any real output values less than -3 because -3 is the lowest value it reaches on the y-axis.

These same answers for domain and range can be found by observing a table. The table below shows that from input values $x = -1$ to $x = 1$, the output results in a minimum of -3. On each side of $x = 0$, the numbers increase, showing that the range is all real numbers greater than or equal to -3.

x (domain/input)	y (range/output)
-2	1
-1	-2
0	-3
-1	-2
2	1

Function Behavior

Different types of functions behave in different ways. A function is defined to be increasing over a subset of its domain if for all $x_1 \geq x_2$ in that interval, $f(x_1) \geq f(x_2)$. Also, a function is decreasing over an interval if for all $x_1 \geq x_2$ in that interval, $f(x_1) \leq f(x_2)$. A point in which a function changes from increasing to decreasing can also be labeled as the **maximum value** of a function if it is the largest point the graph reaches on the y-axis. A point in which a function changes from decreasing to increasing can be labeled as the minimum value of a function if it is the smallest point the graph reaches on the y-axis. Maximum values are also known as **extreme values**. The graph of a continuous function does not have any breaks or jumps in the graph. This description is not true of all functions. A radical function, for example, $f(x) = \sqrt{x}$, has a restriction for the domain and range because there are no real negative inputs or outputs for this function. The domain can be stated as $x \geq 0$, and the range is $y \geq 0$.

A piecewise-defined function also has a different appearance on the graph. In the following function, there are three equations defined over different intervals. It is a function because there is only one y-value for each x-value, passing the Vertical Line Test. The domain is all real numbers less than or equal to 6. The range is all real numbers greater than zero. From left to right, the graph decreases to zero, then increases to almost 4, and then jumps to 6.

From input values greater than 2, the input decreases just below 8 to 4, and then stops.

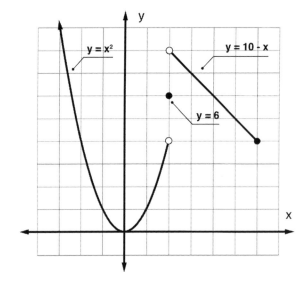

Logarithmic and exponential functions also have different behavior than other functions. These two types of functions are inverses of each other. The **inverse** of a function can be found by switching the place of x and y, and solving for y. When this is done for the exponential equation, $y = 2^x$, the function $y = \log_2 x$ is found. The general form of a **logarithmic function** is $y = \log_b x$, which says b raised to the y power equals x.

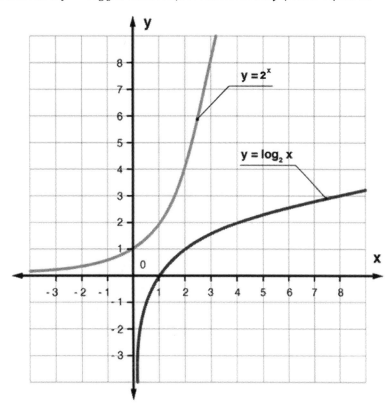

The thick black line on the graph above represents the logarithmic function:

$$y = \log_2 x$$

This curve passes through the point $(1, 0)$, just as all log functions do, because any value $b^0 = 1$. The graph of this logarithmic function starts very close to zero but does not touch the y-axis. The output value will never be zero by the definition of logarithms. The thinner gray line seen above represents the exponential function $y = 2^x$. The behavior of this function is opposite the logarithmic function because the graph of an inverse function is the graph of the original function flipped over the line $y = x$. The curve passes through the point $(0, 1)$ because any number raised to the zero power is one. This curve also gets very close to the x-axis but never touches it because an exponential expression never has an output of zero. The x-axis on this graph is called a horizontal asymptote. An **asymptote** is a line that represents a boundary for a function. It shows a value that the function will get close to, but never reach.

Functions can also be described as being even, odd, or neither. If $f(-x) = f(x)$, the function is even. For example, the following function is even:

$$f(x) = x^2 - 2$$

Plugging in $x = 2$ yields an output of $y = 2$. After changing the input to $x = -2$, the output is still $y = 2$. The output is the same for opposite inputs. Another way to observe an even function is by the symmetry of the graph. If the graph is symmetrical about the axis, then the function is even. If the graph is symmetric about the origin, then the function is odd. Algebraically, if $f(-x) = -f(x)$, the function is odd.

125

Also, a function can be described as **periodic** if it repeats itself in regular intervals. Common periodic functions are trigonometric functions. For example, $y = \sin x$ is a periodic function with period 2π because it repeats itself every 2π units along the x-axis.

Common Functions

Three common functions used to model different relationships between quantities are linear, quadratic, and exponential functions. **Linear functions** are the simplest of the three, and the independent variable x has an exponent of 1. Written in the most common form, $y = mx + b$, the coefficient of x indicates how fast the function grows at a constant rate, and the b-value denotes the starting point. A **quadratic** function has an exponent of 2 on the independent variable x. Standard form for this type of function is:

$$y = ax^2 + bx + c$$

The graph is a parabola. These type functions grow at a changing rate. An **exponential** function has an independent variable in the exponent $y = ab^x$. The graph of these types of functions is described as **growth** or **decay**, based on whether the base, b, is greater than or less than 1. These functions are different from quadratic functions because the base stays constant. A common base is base e.

The following three functions model a linear, quadratic, and exponential function respectively: $y = 2x$, $y = x^2$, and $y = 2^x$. Their graphs are shown below. The first graph, modeling the linear function, shows that the growth is constant over each interval. With a horizontal change of 1, the vertical change is 2. It models constant positive growth. The second graph shows the quadratic function, which is a curve that is symmetric across the y-axis. The growth is not constant, but the change is mirrored over the axis. The last graph models the exponential function, where the horizontal change of 1 yields a vertical change that increases more and more with each iteration of horizontal change. The exponential graph gets very close to the x-axis, but never touches it, meaning there is an asymptote there. The y-value can never be zero because the base of 2 can never be raised to an input value that yields an output of zero.

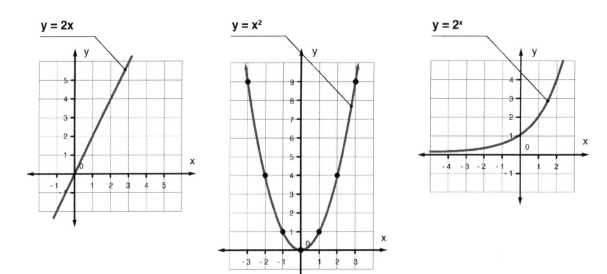

The three tables below show specific values for three types of functions. The third column in each table shows the change in the y-values for each interval. The first table shows a constant change of 2 for each equal interval, which matches the slope in the equation $y = 2x$. The second table shows an increasing change, but it also has a pattern.

The increase is changing by 2 more each time, so the change is quadratic. The third table shows the change as factors of the base, 2. It shows a continuing pattern of factors of the base.

$y = 2x$				$y = x^2$				$y = 2^x$		
x	y	Δy		x	y	Δy		x	y	Δy
1	2			1	1			1	2	
2	4	2		2	4	3		2	4	2
3	6	2		3	9	5		3	8	4
4	8	2		4	16	7		4	16	8
5	10	2		5	25	9		5	32	16

Given a table of values, the type of function can be determined by observing the change in y over equal intervals. For example, the tables below model two functions. The changes in interval for the x-values is 1 for both tables. For the first table, the y-values increase by 5 for each interval. Since the change is constant, the situation can be described as a linear function. The equation would be:

$$y = 5x + 3$$

For the second table, the change for y is 20, 100, and 500, respectively. The increases are multiples of 5, meaning the situation can be modeled by an exponential function. The equation below models this situation:

$$y = 5^x + 3$$

$y = 5x + 3$		$y = 5^x + 3$	
x	y	x	y
1	8	1	8
2	13	2	28
3	18	3	128
4	23	4	628

Quadratic equations can be used to model real-world area problems. For example, a farmer may have a rectangular field that he needs to sow with seed. The field has length $x + 8$ and width $2x$. The formula for area should be used: $A = lw$. Therefore:

$$A = (x + 8) \times 2x = 2x^2 + 16x$$

The possible values for the length and width can be shown in a table, with input x and output A. If the equation was graphed, the possible area values can be seen on the y-axis for given x-values.

Exponential growth and decay can be found in real-world situations. For example, if a piece of notebook paper is folded 25 times, the thickness of the paper can be found. To model this situation, a table can be used. The initial point is one-fold, which yields a thickness of 2 papers. For the second fold, the thickness is 4. Since the thickness doubles each time, the table below shows the thickness for the next few folds. Notice the thickness changes by the same factor each time. Since this change for a constant interval of folds is a factor of 2, the function is exponential. The equation for this is $y = 2^x$. For twenty-five folds, the thickness would be 33,554,432 papers.

x (folds)	y (paper thickness)
0	1
1	2
2	4
3	8
4	16
5	32

One exponential formula that is commonly used is the **interest formula**: $A = Pe^{rt}$. In this formula, interest is compounded continuously. A is the value of the investment after the time, t, in years. P is the initial amount of the investment, r is the interest rate, and e is the constant equal to approximately 2.718. Given an initial amount of $200 and a time of 3 years, if interest is compounded continuously at a rate of 6%, the total investment value can be found by plugging each value into the formula. The invested value at the end is $239.44. In more complex problems, the final investment may be given, and the rate may be the unknown. In this case, the formula becomes $239.44 = 200e^{r3}$. Solving for r requires isolating the exponential expression on one side by dividing by 200, yielding the equation $1.20 = e^{r3}$. Taking the natural log of both sides results in $\ln(1.2) = r3$. Using a calculator to evaluate the logarithmic expression, $r = 0.06 = 6\%$.

When working with logarithms and exponential expressions, it is important to remember the relationship between the two. In general, the logarithmic form is $y = log_b x$ for an exponential form $b^y = x$. Logarithms and exponential functions are inverses of each other.

Interpreting and Building a Function Within a Context

Functions can be built out of the context of a situation. For example, the relationship between the money paid for a gym membership and the months that someone has been a member can be described through a function. If the one-time membership fee is $40 and the monthly fee is $30, then the function can be written:

$$f(x) = 30x + 40$$

The x-value represents the number of months the person has been part of the gym, while the output is the total money paid for the membership. The table below shows this relationship. It is a representation of the function because the initial cost is $40 and the cost increases each month by $30.

x (months)	y (money paid to gym)
0	40
1	70
2	100
3	130

Functions can also be built from existing functions. For example, a given function $f(x)$ can be transformed by adding a constant, multiplying by a constant, or changing the input value by a constant. The new function below represents a vertical shift of the original function:

$$g(x) = f(x) + k$$

In $f(x) = 3x - 2$, a vertical shift 4 units up would be:

$$g(x) = 3x - 2 + 4 = 3x + 2$$

Multiplying the function times a constant k represents a vertical stretch, based on whether the constant is greater than or less than 1. The function

$$g(x) = kf(x) = 4(3x - 2) = 12x - 8$$

represents a stretch. Changing the input x by a constant, forms the function:

$$g(x) = f(x + k) = 3(x + 4) - 2 = 3x + 12 - 2 = 3x + 10$$

and this represents a horizontal shift to the left 4 units. If $(x - 4)$ was plugged into the function, it would represent a vertical shift.

A composition function can also be formed by plugging one function into another. In function notation, this is written:

$$(f \circ g)(x) = f(g(x))$$

For two functions $f(x) = x^2$ and $g(x) = x - 3$, the composition function becomes:

$$f(g(x)) = (x - 3)^2 = x^2 - 6x + 9$$

The composition of functions can also be used to verify if two functions are inverses of each other. Given the two functions:

$$f(x) = 2x + 5 \text{ and } g(x) = \frac{x - 5}{2}$$

The composition function can be found $(f \circ g)(x)$. Solving this equation yields:

$$f(g(x)) = 2\left(\frac{x - 5}{2}\right) + 5 = x - 5 + 5 = x$$

It also is true that $g(f(x)) = x$. Since the composition of these two functions gives a simplified answer of x, this verifies that $f(x)$ and $g(x)$ are inverse functions. The domain of $f(g(x))$ is the set of all x-values in the domain of $g(x)$ such that $g(x)$ is in the domain of $f(x)$. Basically, both $f(g(x))$ and $g(x)$ have to be defined.

To build an inverse of a function, $f(x)$ needs to be replaced with y, and the x- and y-values need to be switched. Then, the equation can be solved for y. For example, given the equation $y = e^{2x}$, the inverse can be found by rewriting the equation $x = e^{2y}$. The natural logarithm of both sides is taken down, and the exponent is brought down to form the equation:

$$\ln(x) = \ln(e)\,2y$$

ln (e)=1, which yields the equation $\ln(x) = 2y$. Dividing both sides by 2 yields the inverse equation

$$\frac{\ln(x)}{2} = y = f^{-1}(x)$$

The domain of an inverse function is the range of the original function, and the range of an inverse function is the domain of the original function. Therefore, an ordered pair (x, y) on either a graph or a table corresponding to $f(x)$ means that the ordered pair (y, x) exists on the graph of $f^{-1}(x)$.

Basically, if $f(x) = y$, then $f^{-1}(y) = x$

For a function to have an inverse, it must be one-to-one. That means it must pass the **Horizontal Line Test**, and if any horizontal line passes through the graph of the function twice, a function is not one-to-one. The domain of a function that is not one-to-one can be restricted to an interval in which the function is one-to-one, to be able to define an inverse function.

Functions can also be formed from combinations of existing functions.

Given $f(x)$ and $g(x)$, the following can be built:

$$f + g$$

$$f - g$$

$$fg$$

$$\frac{f}{g}$$

The domains of $f + g$, $f - g$, and fg are the intersection of the domains of f and g. The domain of $\frac{f}{g}$ is the same set, excluding those values that make $g(x) = 0$.

For example, if:

$$f(x) = 2x + 3$$

$$g(x) = x + 1$$

then

$$\frac{f}{g} = \frac{2x + 3}{x + 1}$$

Its domain is all real numbers except -1.

Radical and Rational Equations

Radical Equations

Equations with radicals containing numbers only as the radicand are solved the same way that an equation without a radical would be. For example, $3x + \sqrt{81} = 45$ would be solved using the same steps as if solving $2x + 4 = 12$. Radical equations are those in which the variable is part of the radicand. For example, the following would be considered radical equations:

$$\sqrt{5x + 1} - 6 = 0 \text{ and } \sqrt{x - 3} + 5 = x$$

To solve a radical equation, the radical should be isolated and both sides of the equation should be raised to the same power to cancel the radical. Raising both sides to the second power will cancel a square root, raising to the third power will cancel a cube root, etc. Consider the following:

$$\sqrt{5x + 1} - 6 = 0$$

To solve, the radical should be isolated first:

$$\sqrt{5x + 1} = 6$$

Then both sides should be raised to the second power:

$$(\sqrt{5x + 1})^2 = (6)^2 \rightarrow 5x + 1 = 36$$

Lastly, the linear equation should be solved: $x = 7$.

If a radical equation contains a variable in the radicand and a variable outside of the radicand, it must be checked for extraneous solutions. An extraneous solution is one obtained by following the proper process for solving an equation but does not "check out" when substituted into the original equation. Here's a sample equation:

$$\sqrt{x - 3} + 5 = x$$

Isolating the radical yields $\sqrt{x - 3} = x - 5$.

Next, both sides should be squared to cancel the radical:

$$(\sqrt{x - 3})^2 = (x - 5)^2 \rightarrow x - 3 = (x - 5)(x - 5)$$

The binomials should be multiplied:

$$x - 3 = x^2 - 10x + 25$$

The quadratic equation is then solved:

$$0 = x^2 - 11x + 28 \rightarrow 0 = (x - 7)(x - 4) \rightarrow x - 7 = 0; x - 4 = 0 \rightarrow x = 7 \text{ or } x = 4$$

To check for extraneous solutions, each answer can be substituted, one at a time, into the original equation. Substituting 7 for x, results in $7 = 7$. Therefore, 7 is a solution. Substituting 4 for x results in $6 = 4$. This is false; therefore, 4 is an extraneous solution.

Rational Expressions, Equations, and Functions

Rational Expressions
A **rational expression** is a fraction where the numerator and denominator are both polynomials. Some examples of rational expressions include the following:

$$\frac{4x^3y^5}{3z^4}, \frac{4x^3 + 3x}{x^2}, and \frac{x^2 + 7x + 10}{x + 2}$$

Since these refer to expressions and not equations, they can be simplified but not solved. Exponents on the variables are restricted to whole numbers, which means roots and negative exponents are not included in rational expressions.

Rational expressions can be transformed by factoring. For example, the expression below can be rewritten by factoring the numerator:

$$\frac{x^2 - 5x + 6}{(x - 3)}$$

$$\frac{(x - 3)(x - 2)}{(x - 3)}$$

131

Therefore, the common binomial $(x - 3)$ can cancel so that the simplified expression is:

$$\frac{(x - 2)}{1} = (x - 2)$$

Additionally, other rational expressions can be rewritten to take on different forms. Some may be factorable in themselves, while others can be transformed through arithmetic operations. Rational expressions are closed under addition, subtraction, multiplication, and division by a nonzero expression. **Closed** means that if any one of these operations is performed on a rational expression, the result will still be a rational expression. The set of all real numbers is another example of a set closed under all four operations.

Adding and subtracting rational expressions is based on the same concepts as adding and subtracting simple fractions. For both concepts, the denominators must be the same for the operation to take place. For example, here are two rational expressions:

$$\frac{x^3 - 4}{(x - 3)} + \frac{x + 8}{(x - 3)}$$

Since the denominators are both $(x - 3)$, the numerators can be combined by collecting like terms to form:

$$\frac{x^3 + x + 4}{(x - 3)}$$

If the denominators are different, they need to be made common (the same) by using the Least Common Denominator (LCD). Each denominator needs to be factored, and the LCD contains each factor that appears in any one denominator the greatest number of times it appears in any denominator. The original expressions need to be multiplied times a form of 1, which will turn each denominator into the LCD. This process is like adding fractions with unlike denominators. It is also important when working with rational expressions to define what value of the variable makes the denominator zero. For this particular value, the expression is undefined.

Multiplication of rational expressions is performed like multiplication of fractions. The numerators are multiplied; then, the denominators are multiplied. The final fraction is then simplified. The expressions are simplified by factoring and cancelling out common terms. In the following example, the numerator of the second expression can be factored first to simplify the expression before multiplying:

$$\frac{x^2}{(x - 4)} \times \frac{x^2 - x - 12}{2}$$

$$\frac{x^2}{(x - 4)} \times \frac{(x - 4)(x + 3)}{2}$$

The $(x - 4)$ on the top and bottom cancel out:

$$\frac{x^2}{1} \times \frac{(x + 3)}{2}$$

Then multiplication is performed, resulting in:

$$\frac{x^3 + 3x^2}{2}$$

Dividing rational expressions is similar to the division of fractions, where division turns into multiplying by a reciprocal. So the following expression can be rewritten as a multiplication problem:

$$\frac{x^2 - 3x + 7}{x - 4} \div \frac{x^2 - 5x + 3}{x - 4}$$

$$\frac{x^2 - 3x + 7}{x - 4} \times \frac{x - 4}{x^2 - 5x + 3}$$

The $x - 4$ cancels out, leaving:

$$\frac{x^2 - 3x + 7}{x^2 - 5x + 3}$$

The final answers should always be completely simplified. If a function is composed of a rational expression, the zeros of the graph can be found from setting the polynomial in the numerator as equal to zero and solving. The values that make the denominator equal to zero will either exist on the graph as a hole or a vertical asymptote.

The following problem is an example of using rational expressions:

Reggie wants to lay sod in his rectangular backyard. The length of the yard is given by the expression $4x + 2$, and the width is unknown. The area of the yard is $20x + 10$. Reggie needs to find the width of the yard. Knowing that the area of a rectangle is length multiplied by width, an expression can be written to find the width (area divided by length):

$$\frac{20x + 10}{4x + 2}$$

Simplifying this expression by factoring out 10 on the top and 2 on the bottom leads to this expression:

$$\frac{10(2x + 1)}{2(2x + 1)}$$

Cancelling out the $2x + 1$ results in $\frac{10}{2} = 5$. The width of the yard is found to be 5 by simplifying the rational expression.

Rational Equations

A **rational equation** can be as simple as an equation with a ratio of polynomials, $\frac{p(x)}{q(x)}$, set equal to a value, where $p(x)$ and $q(x)$ are both polynomials. A rational equation has an equal sign, which is different from expressions. This leads to solutions, or numbers that make the equation true.

It is possible to solve rational equations by trying to get all of the x terms out of the denominator and then isolating them on one side of the equation. For example:

$$\frac{3x + 2}{2x + 3} = 4$$

To solve the equation, both sides get multiplied by $(2x + 3)$. This will cancel on the left side to yield:

$$3x + 2 = 4(2x + 3) \text{ then } 3x + 2 = 8x + 12$$

Now, subtract $8x$ from both sides, which yields:

$$-5x + 2 = 12$$

133

Subtracting 2 from both sides results in $-5x = 10$. Finally, both sides get divided by -5 to obtain $x = -2$.

Sometimes, when solving rational equations, it can be easier to try to simplify the rational expression by factoring the numerator and denominator first, then cancelling out common factors. For example,

$$\frac{2x^2 - 8x + 6}{x^2 - 3x + 2} = 1$$

To solve, the first step is to factor:

$$2x^2 - 8x + 6 = 2(x^2 - 4x + 3) = 2(x - 1)(x - 3)$$

Then, factor $x^2 - 3x + 2$ into $(x - 1)(x - 2)$.

This turns the original equation into:

$$\frac{2(x - 1)(x - 3)}{(x - 1)(x - 2)} = 1$$

The common factor of $(x - 1)$ can be canceled, leaving:

$$\frac{2(x - 3)}{x - 2} = 1$$

Now the same method used in the previous example can be followed. Multiplying both sides by $x - 1$ and performing the multiplication on the left yields:

$$2x - 6 = x - 2$$

This can be simplified to $x = 4$.

Rational Functions

A **rational function** is similar to an equation, but it includes two variables. In general, a rational function is in the form:

$$f(x) = \frac{p(x)}{q(x)}$$

The variables $p(x)$ and $q(x)$ are polynomials. Rational functions are defined everywhere except where the denominator is equal to zero. When the denominator is equal to zero, this indicates either a hole in the graph or an asymptote. An example of a function with an asymptote is shown below.

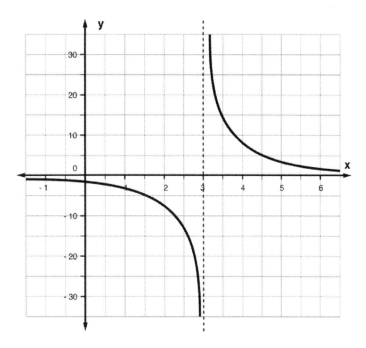

Polynomial Equations

Polynomials

An expression of the form ax^n, where n is a non-negative integer, is called a **monomial** because it contains one term. A sum of monomials is called a **polynomial**. For example, $-4x^3 + x$ is a polynomial, while $5x^7$ is a monomial. A function equal to a polynomial is called a **polynomial function**.

The monomials in a polynomial are also called the **terms** of the polynomial.

The constants that precede the variables are called **coefficients**.

The highest value of the exponent of x in a polynomial is called the **degree** of the polynomial. So, $-4x^3 + x$ has a degree of 3, while $-2x^5$ in the equation below has a degree of 5:

$$-2x^5 + x^3 + 4x + 1$$

When multiplying polynomials, the degree of the result will be the sum of the degrees of the two polynomials being multiplied.

To add polynomials, add the coefficients of like powers of x. For example,

$$(-2x^5 + x^3 + 4x + 1) + (-4x^3 + x)$$

$$-2x^5 + (1 - 4)x^3 + (4 + 1)x + 1$$

$$-2x^5 - 3x^3 + 5x + 1$$

135

Likewise, subtraction of polynomials is performed by subtracting coefficients of like powers of x. So,

$$(-2x^5 + x^3 + 4x + 1) - (-4x^3 + x)$$

$$-2x^5 + (1 + 4)x^3 + (4 - 1)x + 1$$

$$-2x^5 + 5x^3 + 3x + 1$$

To multiply two polynomials, multiply each term of the first polynomial by each term of the second polynomial and add the results. For example,

$$(4x^2 + x)(-x^3 + x)$$

$$4x^2(-x^3) + 4x^2(x) + x(-x^3) + x(x)$$

$$-4x^5 + 4x^3 - x^4 + x^2$$

In the case where each polynomial has two terms, like in this example, some students find it helpful to remember this as multiplying the First terms, then the Outer terms, then the Inner terms, and finally the Last terms, with the mnemonic **FOIL**. For longer polynomials, the multiplication process is the same, but there will be, of course, more terms, and there is no common mnemonic to remember each combination.

The process of **factoring** a polynomial means to write the polynomial as a product of other (generally simpler) polynomials. Here is an example:

$$x^2 - 4x + 3 = (x - 1)(x - 3)$$

If a certain monomial divides every term of the polynomial, factor it out of each term, for example:

$$4x^3 + 16x^2 = 4x^2(x + 4).$$

$$x^2 + 2xy + y^2 = (x + y)^2 \text{ or } x^2 - 2xy + y^2 = (x - y)^2$$

$$x^2 - y^2 = (x + y)(x - y)$$

$$x^3 + y^3 = (x + y)(x^2 - xy + y^2)$$

$$x^3 - y^3 = (x - y)(x^2 + xy + y^2)$$

$$x^3 + 3x^2y + 3xy^2 + y^3 = (x + y)^3 \text{ and } x^3 - 3x^2y + 3xy^2 - y^3 = (x - y)^3$$

It sometimes can be necessary to rewrite the polynomial in some clever way before applying the above rules. Consider the problem of factoring $x^4 - 1$. This does not immediately look like any of the cases for which there are rules. However, it's possible to think of this polynomial as:

$$x^4 - 1 = (x^2)^2 - (1^2)^2$$

Now, apply the third rule in the above list to simplify this:

$$(x^2)^2 - (1^2)^2 = (x^2 + 1^2)(x^2 - 1^2) = (x^2 + 1)(x^2 - 1)$$

Zeros of Polynomials

Finding the zeros of polynomial equations are the points at which the graph of the equation crosses the x-axis. Factors can be used to find the zeros of a polynomial equation or function. The degree of the equation shows the

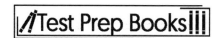
number of possible zeros. If the highest exponent on the independent variable is 4, then the degree is 4, and the number of possible zeros is 4. If there are complex solutions, the number of roots is less than the degree.

Given the equation below, y can be set equal to zero, and the polynomial can be factored:

$$y = x^2 + 7x + 6$$

The equation turns into:

$$0 = (x + 1)(x + 6)$$

Here, $x = -1$ and $x = -6$, which would resolve the expression to 0. Since this is a quadratic equation, the shape of the graph will be a parabola. Knowing that zeros represent the points where the parabola crosses the x-axis, the maximum or minimum point is the only other piece needed to sketch a rough graph of the function. By looking at the function in standard form, the coefficient of x is positive; therefore, the parabola opens *up*. Using the zeros and the minimum, the following rough sketch of the graph can be constructed:

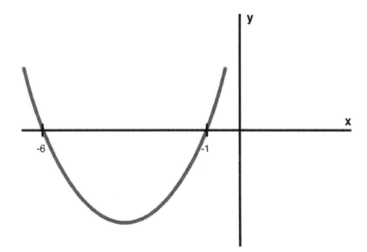

Polynomial Identities

Difference of squares refers to a binomial composed of the difference of two squares. For example, $a^2 - b^2$ is a difference of squares. It can be written $(a)^2 - (b)^2$, and it can be factored into $(a - b)(a + b)$. Recognizing the difference of squares allows the expression to be rewritten easily because of the form it takes. For some expressions, factoring consists of more than one step. When factoring, it's important to always check to make sure that the result cannot be factored further. If it can, then the expression should be split further. If it cannot be, the factoring step is complete, and the expression is completely factored.

A sum and difference of cubes is another way to factor a polynomial expression. When the polynomial takes the form of addition or subtraction of two terms that can be written as a cube, a formula is given. The following graphic shows the factorization of a difference of cubes:

$$a^3 - b^3 = (a - b)(a^2 + ab + b^2)$$

same sign   always +

opposite sign

This form of factoring can be useful in finding the zeros of a function of degree 3. For example, when solving $x^3 - 27 = 0$, this rule needs to be used. $x^3 - 27$ is first written as the difference two cubes, $(x)^3 - (3)^3$ and then factored into:

$$(x - 3)(x^2 + 3x + 9)$$

This expression may not be factored any further. Each factor is then set equal to zero. Therefore, one solution is found to be $x = 3$, and the other two solutions must be found using the quadratic formula. A sum of squares would have a similar process. The formula for factoring a sum of squares is:

$$a^3 + b^3 = (a + b)(a^2 - ab + b^2)$$

The opposite of factoring is multiplying. Multiplying a square of a binomial involves the following rules:

$$(a + b)^2 = a^2 + 2ab + b^2 \text{ and } (a - b)^2 = a^2 - 2ab + b^2$$

The binomial theorem for expansion can be used when the exponent on a binomial is larger than 2, and the multiplication would take a long time. The binomial theorem is given as:

$$(a + b)^n = \sum_{k=0}^{n} \binom{n}{k} a^{n-k} b^k \qquad \binom{n}{k} = \frac{n!}{k!(n-k)!}$$

where

The **Remainder Theorem** can be helpful when evaluating polynomial functions $P(x)$ for a given value of x. A polynomial can be divided by $(x - a)$, if there is a remainder of 0. This also means that $P(a) = 0$ and $(x - a)$ is a factor of $P(x)$. In a similar sense, if P is evaluated at any other number b, $P(b)$ is equal to the remainder of dividing $P(x)$ by $(x - b)$.

Exponential and Logarithmic Equations

Exponential Functions or Equations

An **exponential function** is a function of the form $f(x) = b^x$, where b is a positive real number other than 1. In such a function, b is called the **base**. An exponential equation takes the same form, but is typically written as $y = b^x$.

The **domain** of an exponential function is all real numbers, and the *range* is all positive real numbers. There will always be a horizontal asymptote of $y = 0$ on one side. If b is greater than 1, then the graph will be increasing moving to the right. If b is less than 1, then the graph will be decreasing moving to the right. Exponential functions are one-to-one. The basic exponential function graph will go through the point (0,1).

Example: Solve $5^{x+1} = 25$.

Get the *x* out of the exponent by rewriting the equation so that both sides have a base of 5:

$$5^{x+1} = 5^2$$

Since the bases are the same, the exponents must be equal to each other.

This leaves $x + 1 = 2$ or $x = 1$.

To check the answer, the x-value of 1 can be substituted back into the original equation.

138

Logarithmic Functions and Equations

A **logarithmic function** is an inverse for an exponential function. The inverse of the base b exponential function is written as $\log_b(x)$, and is called the *base b* **logarithm**. The domain of a logarithm is all positive real numbers. It has the properties that:

$$\log_b(b^x) = x$$

For positive real values of x:

$$b^{\log_b(x)} = x$$

When there is no chance of confusion, the parentheses are sometimes skipped for logarithmic functions: $\log_b(x)$ may be written as $\log_b x$. For the special number e, the base e logarithm is called the **natural logarithm** and is written as $\ln x$. Logarithms are one-to-one.

When working with logarithmic functions, it is important to remember the following properties. Each one can be derived from the definition of the logarithm as the inverse to an exponential function:

$$\log_b 1 = 0$$

$$\log_b b = 1$$

$$\log_b b^p = p$$

$$\log_b MN = \log_b M + \log_b N$$

$$\log_b \frac{M}{N} = \log_b M - \log_b N$$

$$\log_b M^p = p \log_b M$$

When solving equations involving exponentials and logarithms, the following fact should be used:

If f is a one-to-one function, $a = b$ is equivalent to $f(a) = f(b)$.

Using this, together with the fact that logarithms and exponentials are inverses, allows manipulations of the equations to isolate the variable.

Example: Solve $4 = \ln(x - 4)$.

Using the definition of a logarithm, the equation can be changed to: $e^4 = e^{\ln(x-4)}$

The functions on the right side cancel with a result of: $e^4 = x - 4$

This then gives: $x = 4 + e^4$

Trigonometry

Trigonometric Functions

Trigonometric functions are built out of two basic functions, the sine and cosine, written as $\sin \theta$ and $\cos \theta$ respectively. Note that similar to logarithms, it is customary to drop the parentheses as long as the result is not confusing.

The sine and cosine are defined using the **unit circle**. If θ is the angle going counterclockwise around the origin from the x-axis, then the point on the unit circle in that direction will have the coordinates $(\cos \theta, \sin \theta)$.

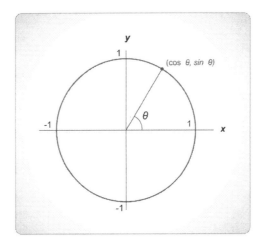

Since the angle returns to the start every 2π radians (or 360 degrees), the graph of these functions will be **periodic**, with period 2π. This means that the graph repeats itself as one moves along the x-axis because:

$$\sin \theta = \sin(\theta + 2\pi)$$

From the unit circle definition, the **sine** function starts at 0 when $\theta = 0$. It grows to 1 as θ grows to $\pi/2$, and then back to 0 at $\theta = \pi$. Then it decreases to -1 as θ grows to $3\pi/2$, and back up to 0 at $\theta = 2\pi$.

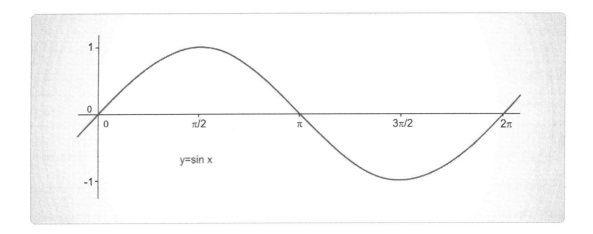

The graph of the **cosine** is similar. The cosine will start at 1, decreasing to 0 at $\pi/2$ and continuing to decrease to -1 at $\theta = \pi$. Then, it grows to 0 as θ grows to $3\pi/2$ and back up to 1 at $\theta = 2\pi$.

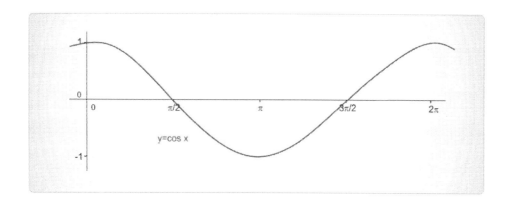

Another trigonometric function, which is frequently used, is the **tangent** function. This is defined as the following equation:

$$\tan\theta = \frac{\sin\theta}{\cos\theta}$$

The tangent function is a period of π rather than 2π because the sine and cosine functions have the same absolute values after a change in the angle of π, but flip their signs. Since the tangent is a ratio of the two functions, the changes in signs cancel.

The tangent function will be zero when the sine is zero, and it will have a vertical asymptote whenever cosine is zero. The following graph shows the tangent function:

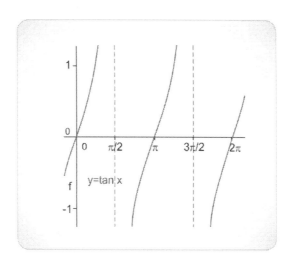

Three other trigonometric functions are sometimes useful. These are the *reciprocal trigonometric functions*, so named because they are just the reciprocals of sine, cosine, and tangent. They are the **cosecant**, defined as $\csc\theta = \frac{1}{\sin\theta}$, the **secant**, $\sec\theta = \frac{1}{\cos\theta}$, and the **cotangent**, $\cot\theta = \frac{1}{\tan\theta}$. Note that from the definition of tangent,

$$\cot\theta = \frac{\cos\theta}{\sin\theta}$$

In addition, there are three identities that relate the trigonometric functions to one another:

$$\cos\theta = \sin(\frac{\pi}{2} - \theta)$$

$$\csc\theta = \sec\left(\frac{\pi}{2} - \theta\right)$$

$$\cot\theta = \tan(\frac{\pi}{2} - \theta)$$

Here is a list of commonly-needed values for trigonometric functions, given in radians, for the first quadrant:

Table for trigonometric functions

$\sin 0 = 0$	$\cos 0 = 1$	$\tan 0 = 0$
$\sin\frac{\pi}{6} = \frac{1}{2}$	$\cos\frac{\pi}{6} = \frac{\sqrt{3}}{2}$	$\tan\frac{\pi}{6} = \frac{\sqrt{3}}{3}$
$\sin\frac{\pi}{4} = \frac{\sqrt{2}}{2}$	$\cos\frac{\pi}{4} = \frac{\sqrt{2}}{2}$	$\tan\frac{\pi}{4} = 1$
$\sin\frac{\pi}{3} = \frac{\sqrt{3}}{2}$	$\cos\frac{\pi}{3} = \frac{1}{2}$	$\tan\frac{\pi}{3} = \sqrt{3}$
$\sin\frac{\pi}{2} = 1$	$\cos\frac{\pi}{2} = 0$	$\tan\frac{\pi}{2} = undefined$
$\csc 0 = undefined$	$\sec 0 = 1$	$\cot 0 = undefined$
$\csc\frac{\pi}{6} = 2$	$\sec\frac{\pi}{6} = \frac{2\sqrt{3}}{3}$	$\cot\frac{\pi}{6} = \sqrt{3}$
$\csc\frac{\pi}{4} = \sqrt{2}$	$\sec\frac{\pi}{4} = \sqrt{2}$	$\cot\frac{\pi}{4} = 1$
$\csc\frac{\pi}{3} = \frac{2\sqrt{3}}{3}$	$\sec\frac{\pi}{3} = 2$	$\cot\frac{\pi}{3} = \frac{\sqrt{3}}{3}$
$\csc\frac{\pi}{2} = 1$	$\sec\frac{\pi}{2} = undefined$	$\cot\frac{\pi}{2} = 0$

To find the trigonometric values in other quadrants, complementary angles can be used. The **complementary angle** is the smallest angle between the x-axis and the given angle.

Once the complementary angle is known, the following rule is used:

For an angle θ with complementary angle x, the absolute value of a trigonometry function evaluated at θ is the same as the absolute value when evaluated at x.

The correct sign is used based on the functions sine and cosine are given by the *x* and *y* coordinates on the unit circle.

- Sine will be positive in quadrants I and II and negative in quadrants III and IV.

- Cosine will be positive in quadrants I and IV, and negative in II and III.

- Tangent will be positive in I and III, and negative in II and IV.

- The signs of the reciprocal functions will be the same as the sign of the function of which they are a reciprocal.

Example: Find $\sin \frac{3\pi}{4}$.

First, the complementary angle must be found.

This angle is in the II quadrant, and the angle between it and the *x*-axis is $\frac{\pi}{4}$.

Now, $\sin \frac{\pi}{4} = \frac{\sqrt{2}}{2}$.

Since this is in the II quadrant, sine takes on positive values (the *y* coordinate is positive in the II quadrant).

Therefore, $\sin \frac{3\pi}{4} = \frac{\sqrt{2}}{2}$.

In addition to the six trigonometric functions defined above, there are inverses for these functions. However, since the trigonometric functions are not one-to-one, one can only construct inverses for them on a restricted domain.

Usually, the domain chosen will be $[0, \pi)$ for cosine and $(-\frac{\pi}{2}, \frac{\pi}{2}]$ for sine. The inverse for tangent can use either of these domains. The inverse functions for the trigonometric functions are also called *arc functions*. In addition to being written with a –1 in the exponent to denote that the function is an inverse, they will sometimes be written with an "a" or "arc" in front of the function name:

$$\cos^{-1} \theta = \mathrm{acos}\,\theta = \mathrm{arccos}\,\theta$$

When solving equations that involve trigonometric functions, there are often multiple solutions. For example, $2 \sin \theta = \sqrt{2}$ can be simplified to $\sin \theta = \frac{\sqrt{2}}{2}$. This has solutions $\theta = \frac{\pi}{4}, \frac{3\pi}{4}$, but in addition, because of the periodicity, any integer multiple of 2π can also be added to these solutions to find another solution.

The full set of solutions for all integer values of *k* is:

$$\theta = \frac{\pi}{4} + 2\pi k \ and \ \frac{3\pi}{4} + 2\pi k$$

It is very important to remember to find all possible solutions when dealing with equations that involve trigonometric functions.

The name *trigonometric* comes from the fact that these functions play an important role in the geometry of triangles, particularly right triangles.

Consider the right triangle shown in this figure:

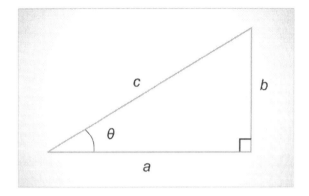

The following hold true:

- $c \sin \theta = b$

- $c \cos \theta = a$

- $\tan \theta = \dfrac{b}{a}$

- $b \csc \theta = c$

- $a \sec \theta = c$

- $\cot \theta = \dfrac{a}{b}$

Remember also the angles of a triangle must add up to π radians (180 degrees).

Solving Trigonometric Functions

Solving trigonometric functions can be done with a knowledge of the unit circle and the trigonometric identities. It requires the use of opposite operations combined with trigonometric ratios for special triangles. For example, the problem may require solving the equation below for the values of x between 0 and 180 degrees:

$$2 \cos^2 x - \sqrt{3} \cos x = 0$$

The first step is to factor out the $\cos x$ term, resulting in $\cos x (2 \cos x - \sqrt{3}) = 0$. By the factoring method of solving, each factor can be set equal to zero: $\cos x = 0$ and $(2 \cos x - \sqrt{3}) = 0$. The second equation can be solved to yield the following equation: $\cos x = \dfrac{\sqrt{3}}{2}$. Now that the value of x is found, the trigonometric ratios can be used to find the solutions of $x = 30$ and 90 degrees.

Solving trigonometric functions requires the use of algebra to isolate the variable and a knowledge of trigonometric ratios to find the value of the variable. The unit circle can be used to find answers for special triangles. Beyond those triangles, a calculator can be used to solve for variables within the trigonometric functions.

Using Graphing Calculators to Solve Trigonometric Problems

In addition to algebraic techniques, problems involving trigonometric functions can be solved using graphing calculators. For example, given an equation, both sides of the equals sign first need to be graphed as separate equations in the same window on the calculator. The point(s) of intersection are then found by zooming into an appropriate window. The points of intersection are the solutions. For example, consider $\cos x = \dfrac{1}{2}$. Solving this

144

equation involves graphing both $y = \cos x$ and $y = \frac{1}{2}$ in the same window. If the calculator is set in Radians mode, the screen zoomed in from $[0, 2\pi]$ on the x-axis would look like:

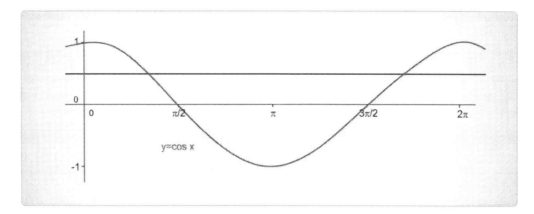

The trace function on the calculator allows the user to zoom into the point of intersection to obtain the two solutions from $[0, 2\pi]$. The periodic nature of the function must then be taken into consideration to obtain the entire solution set, which contains an infinite number of solutions.

Practice Quiz

1. What is the product of the following expression?

$$(4x - 8)(5x^2 + x + 6)$$

   a. $20x^3 - 36x^2 + 16x - 48$
   b. $6x^3 - 41x^2 + 12x + 15$
   c. $20x^3 + 11x^2 - 37x - 12$
   d. $2x^3 - 11x^2 - 32x + 20$

2. What is the y-intercept for $y = x^2 + 3x - 4$?
   a. $y = 1$
   b. $y = -4$
   c. $y = 3$
   d. $y = 4$

3. What is the value of b in the equation: $5b - 4 = 2b + 17$?
   a. 13
   b. 24
   c. 7
   d. 21

4. If $-3(x + 4) \geq x + 8$, what is the value of x?
   a. $x = 4$
   b. $x \geq 2$
   c. $x \geq -5$
   d. $x \leq -5$

5. Karen gets paid a weekly salary and a commission for every sale that she makes. The table below shows the number of sales and her pay for different weeks.

Sales	2	7	4	8
Pay	$380	$580	$460	$620

Which of the following equations represents Karen's weekly pay?
   a. $y = 90x + 200$
   b. $y = 90x - 200$
   c. $y = 40x + 300$
   d. $y = 40x - 300$

See answers on the next page.

146

Answer Explanations

1. A: Finding the product means distributing one polynomial over the other so that each term in the first is multiplied by each term in the second. Then, like terms can be collected. Multiplying the factors yields the expression:

$$20x^3 + 4x^2 + 24x - 40x^2 - 8x - 48$$

Collecting like terms means adding the x^2 terms and adding the x terms. The final answer after simplifying the expression is:

$$20x^3 - 36x^2 + 16x - 48$$

By making this change in position over time into a rate, the speed becomes ten meters in two seconds or five meters in one second.

2. B: The y-intercept of an equation is found where the x-value is zero. Plugging zero into the equation for x, the first two terms cancel out, leaving –4.

3. C: To solve for the value of b, isolate the variable b on one side of the equation.

Start by moving the lower value of –4 to the other side by adding 4 to both sides:

$$5b - 4 = 2b + 17$$

$$5b - 4 + 4 = 2b + 17 + 4$$

$$5b = 2b + 21$$

Then subtract $2b$ from both sides:

$$5b - 2b = 2b + 21 - 2b$$

$$3b = 21$$

Then divide both sides by 3 to get the value of b:

$$\frac{3b}{3} = \frac{21}{3}$$

$$b = 7$$

4. D: When solving a linear inequality, distribution is performed first, if necessary:

$$-3(x + 4) \rightarrow -3x - 12 \geq x + 8$$

The inequality is manipulated to get the variable on one side.

In this case, start by subtracting x from both sides produces:
$$-4x - 12 \geq 8$$

The variable is isolated using inverse operations to undo subtraction. Adding 12 to both sides produces $-4x \geq 20$.

The variable is isolated using inverse operations to undo multiplication/division. Remember, if dividing by a negative number, the relationship of the inequality reverses, so the sign is flipped. In this case, dividing by –4 on both sides produces $x \leq -5$.

5. C: $y = 40x + 300$

In this scenario, the variables are the number of sales and Karen's weekly pay. The weekly pay depends on the number of sales. Therefore, weekly pay is the dependent variable (y), and the number of sales is the independent variable (x). Each pair of values from the table can be written as an ordered pair (x, y): $(2, 380)$, $(7, 580)$, $(4, 460)$, $(8, 620)$.

The ordered pairs can be substituted into the equations to see which create true statements (both sides equal) for each pair. Even if one ordered pair produces equal values for a given equation, the other three ordered pairs must be checked. The only equation which is true for all four ordered pairs is

$$y = 40x + 300$$

$$380 = 40(2) + 300 \rightarrow 380 = 380$$

$$580 = 40(7) + 300 \rightarrow 580 = 580$$

$$460 = 40(4) + 300 \rightarrow 460 = 460$$

$$620 = 40(8) + 300 \rightarrow 620 = 620$$

Reading Test

Information and Ideas

Identifying the Main Idea

Topics and main ideas are critical parts of any writing. The **topic** is the subject matter of the piece, and it is a broader, more general term. The **main idea** is what the writer wants to say about that topic. The topic can be expressed in a word or two, but the main idea should be a complete thought.

The topic and main idea are usually easy to recognize in nonfiction writing. An author will likely identify the topic immediately in the first sentence of a passage or essay. The main idea is also typically presented in the introductory paragraph of an essay. In a single passage, the main idea may be identified in the first or last sentence, but will likely be directly stated and easily recognized by the reader. Because it is not always stated immediately in a passage, it's important to carefully read the entire passage to identify the main idea.

Also remember that when most authors write, they want to make a point or send a message. This point or message of a text is known as the theme. Authors may state themes explicitly, like in *Aesop's Fables*. More often, especially in modern literature, readers must infer the theme based on text details. Usually after carefully reading and analyzing an entire text, the reader can identify the theme. Typically, the longer the piece, the more themes you will encounter, though often one theme dominates the rest, as evidenced by the author's purposeful revisiting of it throughout the passage.

The main idea should not be confused with the thesis statement. A thesis statement is a clear statement of the writer's specific stance, and can often be found in the introduction of a nonfiction piece. The main idea is more of an overview of the entire piece, while the thesis is a specific sentence found in that piece.

In order to illustrate the main idea, a writer will use **supporting details** in a passage. These details can provide evidence or examples to help make a point. Supporting details are most commonly found in nonfiction pieces that seek to inform or persuade the reader.

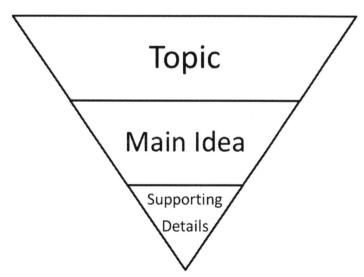

As a reader, you will want to carefully examine the author's supporting details to be sure they are credible. Consider whether they provide evidence of the author's point and whether they directly support the main idea. You might

149

find that an author has used a shocking statistic to grab your attention, but that the statistic doesn't really support the main idea, so it isn't being effectively used in the piece.

Identifying Supporting Details

Supporting details help readers better develop and understand the main idea. Supporting details answer questions like *who, what, where, when, why,* and *how.* Different types of supporting details include examples, facts and statistics, anecdotes, and sensory details.

Persuasive and informative texts often use supporting details. In persuasive texts, authors attempt to make readers agree with their points of view, and supporting details are often used as "selling points." If authors make a statement, they need to support the statement with evidence in order to adequately persuade readers. Informative texts use supporting details such as examples and facts to inform readers. Review the previous "Cheetahs" passage to find examples of supporting details.

Cheetahs

Cheetahs are one of the fastest mammals on the land, reaching up to 70 miles an hour over short distances. Even though cheetahs can run as fast as 70 miles an hour, they usually only have to run half that speed to catch up with their choice of prey. Cheetahs cannot maintain a fast pace over long periods of time because their bodies will overheat. After a chase, cheetahs need to rest for approximately 30 minutes prior to eating or returning to any other activity.

In the example, supporting details include:

- Cheetahs reach up to 70 miles per hour over short distances.
- They usually only have to run half that speed to catch up with their prey.
- Cheetahs will overheat if they exert a high speed over longer distances.
- Cheetahs need to rest for 30 minutes after a chase.

Look at the diagram below (applying the cheetah example) to help determine the hierarchy of topic, main idea, and supporting details.

Identifying Central Ideas or Themes of a Text

The **theme** is the central message of a fictional work, whether that work is structured as prose, drama, or poetry. It is the heart of what an author is trying to say to readers through the writing, and theme is largely conveyed through literary elements and techniques.

In literature, a theme can often be determined by considering the overarching narrative conflict within the work. Though there are several types of conflicts and several potential themes within them, the following are the most common:

A. Individual against the self — relevant to themes of self-awareness, internal struggles, pride, coming of age, facing reality, fate, free will, vanity, loss of innocence, loneliness, isolation, fulfillment, failure, and disillusionment

B. Individual against nature — relevant to themes of knowledge vs. ignorance, nature as beauty, quest for discovery, self-preservation, chaos and order, circle of life, death, and destruction of beauty

C. Individual against society — relevant to themes of power, beauty, good, evil, war, class struggle, totalitarianism, role of men/women, wealth, corruption, change vs. tradition, capitalism, destruction, heroism, injustice, and racism

D. Individual against another individual — relevant to themes of hope, loss of love or hope, sacrifice, power, revenge, betrayal, and honor

151

For example, in Hawthorne's *The Scarlet Letter*, one possible narrative conflict could be the individual against the self, with a relevant theme of internal struggles. This theme is alluded to through characterization—Dimmesdale's moral struggle with his love for Hester and Hester's internal struggles with the truth and her daughter, Pearl. It's also alluded to through plot—Dimmesdale's suicide and Hester helping the very townspeople who initially condemned her.

Sometimes, a text can convey a **message** or **universal lesson**—a truth or insight that the reader infers from the text, based on analysis of the literary and/or poetic elements. This message is often presented as a statement. For example, a potential message in Shakespeare's *Hamlet* could be "Revenge is what ultimately drives the human soul." This message can be immediately determined through plot and characterization in numerous ways, but it can also be determined through the setting of Norway, which is bordering on war.

Authors employ a variety of techniques to present a theme. They may compare or contrast characters, events, places, ideas, or historical or invented settings to speak thematically. They may use analogies, metaphors, similes, allusions, or other literary devices to convey the theme. An author's use of diction, syntax, and tone can also help convey the theme. Authors will often develop themes through the development of characters, use of the setting, repetition of ideas, use of symbols, and through contrasting value systems. Authors of both fiction and nonfiction genres will use a variety of these techniques to develop one or more themes.

Regardless of the literary genre, there are commonalities in how authors, playwrights, and poets develop themes or central ideas.

Authors often do research, the results of which contribute to theme. In prose fiction and drama, this research may include real historical information about the setting the author has chosen or include elements that make fictional characters, settings, and plots seem realistic to the reader. In nonfiction, research is critical since information contained within this literature must be accurate.

In fiction, authors present a narrative conflict that will contribute to the overall theme. This conflict may involve the storyline itself and some trouble within characters that needs resolution. In nonfiction, this conflict may be an explanation or commentary on factual people and events.

Authors will sometimes use character motivation to convey theme, such as in the example from *Hamlet* regarding revenge. In fiction, the characters an author creates will think, speak, and act in ways that effectively convey the theme to readers. In nonfiction, the characters are factual, as in a biography, but authors pay particular attention to presenting those motivations to make them clear to readers.

Authors also use literary devices as a means of conveying theme. For example, the use of moon symbolism in Mary Shelley's *Frankenstein* is significant as its phases can be compared to the phases that the Creature undergoes as he struggles with his identity.

The selected point of view can also contribute to a work's theme. The use of first-person point of view in a fiction or non-fiction work engages the reader's response differently than third person point of view. The central idea or theme from a first-person narrative may differ from a third-person limited text.

In literary nonfiction, authors usually identify the purpose of their writing, which differs from fiction, where the general purpose is to entertain. The purpose of nonfiction is usually to inform, persuade, or entertain the audience. The stated purpose of a non-fiction text will drive how the central message or theme, if applicable, is presented.

Authors identify an audience for their writing, which is critical in shaping the theme of the work. For example, the audience for J.K. Rowling's *Harry Potter* series would be different than the audience for a biography of George Washington. The audience an author chooses to address is closely tied to the purpose of the work. The choice of an audience also drives the choice of language and level of diction an author uses. Ultimately, the intended audience determines the level to which that subject matter is presented and the complexity of the theme.

Central Ideas in Informational Texts

Informational text is specifically designed to relate factual information, and although it is open to a reader's interpretation and application of the facts, the structure of the presentation is carefully designed to lead the reader to a particular conclusion or central idea. When reading informational text, it is important that readers are able to understand its organizational structure as the structure often directly relates to an author's intent to inform and/or persuade the reader.

The first step in identifying the text's structure is to determine the thesis or main idea. The thesis statement and organization of a work are closely intertwined. A **thesis statement** indicates the writer's purpose and may include the scope and direction of the text. It may be presented at the beginning of a text or at the end, and it may be explicit or implicit.

Once a reader has a grasp of the thesis or main idea of the text, he or she can better determine its organizational structure. Test takers are advised to read informational text passages more than once in order to comprehend the material fully. It is also helpful to examine any text features present in the text including the table of contents, index, glossary, headings, footnotes, and visuals. The analysis of these features and the information presented within them can offer additional clues about the central idea and structure of a text.

The following questions should be asked when considering structure:

- How does the author assemble the parts to make an effective whole argument?

- Is the passage linear in nature and if so, what is the timeline or thread of logic?

- What is the presented order of events, facts, or arguments? Are these effective in contributing to the author's thesis?

- How can the passage be divided into sections? How are they related to each other and to the main idea or thesis?

- What key terms are used to indicate the organization?

Next, test takers should skim the passage, noting the first line or two of each body paragraph—the **topic sentences**—and the conclusion. Key **transitional terms**, such as *on the other hand*, *also*, *because*, *however*, *therefore*, *most importantly*, and *first*, within the text can also signal organizational structure. Based on these clues, readers should then be able to identify what type of organizational structure is being used. The following organizational structures are most common:

A. Problem/solution: organized by an analysis/overview of a problem, followed by potential solution(s)

B. Cause/effect: organized by the effects resulting from a cause or the cause(s) of a particular effect

C. Spatial order: organized by points that suggest location or direction—e.g., top to bottom, right to left, outside to inside

D. Chronological/sequence order: organized by points presented to indicate a passage of time or through purposeful steps/stages

E. Comparison/contrast: organized by points that indicate similarities and/or differences between two things or concepts

F. Order of importance: organized by priority of points, often most significant to least significant or vice versa

Summaries of Main Points and Supporting Details

Creating an outline that identifies the **main ideas** of a passage as well as the **supporting details** is a helpful tool in effectively summarizing a text. Most outlines will include a title that reveals the topic of the text and is usually a single phrase or word, such as "whales." If the passage is divided up into paragraphs, or the paragraphs into sections, each paragraph or section will have its own main idea. These "main ideas" are usually depicted in outlines as roman numerals. Next, writers use supporting details in order to support or prove the main ideas. The supporting details should be listed underneath each main idea in the outline.

For example:

> Title: Whales
> I. Killer whales
>> a. Highly social
>> b. Apex predator
> II. Humpback whales
>> a. Males produce "song"
>> b. Targeted for whaling industry
> III. Beluga whales
>> a. Complex sense of hearing
>> b. Slow swimmers

Making an outline is a useful method of summarization because it forces the reader to deconstruct the text as a whole and to identify only the most important parts of the text.

Ideas from a text can also be organized using graphic organizers. A **graphic organizer** is a way to simplify information and take key points from the text. A graphic organizer such as a timeline may have an event listed for a corresponding date on the timeline while an outline may have an event listed under a key point that occurs in the text. Each reader needs to create the type of graphic organizer that works the best for him or her in terms of being able to recall information from a story. Examples include a **spider-map**, which takes a main idea from the story and places it in a bubble with supporting points branching off the main idea. An **outline** is useful for diagramming the main and supporting points of the entire story, and a **Venn diagram** classifies information as separate or overlapping.

Writing a summary is similar to creating an outline. In both instances, the reader wants to relay the most important parts of the text without being too verbose. A **summary** of a text should begin with stating the main idea of that text. Then, the reader must decide which supporting details are absolutely essential to the main idea of the text and leave any irrelevant information out of the summary. A summary shouldn't be too brief—readers should include important details depicted in the text—but it also shouldn't be too long either. The appeal of a summary to an audience is that they are able to receive the message of the text without being distracted by the style or detours of the author.

Another effective reading comprehension strategy is paraphrasing. Paraphrasing is usually longer than a summary. **Paraphrasing** is taking the author's text and rewriting, or "translating," it into their own words. A tip for paraphrasing is to read a passage over three times. Once you read the passage and understand what the author is saying, cover the original passage and begin to write everything you remember from that passage into your own

154

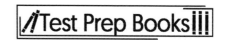
words. Usually, if you understand the content well enough, you will have translated the main idea of the author into your own words with your own writing style. An effective paraphrase will be as long as the original passage but will have a different writing structure.

Summaries of Informational Texts

Informational text is written material that has the primary function of imparting information about a topic. It is often written by someone with expertise in the topic and directed at an audience that has less knowledge of the topic. Informational texts are written in a different fashion from storytelling or narrative texts. Typically, this type of text has several organizational and structural differences from narrative text. In informational texts, there are features such as charts, graphs, photographs, headings and subheadings, glossaries, indexes, bibliographies, or other guidance features. With the aid of technology, embedded hyperlinks and video content are also sometimes included. Informational material may be written to compare and contrast, be explanatory, link cause and effect, provide opinion, persuade the reader, or serve a number of other purposes. Finally, informational texts typically use a different style of language than narrative texts, which instead, focus more on storytelling.

Making Logical Inferences

Critical readers should be able to make inferences. Making an **inference** requires the reader to read between the lines and look for what is implied rather than what is explicitly stated. That is, using information that *is* known from the text, the reader is able to make a logical assumption about information that is not explicitly stated but is probably true. Read the following passage:

"Hey, do you wanna meet my new puppy?" Jonathan asked.

"Oh, I'm sorry but please don't—" Jacinta began to protest, but before she could finish Jonathan had already opened the passenger side door of his car and a perfect white ball of fur came bouncing towards Jacinta.

"Isn't he the cutest?" beamed Jonathan.

"Yes—achoo!—he's pretty—aaaachooo!!—adora—aaa—aaaachoo!" Jacinta managed to say in between sneezes. "But if you don't mind, I—I—achoo!—need to go inside."

Which of the following can be inferred from Jacinta's reaction to the puppy?
    a. She hates animals.
    b. She is allergic to dogs.
    c. She prefers cats to dogs.
    d. She is angry at Jonathan.

An inference requires the reader to consider the information presented and then form their own idea about what is probably true. Based on the details in the passage, what is the best answer to the question? Important details to pay attention to include the tone of Jacinta's dialogue, which is overall polite and apologetic, as well as her reaction itself, which is a long string of sneezes. Choices *A* and *D* both express strong emotions ("hates" and "angry") that are not evident in Jacinta's speech or actions. Choice *C* mentions cats, but there is nothing in the passage to indicate Jacinta's feelings about cats. Choice *B*, "she is allergic to dogs," is the most logical choice. Based on the fact that she began sneezing as soon as a fluffy dog approached her, it makes sense to guess that Jacinta might be allergic to dogs. Using the clues in the passage, it is reasonable to guess that this is true even though Jacinta never directly states, "Sorry, I'm allergic to dogs!"

Making inferences is crucial for readers of literature, because literary texts often avoid presenting complete and direct information to readers about characters' thoughts or feelings, or they present this information in an unclear way, leaving it up to the reader to interpret clues given in the text. In order to make inferences while reading, readers should ask themselves:

- What details are being presented in the text?
- Is there any important information that seems to be missing?
- Based on the information that the author *does* include, what else is probably true?
- Is this inference reasonable based on what is already known?

Critical Thinking Skills

It's important to read any piece of writing critically. The goal is to discover the point and purpose of what the author is writing about through analysis. It's also crucial to establish the point or stance the author has taken on the topic of the piece. After determining the author's perspective, readers can then more effectively develop their own viewpoints on the subject of the piece.

It is important to distinguish between fact and opinion when reading a piece of writing. A **fact** is information that is true. If information can be disproven, it is not a fact. For example, water freezes at or below thirty-two degrees Fahrenheit. An argument stating that water freezes at seventy degrees Fahrenheit cannot be supported by data and is therefore not a fact. Facts tend to be associated with science, mathematics, and statistics. **Opinions** are information open for debate. Opinions are often tied to subjective concepts like feelings, desires, or manners. They can also be controversial.

Authors often use words like *think, feel, believe,* or *in my opinion* when expressing opinion, but these words won't always appear in an opinion piece, especially if it is formally written. An author's opinion may be backed up by facts, which gives it more credibility, but that opinion should not be taken as fact. A critical reader should be wary of an author's opinion, especially if it is only supported by other opinions.

Fact	Opinion
There are 9 innings in a game of baseball.	Baseball games run too long.
James Garfield was assassinated on July 2, 1881.	James Garfield was a good president.
McDonalds has stores in 118 countries.	McDonalds has the best hamburgers.

Critical readers examine the facts used to support an author's argument. They check the facts against other sources to be sure those facts are correct. They also check the validity of the sources used to be sure those sources are credible, academic, and/or peer-reviewed. Consider that when an author uses another person's opinion to support their argument, even if it is an expert's opinion, it is still only an opinion and should not be taken as fact. A strong argument uses valid, measurable facts to support ideas. Even then, the reader may disagree with the argument as it may be rooted in their personal beliefs.

An authoritative argument may use the facts to sway the reader. Because of this, a writer may choose to only use the information and expert opinion that supports their viewpoint.

If the argument is that wind energy is the best solution, the author will use facts that support this idea. That same author may leave out relevant facts on solar energy. The way the author uses facts can influence the reader, so it's important to consider the facts being used, how those facts are being presented, and what information might be left out.

Critical readers should also look for errors in the argument such as logical fallacies and bias. A **logical fallacy** is a flaw in the logic used to make the argument. Logical fallacies include slippery slope, straw man, and begging the question. Authors can also reflect **bias** if they ignore an opposing viewpoint or present their side in an unbalanced way. A strong argument considers the opposition and finds a way to refute it. Critical readers should look for an unfair or one-sided presentation of the argument and be skeptical, as a bias may be present. Even if this bias is unintentional, if it exists in the writing, the reader should be wary of the validity of the argument.

Readers should also look for the use of **stereotypes**. These are the overly simplified beliefs about a person, place, thing, etc. that is indiscriminately applied to a larger group. These can be positive but are usually negative in nature. When a reader comes across the use of stereotypes, they should take that into consideration as they analyze the author's argument. These should generally be avoided. Stereotypes reveal a flaw in the writer's thinking and may suggest a lack of knowledge or understanding about the subject.

Rhetoric

The ACCUPLACER will test a reader's ability to identify an author's use of rhetoric within text passages. **Rhetoric** is the use of positional or persuasive language to convey one or more central ideas. The idea behind the use of rhetoric is to convince the reader of something. Its use is meant to persuade or motivate the reader. An author may choose to appeal to their audience through logic, emotion, the use of ideology, or by conveying that the central idea is timely, and thus, important to the reader. There are a variety of rhetorical techniques an author can use to achieve this goal.

An author may choose to use traditional elements of style to persuade the reader. They may also use a story's setting, mood, characters, or a central conflict to build emotion in the reader. Similarly, an author may choose to use specific techniques such as alliteration, irony, metaphor, simile, hyperbole, allegory, imagery, onomatopoeia, and personification to persuasively illustrate one or more central ideas they wish the reader to adopt. In order to be successful in a standardized reading comprehension test situation, a reader needs to be well acquainted in recognizing rhetoric and rhetorical devices.

Determining How Ideas or Details Inform the Author's Argument

Once a reader has determined an author's thesis or main idea, he or she will need to understand how textual evidence supports interpretation of that thesis or main idea. Test takers will be asked direct questions regarding an author's main idea and may be asked to identify evidence that would support those ideas. This will require test takers to comprehend literal and figurative meanings within the text passage, be able to draw inferences from provided information, and be able to separate important evidence from minor supporting details. It's often helpful to skim test questions and answer options prior to critically reading informational text; however, test takers should avoid the temptation to solely look for the correct answers. Just trying to find the "right answer" may cause test takers to miss important supporting textual evidence. Making mental note of test questions is only helpful as a guide when reading.

After identifying an author's thesis or main idea, a test taker should look at the supporting details that the author provides to back up their assertions, identifying those additional pieces of information that help expand the thesis. From there, test takers should examine the additional information and related details for credibility, the author's use of outside sources, and be able to point to direct evidence that supports the author's claims. It's also imperative that test takers be able to identify what is strong support and what is merely additional information that is nice to know but not necessary. Being able to make this differentiation will help test takers effectively answer questions regarding an author's use of supporting evidence within informational text.

Identifying Elements of Style

A writer's style is unique. The combinations of elements are carefully designed to create an effect on the reader. For example, the novels of J.K. Rowling are very different in style than the novels of Stephen King, yet both are designed to tell a compelling tale and to entertain readers. Furthermore, the articles found in *National Geographic* are vastly different from those a reader may encounter in *People* magazine, yet both have the same objective: to inform the reader. The difference is in the elements of style.

While there are many elements of style an author can employ, it's important to look at three things: the words they choose to use, the voice an author selects, and the fluency of sentence structure. Word choice is critical in persuasive or pictorial writing. While effective authors will choose words that are succinct, different authors will choose various words based on what they are trying to accomplish. For example, a reader would not expect to encounter the same words in a gothic novel that they would read in a scholastic article on gene therapy. An author whose intent is to paint a picture of a foreboding scene, will choose different words than an author who wants to persuade the reader that a particular political party has the most sound, ideological platform. A romance novelist will sound very different than a true crime writer.

The voice an author selects is also important to note. An author's voice is that element of style that indicates their personality. It's important that authors move us as readers; therefore, they will choose a voice that helps them do that. An author's voice may be satirical or authoritative. It may be light-hearted or serious in tone. It may be silly or humorous as well. Voice, as an element of style, can be vague in nature and difficult to identify, since it's also referred to as an author's tone, but it is that element unique to the author. It is the author's "self." A reader can expect an author's voice to vary across literary genres. A non-fiction author will generally employ a more neutral voice than an author of fiction, but use caution when trying to identify voice. Do not confuse an author's voice with a particular character's voice.

Another critical element of style involves how an author structures their sentences. An effective writer—one who wants to paint a vivid picture or strongly illustrate a central idea—will use a variety of sentence structures and sentence lengths. A reader is more likely to be confused if an author uses choppy, unrelated sentences. Similarly, a reader will become bored and lose interest if an author repeatedly uses the same sentence structure. Good writing is fluent. It flows. Varying sentence structure keeps a reader engaged and helps reading comprehension. Consider the following example:

> The morning started off early. It was bright out. It was just daylight. The Moon was still in the sky. He was tired from his sleepless night.

Then consider this text:

> Morning hit hard. He didn't remember the last time light hurt this bad. Sleep had been absent, and the very thought of moving towards the new day seemed like a hurdle he couldn't overcome.

Note the variety in sentence structure. The second passage is more interesting to read because the sentence fluency is more effective. Both passages paint the picture of a central character's reaction to dawn, but the second passage is more effective because it uses a variety of sentences and is more fluent than the first.

Elements of style can also include more recognizable components such as a story's setting, the type of narrative an author chooses, the mood they set, and the character conflicts employed. The ability to effectively understand the use of rhetoric demands the reader take note of an author's word choices, writing voice, and the ease of fluency employed to persuade, entertain, illustrate, or otherwise captivate a reader.

Tone

An author's **tone** is the use of particular words, phrases, and writing style to convey an overall meaning. Tone expresses the author's attitude towards a particular topic. For example, a historical reading passage may begin like the following:

> The presidential election of 1960 ushered in a new era, a new Camelot, a new phase of forward thinking in U.S. politics that embraced brash action and unrest and responded with admirable leadership.

From this opening statement, a reader can draw some conclusions about the author's attitude towards President John F. Kennedy. Furthermore, the reader can make additional, educated guesses about the state of the Union during the 1960 presidential election. By close reading, the test taker can determine that the repeated use of the word *new* and words such as *admirable leadership* indicate the author's tone of admiration regarding President Kennedy's boldness. In addition, the author assesses that the era during President Kennedy's administration was problematic through the use of the words *brash action* and *unrest*. Therefore, if a test taker encountered a test question asking about the author's use of tone and their assessment of the Kennedy administration, the test taker should be able to identify an answer indicating admiration. Similarly, if asked about the state of the Union during the 1960s, a test taker should be able to correctly identify an answer indicating political unrest.

When identifying an author's tone, the following list of words may be helpful. This is not an inclusive list. Generally, parts of speech that indicate attitude will also indicate tone:

- Comical
- Angry
- Ambivalent
- Scary
- Lyrical
- Matter-of-fact
- Judgmental
- Sarcastic
- Malicious
- Objective
- Pessimistic
- Patronizing
- Gloomy
- Instructional
- Satirical
- Formal
- Casual

Message

An author's **message** is the same as the overall meaning of a passage. It is the main idea, or the main concept the author wishes to convey. An author's message may be stated outright, or it may be implied. Regardless, the test taker will need to use careful reading skills to identify an author's message or purpose.

Often, the message of a particular passage can be determined by thinking about why the author wrote the information. Many historical passages are written to inform and to teach readers established, factual information. However, many historical works are also written to convey biased ideas to readers. Gleaning bias from an author's message in a historical passage can be difficult, especially if the reader is presented with a variety of established facts as well. Readers tend to accept historical writing as factual. This is not always the case. Any discerning reader who has tackled historical information on topics such as United States political party agendas can attest that two or more works on the same topic may have completely different messages supporting or refuting the value of the identical policies.

Therefore, it is important to critically assess an author's message separate from factual information. One author, for example, may point to the rise of unorthodox political candidates in an election year based on the failures of the political party in office while another may point to the rise of the same candidates in the same election year based on the current party's successes. The historical facts of what has occurred leading up to an election year are not in refute. Labeling those facts as a failure or a success is a bias within an author's overall message, as is excluding

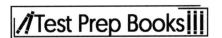

factual information in order to further a particular point. In a standardized testing situation, a reader must be able to critically assess what the author is trying to say separate from the historical facts that surround their message.

Using the example of Lincoln's Gettysburg Address, a test question may ask the following:

What message is the author trying to convey through this address?

Then they will ask the test taker to select an answer that best expresses Lincoln's message to his audience. Based on the options given, a test taker should be able to select the answer expressing the idea that Lincoln's audience should recognize the efforts of those who died in the war as a sacrifice to preserving human equality and self-government.

Effect

An author may want to challenge a reader's intellect, inspire imagination, or spur emotion. An author may present information to appeal to a physical, aesthetic, or transformational sense.

Take the following text as an example:

In 1963, Martin Luther King stated "I have a dream." The gathering at the Lincoln Memorial was the beginning of the Civil Rights movement and, with its reference to the Emancipation Proclamation, Dr. King's words electrified those who wanted freedom and equality while rising from hatred and slavery. It was the beginning of radical change.

The test taker may be asked about the effect this statement might have on King's audience. Through careful reading of the passage, the test taker should be able to choose an answer that best identifies an effect of grabbing the audience's attention. The historical facts are in place: King made the speech in 1963 at the Lincoln Memorial, kicked off the civil rights movement, and referenced the Emancipation Proclamation. The words *electrified* and *radical change* indicate the effect the author wants the reader to understand as a result of King's speech. In this historical passage, facts are facts. However, the author's message goes beyond the facts to indicate the effect the message had on the audience and, in addition, the effect the event should have on the reader.

How an Author's Word Choice Conveys Attitude and Shapes Meaning, Style, and Tone

Authors choose their words carefully in order to artfully depict meaning, style, and tone, which is most commonly inferred through the use of adjectives and verbs. The **tone** is the predominant emotion present in the text and represents the attitude or feelings that an author has towards a character or event.

To review, an **adjective** is a word used to describe something, and usually precedes the **noun**, a person, place, or object. A **verb** is a word describing an action. For example, the sentence "The scary woodpecker ate the spider" includes the adjective "scary," the noun "woodpecker," and the verb "ate." Reading this sentence may rouse some negative feelings, as the word "scary" carries a negative charge. The **charge** is the emotional connotation that can be derived from the adjectives and verbs and is either positive or negative. Recognizing the charge of a particular sentence or passage is an effective way to understand the meaning and tone the author is trying to convey.

Many authors have conflicting charges within the same text, but a definitive tone can be inferred by understanding the meaning of the charges relative to each other. It's important to recognize key **conjunctions**, or words that link sentences or clauses together. There are several types and subtypes of conjunctions. Three are most important for reading comprehension:

- **Cumulative conjunctions** add one statement to another.
  - Examples: *and, both, also, as well as, not only*
  - e.g. The juice is sweet *and* sour.

160

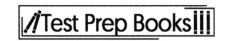

- **Adversative conjunctions** are used to contrast two clauses.
  - Examples: *but, while, still, yet, nevertheless*
  - e.g. She was tired, *but* she was happy.
- **Alternative conjunctions** express two alternatives.
  - Examples: *or, either, neither, nor, else, otherwise*
  - e.g. He must eat, *or* he will die.

Identifying the meaning and tone of a text can be accomplished with the following steps:

- Identify the adjectives and verbs.
- Recognize any important conjunctions.
- Label the adjectives and verbs as positive or negative.
- Understand what the charge means about the text.

To demonstrate these steps, examine the following passage from the classic children's poem, "The Sheep":

Lazy sheep, pray tell me why

In the pleasant fields you lie,

Eating grass, and daisies white,

From the morning till the night?

Everything can something do,

But what kind of use are you?

–Taylor, Jane and Ann. "The Sheep."

This selection is a good example of conflicting charges that work together to express an overall tone. Following the first two steps, identify the adjectives, verbs, and conjunctions within the passage. For this example, the adjectives are underlined, the verbs are in **bold**, and the conjunctions *italicized*:

<u>Lazy</u> sheep, pray **tell** me why

In the <u>pleasant</u> fields you **lie**,

Eating grass, and daisies <u>white,</u>

From the morning till the night?

Everything can something do,

But what kind of use are you?

For step three, read the passage and judge whether feelings of positivity or negativity arose. Then assign a charge to each of the words that were outlined. This can be done in a table format, or simply by writing a + or − next to the word.

The word <u>lazy</u> carries a negative connotation; it usually denotes somebody unwilling to work. To **tell** someone something has an exclusively neutral connotation, as it depends on what's being told, which has not yet been revealed at this point, so a charge can be assigned later. The word <u>pleasant</u> is an inherently positive word. To **lie**

161

could be positive or negative depending on the context, but as the subject (the sheep) is lying in a pleasant field, then this is a positive experience. **Eating** is also generally positive.

After labeling the charges for each word, it might be inferred that the tone of this poem is happy and maybe even admiring or innocuously envious. However, notice the adversative conjunction, "but" and what follows. The author has listed all the pleasant things this sheep gets to do all day, but the tone changes when the author asks, "What kind of use are you?" Asking someone to prove their value is a rather hurtful thing to do, as it implies that the person asking the question doesn't believe the subject has any value, so this could be listed under negative charges. Referring back to the verb **tell**, after reading the whole passage, it can be deduced that the author is asking the sheep to tell what use the sheep is, so this has a negative charge.

+	−
• Pleasant • Lie in fields • From morning to night	• Lazy • Tell me • What kind of use are you

Upon examining the charges, it might seem like there's an even amount of positive and negative emotion in this selection, and that's where the conjunction "but" becomes crucial to identifying the tone. The conjunction "but" indicates there's a contrasting view to the pleasantness of the sheep's daily life, and this view is that the sheep is lazy and useless, which is also indicated by the first line, "lazy sheep, pray tell me why."

It might be helpful to look at questions pertaining to tone. For this selection, consider the following question:

The author of the poem regards the sheep with a feeling of what?
    a. Respect
    b. Disgust
    c. Apprehension
    d. Intrigue

Considering the author views the sheep as lazy with nothing to offer, Choice *A* appears to reflect the opposite of what the author is feeling.

Choice *B* seems to mirror the author's feelings towards the sheep, as laziness is considered a disreputable trait, and people (or personified animals, in this case) with unfavorable traits might be viewed with disgust.

Choice *C* doesn't make sense within context, as laziness isn't usually feared.

Choice *D* is tricky, as it may be tempting to argue that the author is intrigued with the sheep because they ask, "pray tell me why." This is another out-of-scope answer choice as it doesn't *quite* describe the feelings the author experiences and there's also a much better fit in Choice *B*.

An author's choice of words—also referred to as **diction**—helps to convey meaning in a particular way. Through diction, an author can convey a particular tone—e.g., a humorous tone, a serious tone—in order to support the thesis in a meaningful way to the reader.

Connotation and Denotation
Connotation is when an author chooses words or phrases that invoke ideas or feelings other than their literal meaning. An example of the use of connotation is the word *cheap*, which suggests something is poor in value or negatively describes a person as reluctant to spend money. When something or someone is described this way, the

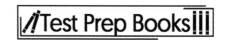

reader is more inclined to have a particular image or feeling. Thus, connotation can be a very effective language tool in creating emotion and swaying opinion. However, connotations are sometimes hard to pin down because varying emotions can be associated with a word. Generally, though, connotative meanings tend to be fairly consistent within a specific cultural group.

Denotation refers to words or phrases that mean exactly what they say. It is helpful when a writer wants to present hard facts or vocabulary terms with which readers may be unfamiliar. Some examples of denotation are the words *inexpensive* and *frugal*. *Inexpensive* refers to the cost of something, not its value, and *frugal* indicates that a person is conscientiously watching their spending. These terms do not elicit the same emotions that *cheap* does.

Authors sometimes choose to use both, but what they choose and when they use it is what critical readers need to differentiate. One method isn't inherently better than the other; however, one may create a better effect, depending upon an author's intent. If, for example, an author's purpose is to inform, to instruct, and to familiarize readers with a difficult subject, their use of connotation may be helpful. However, it may also undermine credibility and confuse readers. An author who wants to create a credible, scholarly effect in their text would most likely use denotation, which emphasizes literal, factual meaning and examples.

Technical Language

Test takers and critical readers alike should be very aware of technical language used within informational text. **Technical language** refers to terminology that is specific to a particular industry and is best understood by those specializing in that industry. This language is fairly easy to differentiate since it will most likely be unfamiliar to readers. It's critical to be able to define technical language either by the author's written definition, through the use of an included glossary—if offered—or through context clues that help readers clarify word meaning.

Analyzing the Structure of a Text

Good writing is not merely a random collection of sentences. No matter how well written, sentences must relate and coordinate appropriately with one another. If not, the writing seems random, haphazard, and disorganized. Therefore, good writing must be organized, where each sentence fits a larger context and relates to the sentences around it.

Transition Words

The writer should act as a guide, showing the reader how all the sentences fit together. Consider this seat belt example:

> Seat belts save more lives than any other automobile safety feature. Many studies show that airbags save lives as well. Not all cars have airbags. Many older cars don't. Air bags aren't entirely reliable. Studies show that in 15% of accidents, airbags don't deploy as designed. Seat belt malfunctions are extremely rare.

There's nothing wrong with any of these sentences individually, but together they're disjointed and difficult to follow. The best way for the writer to communicate information is through the use of transition words. Here are examples of transition words and phrases that tie sentences together, enabling a more natural flow:

> To show causality: *as a result, therefore*, and *consequently*
> To compare and contrast: *however, but,* and *on the other hand*
> To introduce examples: *for instance, namely,* and *including*
> To show order of importance: *foremost, primarily, secondly,* and *lastly*

Note that this is not a complete list of transitions. There are many more that can be used; however, most fit into these or similar categories. The important point is that the words should clearly show the relationship between sentences, supporting information, and the main idea.

Here is an update to the previous example using transition words. These changes make it easier to read and bring clarity to the writer's points:

> Seat belts save more lives than any other automobile safety feature. Many studies show that airbags save lives as well; however, not all cars have airbags. For instance, some older cars don't. Furthermore, air bags aren't entirely reliable. For example, studies show that in 15% of accidents, airbags don't deploy as designed, but, on the other hand, seat belt malfunctions are extremely rare.

Also, test takers should be prepared to analyze whether the writer is using the best transition word or phrase for the situation. For example, the sentence: "As a result, seat belt malfunctions are extremely rare" doesn't make sense in the context above because the writer is trying to show the contrast between seat belts and airbags, not the causality.

Logical Sequence

Even if the writer includes plenty of information to support their point, the writing is only coherent when the information is in a logical order. First, the writer should introduce the main idea, whether for a paragraph, a section, or the entire piece. Second, they should present evidence to support the main idea by using transitional language. This shows the reader how the information relates to the main idea and to the sentences around it. The writer should then take time to interpret the information, making sure necessary connections are obvious to the reader. Finally, the writer can summarize the information in a closing section.

Though most writing follows this pattern, it isn't a set rule. Sometimes writers change the order for effect. For example, the writer can begin with a surprising piece of supporting information to grab the reader's attention, and then transition to the main idea. Thus, if a passage doesn't follow the logical order, don't immediately assume it's wrong. However, most writing usually settles into a logical sequence after a nontraditional beginning.

Introductions and Conclusions

Examining the writer's strategies for introductions and conclusions puts the reader in the right mindset to interpret the rest of the text. Look for methods the writer might use for introductions such as:

> Stating the main point immediately, followed by outlining how the rest of the piece supports this claim.

> Establishing important, smaller pieces of the main idea first, and then grouping these points into a case for the main idea.

> Opening with a quotation, anecdote, question, seeming paradox, or other piece of interesting information, and then using it to lead to the main point.

Whatever method the writer chooses, the introduction should make their intention clear, establish their voice as a credible one, and encourage a person to continue reading.

Conclusions tend to follow a similar pattern. In them, the writer restates their main idea a final time, often after summarizing the smaller pieces of that idea. If the introduction uses a quote or anecdote to grab the reader's attention, the conclusion often makes reference to it again. Whatever way the writer chooses to arrange the conclusion, the final restatement of the main idea should be clear and simple for the reader to interpret. Finally, conclusions shouldn't introduce any new information.

Organization

Depending on what the author is attempting to accomplish, certain formats or text structures work better than others. For example, a sequence structure might work for narration but not for identifying similarities and differences between concepts. Similarly, a comparison-contrast structure is not useful for narration. It's the author's job to put the right information in the correct format.

Readers should be familiar with the five main literary structures:

1. **Sequence** structure (sometimes referred to as the order structure) is when the order of events proceed in a predictable order. In many cases, this means the text goes through the plot elements: exposition, rising action, climax, falling action, and resolution. Readers are introduced to characters, setting, and conflict in the exposition. In the rising action, there's an increase in tension and suspense. The climax is the height of tension and the point of no return. Tension decreases during the falling action. In the resolution, any conflicts presented in the exposition are solved, and the story concludes. An informative text that is structured sequentially will often go in order from one step to the next.

2. In the **problem-solution** structure, authors identify a potential problem and suggest a solution. This form of writing is usually divided into two parts (the problem and the solution) and can be found in informational texts. For example, cell phone, cable, and satellite providers use this structure in manuals to help customers troubleshoot or identify problems with services or products.

3. When authors want to discuss similarities and differences between separate concepts, they arrange thoughts in a **comparison-contrast** paragraph structure. Venn diagrams are an effective graphic organizer for comparison-contrast structures because they feature two overlapping circles that can be used to organize similarities and differences. A comparison-contrast essay organizes one paragraph based on similarities and another based on differences. A comparison-contrast essay can also be arranged with the similarities and differences of individual traits addressed within individual paragraphs. Words such as *however*, *but*, and *nevertheless* help signal a contrast in ideas.

4. **Descriptive** writing structure is designed to appeal to your senses. Much like an artist who constructs a painting, good descriptive writing builds an image in the reader's mind by appealing to the five senses: sight, hearing, taste, touch, and smell. However, overly descriptive writing can become distracting; whereas sparse descriptions can make settings and characters seem flat. Good authors must strike a balance between the two and provide enough detail to enable the reader to really see and experience what is happening in the plot without distracting the reader with excessive details.

5. Passages that use the **cause and effect** structure are simply asking *why* by demonstrating some type of connection between ideas. Words such as *if, since, because, then, or consequently* indicate a cause-and-effect relationship. By switching the order of a complex sentence, the writer can rearrange the emphasis on different clauses. Saying, *If Sheryl is late, we'll miss the dance*, is different from saying *We'll miss the dance if Sheryl is late*. One emphasizes Sheryl's tardiness while the other emphasizes missing the dance. Paragraphs can also be arranged in a cause-and-effect format. Cause-and-effect writing discusses the impact of decisions that have been made or could be made. Researchers often apply this paragraph structure to the scientific method.

Point of View

Point of view is an important writing device to consider. In fiction writing, point of view refers to who tells the story or from whose perspective readers are observing the story. In non-fiction writing, the **point of view** refers to whether authors refer to themselves, their readers, or choose not to refer to either. Whether fiction or nonfiction, the author will carefully consider the impact the perspective will have on the purpose and main point of the writing.

    A. First-person point of view: The story is told from the writer's perspective. In fiction, this would mean that the main character is also the narrator. First-person point of view is easily recognized by the use of personal pronouns such as *I, me, we, us, our, my,* and *myself*.

165

B. Third-person point of view: In a more formal essay, this would be an appropriate perspective because the focus should be on the subject matter, not the writer or the reader. Third-person point of view is recognized using the pronouns *he, she, they,* and *it*. In fiction writing, third-person point of view has a few variations.

C. Third-person limited point of view: Refers to a story told by a narrator who has access to the thoughts and feelings of just one character.

D. Third-person omniscient point of view: The narrator knows the thoughts and emotions of all the characters.

Point of View	Pronouns Used
First person	I, me, we, us, our, my, myself
Second person	You, your, yourself
Third person	He, she, it, they

E. Third-person objective point of view: The narrator is like a fly on the wall and can see and hear what the characters do and say but does not have access to their thoughts and feelings.

F. Second-person point of view: This point of view isn't commonly used in fiction or nonfiction writing because it directly addresses the reader using the pronouns *you, your,* and *yourself*. Second-person perspective is more appropriate in direct communication, such as business letters or emails.

How the Position and Purpose Shape the Text

Readers should always identify the author's position or stance in a text. No matter how objective a piece may seem, assume the author has preconceived beliefs. Reduce the likelihood of accepting an invalid argument by looking for multiple articles on the topic, including those with varying opinions. If several opinions point in the same direction, and are backed by reputable peer-reviewed sources, it's more likely the author has a valid argument. Positions that run contrary to widely held beliefs and existing data should invite scrutiny. There are exceptions to the rule, so be a careful consumer of information.

Though themes, symbols, and motifs are buried deep within the text and can sometimes be difficult to infer, an author's purpose is usually obvious from the beginning. There are four purposes of writing: to inform, to persuade, to describe, and to entertain. Informative writings present facts in an accessible way and are also known as expository writing. Persuasive writing appeals to emotions and logic to inspire the reader to adopt a specific stance. Be wary of this type of writing, as it often lacks objectivity. Descriptive writing is designed to paint a picture in the reader's mind, while texts that entertain are often narratives designed to engage and delight the reader.

The various writing styles are usually blended, with one purpose dominating the rest. For example, a persuasive piece might begin with a humorous tale to make readers more receptive to the persuasive message, or a recipe in a cookbook designed to inform might be preceded by an entertaining anecdote that makes the recipe more appealing.

Determining an Author's Point of View

A **rhetorical strategy**—also referred to as a **rhetorical mode**—is the structural way an author chooses to present their argument. Though the terms noted below are similar to the organizational structures noted earlier, these strategies do not imply that the entire text follows the approach. For example, a cause and effect organizational structure is solely that, nothing more. A persuasive text may use cause and effect as a strategy to convey a singular point. Thus, an argument may include several of the strategies as the author strives to convince their audience to take action or accept a different point of view. It's important that readers are able to identify an author's thesis and

166

position on the topic in order to be able to identify the careful construction through which the author speaks to the reader. The following are some of the more common rhetorical strategies:

- **Cause and effect** — establishing a logical correlation or causation between two ideas
- **Classification/division** — the grouping of similar items together or division of something into parts
- **Comparison/contrast** — the distinguishing of similarities/differences to expand on an idea
- **Definition** — used to clarify abstract ideas, unfamiliar concepts, or to distinguish one idea from another
- **Description** — use of vivid imagery, active verbs, and clear adjectives to explain ideas
- **Exemplification** — the use of examples to explain an idea
- **Narration** — anecdotes or personal experience to present or expand on a concept
- **Problem/solution** — presentation of a problem or problems, followed by proposed solution(s)

Identifying Rhetorical Devices

If a writer feels strongly about a subject, or has a passion for it, strong words and phrases can be chosen. Think of the types of rhetoric (or language) our politicians use. Each word, phrase, and idea is carefully crafted to elicit a response. Hopefully, that response is one of agreement to a certain point of view, especially among voters. Authors use the same types of language to achieve the same results. For example, the word "bad" has a certain connotation, but the words "horrid," "repugnant," and "abhorrent" paint a far better picture for the reader. They're more precise. They're interesting to read and they should all illicit stronger feelings in the reader than the word "bad." An author generally uses other devices beyond mere word choice to persuade, convince, entertain, or otherwise engage a reader.

Rhetorical devices are those elements an author utilizes in painting sensory, and hopefully persuasive ideas to which a reader can relate. They are numerable. Test takers will likely encounter one or more standardized test questions addressing various rhetorical devices. This study guide will address the more common types: alliteration, irony, metaphor, simile, hyperbole, allegory, imagery, onomatopoeia, and personification, providing examples of each.

Alliteration is a device that uses repetitive beginning sounds in words to appeal to the reader. Classic tongue twisters are a great example of alliteration. *She sells sea shells down by the sea shore* is an extreme example of alliteration. Authors will use alliterative devices to capture a reader's attention. It's interesting to note that marketing also utilizes alliteration in the same way. A reader will likely remember products that have the brand name and item starting with the same letter. Similarly, many songs, poems, and catchy phrases use this device. It's memorable. Use of alliteration draws a reader's attention to ideas that an author wants to highlight.

Irony is a device that authors use when pitting two contrasting items or ideas against each other in order to create an effect. It's frequently used when an author wants to employ humor or convey a sarcastic tone. Additionally, it's often used in fictional works to build tension between characters, or between a particular character and the reader. An author may use *verbal irony* (sarcasm), *situational irony* (where actions or events have the opposite effect than what's expected), and *dramatic irony* (where the reader knows something a character does not). Examples of irony include:

- **Dramatic Irony**: An author describing the presence of a hidden killer in a murder mystery, unbeknownst to the characters but known to the reader.

- **Situational Irony**: An author relating the tale of a fire captain who loses her home in a five-alarm conflagration.

- **Verbal Irony**: This is where an author or character says one thing but means another. For example, telling a police officer "Thanks a lot" after receiving a ticket.

Metaphor is a device that uses a figure of speech to paint a visual picture of something that is not literally applicable. Authors relate strong images to readers, and evoke similar strong feelings using metaphors. Most often,

167

authors will mention one thing in comparison to another more familiar to the reader. It's important to note that metaphors do not use the comparative words "like" or "as." At times, metaphors encompass common phrases such as clichés. At other times, authors may use mixed metaphors in making identification between two dissimilar things. Examples of metaphors include:

- An author describing a character's anger as *a flaming sheet of fire.*
- An author relating a politician as having been a folding chair under close questioning.
- A novel's character telling another character to *take a flying hike.*
- Shakespeare's assertion that *all the world's a stage.*

Simile is a device that compares two dissimilar things using the words "like" and "as." When using similes, an author tries to catch a reader's attention and use comparison of unlike items to make a point. Similes are commonly used and often develop into figures of speech and catch phrases.

Examples of similes include:

- An author describing a character as having a complexion like a faded lily.

- An investigative journalist describing his interview subject as being like cold steel and with a demeanor hard as ice.

- An author asserting the current political arena is just like a three-ring circus and as dry as day old bread.

Similes and metaphors can be confusing. When utilizing simile, an author will state one thing is like another. A metaphor states one thing is another. An example of the difference would be if an author states a character is *just like a fierce tiger and twice as angry,* as opposed to stating the character *is a fierce tiger and twice as angry.*

Hyperbole is simply an exaggeration that is not taken literally. A potential test taker will have heard or employed hyperbole in daily speech, as it is a common device we all use. Authors will use hyperbole to draw a reader's eye toward important points and to illicit strong emotional and relatable responses. Examples of hyperbole include:

- An author describing a character as being as big as a house and twice the circumference of a city block.

- An author stating the city's water problem as being old as the hills and more expensive than a king's ransom in spent tax dollars.

- A journalist stating the mayoral candidate died of embarrassment when her tax records were made public.

Allegories are stories or poems with hidden meanings, usually a political or moral one. Authors will frequently use allegory when leading the reader to a conclusion. Allegories are similar to parables, symbols, and analogies. Often, an author will employ the use of allegory to make political, historical, moral, or social observations. As an example, Jonathan Swift's work *Gulliver's Travels into Several Remote Nations of the World* is an allegory in and of itself. The work is a political allegory of England during Jonathan Swift's lifetime. Set in the travel journal style plot of a giant amongst smaller people, and a smaller Gulliver amongst the larger, it is a commentary on Swift's political stance of existing issues of his age. Many fictional works are entire allegories in and of themselves. George Orwell's *Animal Farm* is a story of animals that conquer man and form their own farm society with swine at the top; however, it is not a literal story in any sense. It's Orwell's political allegory of Russian society during and after the Communist revolution of 1917. Other examples of allegory in popular culture include:

- Aesop's fable "The Tortoise and the Hare," which teaches readers that being steady is more important than being fast and impulsive.

- The popular *Hunger Games* by Suzanne Collins that teaches readers that media can numb society to what is truly real and important.

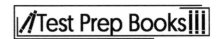

- Dr. Seuss's *Yertle the Turtle* which is a warning against totalitarianism and, at the time it was written, against the despotic rule of Adolf Hitler.

Imagery is a rhetorical device that an author employs when they use visual or descriptive language to evoke a reader's emotion. Use of imagery as a rhetorical device is broader in scope than this study guide addresses, but in general, the function of imagery is to create a vibrant scene in the reader's imagination and, in turn, tease the reader's ability to identify through strong emotion and sensory experience. In the simplest of terms, imagery, as a rhetoric device, beautifies literature.

An example of poetic imagery is below:

> Pain has an element of blank
>
> It cannot recollect
>
> When it began, or if there were
>
> A day when it was not.
>
> It has no future but itself,
>
> Its infinite realms contain
>
> Its past, enlightened to perceive
>
> New periods of pain.

In the above poem, Emily Dickenson uses strong imagery. Pain is equivalent to an "element of blank" or of nothingness. Pain cannot recollect a beginning or end, as if it was a person (see *personification* below). Dickenson appeals to the reader's sense of a painful experience by discussing the unlikelihood that discomfort sees a future, but does visualize a past and present. She simply indicates that pain, through the use of imagery, is cyclical and never ending. Dickenson's theme is one of painful depression, and it is through the use of imagery that she conveys this to her readers.

Onomatopoeia is the author's use of words that create sound. Words like *pop* and *sizzle* are examples of onomatopoeia. When an author wants to draw a reader's attention in an auditory sense, they will use onomatopoeia. An author may also use onomatopoeia to create sounds as interjection or commentary. Examples include:

- An author describing a cat's vocalization as the kitten's chirrup echoed throughout the empty cabin.
- A description of a campfire as crackling and whining against its burning green wood.
- An author relating the sound of a car accident as *metallic screeching against crunching asphalt*.
- A description of an animal roadblock as being *a symphonic melody of groans, baas, and moans*.

Personification is a rhetorical device that an author uses to attribute human qualities to inanimate objects or animals. Once again, this device is useful when an author wants the reader to strongly relate to an idea. As in the example of George Orwell's *Animal Farm*, many of the animals are given the human abilities to speak, reason, apply logic, and otherwise interact as humans do. This helps the reader see how easily it is for any society to segregate into the haves and the have-nots through the manipulation of power. Personification is a device that enables the reader to empathize through human experience.

Examples of personification include:

- An author describing the wind as *whispering through the trees*.

169

- A description of a stone wall as being a hardened, unmovable creature made of cement and brick.

- An author attributing a city building as having slit eyes and an unapproachable, foreboding façade.

- An author describing spring as a beautiful bride, blooming in white, ready for summer's matrimony.

When identifying rhetorical devices, look for words and phrases that capture one's attention. Make note of the author's use of comparison between the inanimate and the animate. Consider words that make the reader feel sounds and envision imagery. Pay attention to the rhythm of fluid sentences and to the use of words that evoke emotion. The ability to identify rhetorical devices is another step in achieving successful reading comprehension and in being able to correctly answer standardized questions related to those devices.

Understanding Methods Used to Appeal to a Specific Audience

In an argument or persuasive text, an author will strive to sway readers to an opinion or conclusion. To be effective, an author must consider their intended audience. Although an author may write text for a general audience, he or she will use methods of appeal or persuasion to convince that audience. Aristotle asserted that there were three methods or modes by which a person could be persuaded. These are referred to as **rhetorical appeals**.

The three main types of rhetorical appeals are shown in the following graphic.

Ethos, also referred to as an **ethical appeal**, is an appeal to the audience's perception of the writer as credible (or not), based on their examination of their ethics and who the writer is, their experience or incorporation of relevant information, or their argument. For example, authors may present testimonials to bolster their arguments. The reader who critically examines the veracity of the testimonials and the credibility of those giving the testimony will be able to determine if the author's use of testimony is valid to their argument. In turn, this will help the reader determine if the author's thesis is valid. An author's careful and appropriate use of technical language can create an overall knowledgeable effect and, in turn, act as a convincing vehicle when it comes to credibility. Overuse of technical language, however, may create confusion in readers and obscure an author's overall intent.

Pathos, also referred to as **emotional appeal**, is an appeal to the audience's sense of identity, self-interest, or emotions. A critical reader will notice when the author is appealing to pathos through anecdotes and descriptions

170

that elicit an emotion such as anger or pity. Readers should also beware of factual information that uses generalization to appeal to the emotions. While it's tempting to believe an author is the source of truth in their text, an author who presents factual information as universally true, consistent throughout time, and common to all groups is using **generalization**. Authors who exclusively use generalizations without specific facts and credible sourcing are attempting to sway readers solely through emotion.

Logos, also referred to as a **logical appeal**, is an appeal to the audience's ability to see and understand the logic in a claim offered by the writer. A critical reader has to be able to evaluate an author's arguments for validity of reasoning and for sufficiency when it comes to argument.

Synthesis

Synthesis

Synthesis in reading involves the ability to fully comprehend text passages, and then going further by making new connections to see things in a new or different way. It involves a full thought process and requires readers to change the way they think about what they read. The ACCUPLACER will require a test taker to integrate new information that he or she already knows, and demonstrate an ability to express new thoughts.

Synthesis goes further than summary. When **summarizing**, a reader collects all of the information an author presents in a text passage, and restates it in an effective manner. Synthesis requires that the test taker not only summarize reading material, but be able to express new ideas based on the author's message. It is a full culmination of all reading comprehension strategies. It will require the test taker to order, recount, summarize, and recreate information into a whole new idea.

In utilizing synthesis, a reader must be able to form mental images about what they read, recall any background information they have about the topic, ask critical questions about the material, determine the importance of points an author makes, make inferences based on the reading, and finally be able to form new ideas based on all of the above skills. Synthesis requires the reader to make connections, visualize concepts, determine their importance, ask questions, make inferences, then fully synthesize all of this information into new thought.

Making Connections in Reading
There are three helpful thinking strategies to keep in mind when attempting to synthesize text passages:

- Think about how the content of a passage relates to life experience.
- Think about how the content of a passage relates to other text.
- Think about how the content of a passage relates to the world in general.

When reading a given passage, the test taker should actively think about how the content relates to their life experience. While the author's message may express an opinion different from what the reader believes, or express ideas with which the reader is unfamiliar, a good reader will try to relate any of the author's details to their own familiar ground. A reader should use context clues to understand unfamiliar terminology, and recognize familiar information they have encountered in prior experience. Bringing prior life experience and knowledge to the test-taking situation is helpful in making connections. The ability to relate an unfamiliar idea to something the reader already knows is critical in understanding unique and new ideas.

When trying to make connections while reading, keep the following questions in mind:

- How does this feel familiar in personal experience?
- How is this similar to or different from other reading?

- How is this familiar in the real world?
- How does this relate to the world in general?

A reader should ask themself these questions during the act of reading in order to actively make connections to past and present experiences. Utilizing the ability to make connections is an important step in achieving synthesis.

Determining Importance in Reading

Being able to determine what is most important while reading is critical to synthesis. It is the difference between being able to tell what is necessary to full comprehension and that which is interesting but not necessary.

When determining the importance of an author's ideas, consider the following:

- Ask how critical an author's particular idea, assertion, or concept is to the overall message.

- Ask "is this an interesting fact or is this information essential to understanding the author's main idea?"

- Make a simple chart. On one side, list all of the important, essential points an author makes and on the other, list all of the interesting yet non-critical ideas.

- Highlight, circle, or underline any dates or data in non-fiction passages. Pay attention to headings, captions, and any graphs or diagrams.

- When reading a fictional passage, delineate important information such as theme, character, setting, conflict (what the problem is), and resolution (how the problem is fixed). Most often, these are the most important aspects contained in fictional text.

- If a non-fiction passage is instructional in nature, take physical note of any steps in the order of their importance as presented by the author. Look for words such as *first*, *next*, *then*, and *last*.

Determining the importance of an author's ideas is critical to synthesis in that it requires the test taker to parse out any unnecessary information and demonstrate they have the ability to make sound determination on what is important to the author, and what is merely a supporting or less critical detail.

Asking Questions While Reading

A reader must ask questions while reading. This demonstrates their ability to critically approach information and apply higher thinking skills to an author's content. Some of these questions have been addressed earlier in this section. A reader must ask what is or isn't important, what relates to their experience, and what relates to the world in general. However, it's important to ask other questions as well in order to make connections and synthesize reading material.

Consider the following partial list of possibilities:

- What type of passage is this? Is it fiction? Non-fiction? Does it include data?

- Based on the type of passage, what information should be noted in order to make connections, visualize details, and determine importance?

- What is the author's message or theme? What is it they want the reader to understand?

- Is this passage trying to convince readers of something? What is it? If so, is the argument logical, convincing, and effective? How so? If not, how not?

- What do readers already know about this topic? Are there other viewpoints that support or contradict it?

- Is the information in this passage current and up to date?

- Is the author trying to teach readers a lesson? If so, what is it? Is there a moral to this story?

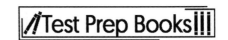

- How does this passage relate to experience?

- What is not as understandable in this passage? What context clues can help with understanding?

- What conclusions can be drawn? What predictions can be made?

Again, the above should be considered only a small example of the possibilities. Any question the reader asks while reading will help achieve synthesis and full reading comprehension.

Connections Between Different Texts

When analyzing two or more texts, there are several different aspects that need to be considered, particularly the styles (or the artful way in which the authors use diction to deliver a theme), points of view, and types of argument. In order to do so, one should compare and contrast the following elements between the texts:

- **Style**: narrative, persuasive, descriptive, informative, etc.
- **Tone**: sarcastic, angry, somber, humorous, etc.
- **Sentence structure**: simple (1 clause) compound (2 clauses), complex-compound (3 clauses)
- **Punctuation choice**: question marks, exclamation points, periods, dashes, etc.
- **Point of view**: first person, second person, third person
- **Paragraph structure**: long, short, both, differences between the two
- **Organizational structure**: compare/contrast, problem/solution, chronological, etc.

The following two poems and the essay concern the theme of death and are presented to demonstrate how to evaluate the above elements:

Poem 1:

How wonderful is Death,

Death, and his brother Sleep!

One, pale as yonder waning moon

With lips of lurid blue;

The other, rosy as the morn

When throned on ocean's wave

It blushes o'er the world;

Yet both so passing wonderful!

"Queen Mab," Percy Bysshe Shelley

Poem 2:

After great pain, a formal feeling comes –

The Nerves sit ceremonious, like Tombs –

The stiff Heart questions 'was it He, that bore,'

And 'Yesterday, or Centuries before'?

The Feet, mechanical, go round –

173

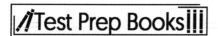

A Wooden way

Of Ground, or Air, or Ought –

Regardless grown,

A Quartz contentment, like a stone –

This is the Hour of Lead –

Remembered, if outlived,

As Freezing persons, recollect the Snow –

First – Chill – then Stupor – then the letting go –

"After Great Pain, A Formal Feeling Comes," Emily Dickinson

Essay 1

The Process of Dying

Death occurs in several stages. The first stage is the pre-active stage, which occurs a few days to weeks before death, in which the desire to eat and drink decreases, and the person may feel restless, irritable, and anxious. The second stage is the active stage, where the skin begins to cool, breathing becomes difficult as the lungs become congested (known as the "death rattle"), and the person loses control of their bodily fluids.

Once death occurs, there are also two stages. The first is clinical death, when the heart stops pumping blood and breathing ceases. This stage lasts approximately 4-6 minutes, and during this time, it is possible for a victim to be resuscitated via CPR or a defibrillator. After 6 minutes however, the oxygen stores within the brain begin to deplete, and the victim enters biological death. This is the point of no return, as the cells of the brain and vital organs begin to die, a process that is irreversible.

Now, using the outline above, the similarities and differences between the two passages are considered:

1. **Style**: The two poems are both descriptive as they focus on descriptions and sensations to convey their messages and do not follow any sort of timeline. The third selection is an expository style, presenting purely factual evidence on death, completely devoid of emotion.

2. **Tone**: Readers should notice the differences in the word choices between the two poems. Percy Shelley's word choices—"wonderful," "rosy," "blushes," "ocean"—surrounding death indicates that he views death in a welcoming manner as his words carry positive charges. The word choices by Dickinson, however, carry negative connotations—"pain," "wooden," "stone," "lead," "chill," "tombs"—which indicates an aversion to death. In contrast, the expository passage has no emotionally-charged words of any kind and seems to view death simply as a process that happens, neither welcoming nor fearing it. The tone in this passage, therefore, is neutral.

3. **Sentence structure**: Shelley's poem is composed mostly of compound sentences, which flow easily into one another. If read aloud, it sounds almost fluid, like the waves of the ocean he describes in his poem. His sentence structure mirrors the ease in which he views death. Dickinson's poem, on the other hand, is mostly simple sentences that are short and curt. They do not flow easily into one another, possibly representing her hesitancy and discomfort in her views of death. The expository passage contains many complex-compound sentences, which are used to accommodate lots of information. The structure of these sentences contributes to the overall informative nature of the selection.

174

4. **Punctuation choice**: Shelley uses commas, semicolons, and exclamation points in his poem, which, combined with his word choices and sentence structure, contributes to the overall positive tone of the poem. Dickinson uses lots of dashes, which make the poem feel almost cutting and jagged, which contributes to the overall negative tone of her poem. The expository text uses only commas and periods, which adds to the overall neutral tone of the selection.

5. **Point of view**: The point of view in all three selections is third person. In the two poems, there are no obvious pronouns; however, they both are presented in the third-person point of view, as Shelley speaks of Death in the third person, and Dickinson refers to "freezing persons." Generally, if there are no first- or second-person pronouns in a selection, the view is third person. The informational selection also uses third-person point of view, as it avoids any first- or second-person pronouns.

6. **Paragraph/stanza structure**: Shelley's poem is one stanza long, making it inherently simple in nature. The simplicity of the single stanza is representative (again) of the comfort in which the author finds the topic of death. Dickinson's poem is much lengthier, and comparatively, could signify the difficulty of letting go of the death of a loved one. The paragraph structure of the essay is much longer than the two and is used to fit in a lot more information than the poems, as the poems are trying to convey emotion, and the essay is presenting facts.

7. **Organizational structure**: Shelley's poem uses a compare and contrast method to illustrate the similarities between death and sleep: that death is merely a paler, bluer brother to the warm and rosy sleep. Dickinson's structure, however, is descriptive, focusing primarily on feelings and sensations. The expository passage, on the other hand, is chronologically-organized, as it follows a timeline of events that occur in stages.

When analyzing the different structures, it may be helpful to make a table and use single words to compare and contrast the texts:

Elements	Queen Mab	After Great Pain	Process of Dying
Style	Descriptive	Descriptive	Expository
Tone	Warm	Cold	Neutral
Sentence Structure	Fluid	Jagged	Long
Punctuation Choice	!	–	.
Point of View	Third	Third	Third
Paragraph Structure	Short	Longer	Longest
Organizational Structure	Compare-Contrast	Descriptive	Chronological

Using this table, the differences become very clear. Although the two poems are both about death, their word tone, sentence structure, punctuation choices, and organization depict differences in how the authors perceive death, while the elements in the expository text clearly indicate an objective view of death. It should be noted that these are only a handful of the endless possible interpretations the reader could make.

Analysis of History/Social Studies Excerpts

The ACCUPLACER will test for the ability to read substantial, historically based excerpts, and then answer comprehension questions based on content. The test taker will likely encounter U.S. history, or social science, passages within the test. One is likely to be from a U.S. founding document or work that has had great impact on history. The test may also include one or more passages from social sciences such as economics, psychology, or sociology.

For these types of questions, the test taker will need to utilize all the reading comprehension skills discussed above, but mastery of further skills will help. This section addresses those skills.

Comprehending Test Questions Prior to Reading

While preparing for a historical passage on a standardized test, first read the test questions, and then quickly scan the test answers prior to reading the passage itself. Notice there is a difference between the terms *read* and *scans*. Reading involves full concentration while addressing every word. Scanning involves quickly glancing at text in chunks, noting important dates, words, and ideas along the way. Reading the test questions will help the test taker know what information to focus on in the historical passage. Scanning answers will help the test taker focus on possible answer options while reading the passage.

When reading standardized test questions that address historical passages, be sure to clearly understand what each question is asking. Is a question asking about vocabulary? Is another asking for the test taker to find a specific historical fact? Do any of the questions require the test taker to draw conclusions, identify an author's topic, tone, or position? Knowing what content to address will help the test taker focus on the information they will be asked about later. However, the test taker should approach this reading comprehension technique with some caution. It is tempting to only look for the right answers within any given passage. However, do not put on "reading blinders" and ignore all other information presented in a passage. It is important to fully read every passage and not just scan it. Strictly looking for what may be the right answers to test questions can cause the test taker to ignore important contextual clues that actually require critical thinking in order to identify correct answers. Scanning a passage for what appears to be wrong answers can have a similar result.

When reading the test questions prior to tackling a historical passage, be sure to understand what skills the test is assessing, and then fully read the related passage with those skills in mind. Focus on every word in both the test questions and the passage itself. Read with a critical eye and a logical mind.

Reading for Factual Information

Standardized test questions that ask for factual information are usually straightforward. These types of questions will either ask the test taker to confirm a fact by choosing a correct answer, or to select a correct answer based on a negative fact question.

For example, the test taker may encounter a passage from Lincoln's Gettysburg Address. A corresponding test question may ask the following:

Which war is Abraham Lincoln referring to in the following passage?:

Now we are engaged in a great civil war, testing whether that nation, or any nation so conceived and so dedicated, can long endure.

This type of question is asking the test taker to confirm a simple fact. Given options such as World War I, the War of Spanish Succession, World War II, and the American Civil War, the test taker should be able to correctly identify the American Civil War based on the words "civil war" within the passage itself, and, hopefully, through general knowledge. In this case, reading the test question and scanning answer options ahead of reading the Gettysburg

176

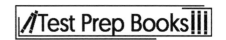

Address would help quickly identify the correct answer. Similarly, a test taker may be asked to confirm a historical fact based on a negative fact question. For example, a passage's corresponding test question may ask the following:

> Which option is incorrect based on the above passage?

Given a variety of choices speaking about which war Abraham Lincoln was addressing, the test taker would need to eliminate all correct answers pertaining to the American Civil War and choose the answer choice referencing a different war. In other words, the correct answer is the one that contradicts the information in the passage.

It is important to remember that reading for factual information is straightforward. The test taker must distinguish fact from bias. Factual statements can be proven or disproven independent of the author and from a variety of other sources. Remember, successfully answering questions regarding factual information may require the test taker to re-read the passage, as these types of questions test for attention to detail.

Analysis of Science Excerpts

The ACCUPLACER usually contains at includes at least two science passages that address the fundamental concepts of Earth science, biology, chemistry, and/or physics. While prior general knowledge of these subjects is helpful in determining correct test answers, the test taker's ability to comprehend the passages is key to success. When reading scientific excerpts, the test taker must be able to examine quantitative information, identify hypotheses, interpret data, and consider implications of the material they are presented with. It is helpful, at this point, to reference the above section on comprehending test questions prior to reading. The same rules apply: read questions and scan questions, along with their answers, prior to fully reading a passage. Be informed prior to approaching a scientific text. A test taker should know what they will be asked and how to apply their reading skills. In this section of the test, it is also likely that a test taker will encounter graphs and charts to assess their ability to interpret scientific data with an appropriate conclusion. This section may use the identification of hypotheses, the reading and examination of data, and the interpretation of data representation passages to determine the skill levels of test takers in the comprehension of scientific data.

Examine Hypotheses

When presented with fundamental, scientific concepts, it is important to read for understanding. The most basic skill in achieving this literacy is to understand the concept of hypothesis and, moreover, to be able to identify it in a particular passage. A hypothesis is a proposed idea that needs further investigation in order to be proven true or false. While it can be considered an educated guess, a hypothesis goes more in depth in its attempt to explain something that is not currently accepted within scientific theory. It requires further experimentation and data gathering to test its validity and is subject to change, based on scientifically conducted test results. Being able to read a science passage and understand its main purpose, including any hypotheses, helps the test taker understand data-driven evidence. It helps the test taker to be able to correctly answer questions about the science excerpt they are asked to read.

When reading to identify a hypothesis, a test taker should ask, "What is the passage trying to establish? What is the passage's main idea? What evidence does the passage contain that either supports or refutes this idea?" Asking oneself these questions will help identify a hypothesis. Additionally, hypotheses are logical statements that are testable and use very precise language.

Review the following hypothesis example:

> Consuming excess sugar in the form of beverages has a greater impact on childhood obesity and subsequent weight gain than excessive sugar from food.

177

While this is likely a true statement, it is still only a conceptual idea in a text passage regarding how sugar consumption affects childhood obesity, unless the passage also contains tested data that either proves or disproves the statement. A test taker could expect the rest of the passage to cite data proving that children who drink empty calories gain more weight and are more likely to be obese than children who eat sugary snacks.

A hypothesis goes further in that, given its ability to be proven or disproven, it may result in further hypotheses that require extended research. For example, the hypothesis regarding sugar consumption in drinks, after undergoing rigorous testing, may lead scientists to state another hypothesis such as the following:

> Consuming excess sugar in the form of beverages as opposed to food items is a habit found in mostly sedentary children.

This new, working hypothesis further focuses not just on the source of an excess of calories, but tries an "educated guess" that empty caloric intake has a direct, subsequent impact on physical behavior.

The data-driven chart below is similar to an illustration a test taker might see in relation to the hypothesis on sugar consumption in children:

Behaviors of Healthy and Unhealthy Kids

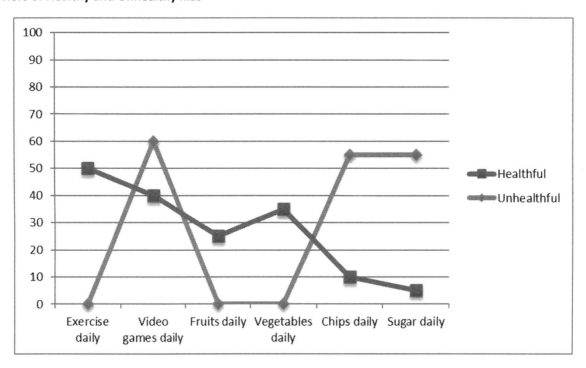

While this guide will address other data-driven passages a test taker could expect to see within a given science excerpt, note that the hypothesis regarding childhood sugar intake and rate of exercise has undergone scientific examination and yielded results that support its truth.

When reading a science passage to determine its hypothesis, a test taker should look for a concept that attempts to explain a phenomenon, is testable, is logical, is precisely worded, and yields data-driven results. The test taker should scan the presented passage for any word or data-driven clues that will help identify the hypothesis, and then be able to correctly answer test questions regarding the hypothesis by using their critical thinking skills.

Interpreting Data and Considering Implications

The ACCUPLACER is likely to contain one or more data-driven science passages that require the test taker to examine evidence within a particular type of graphic. The test taker will then be required to interpret the data and answer questions demonstrating their ability to draw logical conclusions.

In general, there are two types of data: qualitative and quantitative. Science passages may contain both, but simply put, quantitative data is reflected numerically and qualitative is not. Qualitative data is based on its qualities. In other words, qualitative data tends to present information more in subjective generalities (for example, relating to size or appearance). Quantitative data is based on numerical findings such as percentages. Quantitative data will be described in numerical terms. While both types of data are valid, the test taker will more likely be faced with having to interpret quantitative data through one or more graphic(s), and then be required to answer questions regarding the numerical data. The section of this study guide briefly addresses how data may be displayed in line graphs, bar charts, circle graphs, and scatter plots. A test taker should take the time to learn the skills it takes to interpret quantitative data. An example of a line graph is as follows:

Cell Phone Use in Kiteville, 2000-2006

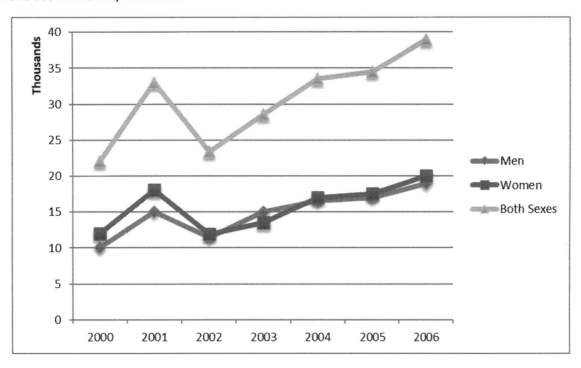

A line graph presents quantitative data on both horizontal (side to side) and vertical (up and down) axes. It requires the test taker to examine information across varying data points. When reading a line graph, a test taker should pay attention to any headings, as these indicate a title for the data it contains. In the above example, the test taker can anticipate the line graph contains numerical data regarding the use of cellphones during a certain time period. From there, a test taker should carefully read any outlying words or phrases that will help determine the meaning of data within the horizontal and vertical axes. In this example, the vertical axis displays the total number of people in increments of 5,000. Horizontally, the graph displays yearly markers, and the reader can assume the data presented accounts for a full calendar year. In addition, the line graph also uses different shapes to mark its data points. Some data points represent the number of men. Some data points represent the number of women, and a third type of data point represents the number of both sexes combined.

A test taker may be asked to read and interpret the graph's data, then answer questions about it. For example, the test may ask, *In which year did men seem to decrease cellphone use?* then require the test taker to select the correct answer. Similarly, the test taker may encounter a question such as *Which year yielded the highest number of cellphone users overall?* The test taker should be able to identify the correct answer as 2006.

A **bar graph** presents quantitative data through the use of lines or rectangles. The height and length of these lines or rectangles corresponds to the magnitude of the numerical data for that particular category or attribute. The data presented may represent information over time, showing shaded data over time or over other defined parameters. A bar graph will also utilize horizontal and vertical axes. An example of a bar graph is as follows:

Population Growth in Major U.S. Cities

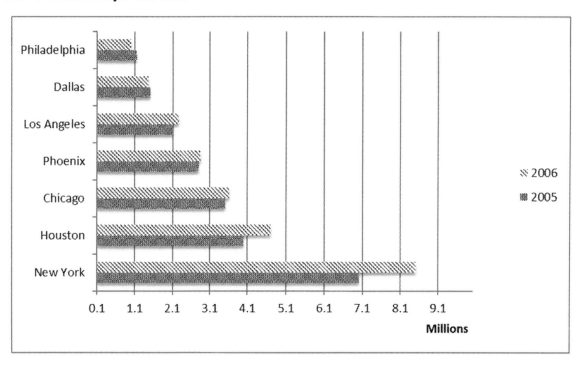

Reading the data in a bar graph is similar to the skills needed to read a line graph. The test taker should read and comprehend all heading information, as well as information provided along the horizontal and vertical axes. Note that the graph pertains to the population of some major U.S. cities. The "values" of these cities can be found along the left side of the graph, along the vertical axis. The population values can be found along the horizontal axes. Notice how the graph uses shaded bars to depict the change in population over time, as the heading indicates. Therefore, when the test taker is asked a question such as, *Which major U.S. city experienced the greatest amount of population growth during the depicted two year cycle,* the reader should be able to determine a correct answer of New York. It is important to pay particular attention to color, length, data points, and both axes, as well as any outlying header information in order to be able to answer graph-like test questions.

A circle graph (also sometimes referred to as a pie chart) presents quantitative data in the form of a circle. The same principles apply: the test taker should look for numerical data within the confines of the circle itself but also note any outlying information that may be included in a header, footer, or to the side of the circle. A circle graph will not depict horizontal or vertical axis information, but will instead rely on the reader's ability to visually take note of segmented circle pieces and apply information accordingly. An example of a circle graph is as follows:

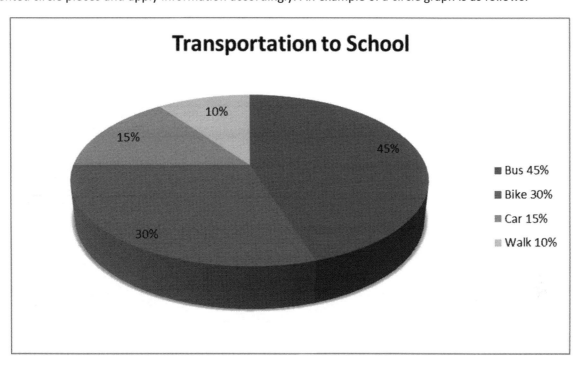

Notice the heading "Transportation to School." This should indicate to the test taker that the topic of the circle graph is how people traditionally get to school. To the right of the graph, the reader should comprehend that the data percentages contained within it directly correspond to the method of transportation. In this graph, the data is represented through the use shades and pattern. Each transportation method has its own shade. For example, if the test taker was then asked, *Which method of school transportation is most widely utilized,* the reader should be able to identify school bus as the correct answer.

Be wary of test questions that ask test takers to draw conclusions based on information that is not present. For example, it is not possible to determine, given the parameters of this circle graph, whether the population presented is of a particular gender or ethnic group. This graph does not represent data from a particular city or school district. It does not distinguish between student grade levels and, although the reader could infer that the typical student must be of driving age if cars are included, this is not necessarily the case. Elementary school students may rely on parents or others to drive them by personal methods. Therefore, do not read too much into data that is not presented. Only rely on the quantitative data that is presented in order to answer questions.

A scatter plot or scatter diagram is a graph that depicts quantitative data across plotted points. It will involve at least two sets of data. It will also involve horizontal and vertical axes.

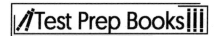

An example of a scatter plot is as follows:

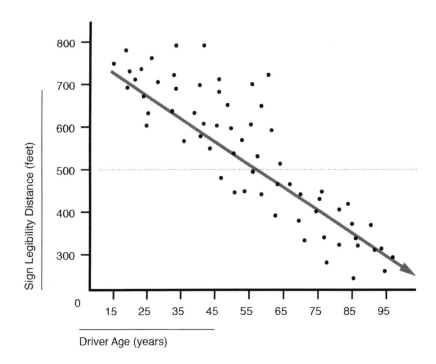

Driver Age (years)

The skills needed to address a scatter plot are essentially the same as in other graph examples. Note any topic headings, as well as horizontal or vertical axis information. In the sample above, the reader can determine the data addresses a driver's ability to correctly and legibly read road signs as related to their age. Again, note the information that is absent. The test taker is not given the data to assess a time period, location, or driver gender. It simply requires the reader to note an approximate age to the ability to correctly identify road signs from a distance measured in feet. Notice that the overall graph also displays a trend. In this case, the data indicates a negative one and possibly supports the hypothesis that as a driver ages, their ability to correctly read a road sign at over 500 feet tends to decline over time. If the test taker were to be asked, *At what approximation in feet does a sixteen-year-old driver correctly see and read a street sign,* the answer would be the option closest to 700 feet.

Reading and examining scientific data in excerpts involves all of a reader's contextual reading, data interpretation, drawing logical conclusions based only on the information presented, and their application of critical thinking skills across a set of interpretive questions. Thorough comprehension and attention to detail is necessary to achieve test success.

Vocabulary

Identifying Roots

By analyzing and understanding Latin, Greek, and Anglo-Saxon word roots and structure, authors better convey the thoughts they want to express to the readers of their words and help them to determine their meanings within the flow and without missing a beat. For instance, **context**—how words are used in sentences—is from the Latin for *contextus*, which means "together" + "to weave," and gives readers a graphic for the minds' eyes to see the coming together of their usage. Like every other topic discussed herein, context is needed for understanding. This element actually has a second, crucial meaning. Context is not only the *how*, but the revealed moment of the *why* a writing has been composed; it is the "Aha" moment.

182

The way *how* words are used in sentences is important because it also gives meaning and cohesion from sentence to sentence, paragraph to paragraph, and page after page. In other words, it gives the document continuity.

Another upside of the how side is that readers have opportunities to understand new words with which they are unfamiliar. Of course, people can always look words up if a dictionary or thesaurus, if available, but meaning might be gleaned on the spot in a piece that is well-written. **Synonyms** (words or phrases that mean about the same) and **antonyms** (words or phrases that mean the opposite of the specific word) in context give clues to meanings, and sometimes reiteration of a word might add clarification. Repetition, wisely used, can also serve as a part of how a piece flows.

The revealed moment of the *why* is important because context, up to that moment, has determined the shape of the text. This is, essentially, to bring out what it is all about.

Prefixes

A **prefix** is a word, letter, or number that is placed before another. It adjusts or qualifies the original word's meaning.

Four prefixes represent 97 percent of English words with prefixes. They are:

- *dis-* means "not" or "opposite of"; *dis*abled
- in-, im-, il-, ir- mean "not"; *il*literate
- *re-* means "again"; *re*turn
- *un-* means "not"; *un*predictable

Other commons prefixes include:

- *anti-* means "against"; antibacterial
- *fore-* means "before"; forefront
- *mis-* means "wrongly"; misunderstand
- *non-* means "not"; nonsense
- *over-* means "over"; overabundance
- *pre-* means "before"; preheat
- *super-* means "above"; superman

Suffixes

The official definition of a **suffix** is "a morpheme added at the end of a word to form a derivative." In simpler terms, that means a suffix is a letter or group of letters added at the end of a word to form another word. The word created with the addition is either a different tense of the same word (*help + ed = helped*) or a new word (*help + ful = helpful*).

They are:

- *-ed* is used to make present tense verbs into past tense verbs; wash*ed*
- *-ing* is used to make a present tense verb into a present participle verb; wash*ing*
- *-ly* is used to make characteristic of; love*ly*
- *-s* or *-es* are used to make more than one; chair*s* or box*es*

Other common suffixes include:

- *-able* means can be done; deplor*able*
- *-al* means having characteristics of; comic*al*

183

- *-est* means comparative; great*est*
- *-ful* means full of; wonder*ful*
- *-ism* means belief in; commun*ism*
- *-less* means without; faith*less*
- *-ment* means action or process; accomplish*ment*
- *-ness* means state of; happi*ness*
- *-ize* means to render, to make; terror*ize*, steril*ize*
- *-ise* is primarily the British variant of *–ize;* surpr*ise,* advert*ise*
- *-ced* means go; spelling variations include -cede (concede, recede); -ceed (only three: proceed, exceed, succeed); -sede (the only one: supersede)

(Note: In some of the examples above, the *e* has been deleted.)

Finding the Meaning of Words and Phrases in Context

There will be many occasions in one's reading career in which an unknown word or a word with multiple meanings will pop up. There are ways of determining what these words or phrases mean that do not require the use of the dictionary, which is especially helpful during a test where one may not be available. Even outside of the exam, knowing how to derive an understanding of a word via **context clues** will be a critical skill in the real world. The context is the circumstances in which a story or a passage is happening, and can usually be found in the series of words directly before or directly after the word or phrase in question. The clues are the words that hint towards the meaning of the unknown word or phrase. The author may use synonyms or antonyms that you can use. **Synonyms** refer to words that have the same meaning as another word (e.g., instructor/teacher/educator, canine/dog, feline/cat, herbivore/vegetarian). **Antonyms** refer to words that have the opposite meaning as another word (e.g., true/false, up/down, in/out, right/wrong).

There may be questions that ask about the meaning of a particular word or phrase within a passage. There are a couple ways to approach these kinds of questions:

- Define the word or phrase in a way that is easy to comprehend (using context clues).
- Try out each answer choice in place of the word.

To demonstrate, here's an example from *Alice in Wonderland*:

> Alice was beginning to get very tired of sitting by her sister on the bank, and of having nothing to do: once or twice she <u>peeped</u> into the book her sister was reading, but it had no pictures or conversations in it, "and what is the use of a book," thought Alice, "without pictures or conversations?"

Q: As it is used in the selection, the word <u>peeped</u> means:

Using the first technique, before looking at the answers, define the word *peeped* using context clues and then find the matching answer. Then, analyze the entire passage in order to determine the meaning, not just the surrounding words.

To begin, imagine a blank where the word should be and put a synonym or definition there: "once or twice she ___ into the book her sister was reading." The context clue here is the book. It may be tempting to put *read* where the blank is, but notice the preposition word, *into*. One does not read *into* a book, one simply reads a book, and since reading a book requires that it is seen with a pair of eyes, then *look* would make the most sense to put into the blank: "once or twice she <u>looked </u>into the book her sister was reading."

Once an easy-to-understand word or synonym has been supplanted, check to make sure it makes sense with the rest of the passage. What happened after she looked into the book? She thought to herself how a book without pictures or conversations is useless. This situation in its entirety makes sense.

Now check the answer choices for a match:
- a. To make a high-pitched cry
- b. To smack
- c. To look curiously
- d. To pout

Since the word was already defined, answer choice (c) is the best option.

Using the second technique, replace the figurative blank with each of the answer choices and determine which one is the most appropriate. Remember to look further into the passage to clarify that they work, because they could still make sense out of context.

Once or twice, she made a high pitched cry into the book her sister was reading.

Once or twice, she smacked the book her sister was reading.

Once or twice, she looked curiously into the book her sister was reading.

Once or twice, she pouted into the book her sister was reading.

For Choice A, it does not make much sense in any context for a person to cry into a book, unless maybe something terrible has happened in the story. Given that afterward Alice thinks to herself how useless a book without pictures is, this option does not make sense within context.

For Choice B, smacking a book someone is reading may make sense if the rest of the passage indicates there a reason for doing so. If Alice was angry or her sister had shoved it in her face, then maybe smacking the book would make sense within context. However, since whatever she does with the book causes her to think, "what is the use of a book without pictures or conversations?" then answer Choice B is not an appropriate answer.

Answer Choice C fits well within context, given her subsequent thoughts on the matter.

Answer Choice D does not make sense in context or grammatically, as people do not *pout into* things.

This is a simple example to illustrate the techniques outlined above. There may, however, be a question in which all of the definitions are correct and also make sense out of context, in which the appropriate context clues will really need to be honed in on in order to determine the correct answer. For example, here is another passage from *Alice in Wonderland*:

... but when the Rabbit actually took a watch out of its waistcoat pocket, and looked at it, and then hurried on, Alice started to her feet, for it flashed across her mind that she had never before seen a rabbit with either a waistcoat-pocket or a watch to take out of it, and burning with curiosity, she ran across the field after it, and was just in time to see it pop down a large rabbit-hole under the hedge.

Q: As it is used in the passage, the word started means:
- a. To turn on
- b. To begin
- c. To move quickly
- d. To be surprised

All of these words qualify as a definition of start, but using context clues, the correct answer can be identified using one of the two techniques above. It's easy to see that one does not turn on, begin, or be surprised to one's feet. The selection also states that she "ran across the field after it," indicating that she was in a hurry. Therefore, to move quickly would make the most sense in this context.

The same strategies can be applied to vocabulary that may be completely unfamiliar. In this case, focus on the words before or after the unknown word in order to determine its definition. Take this sentence, for example:

"Sam was such a <u>miser</u> that he forced Andrew to pay him twelve cents for the candy, even though he had a large inheritance and he knew his friend was poor."

Unlike with assertion questions, for vocabulary questions, it may be necessary to apply some critical thinking skills when something isn't explicitly stated within the passage. Think about the implications of the passage, or what the text is trying to say. With this example, it is important to realize that it is considered unusually stingy for a person to demand so little money from someone instead of just letting their friend have the candy, especially if this person is already wealthy. Hence, a <u>miser</u> is a greedy or stingy individual.

Questions about complex vocabulary may not be explicitly asked, but this is a useful skill to know. If there is an unfamiliar word while reading a passage and its definition goes unknown, it is possible to miss out on a critical message that could inhibit the ability to appropriately answer the questions. Practicing this technique in daily life will sharpen this ability to derive meanings from context clues with ease.

Practice Quiz

Questions 1-5 are based upon the following passage:
The Myth of Head Heat Loss

It has recently been brought to my attention that most people believe that 75% of your body heat is lost through your head. I had certainly heard this before, and I'm not going to attempt to say I didn't believe it when I first heard it. It is natural to be gullible to anything said with enough authority. But the "fact" that the majority of your body heat is lost through your head is a lie.

Let me explain. Heat loss is proportional to surface area exposed. An elephant loses a great deal more heat than an anteater because it has a much greater surface area than an anteater. Each cell has mitochondria that produce energy in the form of heat, and it takes a lot more energy to run an elephant than an anteater.

So, each part of your body loses its proportional amount of heat in accordance with its surface area. The human torso probably loses the most heat, though the legs lose a significant amount as well. Some people have asked, "Why does it feel so much warmer when you cover your head than when you don't?" Well, that's because your head, because it is not clothed, is losing a lot of heat while the clothing on the rest of your body provides insulation. If you went outside with a hat and pants but no shirt, not only would you look stupid but your heat loss would be significantly greater because so much more of you would be exposed. So, if given the choice to cover your chest or your head in the cold, choose the chest. It could save your life.

1. What is the primary purpose of this passage?
    a. To provide evidence that disproves a myth
    b. To compare elephants and anteaters
    c. To explain why it is appropriate to wear clothes in winter
    d. To show how people are gullible

2. Which of the following best describes the main idea of the passage?
    a. It is better to wear a shirt than a hat.
    b. Heat loss is proportional to surface area exposed.
    c. It is natural to be gullible.
    d. The human chest loses the most heat.

3. Why does the author compare elephants and anteaters?
    a. To express an opinion
    b. To give an example that helps clarify the main point
    c. To show the differences between them
    d. To persuade why one is better than the other

4. Which of the following best describes the tone of the passage?
    a. Harsh
    b. Angry
    c. Casual
    d. Indifferent

187

5. Which of the following sentences provides the best evidence to support the main idea?
   a. "It is natural to be gullible to anything said with enough authority."
   b. "Each part of your body loses its proportional amount of heat in accordance with its surface area."
   c. "If given the choice to cover your chest or your head in the cold, choose the chest."
   d. "But the 'fact' that the majority of your body heat is lost through your head is a lie."

Answer Explanations

1. A: Not only does the article provide examples to disprove a myth, the title also suggests that the article is trying to disprove a myth. Further, the sentence, "But the 'fact' that the majority of your body heat is lost through your head is a lie," and then the subsequent "let me explain," demonstrates the author's intention in disproving a myth. Choice *B* is incorrect because although the selection does compare elephants and anteaters, it does so in order to prove a point, and is not the primary reason that the selection was written. Choice *C* is incorrect because even though the article mentions somebody wearing clothes in the winter, and that doing so could save your life, wearing clothes in the winter is not the primary reason this article was written. Choice *D* is incorrect because the article only mentions that people are gullible once and makes no further comment on the matter, so this cannot be the primary purpose.

2. B: If the myth is that most of one's body heat is lost through their head, then the fact that heat loss is proportional to surface area exposed is the best evidence that disproves it, since one's head is a great deal less surface area than the rest of the body, making Choice *B* the correct choice. "It is better to wear a shirt than a hat" does not provide evidence that disproves the fact that the head loses more heat than the rest of the body. Thus, Choice *A* is incorrect. Choice *C* is incorrect because gullibility is mentioned only once in this passage and the rest of the article ignores this statement, so clearly it is not the main idea. Finally, Choice *D* is incorrect because though the article mentions that the human chest probably loses the most heat, it is to provide an example of the evidence that heat loss is proportional to surface area exposed, so this is not the main idea of the passage.

3. B: Choice *B* is correct because the author is trying to demonstrate the main idea, which is that heat loss is proportional to surface area, and so they compare two animals with different surface areas to clarify the main point. Choice *A* is incorrect because the author uses elephants and anteaters to prove a point that heat loss is proportional to surface area, not to express an opinion. Choice *C* is incorrect because though the author does use them to show differences, they do so in order to give examples that prove the above points. Choice *D* is incorrect because there is no language to indicate favoritism between the two animals.

4. C: Because of the way the author addresses the reader and the colloquial language the author uses (e.g., "let me explain," "so," "well," "didn't," "you would look stupid"), Choice *C* is the best answer because it has a much more casual tone than the usual informative article. Choice *A* may be a tempting choice because the author says the "fact" that most of one's heat is lost through their head is a "lie" and that someone who does not wear a shirt in the cold looks stupid. However, this only happens twice within the passage, and the passage does not give an overall tone of harshness. Choice *B* is incorrect because again, while not necessarily nice, the language does not carry an angry charge. The author is clearly not indifferent to the subject because of the passionate language that they use, so Choice *D* is incorrect.

5. B: The primary purpose of the article is to provide evidence to disprove the myth that most of a person's heat is lost through their head. The fact that each part of the body loses heat in proportion to its surface area is the best evidence to disprove this myth. Choice *A* is incorrect because again, gullibility is not a main contributor to this article, but it may be common to see questions on the test that give the same wrong answer in order to try and trick the test taker. Choice *C* only suggests what you should do with this information; it is not the primary evidence itself. Choice *D*, while tempting, is actually not evidence. It does not give any reason for why it is a lie; it simply states that it is. Evidence is factual information that supports a claim.

189

Writing

Expression of Ideas

Development

for words that are close together with the same (or similar) meanings.

Proposition

The **proposition** (also called the **claim** since it can be true or false) is a clear statement of the point or idea the writer is trying to make. The length or format of a proposition can vary, but it often takes the form of a **topic sentence**. A good topic sentence is:

- Clear: does not weave a complicated web of words for the reader to decode or unwrap

- Concise: presents only the information needed to make the claim and doesn't clutter up the statement with unnecessary details

- Precise: clarifies the exact point the writer wants to make and doesn't use broad, overreaching statements

Look at the following example:

> The civil rights movement, from its genesis in the Emancipation Proclamation to its current struggles with de facto discrimination, has changed the face of the United States more than any other factor in its history.

Is the statement clear? Yes, the statement is fairly clear, although other words can be substituted for "genesis" and "de facto" to make it easier to understand.

Is the statement concise? No, the statement is not concise. Details about the Emancipation Proclamation and the current state of the movement are unnecessary for a topic sentence. Those details should be saved for the body of the text.

Is the statement precise? No, the statement is not precise. What exactly does the writer mean by "changed the face of the United States"? The writer should be more specific about the effects of the movement. Also, suggesting that something has a greater impact than anything else in U.S. history is far too ambitious a statement to make.

A better version might look like this:

> The civil rights movement has greatly increased the career opportunities available for Black Americans.

The unnecessary language and details are removed, and the claim can now be measured and supported.

Support

Once the main idea or proposition is stated, the writer attempts to prove or **support** the claim with text evidence and supporting details.

Take for example the sentence, "Seat belts save lives." Though most people can't argue with this statement, its impact on the reader is much greater when supported by additional content. The writer can support this idea by:

- Providing statistics on the rate of highway fatalities alongside statistics for estimated seat belt usage.

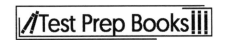
- Explaining the science behind a car accident and what happens to a passenger who doesn't use a seat belt.
- Offering anecdotal evidence or true stories from reliable sources on how seat belts prevent fatal injuries in car crashes.

However, using only one form of supporting evidence is not nearly as effective as using a variety to support a claim. Presenting only a list of statistics can be boring to the reader, but providing a true story that's both interesting and humanizing helps. In addition, one example isn't always enough to prove the writer's larger point, so combining it with other examples is extremely effective for the writing. Thus, when reading a passage, don't just look for a single form of supporting evidence.

Another key aspect of supporting evidence is a *reliable source*. Does the writer include the source of the information? If so, is the source well known and trustworthy? Is there a potential for bias? For example, a seat belt study done by a seat belt manufacturer may have its own agenda to promote.

Focus
Good writing stays focused and on topic. During the test, determine the main idea for each passage and then look for times when the writer strays from the point they're trying to make. Let's go back to the seat belt example. If the writer suddenly begins talking about how well airbags, crumple zones, or other safety features work to save lives, they might be losing focus from the topic of "safety belts."

Focus can also refer to individual sentences. Sometimes the writer does address the main topic, but in a confusing way. For example:

> Thanks to seat belt usage, survival in serious car accidents has shown a consistently steady increase since the development of the retractable seat belt in the 1950s.

This statement is definitely on topic, but it's not easy to follow. A simpler, more focused version of this sentence might look like this:

> Seat belts have consistently prevented car fatalities since the 1950s.

Providing adequate information is another aspect of focused writing. Statements like "seat belts are important" and "many people drive cars" are true, but they're so general that they don't contribute much to the writer's case. When reading a passage, watch for these kinds of unfocused statements.

Organization

Good writing is not merely a random collection of sentences. No matter how well written, sentences must relate and coordinate appropriately with one another. If not, the writing seems random, haphazard, and disorganized. Therefore, good writing must be organized, where each sentence fits a larger context and relates to the sentences around it.

Logical Sequence
Even if the writer includes plenty of information to support their point, the writing is only effective when the information is in a logical order. **Logical sequencing** is really just common sense, but it's also an important writing technique. First, the writer should introduce the main idea, whether for a paragraph, a section, or the entire piece. Second, they should present evidence to support the main idea by using transitional language. This shows the reader how the information relates to the main idea and to the sentences around it. The writer should then take time to interpret the information, making sure necessary connections are obvious to the reader. Finally, the writer can summarize the information in a closing section.

Although most writing follows this pattern, it isn't a set rule. Sometimes writers change the order for effect. For example, the writer can begin with a surprising piece of supporting information to grab the reader's attention, and then transition to the main idea. Thus, if a passage doesn't follow the logical order, don't immediately assume it's wrong. However, most writing usually settles into a logical sequence after a nontraditional beginning.

Introductions and Conclusions

Examining the writer's strategies for introductions and conclusions puts the reader in the right mindset to interpret the rest of the passage. Look for methods the writer might use for introductions such as:

- Stating the main point immediately, followed by outlining how the rest of the piece supports this claim.

- Establishing important, smaller pieces of the main idea first, and then grouping these points into a case for the main idea.

- Opening with a quotation, anecdote, question, seeming paradox, or other piece of interesting information, and then using it to lead to the main point.

Whatever method the writer chooses, the introduction should make their intention clear, establish their voice as a credible one, and encourage a person to continue reading.

Conclusions tend to follow a similar pattern. In them, the writer restates their main idea a final time, often after summarizing the smaller pieces of that idea. If the introduction uses a quote or anecdote to grab the reader's attention, the conclusion often makes reference to it again. Whatever way the writer chooses to arrange the conclusion, the final restatement of the main idea should be clear and simple for the reader to interpret.

Finally, conclusions shouldn't introduce any new information.

Transition Words

The writer should act as a guide, showing the reader how all the sentences fit together. Consider this example concerning seat belts:

> Seat belts save more lives than any other automobile safety feature. Many studies show that airbags save lives as well. Not all cars have airbags. Many older cars don't. Air bags aren't entirely reliable. Studies show that in 15 percent of accidents, airbags don't deploy as designed. Seat belt malfunctions are extremely rare.

There's nothing wrong with any of these sentences individually, but together they're disjointed and difficult to follow. The best way for the writer to communicate information is through the use of transition words. Here are examples of transition words and phrases that tie sentences together, enabling a more natural flow:

- To show causality: as a result, therefore, and consequently
- To compare and contrast: *however, but*, and *on the other hand*
- To introduce examples: *for example, namely*, and *including*
- To show order of importance: *foremost, primarily, secondly*, and *lastly*

Note that this is not a complete list of transitions. There are many more that can be used; however, most fit into these or similar categories. The important point is that the words should clearly show the relationship between sentences, supporting information, and the main idea.

Here is an update to the previous example using transition words. These changes make it easier to read and bring clarity to the writer's points:

> Seat belts save more lives than any other automobile safety feature. Many studies show that airbags save lives as well; however, not all cars have airbags. For example, some older cars don't. Furthermore, air bags

aren't entirely reliable. For example, studies show that in 15 percent of accidents, airbags don't deploy as designed, but, on the other hand, seat belt malfunctions are extremely rare.

Also, be prepared to analyze whether the writer is using the best transition word or phrase for the situation. Take this sentence for example: "As a result, seat belt malfunctions are extremely rare." This sentence doesn't make sense in the context above because the writer is trying to show the contrast between seat belts and airbags, not the causality.

Forming Paragraphs

A good **paragraph** should have the following characteristics:

- Be logical with organized sentences
- Have a *unified* purpose within itself
- Use sentences as *building blocks*
- Be a *distinct section* of a piece of writing
- Present a *single theme* introduced by a *topic sentence*
- Maintain a *consistent flow* through subsequent, relevant, well-placed sentences
- *Tell a story* of its own or have its own purpose, yet connect with what is written before and after
- Enlighten, entertain, and/or inform

Though certainly not set in stone, the length should be a consideration for the reader's sake, not merely for the sake of the topic. When paragraphs are especially short, the reader might experience an irregular, uneven effect; when they're much longer than 250 words, the reader's attention span, and probably their retention, is challenged. While a paragraph can technically be a sentence long, a good rule of thumb is for paragraphs to be at least three sentences long and no more than ten sentence long. An optimal word length is 100 to 250 words.

Relevance of Content

A reader must be able to evaluate the argument or point the author is trying to make and determine if it is adequately supported. The first step is to determine the main idea. The main idea is what the author wants to say about a specific topic. The next step is to locate the supporting details. An author uses supporting details to illustrate the main idea. These are the details that provide evidence or examples to help make a point. Supporting details often appear in the form of quotations, paraphrasing, or analysis. Test takers should then examine the text to make sure the author connects details and analysis to the main point. These steps are crucial to understanding the text and evaluating how well the author presents their argument and evidence. The following graphic demonstrates the connection between the main idea and the supporting details.

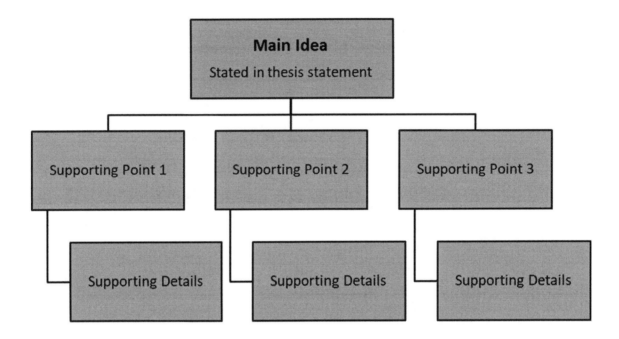

It is important to evaluate the author's supporting details to be sure that they are credible, provide evidence of the author's point, and directly support the main idea. Critical readers examine the facts used to support an author's argument and check those facts against other sources to be sure they are correct. They also check the validity of the sources used to be sure those sources are credible, academic, and/or peer-reviewed. A strong argument uses valid, measurable facts to support ideas.

Effective Language Use

Precision

People often think of **precision** in terms of math, but precise word choice is another key to successful writing. Since language itself is imprecise, it's important for the writer to find the exact word or words to convey the full, intended meaning of a given situation. For example:

> The number of deaths has gone down since seat belt laws started.

There are several problems with this sentence. First, the word *deaths* is too general. From the context, it's assumed that the writer is referring only to *deaths* caused by car accidents. However, without clarification, the sentence lacks impact and is probably untrue. The phrase "gone down" might be accurate, but a more precise word could provide more information and greater accuracy. Did the numbers show a slow and steady decrease of highway fatalities or a sudden drop? If the latter is true, the writer is missing a chance to make their point more dramatically. Instead of

194

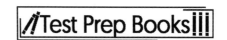

"gone down" they could substitute *plummeted, fallen drastically,* or *rapidly diminished* to bring the information to life. Also, the phrase "seat belt laws" is unclear. Does it refer to laws requiring cars to include seat belts or to laws requiring drivers and passengers to use them? Finally, *started* is not a strong verb. Words like *enacted* or *adopted* are more direct and make the content more real. When put together, these changes create a far more powerful sentence:

> The number of highway fatalities has plummeted since laws requiring seat belt usage were enacted.

However, it's important to note that precise word choice can sometimes be taken too far. If the writer of the sentence above takes precision to an extreme, it might result in the following:

> The incidence of high-speed, automobile accident related fatalities has decreased 75% and continued to remain at historical lows since the initial set of federal legislations requiring seat belt use were enacted in 1992.

This sentence is extremely precise, but it takes so long to achieve that precision that it suffers from a lack of clarity. Precise writing is about finding the right balance between information and flow. This is also an issue of *conciseness* (discussed in the next section).

The last thing to consider with precision is a word choice that's not only unclear or uninteresting, but also confusing or misleading. For example:

> The number of highway fatalities has become hugely lower since laws requiring seat belt use were enacted.

In this case, the reader might be confused by the word *hugely*. Huge means large, but here the writer uses *hugely* to describe something small. Though most readers can decipher this, doing so disconnects them from the flow of the writing and makes the writer's point less effective.

On the test, there can be questions asking for alternatives to the writer's word choice. In answering these questions, always consider the context and look for a balance between precision and flow.

Conciseness

"Less is more" is a good rule to follow when writing a sentence. Unfortunately, writers often include extra words and phrases that seem necessary at the time, but add nothing to the main idea. This confuses the reader and creates unnecessary repetition. Writing that lacks **conciseness** is usually guilty of excessive wordiness and redundant phrases. Here's an example containing both of these issues:

> When legislators decided to begin creating legislation making it mandatory for automobile drivers and passengers to make use of seat belts while in cars, a large number of them made those laws for reasons that were political reasons.

There are several empty or "fluff" words here that take up too much space. These can be eliminated while still maintaining the writer's meaning. For example:

- "decided to begin" could be shortened to "began"
- "making it mandatory for" could be shortened to "requiring"
- "make use of" could be shortened to "use"
- "a large number" could be shortened to "many"

In addition, there are several examples of redundancy that can be eliminated:

- "legislators decided to begin creating legislation" and "made those laws"
- "automobile drivers and passengers" and "while in cars"

195

- "reasons that were political reasons"

These changes are incorporated as follows:

> When legislators began requiring drivers and passengers to use seat belts, many of them did so for political reasons.

There are many examples of redundant phrases, such as "add an additional," "complete and total," "time schedule," and "transportation vehicle." If asked to identify a redundant phrase on the test, look for words that are close together with the same (or similar) meanings.

Style, Tone, and Mood
Style, tone, and mood are often thought to be the same thing. Though they're closely related, there are important differences to keep in mind. The easiest way to do this is to remember that style "creates and affects" tone and mood. More specifically, style is *how the writer uses words* to create the desired tone and mood for their writing.

Style
Style can include any number of technical writing choices, and some may have to be analyzed on the test. A few examples of style choices include:

- Sentence Construction: When presenting facts, does the writer use shorter sentences to create a quicker sense of the supporting evidence, or do they use longer sentences to elaborate and explain the information?

- Technical Language: Does the writer use jargon to demonstrate their expertise in the subject, or do they use ordinary language to help the reader understand things in simple terms?

- Formal Language: Does the writer refrain from using contractions such as *won't* or *can't* to create a more formal tone, or do they use a colloquial, conversational style to connect to the reader?

- Formatting: Does the writer use a series of shorter paragraphs to help the reader follow a line of argument, or do they use longer paragraphs to examine an issue in great detail and demonstrate their knowledge of the topic?

On the test, examine the writer's style and how their writing choices affect the way the passage comes across.

Tone
Tone refers to the writer's attitude toward the subject matter. Tone conveys how the writer feels about characters, situations, events, ideas, etc. Nonfiction writing is sometimes thought to have no tone at all, but this is incorrect.

A lot of nonfiction writing has a neutral tone, which is an extremely important tone for the writer to take. A neutral tone demonstrates that the writer is presenting a topic impartially and letting the information speak for itself. On the other hand, nonfiction writing can be just as effective and appropriate if the tone isn't neutral. For instance, take the previous examples involving seat belt use. In them, the writer mostly chooses to retain a neutral tone when presenting information. If the writer would instead include their own personal experience of losing a friend or family member in a car accident, the tone would change dramatically. The tone would no longer be neutral. Now it would show that the writer has a personal stake in the content, allowing them to interpret the information in a different way. When analyzing tone, consider what the writer is trying to achieve in the passage, and how they *create* the tone using style.

Mood
Mood refers to the feelings and atmosphere that the writer's words create for the reader. Like tone, many nonfiction pieces can have a neutral mood. To return to the previous example, if the writer would choose to include

information about a person they know being killed in a car accident, the passage would suddenly carry an emotional component that is absent in the previous examples. Depending on how they present the information, the writer can create a sad, angry, or even hopeful mood. When analyzing the mood, consider what the writer wants to accomplish and whether the best choice was made to achieve that end.

Consistency

Whatever style, tone, and mood the writer uses, good writing should remain **consistent** throughout. If the writer chooses to include the tragic, personal experience above, it would affect the style, tone, and mood of the entire piece. It would seem out of place for such an example to be used in the middle of a neutral, measured, and analytical piece. To adjust the rest of the piece, the writer needs to make additional choices to remain consistent. For example, the writer might decide to use the word *tragedy* in place of the more neutral *fatality*, or they could describe a series of car-related deaths as an *epidemic*. Adverbs and adjectives such as *devastating* or *horribly* could be included to maintain this consistent attitude toward the content. When analyzing writing, look for sudden shifts in style, tone, and mood, and consider whether the writer would be wiser to maintain the prevailing strategy.

Syntax

Syntax is the order of words in a sentence. While most of the writing on the test has proper syntax, there may be questions on ways to vary the syntax for effectiveness. One of the easiest writing mistakes to spot is **repetitive sentence structure**. For example:

> Seat belts are important. They save lives. People don't like to use them. We have to pass seat belt laws. Then more people will wear seat belts. More lives will be saved.

What's the first thing that comes to mind when reading this example? The short, choppy, and repetitive sentences! In fact, most people notice this syntax issue more than the content itself. By combining some sentences and changing the syntax of others, the writer can create a more effective writing passage:

> Seat belts are important because they save lives. Since people don't like to use seat belts, though, more laws requiring their usage need to be passed. Only then will more people wear them and only then will more lives be saved.

Many rhetorical devices can be used to vary syntax (more than can possibly be named here). These often have intimidating names like *anadiplosis*, *metastasis*, and *paremptosis*. The test questions don't ask for definitions of these tricky techniques, but they can ask how the writer plays with the words and what effect that has on the writing. For example, *anadiplosis* is when the last word (or phrase) from a sentence is used to begin the next sentence:

> Cars are driven by people. People cause accidents. Accidents cost taxpayers money.

The test doesn't ask for this technique by name, but be prepared to recognize what the writer is doing and why they're using the technique in this situation. In this example, the writer is probably using *anadiplosis* to demonstrate causation.

Standard English Conventions

Sentence Structure

First, let's review the basic elements of sentences.

A **sentence** is a set of words that make up a grammatical unit. The words must have certain elements and be spoken or written in a specific order to constitute a complete sentence that makes sense.

> 1. A sentence must have a **subject** (a noun or noun phrase). The subject tells whom or what the sentence is addressing (i.e., what it is about).

> 2. A sentence must have an **action** or **state of being** (*a* verb). To reiterate: A verb forms the main part of the predicate of a sentence. This means that it explains what the noun is doing.

> 3. A sentence must convey a complete thought.

When examining writing, be mindful of grammar, structure, spelling, and patterns. Sentences can come in varying sizes and shapes; so, the point of grammatical correctness is not to stamp out creativity or diversity in writing. Rather, grammatical correctness ensures that writing will be enjoyable and clear. One of the most common methods for catching errors is to mouth the words as you read them. Many typos are fixed automatically by our brain, but mouthing the words often circumvents this instinct and helps one read what's actually on the page. Often, grammar errors are caught not by memorization of grammar rules but by the training of one's mind to know whether something *sounds* right or not.

Types of Sentences
There isn't an overabundance of absolutes in grammar, but here is one: every sentence in the English language falls into one of four categories.

- Declarative: a simple statement that ends with a period

  The price of milk per gallon is the same as the price of gasoline.

- Imperative: a command, instruction, or request that ends with a period

  Buy milk when you stop to fill up your car with gas.

- Interrogative: a question that ends with a question mark

  Will you buy the milk?

- Exclamatory: a statement or command that expresses emotions like anger, urgency, or surprise and ends with an exclamation mark

  Buy the milk now!

Declarative sentences are the most common type, probably because they are comprised of the most general content, without any of the bells and whistles that the other three types contain. They are, simply, declarations or statements of any degree of seriousness, importance, or information.

Imperative sentences often seem to be missing a subject. The subject is there, though; it is just not visible or audible because it is *implied*. Look at the imperative example sentence.

  Buy the milk when you fill up your car with gas.

198

You is the implied subject, the one to whom the command is issued. This is sometimes called *the understood you* because it is understood that *you* is the subject of the sentence.

Interrogative sentences—those that ask questions—are defined as such from the idea of the word *interrogation*, the action of questions being asked of suspects by investigators. Although that is serious business, interrogative sentences apply to all kinds of questions.

To exclaim is at the root of **exclamatory sentences**. These are made with strong emotions behind them. The only technical difference between a declarative or imperative sentence and an exclamatory one is the exclamation mark at the end. The example declarative and imperative sentences can both become an exclamatory one simply by putting an exclamation mark at the end of the sentences.

> The price of milk per gallon is the same as the price of gasoline!
> Buy milk when you stop to fill up your car with gas!

After all, someone might be really excited by the price of gas or milk, or they could be mad at the person that will be buying the milk! However, as stated before, exclamation marks in abundance defeat their own purpose! After a while, they begin to cause fatigue! When used only for their intended purpose, they can have their expected and desired effect.

Independent and Dependent Clauses

Independent and dependent clauses are strings of words that contain both a subject and a verb. An **independent clause** *can* stand alone as complete thought, but a **dependent clause** *cannot*. A dependent clause relies on other words to be a complete sentence.

> Independent clause: The keys are on the counter.
> Dependent clause: If the keys are on the counter

Notice that both clauses have a subject (*keys*) and a verb (*are*). The independent clause expresses a complete thought, but the word *if* at the beginning of the dependent clause makes it *dependent* on other words to be a complete thought.

> Independent clause: If the keys are on the counter, please give them to me.

This presents a complete sentence since it includes at least one verb and one subject and is a complete thought. In this case, the independent clause has two subjects (*keys* & an implied *you*) and two verbs (*are* & *give*).

> Independent clause: I went to the store.
> Dependent clause: Because we are out of milk,
> Complete Sentence: Because we are out of milk, I went to the store.
> Complete Sentence: I went to the store because we are out of milk.

Sentence Structures

A **simple sentence** has one independent clause.

> I am going to win.

A **compound sentence** has two independent clauses. A conjunction—*for, and, nor, but, or, yet, so*—links them together. Note that each of the independent clauses has a subject and a verb.

> I am going to win, but the odds are against me.

A **complex sentence** has one independent clause and one or more dependent clauses.

> I am going to win, even though I don't deserve it.

Even though I don't deserve it is a dependent clause. It does not stand on its own. Some conjunctions that link an independent and a dependent clause are *although, because, before, after, that, when, which,* and *while.*

A **compound-complex sentence** has at least three clauses, two of which are independent and at least one that is a dependent clause.

> While trying to dance, I tripped over my partner's feet, but I regained my balance quickly.

The dependent clause is *While trying to dance.*

Run-Ons and Fragments
Run-Ons
A common mistake in writing is the run-on sentence. A **run-on** is created when two or more independent clauses are joined without the use of a conjunction, a semicolon, a colon, or a dash. We don't want to use commas where periods belong. Here is an example of a run-on sentence:

> Making wedding cakes can take many hours I am very impatient, I want to see them completed right away.

There are a variety of ways to correct a run-on sentence. The method you choose will depend on the context of the sentence and how it fits with neighboring sentences:

> Making wedding cakes can take many hours. I am very impatient. I want to see them completed right away. (Use periods to create more than one sentence.)

> Making wedding cakes can take many hours; I am very impatient—I want to see them completed right away. (Correct the sentence using a semicolon, colon, or dash.)

> Making wedding cakes can take many hours, and I am very impatient and want to see them completed right away. (Correct the sentence using coordinating conjunctions.)

> I am very impatient because I would rather see completed wedding cakes right away than wait for it to take many hours. (Correct the sentence by revising.)

Fragments
Remember that a complete sentence must have both a subject and a verb. Complete sentences consist of at least one independent clause. Incomplete sentences are called **sentence fragments**. A sentence fragment is a common error in writing. Sentence fragments can be independent clauses that start with subordinating words, such as *but, as, so that,* or *because,* or they could simply be missing a subject or verb.

A fragment error can be corrected by adding the fragment to a nearby sentence or by adding or removing words to make it an independent clause. For example:

> Dogs are my favorite animals. Because cats are too lazy. (Incorrect; the word because creates a sentence fragment)

> Dogs are my favorite animals because cats are too lazy. (Correct; this is a dependent clause.)

> Dogs are my favorite animals. Cats are too lazy. (Correct; this is a simple sentence.)

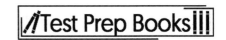

Subject and Predicate

Every complete sentence can be divided into two parts: the subject and the predicate.

Subjects: Subjects are needed in sentences to tell the reader who or what the sentence describes. Subjects can be simple or complete, and they can be direct or indirect. There can also be compound subjects.

Simple subjects are the noun or pronouns the sentence describes, without modifiers. The simple subject can come before or after the verb in the sentence:

>   The big brown <u>dog</u> is the calmest one.

Complete subjects are the subject together with all of its describing words or modifiers.

>   The <u>big brown dog</u> is the calmest one. (The complete subject is big brown dog.)

Direct subjects are subjects that appear in the text of the sentence, as in the example above. **Indirect subjects** are implied. The subject is "you," but the word *you* does not appear.

Indirect subjects are usually in imperative sentences that issue a command or order:

>   Feed the short skinny dog first. (The understood you is the subject.)

>   Watch out—he's really hungry! (The sentence warns you to watch out.)

Compound subjects occur when two or more nouns join together to form a plural subject.

>   <u>Carson</u> and <u>Emily</u> make a great couple.

Predicates: Once we have identified the subject of the sentence, the rest of the sentence becomes the predicate. Predicates are formed by the verb, the direct object, and all words related to it.

>   We <u>went to see the Cirque du' Soleil performance</u>.

>   The gigantic green character <u>was funnier than all the rest</u>.

A **predicate nominative** renames the subject:

>   John is a <u>carpenter</u>.

A **predicate adjective** describes the subject:

>   Margaret is <u>beautiful</u>.

Direct objects are the nouns in the sentence that are receiving the action. Sentences don't necessarily need objects. Sentences only need a subject and a verb.

>   The clown brought the acrobat the hula-hoop. (What is being brought? the hula-hoop)

>   Then he gave the trick pony <u>a soapy bath</u>. (What is being given? a soapy bath)

Indirect objects are words that tell us to or for whom or what the action is being done. For there to be an indirect object, there first must always be a direct object.

   The clown brought <u>the acrobat</u> the hula-hoop. (Who is getting the direct object? the hula-hoop)

   Then he gave <u>the trick pony</u> a soapy bath. (What is getting the bath? a trick pony)

Phrases

A **phrase** is a group of words that go together but do not include both a subject and a verb. They are used to add information, explain something, or make the sentence easier for the reader to understand. Unlike clauses, phrases can never stand alone as their own sentence. They do not form complete thoughts. There are noun phrases, prepositional phrases, verbal phrases, appositive phrases, and absolute phrases. Here are some examples of phrases:

   I know <u>all the shortest routes</u>.

   <u>Before the sequel</u>, we wanted to watch the first movie. (introductory phrase)

   The jumpers have hot cocoa <u>to drink right away</u>.

Complements

A **complement** completes the meaning of an expression. A complement can be a pronoun, noun, or adjective. A verb complement refers to the direct object or indirect object in the sentence. An object complement gives more information about the direct object:

   The magician got the kids excited.

Kids is the direct object, and *excited* is the object complement.

A *subject complement* comes after a linking verb. It is typically an adjective or noun that gives more information about the subject:

   The king was noble and spared the thief's life.

Noble describes the *king* and follows the linking verb *was*.

Subject-Verb Agreement

The subject of a sentence and its verb must agree. The cornerstone rule of subject-verb agreement is that subject and verb must agree in number. Whether the subject is singular or plural, the verb must follow suit.

   Incorrect: The houses is new.

   Correct: The houses are new.

   Also Correct: The house is new.

In other words, a singular subject requires a singular verb; a plural subject requires a plural verb.

The words or phrases that come between the subject and verb do not alter this rule.

   Incorrect: The houses built of brick is new.

   Correct: The houses built of brick are new.

202

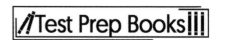

Incorrect: The houses with the sturdy porches is new.

Correct: The houses with the sturdy porches are new.

The subject will always follow the verb when a sentence begins with *here* or *there*. Identify these with care.

Incorrect: Here *is* the *houses* with sturdy porches.

Correct: Here *are* the *houses* with sturdy porches.

The subject in the sentences above is not *here*, it is *houses*. Remember, *here* and *there* are never subjects. Be careful that contractions such as *here's* or *there're* do not cause confusion!

Two subjects joined by *and* require a plural verb form, except when the two combine to make one thing:

Incorrect: Garrett and Jonathan is over there.

Correct: Garrett and Jonathan are over there.

Incorrect: Spaghetti and meatballs are a delicious meal!

Correct: Spaghetti and meatballs is a delicious meal!

In the example above, *spaghetti and meatballs* is a compound noun. However, *Garrett and Jonathan* is not a compound noun.

Two singular subjects joined by *or, either/or,* or *neither/nor* call for a singular verb form.

Incorrect: Butter or syrup are acceptable.

Correct: Butter or syrup is acceptable.

Plural subjects joined by *or, either/or,* or *neither/nor* are, indeed, plural.

The chairs or the boxes are being moved next.

If one subject is singular and the other is plural, the verb should agree with the closest noun.

Correct: The chair or the boxes are being moved next.

Correct: The chairs or the box is being moved next.

Some plurals of money, distance, and time call for a singular verb.

Incorrect: Three dollars *are* enough to buy that.

Correct: Three dollars *is* enough to buy that.

For words declaring degrees of quantity such as *many of, some of,* or *most of,* let the noun that follows *of* be the guide:

> Incorrect: Many of the books is in the shelf.

> Correct: Many of the books are in the shelf.

> Incorrect: Most of the pie *are* on the table.

> Correct: Most of the pie *is* on the table.

For indefinite pronouns like anybody or everybody, use singular verbs.

> Everybody *is* going to the store.

However, the pronouns *few, many, several, all, some,* and *both* have their own rules and use plural forms.

> Some *are* ready.

Some nouns like *crowd* and *congress* are called *collective nouns* and they require a singular verb form.

> Congress *is* in session.

> The news *is* over.

Books and movie titles, though, including plural nouns such as *Great Expectations*, also require a singular verb. Remember that only the subject affects the verb. While writing tricky subject-verb arrangements, say them aloud. Listen to them. Once the rules have been learned, one's ear will become sensitive to them, making it easier to pick out what's right and what's wrong.

Dangling and Misplaced Modifiers

A **modifier** is a word or phrase meant to describe or clarify another word in the sentence. When a sentence has a modifier but is missing the word it describes or clarifies, it's an error called a **dangling modifier**. We can fix the sentence by revising to include the word that is being modified.

Consider the following examples with the modifier underlined:

> Incorrect: <u>Having walked five miles</u>, this bench will be the place to rest. (This implies that the bench walked the miles, not the person.)

> Correct: <u>Having walked five miles</u>, Matt will rest on this bench. (*Having walked five miles* correctly modifies *Matt*, who did the walking.)

> Incorrect: <u>Since midnight</u>, my dreams have been pleasant and comforting. (The adverb clause *since midnight* cannot modify the noun *dreams*.)

> Correct: <u>Since midnight</u>, I have had pleasant and comforting dreams. (*Since midnight* modifies the verb have had, telling us when the dreams occurred.)

Sometimes the modifier is not located close enough to the word it modifies for the sentence to be clearly understood. In this case, we call the error a **misplaced modifier**. Here is an example with the modifier underlined.

Incorrect: We gave the hot cocoa to the children <u>that was filled with marshmallows</u>. (This sentence implies that the children are what are filled with marshmallows.)

Correct: We gave the hot cocoa <u>that was filled with marshmallows</u> to the children. (The cocoa is filled with marshmallows. The modifier is near the word it modifies.)

Parallel Structure in a Sentence

Parallel structure, also known as **parallelism**, refers to using the same grammatical form within a sentence. This is important in lists and for other components of sentences.

Incorrect: At the recital, the boys and girls were dancing, singing, and played musical instruments.
Correct: At the recital, the boys and girls were dancing, singing, and playing musical instruments.

Notice that in the second example, *played* is not in the same verb tense as the other verbs nor is it compatible with the helping verb *were*. To test for parallel structure in lists, try reading each item as if it were the only item in the list.

The boys and girls were dancing.
The boys and girls were singing.
The boys and girls were played musical instruments.

Suddenly, the error in the sentence becomes very clear. Here's another example:

Incorrect: After the accident, I informed the police *that Mrs. Holmes backed* into my car, *that Mrs. Holmes got out* of her car to look at the damage, and *she was driving* off without leaving a note.

Correct: After the accident, I informed the police *that Mrs. Holmes backed* into my car, *that Mrs. Holmes got out* of her car to look at the damage, and *that Mrs. Holmes drove off* without leaving a note.

Correct: After the accident, I informed the police that Mrs. Holmes *backed* into my car, *got out* of her car to look at the damage, and *drove off* without leaving a note.

Note that there are two ways to fix the nonparallel structure of the first sentence. The key to parallelism is consistent structure.

Usage

Parts of Speech

Nouns

A **common noun** is a word that identifies any of a class of people, places, or things. Examples include numbers, objects, animals, feelings, concepts, qualities, and actions. *A, an,* or *the* usually precedes the common noun. These parts of speech are called *articles*. Here are some examples of sentences using nouns preceded by articles.

A building is under construction.

The girl would like to move to *the* city.

An **abstract noun** is an idea, state, or quality. It is something that can't be touched, such as happiness, courage, evil, or humor.

A **proper noun** (also called a **proper name**) is used for the specific name of an individual person, place, or organization. The first letter in a proper noun is capitalized. "My name is *Mary*." "I work for *Walmart*."

Nouns sometimes serve as adjectives (which themselves describe nouns), such as "hockey player" and "state government."

Pronouns

A word used in place of a noun is known as a **pronoun**. Pronouns are words like *I, mine, hers,* and *us.*

Pronouns can be split into different classifications (as shown below) which make them easier to learn; however, it's not important to memorize the classifications.

- **Personal pronouns:** refers to people, places, things, etc.

- **First person pronouns:** we, I, our, mine

- **Second person pronouns:** you, yours

- **Third person pronouns:** he, she, they, them, it

- **Possessive pronouns:** demonstrate ownership (mine, his, hers, its, ours, theirs, yours)

- **Interrogative pronouns:** ask questions (what, which, who, whom, whose)

- **Relative pronouns:** include the five interrogative pronouns and others that are relative (whoever, whomever, that, when, where)

- **Demonstrative pronouns:** replace something specific (this, that, those, these)

- **Reciprocal pronouns:** indicate something was done or given in return (each other, one another)

- **Indefinite pronouns:** have a nonspecific status (anybody, whoever, someone, everybody, somebody)

Indefinite pronouns such as *anybody, whoever, someone, everybody,* and *somebody* command a singular verb form, but others such as *all, none,* and *some* could require a singular or plural verb form.

Antecedents

An **antecedent** is the noun to which a pronoun refers; it needs to be written or spoken before the pronoun is used. For many pronouns, antecedents are imperative for clarity. In particular, a lot of the personal, possessive, and demonstrative pronouns need antecedents. Otherwise, it would be unclear who or what someone is referring to when they use a pronoun like *he* or *this.*

Pronoun reference means that the pronoun should refer clearly to one, clear, unmistakable noun (the antecedent).

Pronoun-antecedent agreement refers to the need for the antecedent and the corresponding pronoun to agree in gender, person, and number. Here are some examples:

The *kidneys* (plural antecedent) are part of the urinary system. *They* (plural pronoun) serve several roles."

The kidneys are part of the *urinary system* (singular antecedent). *It* (singular pronoun) is also known as the renal system.

Pronoun Cases

The **subjective pronouns** —*I, you, he/she/it, we, they,* and *who*—are the subjects of the sentence.

Example: *They* have a new house.

The **objective pronouns**—*me, you* (*singular*), *him/her, us, them,* and *whom*—are used when something is being done for or given to someone; they are objects of the action.

Example: The teacher has an apple for *us.*

The **possessive pronouns**—*mine, my, your, yours, his, hers, its, their, theirs, our,* and *ours*—are used to denote that something (or someone) belongs to someone (or something).

Example: It's *their* chocolate cake.

Even Better Example: It's *my* chocolate cake!

One of the greatest challenges and worst abuses of pronouns concerns *who* and *whom.* Just knowing the following rule can eliminate confusion. *Who* is a subjective-case pronoun used only as a subject or subject complement. *Whom* is only objective-case and, therefore, the object of the verb or preposition.

Who is going to the concert?

You are going to the concert with *whom*?

Hint: When using *who* or *whom,* think of whether someone would say *he* or *him.* If the answer is *he,* use *who.* If the answer is *him,* use *whom.* This trick is easy to remember because *he* and *who* both end in vowels, and *him* and *whom* both end in the letter *M.*

Many possessive pronouns sound like contractions. For example, many people get *it's* and *its* confused. The word *it's* is the contraction for *it is.* The word *its* without an apostrophe is the possessive form of *it.*

I love that wooden desk. It's beautiful. (contraction)

I love that wooden desk. Its glossy finish is beautiful. (possessive)

If you are not sure which version to use, replace *it's/its* with *it is* and see if that sounds correct. If so, use the contraction (*it's*). That trick also works for *who's/whose, you're/your,* and *they're/their.*

Adjectives
"The *extraordinary* brain is the *main* organ of the central nervous system." The adjective *extraordinary* describes the brain in a way that causes one to realize it is more exceptional than some of the other organs while the adjective *main* defines the brain's importance in its system.

An **adjective** is a word or phrase that names an attribute that describes or clarifies a noun or pronoun. This helps the reader visualize and understand the characteristics—size, shape, age, color, origin, etc.—of a person, place, or thing that otherwise might not be known. Adjectives breathe life, color, and depth into the subjects they define. Life would be *drab* and *colorless* without adjectives!

Adjectives often precede the nouns they describe.

She drove her <u>new</u> car.

However, adjectives can also come later in the sentence.

Her car is <u>new</u>.

207

Adjectives using the prefix *a–* can only be used after a verb.

Correct: The dog was *alive* until the car ran up on the curb and hit him.

Incorrect: The *alive* dog was hit by a car that ran up on the curb.

Other examples of this rule include *awake, ablaze, ajar, alike,* and *asleep.*

Other adjectives used after verbs concern states of health.

The girl was finally *well* after a long bout of pneumonia.

The boy was *fine* after the accident.

An adjective phrase is not a bunch of adjectives strung together, but a group of words that describes a noun or pronoun and, thus, functions as an adjective. Very happy is an adjective phrase; so are way too hungry and passionate about traveling.

Possessives

In grammar, **possessive nouns** and **possessive pronouns** show ownership.

Singular nouns are generally made possessive with an apostrophe and an *s* (*'s*).

My *uncle's* new car is silver.

The *dog's* bowl is empty.

James's ties are becoming outdated.

Plural nouns ending in *s* are generally made possessive by just adding an apostrophe ('):

The pistachio nuts' saltiness is added during roasting. (The saltiness of pistachio nuts is added during roasting.)

The students' achievement tests are difficult. (The achievement tests of the students are difficult.)

If the plural noun does not end in an *s* such as *women,* then it is made possessive by adding an *apostrophe s* (*'s*)— *women's.*

Possessive pronouns can be first person (*mine*), second person (*yours*), or third person (*theirs*). Indefinite possessive pronouns such as *nobody* or *someone* become possessive by adding an *apostrophe s* to become *nobody's* or *someone's.*

Verbs

A **verb** is the part of speech that describes an action, state of being, or occurrence.

A verb forms the main part of a predicate of a sentence. This means that the verb explains what the noun (which will be discussed shortly) is doing. A simple example is *time <u>flies</u>.* The verb *flies* explains what the action of the noun, *time,* is doing. This example is a *main* verb.

Helping (auxiliary) verbs are words like *have, do, be, can, may, should, must,* and *will.* "I *should* go to the store." Helping verbs assist main verbs in expressing tense, ability, possibility, permission, or obligation.

Particles are minor function words like *not, in, out, up,* or *down* that become part of the verb itself. "I might *not.*"

Participles are words formed from verbs that are often used to modify a noun, noun phrase, verb, or verb phrase.

The *running* teenager collided with the cyclist.

Participles can also create compound verb forms.

He is *speaking*.

Participial phrases are made up of the participle and modifiers, complements, or objects.

Crying for most of an hour, the baby didn't seem to want to nap.

Having already taken this course, the student was bored during class.

Verbs have five basic forms: the **base** form, the **-s** form, the **-ing** form, the **past** form, and the **past participle** form.

The past forms are either **regular** (*love/loved; hate/hated*) or **irregular** because they don't end by adding the common past tense suffix "-ed" (*go/went; fall/fell; set/set*).

Adverbs

Adverbs have more functions than adjectives because they modify or qualify verbs, adjectives, or other adverbs as well as word groups that express a relation of place, time, circumstance, or cause. Therefore, adverbs answer any of the following questions: *How, when, where, why, in what way, how often, how much, in what condition*, and/or *to what degree. How good looking is he? He is* <u>very</u> *handsome.*

Here are some examples of adverbs for different situations:

- how: quickly
- when: daily
- where: there
- in what way: easily
- how often: often
- how much: much
- in what condition: badly
- what degree: hardly

As one can see, for some reason, many adverbs end in *-ly*.

Adverbs do things like emphasize (*really, simply,* and *so*), amplify (*heartily, completely,* and *positively*), and tone down (*almost, somewhat,* and *mildly*).

Adverbs also come in phrases.

The dog ran as <u>though his life depended on it.</u>

Prepositions

Prepositions are connecting words and, while there are only about 150 of them, they are used more often than any other individual groups of words. They describe relationships between other words. They are placed before a noun or pronoun, forming a phrase that modifies another word in the sentence. **Prepositional phrases** begin with a preposition and end with a noun or pronoun, the **object of the preposition.** *A pristine lake is <u>near the store</u> and <u>behind the bank</u>.*

Some commonly used prepositions are *about, after, anti, around, as, at, behind, beside, by, for, from, in, into, of, off, on, to,* and *with.*

Complex prepositions, which also come before a noun or pronoun, consist of two or three words such as *according to, in regards to,* and *because of.*

Interjections

Interjections are words used to express emotion. Examples include *wow, ouch,* and *hooray.* Interjections are often separate from sentences; in those cases, the interjection is directly followed by an exclamation point. In other cases, the interjection is included in a sentence and followed by a comma. The punctuation plays a big role in the intensity of the emotion that the interjection is expressing. Using a comma or semicolon indicates less excitement than using an exclamation mark.

Conjunctions

Conjunctions are vital words that connect words, phrases, thoughts, and ideas. Conjunctions show relationships between components. There are two types:

Coordinating conjunctions are the primary class of conjunctions placed between words, phrases, clauses, and sentences that are of equal grammatical rank; the coordinating conjunctions are *for, and, nor, but, or, yet,* and *so.* A useful memorization trick is to remember that all the first letters of these conjunctions collectively spell the word fanboys.

> I need to go shopping, *but* I must be careful to leave enough money in the bank.

> She wore a black, red, *and* white shirt.

Subordinating conjunctions are the secondary class of conjunctions. They connect two unequal parts, one **main** (or **independent**) and the other **subordinate** (or **dependent**). I must go to the store *even though* I do not have enough money in the bank.

> *Because* I read the review, I do not want to go to the movie.

Notice that the presence of subordinating conjunctions makes clauses dependent. *I read the review* is an independent clause, but *because* makes the clause dependent. Thus, it needs an independent clause to complete the sentence.

Shifts in Construction

It's been said several times already that *good writing must be consistent.* Another common writing mistake occurs when the writer unintentionally shifts verb tense, voice, or noun-pronoun agreement. This shift can take place within a sentence, within a paragraph, or over the course of an entire piece of writing. On the test, questions may ask that this kind of error be identified. Here are some examples.

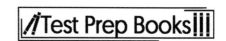

Shift in Verb Tense

Verb tense reflects when an action occurred or a state existed. For example, the tense known as **simple present** expresses something that is happening right now or that happens regularly:

> She *works* in a hospital.

Present continuous tense expresses something in progress. It is formed by to be + verb + -ing.

> Sorry, I can't go out right now. I *am doing* my homework.

Past tense is used to describe events that previously occurred. However, in conversational English, speakers often use present tense or a mix of past and present tense when relating past events because it gives the narrative a sense of immediacy. In formal written English, though, consistency in verb tense is necessary to avoid reader confusion.

> I traveled to Europe last summer. As soon as I stepped off the plane, I feel like I'm in a movie! I'm surrounded by quaint cafes and impressive architecture.

The passage above abruptly switches from past tense—*traveled, stepped*—to present tense—*feel, am surrounded*.

> I *traveled* to Europe last summer. As soon as I *stepped* off the plane, I *felt* like I was in a movie! I *was surrounded* by quaint cafes and impressive architecture.

All verbs are in past tense, so this passage now has consistent verb tense.

Shift in Voice

Sometimes the writer accidentally slips from active voice to passive voice in the middle of a sentence. This is a difficult mistake to catch because it's something people often do when speaking to one another. First, it's important to understand the difference between active and passive voice. Most sentences are written in **active voice**, which means that the noun is doing what the verb in the sentence says. For example:

> Seat belts save lives.

Here, the noun (*seat belt*) is doing the saving. However, in **passive voice**, the verb is doing something to the noun:

> Lives are saved.

In this case, the noun (*lives*) is the thing *being saved*. Passive voice is difficult for many people to identify and understand, but there's a simple (and memorable) way to check: simply add "by zombies" to the end of the verb and, if it makes sense, then the verb is written in passive voice. For example: "My car was wrecked...by zombies." Also, in the above example, "Lives are saved...by zombies." If the zombie trick doesn't work, then the sentence is in active voice.

Here's what a shift in voice looks like in a sentence:

> When Amy buckled her seat belt, a satisfying click was heard.

The writer shifts from active voice in the beginning of the sentence to passive voice after the comma (remember, "a satisfying click was heard...by zombies"). To fix this mistake, the writer must remain in active voice throughout:

> When Amy buckled her seat belt, she heard a satisfying click.

This sentence is now grammatically correct, easier to read...and zombie free!

Shift in Noun-Pronoun Agreement

Pronouns are used to replace nouns so sentences don't have a lot of unnecessary repetition. This repetition can make a sentence seem awkward as in the following example:

> Seat belts are important because seat belts save lives, but seat belts can't do so unless seat belts are used.

Replacing some of the nouns (*seat belts*) with a pronoun (*they*) improves the flow of the sentence:

> Seat belts are important because they save lives, but they can't do so unless they are used.

A pronoun should agree in number (singular or plural) with the noun that precedes it. Another common writing error is the shift in **noun-pronoun agreement**. Here's an example:

> When people are getting in a car, he should always remember to buckle his seatbelt.

The first half of the sentence talks about a plural (*people*), while the second half refers to a singular person (*he* and *his*). These don't agree, so the sentence should be rewritten as:

> When people are getting in a car, they should always remember to buckle their seatbelt.

Split Infinitives

The **infinitive form** of a verb consists of "to + base verb"—e.g., to walk, to sleep, to approve. A **split infinitive** occurs when another word, usually an adverb, is placed between *to* and the verb:

> I decided *to simply walk* to work to get more exercise every day.

The infinitive *to walk* is split by the adverb *simply*.

> It was a mistake *to hastily approve* the project before conducting further preliminary research.

The infinitive *to approve* is split by *hastily*.

Although some grammarians still advise against split infinitives, this syntactic structure is common in both spoken and written English and is widely accepted in standard usage.

Pronouns

Pronoun Person

Pronoun person refers to the narrative voice the writer uses in a piece of writing. A great deal of nonfiction is written in third person, which uses pronouns like *he, she, it,* and *they* to convey meaning. Occasionally a writer uses first person (*I, me, we,* etc.) or second person (*you*). Any choice of pronoun person can be appropriate for a particular situation, but the writer must remain consistent and logical.

Test questions may cover examining samples that should stay in a single pronoun person, be it first, second, or third. Look out for shifts between words like *you* and *I* or *he* and *they*.

Pronoun Clarity

Pronouns always refer back to a noun. However, as the writer composes longer, more complicated sentences, the reader may be unsure which noun the pronoun should replace. For example:

> An amendment was made to the bill, but now it has been voted down.

212

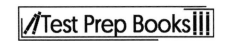

Was the amendment voted down or the entire bill? It's impossible to tell from this sentence. To correct this error, the writer needs to restate the appropriate noun rather than using a pronoun:

An amendment was made to the bill, but now the bill has been voted down.

Pronouns in Combination

Writers often make mistakes when choosing pronouns to use in combination with other nouns. The most common mistakes are found in sentences like this:

Please join Senator Wilson and I at the event tomorrow.

Notice anything wrong? Though many people think the sentence sounds perfectly fine, the use of the pronoun *I* is actually incorrect. To double-check this, take the other person out of the sentence:

Please join I at the event tomorrow.

Now the sentence is obviously incorrect, as it should read, "Please join *me* at the event tomorrow." Thus, the first sentence should replace *I* with *me*:

Please join Senator Wilson and me at the event tomorrow.

For many people, this sounds wrong because they're used to hearing and saying it incorrectly. Take extra care when answering this kind of question and follow the double-checking procedure.

Agreement

In English writing, certain words connect to other words. People often learn these connections (or **agreements**) as young children and use the correct combinations without a second thought. However, the questions on the test dealing with agreement probably aren't simple ones.

Subject-Verb Agreement

Which of the following sentences is correct?

A large crowd of protesters was on hand.

A large crowd of protesters were on hand.

Many people would say the second sentence is correct, but they'd be wrong. However, they probably wouldn't be alone. Most people just look at two words: *protesters were*. Together they make sense. They sound right. The problem is that the verb *were* doesn't refer to the word *protesters*. Here, the word *protesters* is part of a prepositional phrase that clarifies the actual subject of the sentence (*crowd*). Take the phrase "of protesters" away and re-examine the sentences:

A large crowd was on hand.

A large crowd were on hand.

Without the prepositional phrase to separate the subject and verb, the answer is obvious. The first sentence is correct. On the test, look for confusing prepositional phrases when answering questions about subject-verb agreement. Take the phrase away, and then recheck the sentence.

Noun Agreement

Nouns that refer to other nouns must also match in number. Take the following example:

John and Emily both served as an intern for Senator Wilson.

Two people are involved in this sentence: John and Emily. Therefore, the word *intern* should be plural to match. Here is how the sentence should read:

John and Emily both served as interns for Senator Wilson.

Frequently Confused Words

The English language is interesting because many of its words sound so similar or identical that they confuse readers and writers alike. Errors involving these words are hard to spot because they *sound* right even when they're wrong. Also, because these mistakes are so pervasive, many people think they're correct. Here are a few examples that may be encountered on the test:

They're vs. Their vs. There

This set of words is probably the all-time winner of misuse. The word *they're* is a contraction of "they are." Remember that contractions combine two words, using an apostrophe to replace any eliminated letters. If a question asks whether the writer is using the word *they're* correctly, change the word to "they are" and reread the sentence. Look at the following example:

Legislators can be proud of they're work on this issue.

This sentence *sounds* correct, but replace the contraction *they're* with "they are" to see what happens:

Legislators can be proud of they are work on this issue.

The result doesn't make sense, which shows that it's an incorrect use of the word *they're*. Did the writer mean to use the word *their* instead? The word *their* indicates possession because it shows that something *belongs* to something else. Now put the word *their* into the sentence:

Legislators can be proud of their work on this issue.

To check the answer, find the word that comes right after the word *their* (which in this case is *work*). Pose this question: whose *work* is it? If the question can be answered in the sentence, then the word signifies possession. In the sentence above, it's the legislators' work. Therefore, the writer is using the word *their* correctly.

If the words *they're* and *their* don't make sense in the sentence, then the correct word is almost always *there*. The word *there* can be used in many different ways, so it's easy to remember to use it when *they're* and *their* don't work. Now test these methods with the following sentences:

Their going to have a hard time passing these laws.

Enforcement officials will have there hands full.

They're are many issues to consider when discussing car safety.

In the first sentence, asking the question "Whose going is it?" doesn't make sense. Thus the word *their* is wrong. However, when replaced with the conjunction *they're* (or *they are*), the sentence works. Thus the correct word for the first sentence should be *they're*.

In the second sentence, ask this question: "Whose hands are full?" The answer (*enforcement officials*) is correct in the sentence. Therefore, the word *their* should replace *there* in this sentence.

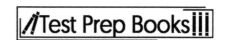

In the third sentence, changing the word *they're* to "they are" ("They are are many issues") doesn't make sense. Ask this question: "Whose are is it?" This makes even less sense, since neither of the words *they're* or *their* makes sense. Therefore, the correct word must be *there*.

Who's vs. Whose

Who's is a contraction of "who is" while the word *whose* indicates possession. Look at the following sentence:

Who's job is it to protect America's drivers?

The easiest way to check for correct usage is to replace the word *who's* with "who is" and see if the sentence makes sense:

Who is job is it to protect America's drivers?

By changing the contraction to "Who is" the sentence no longer makes sense. Therefore, the correct word must be *whose*.

Your vs. You're

The word *your* indicates possession, while *you're* is a contraction for "you are." Look at the following example:

Your going to have to write your congressman if you want to see action.

Again, the easiest way to check correct usage is to replace the word *Your* with "You are" and see if the sentence still makes sense.

You are going to have to write your congressman if you want to see action.

By replacing Your with "You are," the sentence still makes sense. Thus, in this case, the writer should have used "You're."

Its vs. It's

Its is a word that indicates possession, while the word *it's* is a contraction of "it is." Once again, the easiest way to check for correct usage is to replace the word with "it is" and see if the sentence makes sense. Look at the following sentence:

It's going to take a lot of work to pass this law.

Replacing *it's* with "it is" results in this: "It is going to take a lot of work to pass this law." This makes sense, so the contraction (*it's*) is correct. Now look at another example:

The car company will have to redesign it's vehicles.

Replacing *it's* with "it is" results in this: "The car company will have to redesign it is vehicles." This sentence doesn't make sense, so the contraction (*it's*) is incorrect.

Than vs. Then

Than is used in sentences that involve comparisons, while *then* is used to indicate an order of events. Consider the following sentence:

Japan has more traffic fatalities than the U.S.

The use of the word *than* is correct because it compares Japan to the U.S. Now look at another example:

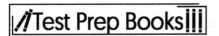

Laws must be passed, and then we'll see a change in behavior.

Here the use of the word *then* is correct because one thing happens after the other.

Affect vs. Effect
Affect is a verb that means to change something, while *effect* is a noun that indicates such a change. Look at the following sentence:

There are thousands of people affected by the new law.

This sentence is correct because *affected* is a verb that tells what's happening. Now look at this sentence:

The law will have a dramatic effect.

This sentence is also correct because *effect* is a noun and the thing that happens.

Note that a noun version of *affect* is occasionally used. It means "emotion" or "desire," usually in a psychological sense.

Two vs. Too vs. To
Two is the number (2). *Too* refers to an amount of something, or it can mean *also*. *To* is used for everything else. Look at the following sentence:

Two senators still haven't signed the bill.

This is correct because there are *two* (2) senators. Here's another example:

There are too many questions about this issue.

In this sentence, the word *too* refers to an amount ("too many questions"). Now here's another example:

Senator Wilson is supporting this legislation, too.

In this sentence, the word *also* can be substituted for the word *too*, so it's also correct. Finally, one last example:

I look forward to signing this bill into law.

In this sentence, the tests for *two* and *too* don't work. Thus the word *to* fits the bill!

Other Common Writing Confusions
In addition to all of the above, there are other words that writers often misuse. This doesn't happen because the words sound alike, but because the writer is not aware of the proper way to use them.

Logical Comparison
Writers often make comparisons in their writing. However, it's easy to make mistakes in sentences that involve comparisons, and those mistakes are difficult to spot. Try to find the error in the following sentence:

Senator Wilson's proposed seat belt legislation was similar to Senator Abernathy.

Can't find it? First, ask what two things are actually being compared. It seems like the writer *wants* to compare two different types of legislation, but the sentence actually compares legislation ("Senator Wilson's proposed seat belt legislation") to a person ("Senator Abernathy"). This is a strange and illogical comparison to make.

So how can the writer correct this mistake? The answer is to make sure that the second half of the sentence logically refers back to the first half. The most obvious way to do this is to repeat words:

> Senator Wilson's proposed seat belt legislation was similar to Senator Abernathy's seat belt legislation.

Now the sentence is logically correct, but it's a little wordy and awkward. A better solution is to eliminate the word-for-word repetition by using suitable replacement words:

> Senator Wilson's proposed seat belt legislation was similar to that of Senator Abernathy.

> Senator Wilson's proposed seat belt legislation was similar to the bill offered by Senator Abernathy.

Here's another similar example:

> More lives in the U.S. are saved by seat belts than Japan.

The writer probably means to compare lives saved by seat belts in the U.S. to lives saved by seat belts in Japan. Unfortunately, the sentence's meaning is garbled by an illogical comparison, and instead refers to U.S. lives saved *by Japan* rather than *in Japan.* To resolve this issue, first repeat the words and phrases needed to make an identical comparison:

> More lives in the U.S. are saved by seat belts than lives in Japan are saved by seat belts.

Then, use a replacement word to clean up the repetitive text:

> More lives in the U.S. are saved by seat belts than in Japan.

Capitalization
Capitalize the first word in a sentence and the first word in a quotation:

> The realtor showed them the house.

> Robert asked, "When can we get together for dinner again?"

- Capitalize proper nouns and words derived from them:

  > We are visiting Germany in a few weeks.

  > We will stay with our German relatives on our trip.

- Capitalize days of the week, months of the year, and holidays:

  > The book club meets the last Thursday of every month.

  > The baby is due in June.

  > I decided to throw a Halloween party this year.

- Capitalize the main words in titles (referred to as *title case*), but not the articles, conjunctions, or prepositions:

  > *A Raisin in the Sun*

  > *To Kill a Mockingbird*

- Capitalize directional words that are used as names, but not when referencing a direction:

  The North won the Civil War.

  After making a left, go north on Rt. 476.

  She grew up on the West Coast.

  The winds came in from the west.

- Capitalize titles that go with names:

  Mrs. McFadden   Sir Alec Guinness   Lt. Madeline Suarez

- Capitalize familial relationships when referring to a *specific* person:

  I worked for my Uncle Steven last summer.

  Did you work for your uncle last summer?

Idiomatic Usage

A **figure of speech** (sometimes called an **idiom**) is a rhetorical device. It's a phrase that is not intended to be taken literally.

When the writer uses a figure of speech, their intention must be clear if it's to be used effectively. Some phrases can be interpreted in a number of ways, causing confusion for the reader. Look for clues to the writer's true intention to determine the best replacement. Likewise, some figures of speech may seem out of place in a more formal piece of writing. To show this, here is another example involving seat belts:

Seat belts save more lives than any other automobile safety feature. Many studies show that airbags save lives as well, however not all cars have airbags. For example, some older cars don't. In addition, air bags aren't entirely reliable. For example, studies show that in 15 percent of accidents, airbags don't deploy as designed, but, on the other hand, seat belt malfunctions happen once in a blue moon.

Most people know that "once in a blue moon" refers to something that rarely happens. However, because the rest of the paragraph is straightforward and direct, using this figurative phrase distracts the reader. In this example, the earlier version is much more effective.

Now it's important to take a moment and review the meaning of the word *literally*. This is because it's one of the most misunderstood and misused words in the English language. *Literally* means that something is exactly what it says it is, and there can be no interpretation or exaggeration. Unfortunately, *literally* is often used for emphasis as in the following example:

This morning, I literally couldn't get out of bed.

This sentence meant to say that the person was extremely tired and wasn't able to get up. However, the sentence can't *literally* be true unless that person was tied down to the bed, paralyzed, or affected by a strange situation that the writer (most likely) didn't intend. Here's another example:

I literally died laughing.

The writer tried to say that something was very funny. However, unless they're writing this from beyond the grave, it can't *literally* be true.

Note that this doesn't mean that writers can't use figures of speech. The colorful use of language and idioms make writing more interesting and draw in the reader. However, for these kinds of expressions to be used correctly, they cannot include the word *literally*.

Punctuation

Commas

A **comma** (,) is the punctuation mark that signifies a pause—breath—between parts of a sentence. It denotes a break of flow. As with so many aspects of writing structure, authors will benefit by memorizing all of the different ways in which commas can be used so as not to abuse them.

In a complex sentence—one that contains a subordinate (dependent) clause or clauses—the use of a comma is dictated by where the subordinate clause is located. If the subordinate clause is located before the main clause, a comma is needed between the two clauses.

> I will not pay for the steak, *because I don't have that much money.*

Generally, if the subordinate clause is placed after the main clause, no punctuation is needed.

> I did well on my exam because I studied two hours the night before.

Notice how the last clause is dependent because it earlier independent clauses to make sense.

Use a comma on both sides of an interrupting phrase.

> I will pay for the ice cream, *chocolate and vanilla*, and then will eat it all myself.

The words forming the phrase in italics are nonessential (extra) information. To determine if a phrase is nonessential, try reading the sentence without the phrase and see if it's still coherent.

A comma is not necessary in this next sentence because no interruption—nonessential or extra information—has occurred. Read sentences aloud when uncertain.

I will pay for his chocolate and vanilla ice cream and then will eat it all myself.

If the nonessential phrase comes at the beginning of a sentence, a comma should only go at the end of the phrase. If the phrase comes at the end of a sentence, a comma should only go at the beginning of the phrase.

Other types of interruptions include the following:

- interjections: Oh no, I am not going.
- abbreviations: Barry Potter, M.D., specializes in heart disorders.
- direct addresses: Yes, Claudia, I am tired and going to bed.
- parenthetical phrases: His wife, lovely as she was, was not helpful.
- transitional phrases: Also, it is not possible.

The second comma in the following sentence is called an Oxford comma.

> I will pay for ice cream, syrup, and pop.

It is a comma used after the second-to-last item in a series of three or more items. It comes before the word *or* or *and*. Not everyone uses the Oxford comma; it is optional, but many believe it is needed. The comma functions as a tool to reduce confusion in writing. So, if omitting the Oxford comma would cause confusion, then it's best to include it.

Commas are used in math to mark the place of thousands in numerals, breaking them up so they are easier to read. Other uses for commas are in dates (*March 19, 2016*), letter greetings (*Dear Sally,*), and in between cities and states (*Louisville, KY*).

Apostrophes

This punctuation mark, the apostrophe ('), is a versatile little mark. It has a few different functions:

- Quotes: Apostrophes are used when a second quote is needed within a quote.

- In my letter to my friend, I wrote, "The girl had to get a new purse, and guess what Mary did? She said, 'I'd like to go with you to the store.' I knew Mary would buy it for her."

- Contractions: Another use for an apostrophe in the quote above is a contraction. *I'd* is used for *I would*.

  The basic rule for making *contractions* is one area of spelling that is pretty straightforward: combine the two words by inserting an apostrophe (') in the space where a letter is omitted. For example, to combine *you* and *are*, drop the *a* and put the apostrophe in its place: *you're*.

    he + is = he's

    you + all = y'all (informal but often misspelled)

- Possession: An apostrophe followed by the letter *s* shows possession (*Mary's* purse). If the possessive word is plural, the apostrophe generally just follows the word.

- The trees' leaves are all over the ground.

Ellipses

An **ellipsis** (...) is used to show that there is more to the quoted text than is necessary for the current discussion. Writers use them in place of words, lines, phrases, list content, or paragraphs that might just as easily have been omitted from a passage of writing. This can be done to save space or to focus only on the specifically relevant material.

    Exercise is good for some unexpected reasons. Watkins writes, "Exercise has many benefits such as...reducing cancer risk."

In the example above, the ellipsis takes the place of the other benefits of exercise that are more expected.

The ellipsis may also be used to show a pause in sentence flow.

    "I'm wondering...how this could happen," Dylan said in a soft voice.

Semicolons

The **semicolon** (;) might be described as a heavy-handed comma. Take a look at these two examples:

    I will pay for the ice cream, but I will not pay for the steak.
    I will pay for the ice cream; I will not pay for the steak.

What's the difference? The first example has a comma and a conjunction separating the two independent clauses. The second example does not have a conjunction, but there are two independent clauses in the sentence, so something more than a comma is required. In this case, a semicolon is used.

Two independent clauses can only be joined in a sentence by either a comma and conjunction or a semicolon. If one of those tools is not used, the sentence will be a run-on. Remember that while the clauses are independent, they need to be closely related in order to be contained in one sentence.

Another use for the semicolon is to separate items in a list when the items themselves require commas.

> The family lived in Phoenix, Arizona; Oklahoma City, Oklahoma; and Raleigh, North Carolina.

Colons

Colons (:) have many miscellaneous functions. Colons can be used to precede further information or a list. In these cases, a colon should only follow an independent clause.

> Humans take in sensory information through five basic senses: sight, hearing, smell, touch, and taste.

The meal includes the following components:

- Caesar salad
- spaghetti
- garlic bread
- cake

Colons can also be used to introduce an appositive.

> The family got what they needed: a reliable vehicle.

While a comma is more common, a colon can also precede a formal quotation.

> He said to the crowd: "Let's begin!"

The colon is used after the greeting in a formal letter.

> Dear Sir:
> To Whom It May Concern:

In the writing of time, the colon separates the minutes from the hour (*4:45 p.m.*). The colon can also be used to indicate a ratio between two numbers (*50:1*).

Hyphens

The **hyphen** (-) is a small dash mark that can be used to join words to show that they are linked.

Hyphens can connect two words that work together as a single adjective (a compound adjective).

> honey-covered biscuits

Some words always require hyphens even if not serving as an adjective.

> merry-go-round

Hyphens always go after certain prefixes like *anti-* & *all-*.

Hyphens should also be used when the absence of the hyphen would cause a strange vowel combination (*semi-engineer*) or confusion. For example, *re-collect* should be used to describe something being gathered twice rather than being written as *recollect*, which means to remember.

Parentheses and Dashes

Parentheses are half-round brackets that look like this: ( ). They set off a word, phrase, or sentence that is an afterthought, explanation, or side note relevant to the surrounding text but not essential. A pair of commas is often used to set off this sort of information, but parentheses are generally used for information that would not fit well within a sentence or that the writer deems not important enough to be structurally part of the sentence.

> The picture of the heart (see above) shows the major parts you should memorize.
> Mount Everest is one of three mountains in the world that are over 28,000 feet high (K2 and Kanchenjunga are the other two).

See how the sentences above are complete without the parenthetical statements? In the first example, *see above* would not have fit well within the flow of the sentence. The second parenthetical statement could have been a separate sentence, but the writer deemed the information not pertinent to the topic.

The **em-dash** (—) is a mark longer than a hyphen used as a punctuation mark in sentences and to set apart a relevant thought. Even after plucking out the line separated by the dash marks, the sentence will be intact and make sense.

> Looking out the airplane window at the landmarks—Lake Clarke, Thompson Community College, and the bridge—she couldn't help but feel excited to be home.

The dashes use is similar to that of parentheses or a pair of commas. So, what's the difference? Many believe that using dashes makes the clause within them stand out while using parentheses is subtler. It's advised to not use dashes when commas could be used instead.

Quotation Marks

Quotation marks ("") are used in a number of ways. Here are some instances where quotation marks should be used: to indicate a quote that was taken from somewhere else, either from a verbal or written source...

- Dialogue for characters in narratives. When characters speak, the first word should always be capitalized, and the punctuation goes inside the quotes. For example:

  > Janie said, "The tree fell on my car during the hurricane."

- Around titles of songs, short stories, essays, and chapter in books
- To emphasize a certain word
- To refer to a word as the word itself

Capitalization Rules

Here's a non-exhaustive list of things that should be capitalized:

- The first word of every sentence
- The first word of every line of poetry
- The first letter of proper nouns (World War II)
- Holidays (Valentine's Day)
- The days of the week and months of the year (Tuesday, March)
- The first word, last word, and all major words in the titles of books, movies, songs, and other creative works (In the novel, *To Kill a Mockingbird*, note that *a* is lowercase since it's not a major word, but *to* is capitalized since it's the first word of the title.)
- Titles when preceding a proper noun (President Roberto Gonzales, Aunt Judy)

When simply using a word such as president or secretary, though, the word is not capitalized.

> Officers of the new business must include a *president* and *treasurer*.

Seasons—spring, fall, etc.—are not capitalized.

North, *south*, *east*, and *west* are capitalized when referring to regions but are not when being used for directions. In general, if it's preceded by *the* it should be capitalized.

> I'm from the South.
> I drove south.

Homonyms

Homonyms are words that sound the same but are spelled differently, and they have different meanings. There are several common homonyms that give writers trouble.

There, They're, and *Their*

The word *there* can be used as an adverb, adjective, or pronoun:

> *There* are ten children on the swim team this summer.

> I put my book over *there*, but now I can't find it.

The word *they're* is a contraction of the words *they* and *are*:

> *They're* flying in from Texas on Tuesday.

The word *their* is a possessive pronoun:

> I store *their* winter clothes in the attic.

Its and *It's*

Its is a possessive pronoun:

> The cat licked *its* injured paw.

It's is the contraction for the words *it* and *is*:

> *It's* unbelievable how many people opted not to vote in the last election.

Your and You're

Your is a possessive pronoun:

> Can I borrow *your* lawnmower this weekend?

You're is a contraction for the words *you* and *are*:

> *You're* about to embark on a fantastic journey.

To, Too, and *Two*

To is an adverb or a preposition used to show direction, relationship, or purpose:

> We are going *to* New York.

> They are going *to* see a show.

223

Too is an adverb that means more than enough, also, and very:

> You have had *too* much candy.

> We are on vacation that week, *too*.

Two is the written-out form of the numeral 2:

> *Two* of the shirts didn't fit, so I will have to return them.

New and *Knew*

New is an adjective that means recent:

> There's a *new* customer on the phone.

Knew is the past tense of the verb *know*:

> I *knew* you'd have fun on this ride.

Affect and *Effect*

Affect and *effect* are complicated because they are used as both nouns and verbs, have similar meanings, and are pronounced the same.

	Affect	Effect
Noun Definition	emotional state	result
Noun Example	The patient's affect was flat.	The effects of smoking are well documented.
Verb Definition	to influence	to bring about
Verb Example	The pollen count affects my allergies.	The new candidate hopes to effect change.

Independent and Dependent Clauses

Independent and *dependent* clauses are strings of words that contain both a subject and a verb. An independent clause *can* stand alone as complete thought, but a dependent clause *cannot*. A dependent clause relies on other words to be a complete sentence.

> Independent clause: The keys are on the counter.
> Dependent clause: If the keys are on the counter

Notice that both clauses have a subject (*keys*) and a verb (*are*). The independent clause expresses a complete thought, but the word *if* at the beginning of the dependent clause makes it *dependent* on other words to be a complete thought.

> Independent clause: If the keys are on the counter, please give them to me.

This example constitutes a complete sentence since it includes at least one verb and one subject and is a complete thought. In this case, the independent clause has two subjects (*keys* & an implied *you*) and two verbs (*are* & *give*).

> Independent clause: I went to the store.
> Dependent clause: Because we are out of milk,
> Complete Sentence: Because we are out of milk, I went to the store.
> Complete Sentence: I went to the store because we are out of milk.

Phrases

A *phrase* is a group of words that do not make a complete thought or a clause. They are parts of sentences or clauses. Phrases can be used as nouns, adjectives, or adverbs. A phrase does not contain both a subject and a verb.

Prepositional Phrases

A *prepositional phrase* shows the relationship between a word in the sentence and the object of the preposition. The object of the preposition is a noun that follows the preposition.

> The orange pillows are on the couch.

On is the preposition, and *couch* is the object of the preposition.

> She brought her friend with the nice car.

With is the preposition, and *car* is the object of the preposition. Here are some common prepositions:

about	as	at	after
by	for	from	in
of	on	to	with

Verbals and Verbal Phrases

Verbals are forms of verbs that act as other parts of speech. They can be used as nouns, adjectives, or adverbs. Though they are verb forms, they are not to be used as the verb in the sentence. A word group that is based on a verbal is considered a *verbal phrase*. There are three major types of verbals: *participles, gerunds,* and *infinitives.*

Participles are verbals that act as adjectives. The present participle ends in –*ing,* and the past participle ends in –*d, -ed, -n, or-t.*

Verb	**Present Participle**	**Past Participle**
walk	walking	walked
share	sharing	shared

Participial phrases are made up of the participle and modifiers, complements, or objects.

> Crying for most of an hour, the baby didn't seem to want to nap.

> Having already taken this course, the student was bored during class.

> *Crying for most of an hour* and *Having already taken this course* are the participial phrases.

Gerunds are verbals that are used as nouns and end in –*ing.* A gerund can be the subject or object of the sentence like a noun. Note that a present participle can also end in –*ing,* so it is important to distinguish between the two. The gerund is used as a noun, while the participle is used as an adjective.

> Swimming is my favorite sport.

> I wish I were sleeping.

A *gerund phrase* includes the gerund and any modifiers or complements, direct objects, indirect objects, or pronouns.

Cleaning the house is my least favorite weekend activity.

Cleaning the house is the gerund phrase acting as the subject of the sentence.

The most important goal this year is raising money for charity.

Raising money for charity is the gerund phrase acting as the direct object.

The police accused the woman of stealing the car.

The *gerund* phrase *stealing the car* is the object of the preposition in this sentence.

An *infinitive* is a verbal made up of the word to and a verb. Infinitives can be used as nouns, adjectives, or adverbs.

Examples: To eat, to jump, to swim, to lie, to call, to work

An *infinitive phrase* is made up of the infinitive plus any complements or modifiers. The infinitive phrase *to wait* is used as the subject in this sentence:

To wait was not what I had in mind.

The infinitive phrase *to sing* is used as the subject complement in this sentence:

Her dream is to sing.

The infinitive phrase *to grow* is used as an adverb in this sentence:

Children must eat to grow.

Appositive Phrases

An *appositive* is a noun or noun phrase that renames a noun that comes immediately before it in the sentence. An appositive can be a single word or several words. These phrases can be *essential* or *nonessential*. An essential appositive phrase is necessary to the meaning of the sentence and a nonessential appositive phrase is not. It is important to be able to distinguish these for purposes of comma use.

Essential: My sister Christina works at a school.

Naming which sister is essential to the meaning of the sentence, so no commas are needed.

Nonessential: My sister, who is a teacher, is coming over for dinner tonight.

Who is a teacher is not essential to the meaning of the sentence, so commas are required.

Absolute Phrases

An *absolute phrase* modifies a noun without using a conjunction. It is not the subject of the sentence and is not a complete thought on its own. Absolute phrases are set off from the independent clause with a comma.

Arms outstretched, she yelled at the sky.

All things considered, this has been a great day.

The Four Types of Sentence Structures

A *simple sentence* has one independent clause.

> I am going to win.

A *compound sentence* has two independent clauses. A conjunction—*for, and, nor, but, or, yet, so*—links them together. Note that each of the independent clauses has a subject and a verb.

> I am going to win, but the odds are against me.

A *complex sentence* has one independent clause and one or more dependent clauses.

> I am going to win, even though I don't deserve it.

Even though I don't deserve it is a dependent clause. It does not stand on its own. Some conjunctions that link an independent and a dependent clause are *although, because, before, after, that, when, which,* and *while*.

A *compound-complex sentence* has at least three clauses, two of which are independent and at least one that is a dependent clause.

> While trying to dance, I tripped over my partner's feet, but I regained my balance quickly.

> The dependent clause is *While trying to dance*.

Sentence Fragments

A *sentence fragment* is an incomplete sentence. An independent clause is made up of a subject and a predicate, and both are needed to make a complete sentence.

Sentence fragments often begin with relative pronouns (when, which), subordinating conjunctions (because, although) or gerunds (trying, being, seeing). They might be missing the subject or the predicate.

The most common type of fragment is the isolated dependent clause, which can be corrected by joining it to the independent clause that appears before or after the fragment:

> Fragment: While the cookies baked.

> Correction: While the cookies baked, we played cards. (We played cards while the cookies baked.)

Run-on Sentences

A *run-on sentence* is created when two independent clauses (complete thoughts) are joined without correct punctuation or a conjunction. Run-on sentences can be corrected in the following ways:

- Join the independent clauses with a comma and coordinating conjunction.

> Run-on: We forgot to return the library books we had to pay a fine.

> Correction: We forgot to return the library books, so we had to pay a fine.

- Join the independent clauses with a semicolon, dash, or colon when the clauses are closely related in meaning.

    Run-on: I had a salad for lunch every day this week I feel healthier already.

    Correction: I had a salad for lunch every day this week; I feel healthier already.

- Join the independent clauses with a *semicolon and a conjunctive adverb.*

    Run-on: We arrived at the animal shelter on time however the dog had already been adopted.

    Correction: We arrived at the animal shelter on time; however, the dog had already been adopted.

- Separate the independent clauses into two sentences *with a period.*

    Run-on: He tapes his favorite television show he never misses an episode.

    Correction: He tapes his favorite television show. He never misses an episode.

- *Rearrange the wording* of the sentence to create an independent clause and a dependent clause.

    Run-on: My wedding date is coming up I am getting more excited to walk down the aisle.

    Correction: As my wedding date approaches, I am getting more excited to walk down the aisle.

Dangling and Misplaced Modifiers

A *modifier* is a phrase that describes, alters, limits, or gives more information about a word in the sentence. The two most common issues are dangling and misplaced modifiers.

A *dangling modifier* is created when the phrase modifies a word that is not clearly stated in the sentence.

    Dangling modifier: Having finished dinner, the dishes were cleared from the table.

    Correction: Having finished dinner, Amy cleared the dishes from the table.

In the first sentence, *having finished dinner* appears to modify *the dishes*, which obviously can't finish dinner. The second sentence adds the subject *Amy*, to make it clear who has finished dinner.

    Dangling modifier: Hoping to improve test scores, all new books were ordered for the school.

    Correction: Hoping to improve test scores, administrators ordered all new books for the school.

    Without the subject *administrators*, it appears the books are hoping to improve test scores, which doesn't make sense.

Misplaced modifiers are placed incorrectly in the sentence, which can cause confusion. Compare these examples:

    Misplaced modifier: Rory purchased a new flat screen television and placed it on the wall above the fireplace, with all the bells and whistles.

    Revised: Rory purchased a new flat screen television, with all the bells and whistles, and placed it on the wall above the fireplace.

The bells and whistles should modify the television, not the fireplace.

> Misplaced modifier: The delivery driver arrived late with the pizza, who was usually on time.

> Revised: The delivery driver, who usually was on time, arrived late with the pizza.

This suggests that the delivery driver was usually on time, instead of the pizza.

> Misplaced modifier: We saw a family of ducks on the way to church.

> Revised: On the way to church, we saw a family of ducks.

> The misplaced modifier, here, suggests the *ducks* were on their way to church, instead of the pronoun *we*.

Split Infinitives

An infinitive is made up of the word *to* and a verb, such as: to run, to jump, to ask. A *split infinitive* is created when a word comes between *to* and the verb.

> Split infinitive: To quickly run

> Correction: To run quickly

> Split infinitive: To quietly ask

> Correction: To ask quietly

Double Negatives

A *double negative* is a negative statement that includes two negative elements. This is incorrect in Standard English.

> Incorrect: She hasn't never come to my house to visit.

> Correct: She has never come to my house to visit.

The intended meaning is that she has never come to the house, so the double negative is incorrect. However, it is possible to use two negatives to create a positive statement.

> Correct: She was not unhappy with her performance on the quiz.

In this case, the double negative, *was not unhappy*, is intended to show a positive, so it is correct. This means that she was somewhat happy with her performance.

Faulty Parallelism

It is necessary to use parallel construction in sentences that have multiple similar ideas. Using parallel structure provides clarity in writing. *Faulty parallelism* is created when multiple ideas are joined using different sentence structures. Compare these examples:

> Incorrect: We start each practice with stretches, a run, and fielding grounders.
> Correct: We start each practice with stretching, running, and fielding grounders.

> Incorrect: I watched some television, reading my book, and fell asleep.
> Correct: I watched some television, read my book, and fell asleep.

229

Incorrect: *Some of the readiness skills for Kindergarten are to cut with scissors, to tie shoes, and dressing independently.*
Correct: *Some of the readiness skills for Kindergarten are being able to cut with scissors, to tie shoes, and to dress independently.*

Subordination

If multiple pieces of information in a sentence are not equal, they can be joined by creating an independent clause and a dependent clause. The less important information becomes the *subordinate clause*:

Draft: The hotel was acceptable. We wouldn't stay at the hotel again.

Revised: Though the hotel was acceptable, we wouldn't stay there again.

The more important information (*we wouldn't stay there again*) becomes the main clause, and the less important information (*the hotel was acceptable*) becomes the subordinate clause.

Context Clues

Context clues help readers understand unfamiliar words, and thankfully, there are many types.

Synonyms are words or phrases that have nearly, if not exactly, the same meaning as other words or phrases

Large boxes are needed to pack *big* items.

Antonyms are words or phrases that have opposite definitions. Antonyms, like synonyms, can serve as context clues, although more cryptically.

Large boxes are not needed to pack *small* items.

Definitions are sometimes included within a sentence to define uncommon words.

They practiced the *rumba*, a *type of dance*, for hours on end.

Explanations provide context through elaboration.

Large boxes holding items weighing over 60 pounds were stacked in the corner.

Contrast provides ways in which things are different.

These *minute* creatures were much different than the *huge* mammals that the zoologist was accustomed to dealing with.

Beware of Simplicity

Sometimes the answer may seem very simple. In this case, it's prudent to look more carefully at the question and the possible answer choices. Very brief answers aren't always correct, and the opposite may also be true. The goal is to read all the answer choices carefully, trying to rule out those that don't make sense.

Final Notes

It's best to read every answer choice before making a decision. While some answers may seem plausible, there may be others that are better choices. First instinct is usually right, but reading every answer is recommended. Caution should be taken in choosing an answer that "sounds right." Grammar rules can be tricky, and what sounds right may not be correct. It's best to rely on knowledge of grammar to choose the best answer. Ruling out incorrect responses can help narrow the choices down. Choosing between two choices (after reading them carefully) and selecting the answer that best matches the rules of Standard English is less overwhelming.

Practice Quiz

Read the selection about traveling in an RV and answer Questions 1-5.

(1) I have to admit that when my father bought a recreational vehicle (RV), I thought he was making a huge mistake. (2) I didn't really know anything about RVs, but I knew that my dad was as big a "city slicker" as there was. (3) In fact, I even thought he might have gone a little bit crazy. (4) On trips to the beach, he preferred to swim at the pool, and whenever he went hiking, he avoided touching any plants for fear that they might be poison ivy. (5) Why would this man, with an almost irrational fear of the outdoors, want a 40-foot camping behemoth?

(6) The RV was a great purchase for our family and brought us all closer together. (7) Every morning we would wake up, eat breakfast, and broke camp. (8) We laughed at our own comical attempts to back The Beast into spaces that seemed impossibly small. (9) We rejoiced as "hackers." (10) When things inevitably went wrong and we couldn't solve the problems on our own, we discovered the incredible helpfulness and friendliness of the RV community. (11) We even made some new friends in the process.

(12) Above all, it allowed us to share adventures. (13) While traveling across America, which we could not have experienced in cars and hotels. (14) Enjoying a campfire on a chilly summer evening with the mountains of Glacier National Park in the background, or waking up early in the morning to see the Sun rising over the distant spires of Arches National Park are memories that will always stay with me and our entire family.

1. Which of the following would be the best choice for this sentence?

   <u>In fact, I even thought he might have gone a little bit crazy.</u>

   a. Leave it where it is now.
   b. Move the sentence so that it comes before the preceding sentence.
   c. Move the sentence to the end of the first paragraph.
   d. Omit the sentence.

2. Which of the following would be the best choice for the underlined portion of Sentence 6 (reproduced below)?
   <u>The RV</u> was a great purchase for our family and brought us all closer together.
   a. NO CHANGE
   b. Not surprisingly, the RV
   c. Furthermore, the RV
   d. As it turns out, the RV

3. Which of the following would be the best choice for the underlined portion of Sentence 7 (reproduced below)?
   Every morning <u>we would wake up, eat breakfast, and broke camp.</u>
   a. NO CHANGE
   b. we would wake up, eat breakfast, and break camp.
   c. would we wake up, eat breakfast, and break camp?
   d. we are waking up, eating breakfast, and breaking camp.

4. Which of the following would be the best choice for Sentence 9 (reproduced below)?

We rejoiced as "hackers."

a. NO CHANGE

b. To a nagging problem of technology, we rejoiced as "hackers."

c. We rejoiced when we figured out how to "hack" a solution to a nagging technological problem.

d. To "hack" our way to a solution, we had to rejoice.

5. Which of the following would be the best choice for Sentences 12 and 13 (reproduced below)?

<u>Above all, it allowed us to share adventures. While traveling across America,</u> which we could not have experienced in cars and hotels.

a. NO CHANGE

b. Above all, it allowed us to share adventures while traveling across America

c. Above all, it allowed us to share adventures; while traveling across America

d. Above all, it allowed us to share adventures—while traveling across America

See answers on the next page.

Answer Explanations

1. B: For this question, the underlined sentence in each prospective choice's position. Leaving the sentence in place is incorrect because the father "going crazy" doesn't logically follow the fact that he was a "city slicker." Choice *C* is incorrect because the sentence in question is not a concluding sentence and does not transition smoothly into the second paragraph. Choice *D* is incorrect because the sentence doesn't necessarily need to be omitted since it logically follows the very first sentence in the passage.

2. D: Choice *D* is correct because "As it turns out" indicates a contrast from the previous sentiment, that the RV was a great purchase. Choice *A* is incorrect because the sentence needs an effective transition from the paragraph before. Choice *B* is incorrect because the text indicates it *is* surprising that the RV was a great purchase because the author was skeptical beforehand. Choice *C* is incorrect because the transition "furthermore" does not indicate a contrast.

3. B: This sentence calls for parallel structure. Choice *B* is correct because the verbs "wake," "eat," and "break" are consistent in tense and parts of speech. Choice *A* is incorrect because the words "wake" and "eat" are present tense while the word "broke" is in past tense. Choice *C* is incorrect because this turns the sentence into a question, which doesn't make sense within the context. Choice *D* is incorrect because it breaks tense with the rest of the passage. "Waking," "eating," and "breaking" are all present participles, and the context around the sentence is in past tense.

4. C: Choice *C* is correct because it is clear and fits within the context of the passage. Choice *A* is incorrect because it does not explain what was meant by "hackers" or why it was a cause for rejoicing. Choice *B* is incorrect because it does not mention a solution being found and is therefore not specific enough. Choice *D* is incorrect because the meaning is eschewed by the helping verb "had to rejoice," and the sentence suggests that rejoicing was necessary to "hack" a solution.

5. B: Choice *B* is correct because there is no punctuation needed if a dependent clause ("while traveling across America") is located behind the independent clause ("it allowed us to share adventures"). Choice *A* is incorrect because there are two dependent clauses connected and no independent clause, and a complete sentence requires at least one independent clause. Choice *C* is incorrect because of the same reason as Choice *A*. Semicolons have the same function as periods: there must be an independent clause on either side of the semicolon. Choice *D* is incorrect because the dash simply interrupts the complete sentence.

WriterPlacer (Written Essay)

Brainstorming

One of the most important steps in writing an essay is prewriting. Before drafting an essay, it's helpful to think about the topic for a moment or two, in order to gain a more solid understanding of the task. Then, spending about five minutes jotting down the immediate ideas that could work for the essay is recommended. It is a way to get some words on the page and offer a reference for ideas when drafting. Scratch paper is provided for writers to use any prewriting techniques such as webbing, free writing, or listing. The goal is to get ideas out of the mind and onto the page.

Considering Opposing Viewpoints

In the planning stage, it's important to consider all aspects of the topic, including different viewpoints on the subject. There are more than two ways to look at a topic, and a strong argument considers those opposing viewpoints. Considering opposing viewpoints can help writers present a fair, balanced, and informed essay that shows consideration for all readers. This approach can also strengthen an argument by recognizing and potentially refuting opposing viewpoint(s).

Drawing from personal experience may help to support ideas. For example, if the goal for writing is a personal narrative, then the story should come from the writer's own life. Many writers find it helpful to draw from personal experience, even in an essay that is not strictly narrative. Personal anecdotes or short stories can help to illustrate a point in other types of essays as well.

Moving from Brainstorming to Planning

Once the ideas are on the page, it's time to turn them into a solid plan for the essay. The best ideas from the brainstorming results can then be developed into a more formal outline. An outline typically has one main point (the thesis) and at least three sub-points that support the main point. Here's an example:

Main Idea

- Point #1
- Point #2
- Point #3

Of course, there will be details under each point, but this approach is the best for dealing with timed writing.

Staying on Track

Basing the essay on the outline aids in both organization and coherence. The goal is to ensure that there is enough time to develop each sub-point in the essay, roughly spending an equal amount of time on each idea. Keeping an eye on the time will help. If there are fifteen minutes left to draft the essay, then it makes sense to spend about 5 minutes on each of the ideas. Staying on task is critical to success, and timing out the parts of the essay can help writers avoid feeling overwhelmed.

Parts of the Essay

The *introduction* has to do a few important things:

- Establish the *topic* of the essay in original wording (i.e., not just repeating the prompt)
- Clarify the significance/importance of the topic or purpose for writing (not too many details, a brief overview)
- Offer a *thesis statement* that identifies the writer's own viewpoint on the topic (typically one-two brief sentences as a clear, concise explanation of the main point on the topic)

Body paragraphs reflect the ideas developed in the outline. Three-four points is probably sufficient for a short essay, and they should include the following:

- A *topic sentence* that identifies the sub-point (e.g., a reason why, a way how, a cause or effect)
- A detailed *explanation* of the point, explaining why the writer thinks this point is valid
- Illustrative examples, such as personal examples or real-world examples, that support and validate the point (i.e., "prove" the point)
- A *concluding sentence* that connects the examples, reasoning, and analysis to the point being made

The *conclusion*, or final paragraph, should be brief and should reiterate the focus, clarifying why the discussion is significant or important. It is important to avoid adding specific details or new ideas to this paragraph. The purpose of the conclusion is to sum up what has been said to bring the discussion to a close.

Don't Panic!

Writing an essay can be overwhelming, and performance panic is a natural response. The outline serves as a basis for the writing and helps to keep writers focused. Getting stuck can also happen, and it's helpful to remember that brainstorming can be done at any time during the writing process. Following the steps of the writing process is the best defense against writer's block.

Timed essays can be particularly stressful, but assessors are trained to recognize the necessary planning and thinking for these timed efforts. Using the plan above and sticking to it helps with time management. Timing each part of the process helps writers stay on track. Sometimes writers try to cover too much in their essays. If time seems to be running out, this is an opportunity to determine whether all of the ideas in the outline are necessary. Three body paragraphs are sufficient, and more than that is probably too much to cover in a short essay.

More isn't always *better* in writing. A strong essay will be clear and concise. It will avoid unnecessary or repetitive details. It is better to have a concise, five-paragraph essay that makes a clear point, than a ten-paragraph essay that doesn't. The goal is to write one-two pages of quality writing. Paragraphs should also reflect balance; if the introduction goes to the bottom of the first page, the writing may be going off-track or be repetitive. It's best to fall into the one-two page range, but a complete, well-developed essay is the ultimate goal.

The Final Steps

Leaving a few minutes at the end to revise and proofread offers an opportunity for writers to polish things up. Putting one's self in the reader's shoes and focusing on what the essay actually says helps writers identify problems—it's a movement from the mindset of writer to the mindset of editor. The goal is to have a clean, clear copy of the essay. The following areas should be considered when proofreading:

- Sentence fragments
- Awkward sentence structure
- Run-on sentences

236

- Incorrect word choice
- Grammatical agreement errors
- Spelling errors
- Punctuation errors
- Capitalization errors

The Short Overview

The essay may seem challenging, but following these steps can help writers focus:

- Take one-two minutes to think about the topic.
- Generate some ideas through brainstorming (three-four minutes).
- Organize ideas into a brief outline, selecting just three-four main points to cover in the essay (eventually the body paragraphs).
- Develop essay in parts:
- Introduction paragraph, with intro to topic and main points
- Viewpoint on the subject at the end of the introduction
- Body paragraphs, based on outline
- Each paragraph: makes a main point, explains the viewpoint, uses examples to support the point
- Brief conclusion highlighting the main points and closing
- Read over the essay (last five minutes).
- Look for any obvious errors, making sure that the writing makes sense.

Practice Prompt

Prepare an essay of about 300-600 words on the topic below.

Some people feel that sharing their lives on social media sites such as Facebook, Instagram, and Snapchat is fine. They share every aspect of their lives, including pictures of themselves and their families, what they ate for lunch, who they are dating, and when they are going on vacation. They even say that if it's not on social media, it didn't happen. Other people believe that sharing so much personal information is an invasion of privacy and could prove dangerous. They think sharing personal pictures and details invites predators, cyberbullying, and identity theft.

Write an essay to someone who is considering whether to participate in social media. Take a side on the issue and argue whether or not he/she should join a social media network. Use specific examples to support your argument.

Practice Test #1

Arithmetic

1. $3.4 + 2.35 + 4 =$
    a. 5.35
    b. 9.2
    c. 9.75
    d. 10.25

2. $5.88 \times 3.2 =$
    a. 18.816
    b. 16.44
    c. 20.352
    d. 17

3. $\frac{3}{25} =$
    a. 0.15
    b. 0.1
    c. 0.9
    d. 0.12

4. Between what two numbers on the number line is the fraction $\frac{22}{3}$ located?
    a. Between 3 and 4
    b. Between 7 and 8
    c. Between 22 and 23
    d. Between 6 and 7

5. Let $x = 6, y = -3, z = 6$, and $h = -11$. Which of the following is true?
    a. $x + y \leq z - h$
    b. $x + y \leq z + h$
    c. $x - y \geq z - h$
    d. $x + y + z \leq h$

6. Which is closest to 17.8×9.9?
    a. 140
    b. 180
    c. 200
    d. 350

7. A student gets an 85% on a test with 20 questions. How many questions did the student solve correctly?
    a. 15
    b. 16
    c. 17
    d. 18

8. It costs Shea $12 to produce 3 necklaces. If he can sell each necklace for $20, how much profit would he make if he sold 60 necklaces?
    a. $240
    b. $360
    c. $960
    d. $1200

9. 6 is 30% of what number?
    a. 18
    b. 20
    c. 24
    d. 26

10. $3\frac{2}{3} - 1\frac{4}{5} =$
    a. $1\frac{13}{15}$
    b. $\frac{14}{15}$
    c. $2\frac{2}{3}$
    d. $\frac{4}{5}$

11. The Cross family is planning a trip to Florida. They will be taking two cars for the trip. One car gets 18 miles to the gallon of gas. The other car gets 25 miles to the gallon. If the total trip to Florida is 450 miles, and the cost of gas is $2.49/gallon, how much will the gas cost for both cars to complete the trip?
    a. $43.00
    b. $44.82
    c. $107.07
    d. $32.33

12. $4\frac{1}{3} + 3\frac{3}{4} =$
    a. $6\frac{5}{12}$
    b. $8\frac{1}{12}$
    c. $8\frac{2}{3}$
    d. $7\frac{7}{12}$

13. An accounting firm charted its income on the following pie graph. If the total income for the year was $500,000, how much of the income was received from Audit and Taxation Services?

Income

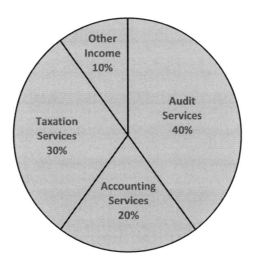

a. $200,000
b. $350,000
c. $150,000
d. $300,000

14. A National Hockey League store in the state of Michigan advertises 50% off all items. Sales tax in Michigan is 6%. How much would a hat originally priced at $32.99 and a jersey originally priced at $64.99 cost during this sale? Round to the nearest penny.
a. $97.98
b. $103.86
c. $51.93
d. $48.99

15. If $\frac{5}{2} \div \frac{1}{3} = n$, then n is between:
a. 5 and 7
b. 7 and 9
c. 9 and 11
d. 3 and 5

16. A closet is filled with red, blue, and green shirts. If $\frac{1}{3}$ of the shirts are green and $\frac{2}{5}$ are red, what fraction of the shirts are blue?

    a. $\frac{4}{15}$

    b. $\frac{1}{5}$

    c. $\frac{7}{15}$

    d. $\frac{1}{2}$

17. What is the solution to $9 \times 9 \div 9 + 9 - 9 \div 9$?

    a.   9
    b.   3.5
    c.   17
    d.   1

18. $\frac{2}{9}$ is equal to which of the following answer choices?

    a.   22%
    b.   4.5%
    c.   450%
    d.   0.22%

19. Paint Inc. charges $2,000 for painting the first 1,800 feet of trim on a house and $1.00 per foot for each foot after. How much would it cost to paint a house with 3,125 feet of trim?

    a. $3,125
    b. $2,000
    c. $5,125
    d. $3,325

20. What is $4 \times 7 + (25 - 21)^2 \div 2$?

    a.   60
    b.   22
    c.   46
    d.   36

Quantitative Reasoning, Algebra, and Statistics

1. Simplify:

$$\frac{4a^{-1}b^3}{a^4b^{-2}} \times \frac{3a}{b}$$

    a. $12a^3b^5$

    b. $12\dfrac{b^4}{a^4}$

    c. $\dfrac{12}{a^4}$

    d. $7\dfrac{b^4}{a}$

2. What would the equation be for six less than three times the sum of twice a number and one?
   a. $2x + 1 - 6$
   b. $3x + 1 - 6$
   c. $3(x + 1) - 6$
   d. $3(2x + 1) - 6$

3. On Monday, Robert mopped the floor in 4 hours. On Tuesday, he did it in 3 hours. If on Monday, his average rate of mopping was p sq. ft. per hour, what was his average rate on Tuesday?
   a. $\frac{4}{3}p$ sq. ft. per hour

   b. $\frac{3}{4}p$ sq. ft. per hour

   c. $\frac{5}{4}p$ sq. ft. per hour

   d. $p + 1$ sq. ft. per hour

4. The phone bill is calculated each month using the equation $c = 50g + 75$. The cost of the phone bill per month is represented by c, and g represents the gigabytes of data used that month. What is the value and interpretation of the slope of this equation?
   a. 75 dollars per day
   b. 75 gigabytes per day
   c. 50 dollars per day
   d. 50 dollars per gigabyte

5. Five of six numbers have a sum of 25. The average of all six numbers is 6. What is the sixth number?
   a. 8
   b. 10
   c. 11
   d. 12

6. Which of the following is an equivalent measurement for 1.3 cm?
   a. 0.13 m
   b. 0.013 m
   c. 0.13 mm
   d. 0.013 mm

7. Jessica buys 10 cans of paint. Red paint costs $1 per can, and blue paint costs $2 per can. In total, she spends $16. How many red cans did she buy?
   a. 2
   b. 3
   c. 4
   d. 5

8. A line passes through the point $(1,2)$ and crosses the y-axis at $y = 1$. Which of the following is an equation for this line?
   a. $y = 2x$
   b. $y = x + 1$
   c. $x + y = 1$
   d. $y = \frac{x}{2} - 2$

243

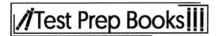
9. A right triangle has a hypotenuse of 10 inches, and one leg is 8 inches. How long is the other leg?
   a. 6 in
   b. 18 in
   c. 80 in
   d. 13 in

10. A rectangle has a length that is 5 feet longer than three times its width. If the perimeter is 90 feet, what is the length in feet?
   a. 10
   b. 20
   c. 25
   d. 35

11. A sample data set contains the following values: 1, 3, 5, 7. What's the standard deviation of the set?
   a. 2.58
   b. 4
   c. 6.23
   d. 1.1

12. A ball is drawn at random from a ball pit containing 8 red balls, 7 yellow balls, 6 green balls, and 5 purple balls. What's the probability that the ball drawn is yellow?
   a. $\frac{1}{26}$
   b. $\frac{19}{26}$
   c. $\frac{7}{26}$
   d. 1

13. If $2x + 6 = 20$, what is x?
   a. 3
   b. 4
   c. 7
   d. 9

14. What's the probability of rolling a 6 at least once in two rolls of a die?
   a. $\frac{1}{3}$
   b. $\frac{1}{36}$
   c. $\frac{1}{6}$
   d. $\frac{11}{36}$

15. A train traveling 50 miles per hour takes a trip lasting 3 hours. If a map has a scale of 1 inch per 10 miles, how many inches apart are the train's starting point and ending point on the map?
   a. 14
   b. 12
   c. 13
   d. 15

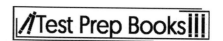

16. Apples cost $2 each, while oranges cost $3 each. Maria purchased 10 fruits in total and spent $22. How many apples did she buy?
    a. 5
    b. 6
    c. 7
    d. 8

17. A truck is carrying three cylindrical barrels. Their bases have a diameter of 2 feet, and they have a height of 3 feet. What is the total volume of the three barrels in cubic feet?
    a. 3π
    b. 9π
    c. 12π
    d. 15π

18. Evaluate:

$$\left(\sqrt{36} \times \sqrt{16}\right) - 3^2$$

    a. 441
    b. 15
    c. 138
    d. -30

19. What is the result of evaluating $\frac{1}{2}\sqrt{16}$?
    a. 0
    b. 1
    c. 2
    d. 4

20. $(4x^2y^4)^{\frac{3}{2}}$ can be simplified to which of the following?
    a. $8x^3y^6$

    b. $4x^{\frac{5}{2}}y$

    c. $4xy$

    d. $32x^{\frac{7}{2}}y^{\frac{11}{2}}$

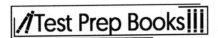
Advanced Algebra and Functions

1. What is the value of x in the following triangle?

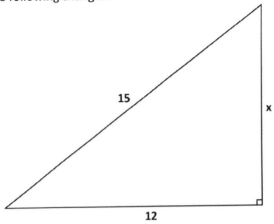

    a. 19.2
    b. 9
    c. 3
    d. 7.5

2. There are $4x + 1$ treats in each party favor bag. If a total of $60x + 15$ treats are distributed, how many bags are given out?
    a. 15
    b. 16
    c. 20
    d. 22

3. Suppose an investor deposits $1,200 into a bank account that accrues 1 percent interest per month. Assuming x represents the number of months since the deposit and y represents the money in the account, which of the following exponential functions models the scenario?
    a. $y = (0.01)(1200^x)$
    b. $y = (1200)(0.01^x)$
    c. $y = (1.01)(1200^x)$
    d. $y = (1200)(1.01^x)$

4. The square and circle have the same center. The circle has a radius of r. What is the area of the shaded region?

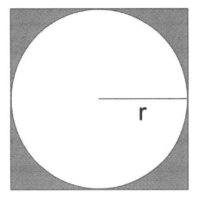

    a. $r^2 - \pi r^2$
    b. $4r^2 - 2\pi r$
    c. $(4 - \pi)r^2$
    d. $(\pi - 1)r^2$

5. If $4x - 3 = 5$, what is the value of x?
    a.   1
    b.   2
    c.   3
    d.   4

6. What are the zeros of the function: $f(x) = x^3 + 4x^2 + 4x$?
    a.   −2
    b.   0, −2
    c.   2
    d.   0, 2

7. Solve the equation $4^{5-x} = 7$
    a. $x = -\dfrac{\ln 7}{\ln 4 + 5}$

    b. $x = -\dfrac{\ln 7}{\ln 4} + 5$

    c. $x = -\ln\dfrac{7}{4} + 5$

    d. $x = \ln\dfrac{7}{4} - 5$

8. A pyramid has a square base with a side length of 6 inches, and the pyramid's height is 9 inches. What is the pyramid's volume?
    a. 324 in^3
    b. 72 in^3
    c. 108 in^3
    d. 18 in^3

9. What is the solution for the equation $\tan(\theta) + 1 = 0$, where $0 \leq \theta < 2\pi$?
   a. $\theta = \frac{3\pi}{4}, \frac{5\pi}{4}$
   b. $\theta = \frac{3\pi}{4}, \frac{\pi}{4}$
   c. $\theta = \frac{5\pi}{4}, \frac{7\pi}{4}$
   d. $\theta = \frac{3\pi}{4}, \frac{7\pi}{4}$

10. Which of the following inequalities is equivalent to $3 - \frac{1}{2}x \geq 2$?
   a. $x \geq 2$
   b. $x \leq 2$
   c. $x \geq 1$
   d. $x \leq 1$

11. For which of the following are $x = 4$ and $x = -4$ solutions?
   a. $x^2 + 16 = 0$
   b. $x^2 + 4x - 4 = 0$
   c. $x^2 - 2x - 2 = 0$
   d. $x^2 - 16 = 0$

12. If x is not zero, then $\frac{3}{x} + \frac{5u}{2x} - \frac{u}{4} =$
   a. $\frac{12 + 10u - ux}{4x}$
   b. $\frac{3 + 5u - ux}{x}$
   c. $\frac{12x + 10u + ux}{4x}$
   d. $\frac{12 + 10u - u}{4x}$

13. Which equation best represents the scatter plot below?

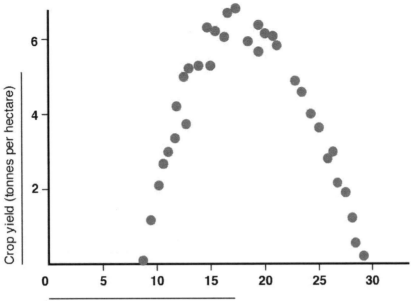

a. $y = 3x - 4$
b. $y = 2x^2 + 7x - 9$
c. $y = (3)(4^x)$
d. $y = -\frac{1}{14}x^2 + 2x - 8$

14. How could the following equation be factored to find the zeros?

$$y = x^3 - 3x^2 - 4x$$

a. $0 = x^2(x - 4), x = 0, 4$
b. $0 = 3x(x + 1)(x + 4), x = 0, -1, -4$
c. $0 = x(x + 1)(x + 6), x = 0, -1, -6$
d. $0 = x(x + 1)(x - 4), x = 0, -1, 4$

15. What is the simplified quotient of $\frac{5x^3}{3x^2y} \div \frac{25}{3y^9}$?

a. $\frac{125x}{9y^{10}}$

b. $\frac{x}{5y^8}$

c. $\frac{5}{xy^8}$

d. $\frac{xy^8}{5}$

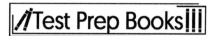
16. Let $f(x) = 2x + 1$, $g(x) = \frac{x-1}{4}$. Find $g(f(x))$.

    a. $\frac{x+1}{2}$

    b. $\frac{x}{2}$

    c. $\frac{2x^2-x-1}{4}$

    d. $3x$

17. What is the simplified form of the expression $tan\theta \ cos\theta$?

    a. $sin\theta$

    b. 1

    c. $csc\theta$

    d. $\frac{1}{sec\theta}$

18. The weight w, in pounds, of the load of a delivery truck is approximated by a linear equation. The truck weighs 25,000 pounds with no load, and each box in a load is approximately 45 pounds. Which of the following equations represents the correct equation that represents w? Let b represent the number of boxes in a load.

    a. $w = 25000b + 45$

    b. $w = 45b + 25000$

    c. $b = 25w + 2500$

    d. $w = 45b - 25000$

19. How could the following function be rewritten to identify the zeros?

$$y = 3x^3 + 3x^2 - 18x$$

    a. $y = 3x(x + 3)(x - 2)$

    b. $y = x(x - 2)(x + 3)$

    c. $y = 3x(x - 3)(x + 2)$

    d. $y = (x + 3)(x - 2)$

20. If $x^2 - x - 3 = 0$, what is the value of $\left(x - \frac{1}{2}\right)^2$?

    a. $\frac{13}{2}$

    b. $\frac{13}{4}$

    c. 13

    d. $\frac{169}{4}$

Reading Comprehension

The next four questions pertain to the following excerpt:

> My gentleness and good behaviour had gained so far on the emperor and his court, and indeed upon the army and people in general, that I began to conceive hopes of getting my liberty in a short time. I took all possible methods to cultivate this favourable disposition. The natives came, by degrees, to be less apprehensive of any danger from me. I would

sometimes lie down, and let five or six of them dance on my hand; and at last the boys and girls would venture to come and play at hide-and-seek in my hair. I had now made a good progress in understanding and speaking the language. The emperor had a mind one day to entertain me with several of the country shows, wherein they exceed all nations I have known, both for dexterity and magnificence. I was diverted with none so much as that of the rope-dancers, performed upon a slender white thread, extended about two feet, and twelve inches from the ground. Upon which I shall desire liberty, with the reader's patience, to enlarge a little.

This diversion is only practised by those persons who are candidates for great employments, and high favour at court. They are trained in this art from their youth, and are not always of noble birth, or liberal education. When a great office is vacant, either by death or disgrace (which often happens), five or six of those candidates petition the emperor to entertain his majesty and the court with a dance on the rope; and whoever jumps the highest, without falling, succeeds in the office. Very often the chief ministers themselves are commanded to show their skill, and to convince the emperor that they have not lost their faculty. Flimnap, the treasurer, is allowed to cut a caper on the straight rope, at least an inch higher than any other lord in the whole empire. I have seen him do the summerset several times together, upon a trencher fixed on a rope which is no thicker than a common packthread in England. My friend Reldresal, principal secretary for private affairs, is, in my opinion, if I am not partial, the second after the treasurer; the rest of the great officers are much upon a par.

Excerpt from an adaptation of Jonathan Swift's Gulliver's Travels into Several Remote Nations of the World.

1. Which of the following statements best summarizes the central purpose of this text?
   a. Gulliver details his fondness for the archaic yet interesting practices of his captors.
   b. Gulliver conjectures about the intentions of the aristocratic sector of society.
   c. Gulliver becomes acquainted with the people and practices of his new surroundings.
   d. Gulliver's differences cause him to become penitent around new acquaintances.

2. What can the reader infer from the following text from *Gulliver's Travels*?
   I would sometimes lie down, and let five or six of them dance on my hand; and at last the boys and girls would venture to come and play at hide-and-seek in my hair.

   a. The children tortured Gulliver.
   b. Gulliver traveled because he wanted to meet new people.
   c. Gulliver is considerably larger than the children who are playing around him.
   d. Gulliver has a genuine love and enthusiasm for people of all sizes.

3. Which of the following sentences from the passage demonstrates the satirical or mocking tone of the piece?
   a. "The natives came, by degrees, to be less apprehensive of any danger from me."
   b. "The emperor had a mind one day to entertain me with several of the country shows, wherein they exceed all nations I have known, both for dexterity and magnificence."
   c. "My friend Reldresal, principal secretary for private affairs, is, in my opinion, if I am not partial, the second after the treasurer; the rest of the great officers are much upon a par."
   d. "When a great office is vacant, either by death or disgrace (which often happens), five or six of those candidates petition the emperor to entertain his majesty and the court with a dance on the rope; and whoever jumps the highest, without falling, succeeds in the office."

4. What effect does the point of view have on the reader of the passage?
   a. The point of view creates distance between the reader and narrator, allowing readers to question the accuracy of the events of the plot.
   b. The point of view presents the plot objectively, allowing readers to draw their own conclusions about the societies with which the narrator interacts.
   c. The point of view takes readers inside Gulliver's experiences and aligns them with his skeptical, often critical perspective on the societies he visits.
   d. The point of view allows readers to access the natives' perspective, causing readers to feel sympathy for them as Gulliver views them with skepticism.

The next four questions pertain to the following set of passages:

Passage I

Lethal force, or deadly force, is defined as the physical means to cause death or serious harm to another individual. The law holds that lethal force is only acceptable when you or another person are in immediate and unavoidable danger of death or severe bodily harm. For example, a person could be beating someone in such a way that the victim is suffering severe trauma that could result in death or serious harm. This would be an instance where lethal force would be acceptable and possibly the only way to save the victim from irrevocable damage.

Another example of when to use lethal force would be when someone enters your home with a deadly weapon. The intruder's presence and possession of the weapon indicate malicious intent and the ability to inflict death or severe injury upon you and your loved ones. Again, lethal force can be used in this situation. Lethal force can also be applied to prevent the harm of another individual. If a woman is being brutally assaulted and is unable to fend off an attacker, lethal force can be used to defend her as a last-ditch effort. If she is in immediate jeopardy of rape, harm, and/or death, lethal force could be the only response that could effectively deter the assailant.

The key to understanding the concept of lethal force is the term *last resort*. Deadly force cannot be taken back; it should be used only to prevent severe harm or death. The law does distinguish whether the means of one's self-defense is fully warranted or if the individual goes out of control in the process. If you continually attack the assailant after they are rendered incapacitated, this would be causing unnecessary harm, and the law can bring charges against you. Likewise, if you kill an attacker unnecessarily after defending yourself, you can be charged with murder. This would move lethal force beyond necessary defense, making it no longer a last resort but rather a use of excessive force.

Passage II

Assault is an unlawful and intentional act that causes reasonable apprehension in another individual, either by an imminent threat or by initiating offensive contact. Assaults can vary, encompassing physical strikes, threatening body language, and even provocative language. In the case of the latter, even if a hand has not been laid, it is still considered an assault because of its threatening nature.

Let's look at an example. A homeowner is angered because his neighbor blows fallen leaves onto his freshly mowed lawn. Irate, the homeowner gestures a fist to his neighbor and threatens to bash his head in for littering on his lawn. The homeowner's physical motions

252

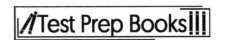
and verbal threats herald a physical threat against the other neighbor. These factors classify the homeowner's reaction as an assault. If the angry neighbor hits the threatening homeowner in retaliation, that would constitute an assault as well because he physically hit the homeowner.

Assault also centers on the involvement of weapons in a conflict. If someone fired a gun at another person, it could be interpreted as an assault, unless the shooter acted in self-defense. If an individual drew a gun or a knife on someone with the intent to harm them, it would be considered assault. However, it's also considered an assault if someone simply aims a weapon, loaded or not, at another person in a threatening manner.

5. Which of the following best describes the way the passages are structured?
   a. Both passages open by defining a legal concept and then continue to describe situations that further explain the concept.
   b. Both passages begin with situations, introduce accepted definitions, and then cite legal ramifications.
   c. Passage I presents a long definition while the Passage II begins by showing an example of assault.
   d. Both cite specific legal doctrines, then proceed to explain the rulings.

6. Based on the passages, what can we infer about the relationship between assault and lethal force?
   a. An act of lethal force always leads to a type of assault.
   b. Assault and lethal force have no conceivable connection.
   c. An assault with deadly intent can lead to an individual using lethal force to preserve their well-being.
   d. If someone uses self-defense in a conflict, it is called deadly force; if actions or threats are intended, it is called assault.

7. What can be inferred about the role of intent in lethal force and assault?
   a. Intent is irrelevant. The law does not take intent into account.
   b. Intent is vital for determining the lawfulness of using lethal force, but not for assault.
   c. Intent is very important for determining both lethal force and assault; intent is examined in both parties and helps determine the severity of the issue.
   d. The intent of the assailant is the main focus for determining legal ramifications; it is used to determine if the defender was justified in using force to respond.

8. Using lethal force would be legal in which of the following situations, according to Passage I?
   a. A disgruntled cashier yells obscenities at a customer.
   b. A thief is seen running away with stolen cash.
   c. A man is attacked in an alley by another man with a knife.
   d. A woman punches another woman in a bar.

The next question pertains to the following passage:

Three years ago, I think there were not many bird-lovers in the United States who believed it possible to prevent the total extinction of both egrets from our fauna. All the known rookeries accessible to plume-hunters had been totally destroyed. Two years ago, the secret discovery of several small, hidden colonies prompted William Dutcher, President of the National Association of Audubon Societies, and Mr. T. Gilbert Pearson, Secretary, to attempt the protection of those colonies. With a fund contributed for the purpose, wardens were hired and duly commissioned. As previously stated, one of those wardens was shot dead in cold blood by a plume hunter. The task of guarding swamp rookeries from the attacks of money-hungry desperadoes, to whom the accursed plumes were worth their weight in gold, is a very chancy proceeding. There is now one warden in Florida who says that "before they get my rookery they will first have to get me."

Thus far, the protective work of the Audubon Association has been successful. Now there are 20 colonies, which contain all told, about 5,000 egrets and about 120,000 herons and ibises which are guarded by the Audubon wardens. One of the most important is on Bird Island, a mile out in Orange Lake, Central Florida, and it is ably defended by Oscar E. Baynard. To-day, the plume hunters who do not dare to raid the guarded rookeries are trying to study out the lines of flight of the birds, to and from their feeding-grounds, and shoot them in transit. Their motto is "Anything to beat the law, and get the plumes." It is there that the state of Florida should take part in the war.

The success of this campaign is attested by the fact that last year a number of egrets were seen in eastern Massachusetts—for the first time in many years. And so to-day the question is, can the wardens continue to hold the plume-hunters at bay?

Excerpt adapted from Our Vanishing Wildlife, by William T. Hornaday

9. What is the central idea of the passage?
   a. That the public must act in preservation of the bird colonies
   b. The effects that hunting egrets has had on the environment
   c. The negative impact that preservation of bird colonies has had on the environment
   d. The success of the protective work of the Audubon Association

The next question pertains to the following passage:

Rainforests cover approximately 6% of the Earth's surface. Tropical rainforests are found in five major areas of the world: Central America, South America, Central Africa, Asia (stretching from India to islands in the Pacific Ocean), and Australia. All of these areas are warm and wet areas within ten degrees of the equator. They do not have a substantial dry season during the year.

Rainforests are large areas of jungle that get an abundance of rain. They comprise four layers, each with unique characteristics. The emergent layer is the highest layer and is made up of the tops of the tall trees. There is very good sunlight in this layer. The canopy layer is the next layer, just under the emergent layer. Here, there is some sun but not as much as the emergent layer. The next layer is the understory layer. This layer does not receive very much sunlight. The plants in this layer need to grow very large leaves to reach the sun. The bottom-most layer is the forest floor. Sunlight generally does not reach this layer, so plants do not grow here.

10. Which of these plants, based on their listed requirements, would thrive in a rainforest climate?
   a. Giant water lily: warm temperatures, wet environment, has ability to grow large leaves
   b. Cactus: dry environment, long, hot season for growth
   c. Pine tree: dry and sandy soil, lots of sunlight
   d. Black-eyed Susan: very hot temperatures, slightly moist soil

The next question pertains to the following passage:

Piloting is a consummate skill to obtain, and for many, it's a skill that remains unattainable. A potential pilot must be so well-versed in flight instruction that studying the requirements can seem overwhelming. In addition, thousands of flight hours must be logged in practice before a pilot can begin a career. The physical and mental demands made on many potential students can be prohibitive. It's a dedicated person who perseveres and becomes successful in the flight industry.

11. Which statement best describes the author's position?
   a. Piloting is a difficult goal requiring serious consideration.
   b. Piloting careers are few and far between.
   c. The physical and mental demands on piloting students should be the main consideration when deciding on a career in flight.
   d. Piloting involves a lot of luck and practice.

The next question pertains to the following passage:

I have thought that an example of the intelligence (instinct?) of a class of fish which has come under my observation during my excursions into the Adirondack region of New York State might possibly be of interest to your readers, especially as I am not aware that anyone except myself has noticed it, or, at least, has given it publicity.

The female sun-fish (called, I believe, in England, the roach or bream) makes a "hatchery" for her eggs in this wise. Selecting a spot near the banks of the numerous lakes in which this region abounds, and where the water is about 4 inches deep, and still, she builds, with her tail and snout, a circular embankment 3 inches in height and 2 thick. The circle, which is as perfect a one as could be formed with mathematical instruments, is usually a foot and a half in diameter; and at one side of this circular wall an opening is left by the fish of just sufficient width to admit her body.

The mother sun-fish, having now built or provided her "hatchery," deposits her spawn within the circular enclosure, and mounts guard at the entrance until the fry are hatched out and are sufficiently large to take charge of themselves. As the embankment, moreover, is built up to the surface of the water, no enemy can very easily obtain an entrance within the enclosure from the top; while there being only one entrance, the fish is able, with comparative ease, to keep out all intruders.

I have, as I say, noticed this beautiful instinct of the sun-fish for the perpetuity of her species more particularly in the lakes of this region; but doubtless the same habit is common to these fish in other waters.

Excerpt from "The 'Hatchery' of the Sun-Fish" — Scientific American, #711

12. The author included the third paragraph in the passage to achieve which of the following effects?
   a. To complicate the subject matter
   b. To express a bias
   c. To insert a counterargument
   d. To conclude a sequence and add a final detail

The next question pertains to the following passage:

Dr. Wilfred Buck, an esteemed First Nations astrophysicist from the Opaskwayak Cree Nation in Manitoba, Canada, has been a trailblazer in integrating traditional indigenous knowledge with modern astrophysics. Notably, Dr. Buck has correlated celestial events (like specific constellations' appearances) with indigenous oral traditions, illuminating the deep astronomical understanding within these communities.

As a dedicated science communicator, Dr. Buck emphasizes the importance of incorporating indigenous perspectives into mainstream science education. Through public lectures, workshops, and educational programs, he has inspired a broader appreciation for the interconnectedness of scientific principles and indigenous wisdom. His efforts showcase the profound contributions that indigenous voices bring to the scientific community, fostering a richer understanding of the cosmos while preserving cultural heritage. Dr. Wilfred Buck stands as a shining example of the synergy between indigenous knowledge and modern science, making invaluable strides in both fields.

13. What inference can a reader reasonably draw from the first paragraph?
    a. Indigenous understanding of space has been largely ignored in modern science.
    b. Dr. Buck's work is highly respected among all astrophysicists.
    c. Stars feature heavily in the stories of most indigenous cultures.
    d. Dr. Buck has made some of the most important astrophysical discoveries of the last fifty years.

The next question pertains to the following passage:

Wedding planners, working behind the scenes to craft clients' dream events, face incredible pressure and require a high degree of flexibility. Wedding planners must balance the needs, budgets, and availability of floral designers, caterers, DJs and other performers, officiants, venue owners, and other essential event stakeholders while prioritizing the wishes of their clients. Balancing various responsibilities—from guest list curation to decor logistics—requires advanced time management and adept problem-solving skills, especially when it comes to last-minute adjustments and changes in plans. Everything from wardrobe malfunctions to unexpected rain showers has the potential to disrupt the happy couple's big day. Despite the fast-paced and often unpredictable nature of the role, the satisfaction for dedicated wedding planners lies in crafting memorable events that bring romantic dreams to life.

14. What is the purpose of the last line of the paragraph?
    a. To explain why wedding planners deserve competitive salaries
    b. To highlight the job's meaningfulness, despite its stress level
    c. To summarize the factors that make wedding planning stressful
    d. To juxtapose wedding planning against other high-stress vocations

The next question pertains to the following passage:

Increasing Appalachian media representation addresses long-standing Hollywood failures in the form of cultural misrepresentation and stereotypes. A more accurate portrayal of life in Appalachia is crucial for dispelling misconceptions and fostering a nuanced understanding of our region's diverse cultural fabric. By incorporating authentic narratives, we contribute to a comprehensive socio-cultural discourse that transcends simplistic, unfair characterizations. Such representation not only empowers individuals within the Appalachian community but also serves as an educational tool for a broader audience.

15. The author's use of "our" and "we" implies that the author:
    a. believes that the misrepresentation of Appalachian culture is less of a problem than some think.
    b. thinks that the harm caused by media stereotypes is overblown.
    c. is a member of both the media and the Appalachian community.
    d. is tired of hearing complaints about Appalachian stereotypes in movies and on TV.

The next question pertains to the following passage:

The Rosetta Stone, often hailed as an iconic artifact for deciphering ancient Egyptian hieroglyphs, has been subject to overblown importance in historical narratives. While undeniably valuable in providing a key to understanding a bygone language, the stone's significance is often exaggerated. Its discovery in 1799 by French soldiers during Napoleon's Egyptian campaign did pave the way for breakthroughs in Egyptology, but its role as the sole catalyst for deciphering hieroglyphs has been overstated. Scholars like Thomas Young and Jean-François Champollion were instrumental in unraveling the mysteries of ancient Egyptian writing; Young made significant strides before the Rosetta Stone's full translation.

Moreover, the stone's inscriptions are primarily a decree affirming the divine cult of the newly crowned Ptolemy V. While shedding light on historical and cultural aspects of Ptolemaic Egypt, it doesn't offer profound insights into broader facets of Egyptian civilization. Elevating the Rosetta Stone to a status beyond its actual contribution risks overshadowing the collective efforts of scholars and diminishes the rich tapestry of Egyptology. It is crucial to recognize the collaborative nature of decipherment and acknowledge the myriad factors that contributed to unlocking the secrets of ancient Egyptian script.

16. Which of the following is an accurate summary of the passage's overall argument?
   a. Jean-François Champollion was a French scholar and linguist renowned for his groundbreaking work in deciphering the Rosetta Stone and unlocking the mysteries of ancient Egyptian hieroglyphs.
   b. Napoleon's campaign to explore Egypt was a military expedition with the dual purpose of disrupting British trade routes and fostering scientific and cultural discovery, resulting in the discovery of the Rosetta Stone by French soldiers in 1799.
   c. The divine cult of Ptolemy V was a religious practice affirming the worship of the newly crowned ruler, emphasizing his divine status and reinforcing political legitimacy in Ptolemaic Egypt.
   d. While the Rosetta Stone facilitated the decipherment of ancient Egyptian hieroglyphs, its importance has been exaggerated, overshadowing the collaborative efforts of influential scholars and the broader context of Egyptology.

The next question pertains to the following passage:

A canyon, a breathtaking geological formation, takes shape through the slow but persistent forces of erosion. Over thousands to millions of years, a combination of water, wind, and other natural processes sculpts the landscape into these deep yet often narrow chasms.

The initial step in canyon formation often involves the work of rivers or streams. As water flows, it gradually wears away the softer rock layers, creating a channel. Over time, this channel deepens through a process called downcutting as water carries sediment and rocks downstream.

Simultaneously, weathering contributes to the widening of the canyon. Windblown sand and debris can erode the canyon walls, while freeze-thaw cycles, especially in colder climates, cause rocks to fracture and break apart.

In some cases, tectonic activity plays a role. Earthquakes and the shifting of the Earth's crust can accelerate the downcutting process, exposing fresh rock surfaces to erosion.

The remarkable features found within canyons, such as towering cliffs and captivating rock layers, can be directly attributed to the resistance of different types of rock to erosion. Take

257

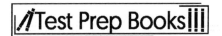
the Grand Canyon as an illustration, where the Colorado River has gradually shaped the landscape over millions of years. The rocks less susceptible to erosion stand prominently, contributing to the awe-inspiring formations that characterize the canyon's unique and intricate topography.

17. Which option describes the overall structure of the passage?
   a. Stages of canyon development are described chronologically.
   b. Stages of canyon development are compared and contrasted.
   c. A series of problem-solution pairs are presented.
   d. Each stage is presented as a cause, with the resulting effect described.

The next question pertains to the following passage:

Cape Cod, with its pristine beaches, charming coastal towns, and vibrant maritime culture, is the quintessential summer vacation destination. It has held a special place in my heart ever since my family began our annual tradition of vacationing there when I was a young child. The sun-kissed beaches stretch for miles, offering a haven for relaxation and countless opportunities for beachside activities.

One can't help but be enchanted by the idyllic charm of towns like Provincetown, with its colorful cottages and bustling art scene. I'll never forget my first time there, during the summer when I was eight. Along Main Street, the aroma of fresh seafood wafts from quaint eateries, tempting taste buds with the catch of the day. It's not just a vacation; it's a sensory experience, and there are enough restaurants to suit young and mature tastes alike.

The Cape's maritime history comes alive in places like the Cape Cod Maritime Museum, where tales of legendary sea captains and their adventures echo through the exhibits. For families like mine, the Cape Cod Rail Trail beckons, winding through picturesque landscapes and providing a perfect backdrop for biking adventures.

The beauty of Cape Cod lies not only in its picturesque landscapes but also in the warmth of its people. One of my favorite aspects of our annual tradition is seeing some of the same faces year after year. From the jovial fisherman sharing tales at the local seafood shack to the welcoming smiles of shopkeepers, the sense of community creates an atmosphere that feels like a home away from home.

In essence, Cape Cod is more than a destination; it's a tapestry of shared moments woven together by multiple generations. It's where the simplicity of beach days and the richness of coastal culture converge, making it the ultimate summer haven for those seeking a retreat filled with memories that linger like the salt-tinged air.

18. In the passage, the author claims that Cape Cod is the ultimate summer vacation destination. Which of the following options best classifies the author's argument?
   a. The author fails to provide any evidence to support the claim, making it unsubstantiated.
   b. The author includes statistics and expert opinions, enhancing the credibility of the claim.
   c. The author attempts to offer universal, objective appeal but ultimately leans too heavily on personal experience.
   d. The author presents counterclaims without offering any evidence to refute them, leaving the argument unbalanced.

For the next two questions, choose the best word to fill in the blank in each sentence.

19. The candidate's political promises were met with _____ reactions from the public, as many questioned the sincerity and feasibility of her proposed policies.
   a. amenable
   b. accepting
   c. exuberant
   d. dubious

20. Despite the challenging circumstances, Jaci approached her new responsibilities with remarkable _____, eager to contribute and have a positive impact on the team.
   a. apathy
   b. alacrity
   c. reluctance
   d. indifference

Writing

The next five questions pertain to the following passage:

(1) One of the icon's of romantic and science fiction literature remains Mary Shelley's classic, *Frankenstein, or The Modern Prometheus*. (2) Schools throughout the world still teach the book in literature and philosophy courses. (3) Scientific communities also engage in discussion on the novel. (4) But why? (5) Besides the novel's engaging writing style the story's central theme remains highly relevant in a world of constant discovery and moral dilemmas. (6) Central to the core narrative is the struggle between enlightenment and the cost of overusing power.

(7) The subtitle, *The Modern Prometheus*, encapsulates the inner theme of the story more than the main title of *Frankenstein*. (8) As with many romantic writers, Shelley invokes the classical myths and symbolism of Ancient Greece and Rome to highlight core ideas. (9) Looking deeper into the myth of Prometheus sheds light not only on the character of Frankenstein but also poses a psychological dilemma with the audience. (10) Prometheus is the titan who gave fire to mankind. (11) However, more than just fire he gave people knowledge and power. (12) The power of fire advanced civilization. (13) Yet, for giving fire to man, Prometheus is punished by the gods bound to a rock and tormented for his act. (14) This is clearly a parallel to Frankenstein—he is the modern Prometheus.

(15) Frankenstein's quest for knowledge becomes an obsession. (16) It leads him to literally create new life, breaking the bounds of conceivable science to illustrate that man can create life out of nothing. (17) Yet he ultimately faltered as a creator, abandoning his progeny in horror of what he created. (18) Frankenstein then suffers his creature's wrath, the result of his pride, obsession for power, and lack of responsibility.

(19) Shelley isn't condemning scientific achievement. (20) Rather, her writing reflects that science and discovery are good things, but, like all power, it must be used wisely.

1. Which of the following would be the best choice for the underlined portion of Sentence 1 (reproduced below)?

> One of the icon's of romantic and science fiction literature remains Mary Shelley's classic, *Frankenstein, or The Modern Prometheus.*

a. NO CHANGE
b. One of the icons of romantic and science fiction literature
c. One of the icon's of romantic, and science fiction literature,
d. The icon of romantic and science fiction literature

2. Which of the following would be the best choice for the underlined portion of Sentence 5 (reproduced below)?

> Besides the novel's engaging writing style the story's central theme remains highly relevant in a world of constant discovery and moral dilemmas.

a. NO CHANGE
b. writing style the central theme of the story
c. writing style, the story's central theme
d. the story's central theme's writing style

3. Which of the following would be the best choice for the underlined portion of Sentence 6 (reproduced below)?

> Central to the core narrative is the struggle between enlightenment and the cost of overusing power.

a. NO CHANGE
b. struggle between enlighten and the cost of overusing power.
c. struggle between enlightenment's cost of overusing power.
d. struggle between enlightening and the cost of overusing power.

4. Which of the following would be the best choice for Sentence 11 (reproduced below)?

> However, more than just fire he gave people knowledge and power.

a. NO CHANGE
b. However, more than just fire he gave people, knowledge, and power.
c. However, more than just fire, he gave people knowledge and power.
d. In addition to fire, Prometheus gave people knowledge and power.

5. Which of the following would be the best choice for the underlined portion of Sentence 13 (reproduced below)?

> Yet, for giving fire to man, Prometheus is punished by the gods bound to a rock and tormented for his act.

a. NO CHANGE
b. punished by the gods, bound to a rock and tormented for his act.
c. bound to a rock and tormented by the gods as punishment.
d. punished for his act by being bound to a rock and tormented as punishment from the gods.

260

The next five questions pertain to the following passage:

(1) The country of Japan is a chain of islands located along the coast of Asia. (2) Japan is made up of four major islands, with Honshu being the largest. (3) Honshu is also the seventh largest island in the world. (4) Underneath Japan, there are many volcanoes, some active and some dormant, but only about 108 of them are active today.

(5) There are many exciting places to visit in Japan. (6) Osaka is home to Dontobori, the main entertainment district. (7) The popular sport of sumo wrestling is often hosted in the town's arena. (8) People from all over Japan ride the Shinkansen or bullet train to Osaka to watch the events. (9) Hakone is famous for black eggs. (10) The town of Hakone sits on top of a mountain near Mount Fuji, the tallest mountain in Japan. (11) The eggs are boiled in a hot spring on the mountainside. (12) The natural water turns the shell of the egg black; however, it does not change the taste of it. (13) Tokyo is the capital city of Japan. (14) The town of Kyoto is full of shrines and temples, some lined with gold. (15) It is also a well-known place for geisha sightings.

(16) Traditional Japanese food consists mostly of fish and rice. (17) Sushi is raw fish and vegetables rolled in rice and wrapped in seaweed. (18) It is typically dipped in a sauce made of soy sauce and wasabi paste. (19) Tempura is a light, crispy batter used to fry fish, chicken, or vegetables. (20) Soba is another traditional Japanese dish. (21) They are a type of noodle that is oftentimes eaten cold and served in a broth made with soy sauce.

6. Which transition sentence should be added to the beginning of Sentence 16 (reproduced below)?

Traditional Japanese food consists mostly of fish and rice.

 a. Typical Japanese lunch boxes are called *bentos* and usually consist of foods such as dried fruit, rice, and sushi.
 b. Japanese cuisine is very different from American cuisine.
 c. Yakisoba is a traditional Japanese noodle dish served with slices of beef.
 d. Gyoza is a traditional Japanese dish that many Americans refer to as *pot stickers*.

7. Which sentence should be moved to follow Sentence 8 to correct the flow of information in the paragraph?
 a. Sentence 5
 b. Sentence 7
 c. Sentence 10
 d. Sentence 15

8. Which revision of Sentence 4 (reproduced below) uses the most concise language?

Underneath Japan, there are many volcanoes, some active and some dormant, but only about 108 of them are active today.

 a. Japan sits just above 108 active volcanos.
 b. Japan has many volcanos, with only 108 being active.
 c. Active volcanos are common in Japan, especially the biggest 108.
 d. Japan lies on a chain of volcanos, and more than 108 of them are active.

9. Which sentence should be revised to correct an error in sentence structure?
   a. Sentence 4
   b. Sentence 8
   c. Sentence 12
   d. Sentence 14

10. Which of the following is the best revision for Sentence 21 (reproduced below)?

   They are a type of noodle that is oftentimes eaten cold and served in a broth made with soy sauce.

   a. NO CHANGE
   b. They are a type of noodle that was oftentimes eaten cold and served in a broth made with soy sauce.
   c. It is a type of noodle that is oftentimes eaten cold and served in a broth made with soy sauce.
   d. It was a type of noodle that is oftentimes eaten cold and served in a broth made with soy sauce.

The next five questions pertain to the following passage:

   (1) Some people confuse Memorial Day with Veterans Day; however, there is a big difference. (2) Veterans Day is a day to celebrate past and present service men and women who have worked to ensure the safety of our nation. (3) Memorial Day is a day of celebration and remembrance of those who lost their lives fighting for our country.

   (4) Memorial Day, originally known as Decoration Day, first began on May 5, 1868 to celebrate the lives of those lost during the Civil War. (5) However, after World War I, the meaning of Decoration Day was changed to honor not just those who had fallen in the Civil War but all those who had fallen fighting for our country. (6) On Decoration Day, families of fallen soldiers visited their loved ones' gravesites to decorate them with flowers, such as the red poppy, which is the official flower of Memorial Day.

   (7) In 1950, Decoration Day was renamed Memorial Day and declared a federal holiday by President Nixon in 1971. (8) Memorial Day is now celebrated on the last Monday in May. (9) All federal buildings, schools, post offices, and banks are closed.

11. Which of the following is the best choice for the underlined part of Sentence 2 (reproduced below)?

   Veterans Day is a day to celebrate all service men and women who have worked or still work to insure the safety of our nation.

   a. NO CHANGE
   b. assure
   c. ensure
   d. DELETE THE WORD

12. Which transition phrase should be added to the beginning of Sentence 9 (reproduced below)?

   All federal buildings, schools, post offices, and banks are closed.

   a. On this day,
   b. So,
   c. Because
   d. If

13. Which sentence should be moved to follow Sentence 1 to correct the flow of information in the paragraph?
   a. Sentence 3
   b. Sentence 4
   c. Sentence 7
   d. Sentence 8

14. Which revision of Sentence 6 (reproduced below) uses the most precise language?

   On Decoration Day, families of fallen soldiers visited their loved ones' gravesites to decorate them with flowers, such as the red poppy, which is the official flower of Memorial Day.

   a. On Decoration Day, families visited graves to decorate them with red poppies.
   b. Red poppies are used to decorate the graves of fallen soldiers during Decoration Day celebrations.
   c. Fallen soldiers get their graves decorated with red poppies by their loved ones on Decoration Day.
   d. On Decoration Day, families of fallen soldiers visited graves and decorated them with flowers, such as the red poppy, the official flower of Memorial Day.

15. Which of the following is the best revision for Sentence 7 (reproduced below)?

   In 1950, Decoration Day was renamed Memorial Day and declared a federal holiday by President Nixon in 1971.

   a. NO CHANGE
   b. In 1950 Decoration Day was renamed Memorial Day, and declared a federal holiday by President Nixon in 1971.
   c. In 1950, Decoration Day was renamed Memorial Day and declared a federal holiday, by President Nixon in 1971.
   d. In 1950, Decoration Day was renamed Memorial Day, and it was declared a federal holiday by President Nixon in 1971.

The next five questions pertain to the following passage:

   (1) While all dogs descend through gray wolves, it's easy to notice that dog breeds come in a variety of shapes and sizes. (2) With such a drastic range of traits, appearances and body types, dogs are one of the most variable and adaptable species on the planet. (3) But why are there so many differences? (4) The answer is that humans have actually played a major role in altering the biology of dogs. (5) This was done through a process called selective breeding.

   (6) Selective breeding is the process in which animals with desired traits are bred to produce offspring that share the same traits, which is also known as artificial selection. (7) In natural evolution, animals must escape from their environments to increase their chance of survival. (8) Over time, certain traits develop in animals that enable them to thrive in these environments. (9) The animals that have more of these traits, or better versions of these traits, gain an advantage over others of their species. (10) Therefore, the animal's chances to mate are increased and these useful genes are passed on to their offspring. (11) With dog breeding, humans select traits that are desired and encourage more of these desired traits in other dogs by breeding dogs that already have these traits.

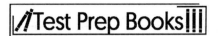
16. Which answer choice is the best replacement for the underlined word in Sentence 1 (reproduced below)?

> While all dogs descend <u>through</u> gray wolves, it's easy to notice that dog breeds come in a variety of shapes and sizes.

    a. NO CHANGE
    b. after
    c. by
    d. from

17. Choose the best revision for Sentence 6 (reproduced below).

> Selective breeding is the process in which animals with desired traits are bred to produce offspring that share the same traits, which is also known as artificial selection.

    a. NO CHANGE
    b. Selective breeding, which is also known as artificial selection, is the process in which animals with desired traits are bred to produce offspring that share the same traits.
    c. Selective breeding is the process in which animals, with desired traits, are bred to produce offspring that share the same traits, which is also known as artificial selection.
    d. Selective breeding is the process in which animals with desired traits are bred to produce offspring that share the same traits which is also known as artificial selection.

18. Choose the best revision for the underlined part of Sentence 2 (reproduced below).

> With such a drastic <u>range of traits, appearances and body types, dogs</u> are one of the most variable and adaptable species on the planet.

    a. NO CHANGE
    b. range of traits; appearances; and body types, dogs
    c. range—of traits, appearances, and body types—dogs
    d. range of traits, appearances, and body types, dogs

19. Considering the entire passage, choose the best revision for the underlined part of Sentence 7 (reproduced below)?

> In natural evolution, animals must <u>escape from</u> their environments to increase their chance of survival.

    a. NO CHANGE
    b. hide in
    c. adapt to
    d. modify

20. Which answer choice is the best version of the underlined portion of Sentence 11 (reproduced below)?

> With dog breeding, <u>humans select traits that are desired and encourage more of these desired traits in other dogs by breeding dogs that already have these traits.</u>

    a. NO CHANGE
    b. humans can encourage desired traits by breeding dogs that already have the desired traits.
    c. selecting and then encouraging desired traits can be accomplished by breeding dogs that already have these traits.

d. and the help of humans, dogs that already have desired traits can pass them on to their offspring.

The next five questions pertain to the following passage:

(1) Early in my career, a professor shared this thought with me "Education is the last bastion of civility." (2) While I did not completely understand the scope of those words at the time, I have since come to realize the depth, breadth, truth, and _____ of what he said. (3) Education provides society with a vehicle for raising its children to be civil, decent human beings with something valuable to contribute to the world. (4) It is really what makes us human and what distinguishes us as civilized creatures. (5) Although, some people would argue that characteristics such as bipedalism make us human.

(6) Being "civilized" humans means being "whole" humans. (7) Education must address the minds, bodies, and souls of students. (8) It would be detrimental to society, only meeting the needs of the mind, if our schools were myopic in their focus. (9) As humans, we are multidimensional, multifaceted beings who need more than head knowledge to survive. (10) The human heart and psyche have to be fed in order for the mind to develop properly, and the body must be maintained and exercised to help fuel the working of the brain. (11) Education is a basic human right, and it allows us to sustain a democratic society in which participation is fundamental to its success. (12) It should inspire students to seek better solutions to world problems and to dream of a more equitable society. (13) Education should never discriminate on any basis, and it should create individuals who are self-sufficient, patriotic, and tolerant of others' ideas.

(14) All children can learn, although not all children learn in the same manner. (15) All children learn best, however, when their basic physical needs are met and they feel safe, secure, and loved. (16) Students are much more responsive to a teacher who values them and shows them respect as individual people. (17) Teachers must model at all times the way they expect students to treat them and their peers. (18) If teachers set high expectations for their students, the students will rise to that high level. (19) Teachers must make the well-being of students their primary focus and must not be afraid to let students learn from their own mistakes.

From the essay "Education is Essential to Civilization"

21. Based on the tone of the passage, which word would be the best choice to fill the blank in Sentence 2 (reproduced below)?

While I did not completely understand the scope of those words at the time, I have since come to realize the depth, breadth, truth, and _____ of what he said.

a. insufficiency
b. awesomeness
c. significance
d. gaiety

22. Which sentence is a digression and should be deleted?
a. Sentence 2
b. Sentence 5
c. Sentence 6
d. Sentence 10

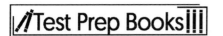

23. Which is the best version of the underlined portion of Sentence 1 (reproduced below)?

> Early in my career, <u>a professor shared this thought with me "Education is the last bastion of civility."</u>

a. NO CHANGE
b. a professor shared this thought with me: "Education is the last bastion of civility."
c. a professor shared this thought with me: "Education is the last bastion of civility".
d. a professor shared this thought with me. "Education is the last bastion of civility."

24. Which is the best version of Sentence 8 (reproduced below)?

> It would be detrimental to society, only meeting the needs of the mind, if our schools were myopic in their focus.

a. NO CHANGE
b. It would be detrimental to society if our schools were myopic in their focus, only meeting the needs of the mind.
c. Only meeting the needs of our mind, our schools were myopic in their focus, detrimental to society.
d. Myopic is the focus of our schools, being detrimental to society for only meeting the needs of the mind.

25. Which of these sentences, if any, should begin a new paragraph?

> The human heart and psyche have to be fed in order for the mind to develop properly, and the body must be maintained and exercised to help fuel the working of the brain. Education is a basic human right, and it allows us to sustain a democratic society in which participation is fundamental to its success. It should inspire students to seek better solutions to world problems and to dream of a more equitable society.

a. NO CHANGE
b. The human heart and psyche have to be fed in order for the mind to develop properly, and the body must be maintained and exercised to help fuel the working of the brain.
c. Education is a basic human right, and it allows us to sustain a democratic society in which participation is fundamental to its success.
d. It should inspire students to seek better solutions to world problems and to dream of a more equitable society.

Written Essay

For-profit institutions of learning should be illegal because they suffer from a conflict of interest between the student receiving the best education and the institution minimizing costs in providing instruction and other services to remain profitable.

Write a response in support or nonsupport of the statement in regard to the position that is taken. To support your stance, evaluate how your position may or may not be true to the argument. Explain how you've come to your position and provide examples in support of your argument.

Answer Explanations #1

Arithmetic

1. C: Line up the decimal points, putting in zeros as needed. Then, add up the numbers just like integers:

$$
\begin{array}{r}
3.40 \\
2.35 \\
+4.00 \\
\hline
9.75
\end{array}
$$

2. A: This problem can be multiplied as 588×32, except at the end, the decimal point needs to be moved three places to the left (because in the problem, we have a total of three digits after decimal points: 88 and 2). Performing the multiplication will give 18,816, and moving the decimal place over three places results in 18.816.

3. D: In this case, since the denominator happens to be 25, we can multiply the numerator and denominator by 4 to get a denominator of 100. That gives us $\frac{3\times4}{25\times4} = \frac{12}{100}$. This is useful because dividing by 100 just moves the decimal point of the numerator two places left: $\frac{12}{100} = 12 \div 100 = 0.12$.

4. B: First, change the improper fraction into a mixed number. Divide 22 by 3 to obtain 7 with a remainder of 1. The 1 becomes the numerator over the denominator of 3. The mixed number is $7\frac{1}{3}$. This value is between 7 and 8.

5. A: Substitute each value for x, y, z, and h into each inequality. Substituting the values into $x + y \leq z - h$ results in $6 + (-3) \leq 6 - (-11)$, which simplifies to $3 \leq 17$. This inequality is true. This is the only correct option.

6. B: Instead of multiplying these out, we can estimate the product by using $18 \times 10 = 180$.

7. C: To get 85% of a number, multiply it by 0.85.

$$
0.85 \times 20 = \frac{85}{100} \times \frac{20}{1}
$$

This can be simplified to:

$$
\frac{17}{20} \times \frac{20}{1} = 17
$$

8. C: In order to calculate the profit, we need to create an equation that models the total income minus the cost of the materials. $60 \times \$20 = \$1,200$ total income. $60 \div 3 = 20$ sets of materials. $20 \times \$12 = \$240$ cost of materials. $\$1,200 - \$240 = \$960$ profit.

9. B: 30% can be converted to the decimal 0.30, which equals $\frac{3}{10}$. If we think of our missing number as having been broken into 10 parts, from the information given, we can conclude that 3 of those 10 parts together equals 6, or $\frac{3}{10} = 6$. To find the value for one tenth, we must divide 6 by 3: $6 \div 3 = 2$

This means that $\frac{1}{10} = 2$, so $\frac{10}{10} = 20$.

267

This material is provided for exam preparation purposes only and does not indicate an endorsement of any specific scientific, political, or religious point of view. © TPB Publishing. You have been licensed one copy of this document for personal use only. Any other reproduction or redistribution is strictly prohibited. All rights reserved.

10. A: First, convert the mixed numbers to improper fractions: $\frac{11}{3} - \frac{9}{5}$. Then, use 15 as a common denominator:

$$\frac{11}{3} - \frac{9}{5} = \frac{55}{15} - \frac{27}{15} = \frac{28}{15} = 1\frac{13}{15}$$

11. C: For the first car, the trip will be 450 miles at 18 miles to the gallon. The total gallons needed for this car will be:

$$450 \div 18 = 25$$

For the second car, the trip will be 450 miles at 25 miles to the gallon, or $450 \div 25 = 18$, which will require 18 gallons of gas. Adding these two amounts of gas gives a total of 43 gallons of gas. If the gas costs \$2.49 per gallon, the cost of the trip for both cars is:

$$43 \times \$2.49 = \$107.07$$

12. B:

$$4\frac{1}{3} + 3\frac{3}{4} = 4 + 3 + \frac{1}{3} + \frac{3}{4}$$

$$7 + \frac{1}{3} + \frac{3}{4}$$

Adding the fractions gives:

$$\frac{1}{3} + \frac{3}{4} = \frac{4}{12} + \frac{9}{12}$$

$$\frac{13}{12} = 1 + \frac{1}{12}$$

Thus:

$$7 + \frac{1}{3} + \frac{3}{4}$$

$$7 + 1 + \frac{1}{12} = 8\frac{1}{12}$$

13. B: \$350,000: Since the total income is \$500,000, then a percentage of that can be found by multiplying the percent of Audit Services as a decimal, or 0.40, by the total of 500,000. This answer is found from the equation:

$$500000 \times 0.4 = 200000$$

The total income from Audit Services is \$200,000.

For the income received from Taxation Services, the following equation can be used:

$$500000 \times 0.3 = 150000$$

The total income from Audit Services and Taxation Services is:

$$150,000 + 200,000 = 350,000$$

Another way of approaching the problem is to calculate the easy percentage of 10% then multiply it by 7 because the total percentage for Audit and Taxation Services was 70%. 10% of 500,000 is 50,000. Then multiplying this number by 7 yields the same income of $350,000.

14. C: $51.93

List the givens.

$$\text{Tax} = 6.0\% = 0.06$$

$$\text{Sale} = 50\% = 0.5$$

$$\text{Hat} = \$32.99$$

$$\text{Jersey} = \$64.99$$

Calculate the sale prices.

$$\text{Hat Sale} = 0.5\,(32.99) = 16.495$$

$$\text{Jersey Sale} = 0.5\,(64.99) = 32.495$$

Total the sales prices.

$$\text{Hat sale} + \text{jersey sale} = 16.495 + 32.495 = 48.99$$

Calculate the tax and add it to the total sales prices.

$$\text{Total after tax} = 48.99 + (48.99 \times 0.06) = \$51.93$$

15. B: $\frac{5}{2} \div \frac{1}{3} = \frac{5}{2} \times \frac{3}{1} = \frac{15}{2} = 7.5$

16. A: The total fraction taken up by green and red shirts will be:

$$\frac{1}{3} + \frac{2}{5} = \frac{5}{15} + \frac{6}{15} = \frac{11}{15}$$

The remaining fraction is:

$$1 - \frac{11}{15} = \frac{15}{15} - \frac{11}{15} = \frac{4}{15}$$

17. C: According to the order of operations, multiplication and division must be completed first from left to right. Then, addition and subtraction are completed from left to right. Therefore:

$$9 \times 9 \div 9 + 9 - 9 \div 9$$

$$81 \div 9 + 9 - 9 \div 9$$

$$9 + 9 - 9 \div 9$$

$$9 + 9 - 1$$

$$18 - 1$$

$$17$$

18. A: 22%

Converting from a fraction to a percentage generally involves two steps. First, the fraction needs to be converted to a decimal.

Divide 2 by 9 which results in $0.\overline{22}$. The top line indicates that the decimal actually goes on forever with an endless amount of 2s.

Second, the decimal needs to be moved two places to the right:

$$22\%$$

19. D: List the givens.

$$1,800 \text{ ft} = \$2,000$$

$$\text{Cost after 1,800 ft} = \$1.00/\text{ft.}$$

Find how many feet left after the first 1,800 feet.

$$\begin{array}{r} 3,125 \text{ ft} \\ -1,800 \text{ ft} \\ \hline 1,325 \text{ ft} \end{array}$$

Calculate the cost for the feet over 1,800 feet.

$$1,325 \text{ ft} \times \frac{\$1.00}{1 \text{ ft}} = \$1,325$$

Add these together to find the total for the entire cost.

$$\$2,000 + \$1,325 = \$3,325$$

20. D: To solve this correctly, keep in mind the order of operations with the mnemonic PEMDAS (Please Excuse My Dear Aunt Sally). This stands for Parentheses, Exponents, Multiplication & Division, Addition & Subtraction. Taking it step by step, solve inside the parentheses first:

$$4 \times 7 + (4)^2 \div 2$$

Then, apply the exponent:

$$4 \times 7 + 16 \div 2$$

Multiplication and division are both performed next:

$$28 + 8$$

Addition and subtraction are done last.

$$28 + 8 = 36$$

The solution is 36.

Quantitative Reasoning, Algebra, and Statistics

1. B: The first step is to make all exponents positive by moving the terms with negative exponents to the opposite side of the fraction. This expression becomes:

$$\frac{4b^3 b^2}{a^1 a^4} \times \frac{3a}{b}$$

Then the rules for exponents can be used to simplify. Multiplying the same bases means the exponents can be added. Dividing the same bases means the exponents are subtracted. Thus, after multiplying the exponents in the first fraction, the expression becomes:

$$\frac{4b^5}{a^5} \times \frac{3a}{b}$$

Therefore, we can first multiply to get:

$$\frac{12ab^5}{a^5 b}$$

Then, simplifying yields:

$$12 \frac{b^4}{a^4}$$

2. D: "Sum" means the result of adding, so "the sum of twice a number and one" can be written as $(2x + 1)$. Next, "three times the sum of twice a number and one" would be $3(2x + 1)$. Finally, "six less than three times the sum of twice a number and one" would be $3(2x + 1) - 6$.

3. A: If s is the size of the floor in square feet and r is the rate on Tuesday, then, based on the information given, $p = \frac{s}{4}$ and $r = \frac{s}{3}$. Solve the Monday rate for s, $s = 4p$, and then substitute that in the expression for Tuesday.

4. D: The slope from this equation is 50, and it is interpreted as the cost per gigabyte used. Since the g-value represents the number of gigabytes and the equation is set equal to the cost in dollars, the slope relates these two values. For every gigabyte used on the phone, the bill goes up 50 dollars.

5. C: The average is calculated by adding all six numbers, then dividing by 6. The first five numbers have a sum of 25. This means $\frac{(25+n)}{6} = 6$, where n is the unknown number. Multiplying both sides by 6, we get $25 + n = 36$, which means $n = 11$.

6. B: 100 cm is equal to 1 m. 1.3 divided by 100 is 0.013. Therefore, 1.3 cm is equal to 0.013 mm. Because 1 cm is equal to 10 mm, 1.3 cm is equal to 13 mm.

7. C: We know that red cans are $1 each and blue cans are $2 each. Since the total cost is $16, we can say that $r \times 1 + b \times 2 = 16$, where r is the number of red cans and b is the number of blue cans. We can write this equation more simply as $r + 2b = 16$.

Because Jessica buys 10 cans total, we know that $r + b = 10$, so $b = 10 - r$. Substituting in $10 - r$ for b in the original equation, we get $r + 2(10 - r) = 16$. Simplifying and solving for r, we find:

$$r + 20 - 2r = 16$$

$$20 - r = 16$$

$$r = 4$$

8. B: We can use slope-intercept form, $y = mx + b$. We are told that the y-intercept (b) is 1, which gives us $y = mx + 1$. Now we can plug in the x and y values from our point, $(1,2)$, to find the slope: $2 = m(1) + 1$, so $m = 1$. This gives us $y = x + 1$.

9. A: The Pythagorean theorem tells us that $8^2 + x^2 = 10^2$, where x is the unknown side. This simplifies to $64 + x^2 = 100$, so $x^2 = 100 - 64 = 36$, and $x = \sqrt{36} = 6$ inches.

10. D: Denote the width as w and the length as l. Then, $l = 3w + 5$. The perimeter is $2w + 2l = 90$. Substituting the first expression for l into the second equation yields:

$$2(3w + 5) + 2w = 90$$

$$6w + 10 + 2w = 90$$

$$8w = 80$$

$$w = 10$$

Putting this into the first equation, it yields:

$$l = 3(10) + 5 = 35$$

11. A: First, the sample mean must be calculated.

$$\bar{x} = \frac{1}{4}(1 + 3 + 5 + 7) = 4$$

The sample standard deviation of the data set is:

$$s = \sqrt{\frac{\sum(x - \bar{x})^2}{n - 1}}$$

$n = 4$ represents the number of data points.

Therefore, the sample standard deviation is:

$$s = \sqrt{\frac{1}{3}[(1 - 4)^2 + (3 - 4)^2 + (5 - 4)^2 + (7 - 4)^2]}$$

$$s = \sqrt{\frac{1}{3}(9 + 1 + 1 + 9)} = 2.58$$

12. C: The sample space is made up of $8 + 7 + 6 + 5 = 26$ balls. The probability of pulling each individual ball is $1/26$. Since there are 7 yellow balls, the probability of pulling a yellow ball is $7/26$.

13. C: Begin by subtracting 6 from both sides to get $2x = 14$. Dividing both sides by 2 results in $x = 7$.

14. D: If we roll a die twice, there are 6 possibilities for the first roll and 6 for the second roll, which gives $6 \times 6 = 36$ total possibilities. Now, how many ways are there to roll exactly one 6? We could get a 6 & 1, or 6 & 2, or 6 & 3, or 6 & 4, or 6 & 5. Or the 6 could come on the second roll; we could get a 1 & 6, or 2 & 6, or 3 & 6, or 4 & 6, or 5 & 6. Counting these up, we find a total of 10 different ways to roll exactly one 6. That means our event happens in 10 out of 36 possible rolls, so the probability is $\frac{10}{36}$, which reduces to $\frac{5}{18}$.

15. D: First, the train's journey in the real world is:

$$3\,\text{h} \times 50\,\frac{\text{mi}}{\text{h}} = 150\,\text{mi}$$

On the map, 1 inch corresponds to 10 miles, so that is equivalent to:

$$150\,\text{mi} \times \frac{1\,\text{in}}{10\,\text{mi}} = 15\,\text{in}$$

Therefore, the start and end points are 15 inches apart on the map.

16. D: Let a be the number of apples, and let b represent the number of oranges. The total number of fruits is $a + b = 10$, and the total cost is $2a + 3b = 22$. To solve this pair of equations, we can multiply the first equation by –3:

$$-3(a + b) = -3(10)$$

$$-3a - 3b = -30$$

Now we can add this to the other equation, and the b terms cancel out:

$$(-3a - 3b = -30)$$

$$+(2a + 3b = 22)$$

$$= (-a = -8)$$

This simplifies to $a = 8$.

17. B: The formula for the volume of a cylinder is $\pi r^2 h$, where r is the radius and h is the height. The diameter is twice the radius, so these barrels have a radius of 1 foot. That means each barrel has a volume of:

$$\pi \times 1^2 \times 3 = 3\pi \text{ ft}^3$$

Since there are three of them, the total is:

$$3 \times 3\pi = 9\pi \text{ ft}^3$$

18. B: Follow the order of operations in order to solve this problem. Evaluate inside the parentheses first, being sure to follow the order of operations inside the parentheses as well. First, simplify the square roots:

$$(6 \times 4) - 3^2$$

Then, multiply inside the parentheses:

$$24 - 3^2$$

Next, simplify the exponent:

$$24 - 9$$

Finally, subtract to get 15.

19. C: The square root of 16 is 4, so this expression simplifies to:

$$\frac{1}{2}\sqrt{16} = \frac{1}{2}(4) = 2$$

Therefore, Choice *C* is correct.

20. A: Simplify this to:

$$(4x^2y^4)^{\frac{3}{2}} = 4^{\frac{3}{2}}(x^2)^{\frac{3}{2}}(y^4)^{\frac{3}{2}}$$

$$4^{\frac{3}{2}} = (\sqrt{4})^3 = 2^3 = 8$$

For the other, recall that the exponents must be multiplied; this yields:

$$8x^{2 \cdot \frac{3}{2}}y^{4 \cdot \frac{3}{2}} = 8x^3y^6$$

Advanced Algebra and Functions

1. B: This problem can be solved using the Pythagorean Theorem. The triangle has a hypotenuse of 15 and one leg of 12. These values can be substituted into the Pythagorean formula to yield:

$$12^2 + b^2 = 15^2$$

$$144 + b^2 = 225$$

$$81 = b^2$$

$$b = 9$$

In this problem, b is represented by x so $x = 9$ is the correct answer.

2. A: The total number of treats distributed will be the number of treats per bag $(4x + 1)$ times the number of bags given out, which can be represented by the variable n. This expression is $n(4x + 1)$. Since this is the amount of treats distributed, set it equal to $60x + 15$. $n(4x + 1) = 60x + 15$. In order to figure out what n is, determine what number times 4 results in 60 $(4n = 60)$ and what number times 1 results in 15 $(1n = 15)$. In both cases, $n = 15$. Therefore, 15 bags are given out.

3. D: Exponential functions can be written in the form: $y = a \times b^x$. The equation for an exponential function can be written given the y-intercept (a) and the growth rate (b).

The y-intercept is the output (y) when the input (x) equals zero. It can be thought of as an "original value," or starting point. The value of b is the rate at which the original value increases $(b > 1)$ or decreases $(b < 1)$.

In this scenario, the y-intercept, a, would be $1200, and the growth rate, b, would be 1.01 (100% of the original value combined with 1% interest, or $100\% + 1\% = 101\% = 1.01$).

4. C: The area of the shaded region is the area of the square minus the area of the circle. The area of the circle is πr^2. The side of the square will be $2r$, so the area of the square will be $4r^2$. Therefore, the difference is:

$$4r^2 - \pi r^2 = (4 - \pi)r^2$$

5. B: When solving for x, add 3 to both sides to get $4x = 8$. Then divide both sides by 4 to get $x = 2$.

6. B: There are two zeros for the given function. They are $x = 0, -2$. The zeros can be found several ways, but this particular equation can be factored into:

$$f(x) = x(x^2 + 4x + 4) = x(x + 2)(x + 2)$$

By setting each factor equal to zero and solving for x, there are two solutions: $x = 0$ and $x = -2$. On a graph, these zeros can be seen where the line crosses the x-axis.

7. B: First, take the natural logarithm of both sides. This results in $\ln(4^{5-x}) = \ln 7$. By properties of logarithms, the exponent can come down in front, resulting in $(5 - x) \ln 4 = \ln 7$. Then, divide both sides by $\ln 4$ to obtain $5 - x = \frac{\ln 7}{\ln 4}$. Finally, subtract 5 off of both sides and divide by -1 to obtain the solution. $x = -\frac{\ln 7}{\ln 4} + 5$.

8. C: The formula for the volume of a pyramid is $V = \frac{lwh}{3}$. Here, the length and width are each 6 in, and the height is 9 in, so we calculate $V = \frac{6 \times 6 \times 9}{3} = 108 \ in^3$.

9. D: Using SOHCAHTOA reminds us that tangent equals the opposite side over the adjacent side. Since $tan(\theta) + 1 = 0$, we are looking for $tan(\theta) = -1$. On the unit circle, "opposite over adjacent" equals 1 or -1 when the angle with the x-axis is 45°, or $\frac{\pi}{4}$. This value is negative in the second and fourth quadrant, which corresponds to $\frac{3\pi}{4}$ and $\frac{7\pi}{4}$.

10. B: To simplify this inequality, subtract 3 from both sides to get:

$$-\frac{1}{2}x \geq -1$$

Then, multiply both sides by -2 (remembering that this flips the direction of the inequality) to get $x \leq 2$.

11. D: There are two ways to approach this problem. Each value can be substituted into each equation. A can be eliminated, since:

$$4^2 + 16 = 32$$

Choice B can be eliminated, since:

$$4^2 + 4 \times 4 - 4 = 28$$

C can be eliminated, since

$$4^2 - 2 \times 4 - 2 = 6$$

But, plugging either value into $x^2 - 16$ gives the following:

$$(\pm 4)^2 - 16 = 16 - 16 = 0$$

12. A: The common denominator here will be $4x$. Rewrite these fractions as:

$$\frac{3}{x} + \frac{5u}{2x} - \frac{u}{4}$$

$$\frac{12}{4x} + \frac{10u}{4x} - \frac{ux}{4x}$$

$$\frac{12x + 10u - ux}{4x}$$

13. D: The shape of the scatter plot is a parabola (U-shaped). This eliminates Choices A (a linear equation that produces a straight line) and C (an exponential equation that produces a smooth curve upward or downward). The value of a for a quadratic function in standard form ($y = ax^2 + bx + c$) indicates whether

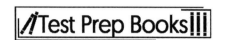
the parabola opens up (U-shaped) or opens down (upside-down U). A negative value for a produces a parabola that opens down; therefore, Choice B can also be eliminated.

14. D: Finding the zeros for a function by factoring is done by setting the equation equal to zero, then completely factoring. Since there is a common x for each term in the provided equation, that should be factored out first to get $x(x^2 - 3x - 4)$. Then the quadratic that is left can be factored into two binomials, which are $(x + 1)(x - 4)$. This gives the factored equation $0 = x(x + 1)(x - 4)$.

15. D: Dividing rational expressions follows the same rule as dividing fractions. The division is changed to multiplication by the reciprocal of the second fraction. This turns the expression into:

$$\frac{5x^3}{3x^2y} \times \frac{3y^9}{25}$$

This can be simplified by finding common factors in the numerators and denominators of the two fractions.

$$\frac{x^3}{x^2y} \times \frac{y^9}{5}$$

Multiplying across creates:

$$\frac{x^3y^9}{5x^2y}$$

Simplifying leads to the final expression of:

$$\frac{xy^8}{5}$$

16. B: Recall that to compose functions, replace the x in the expression for g with the expression for f everywhere there is x. So:

$$g(f(x)) = \frac{f(x) - 1}{4} = \frac{2x + 1 - 1}{4} = \frac{2x}{4} = \frac{x}{2}$$

17. A: Using the trigonometric identity $\tan(\theta) = \frac{\sin(\theta)}{\cos(\theta)}$, the expression becomes $\frac{\sin\theta}{\cos\theta}\cos\theta$. The factors that are the same on the top and bottom cancel out, leaving the simplified expression $\sin\theta$.

18. B: The truck weighs 25,000 pounds without any boxes added to the load. This is equivalent to the y-intercept in the equation since the number of boxes $b = 0$. The weight changes when boxes are added. The weight of each box, 45, is equal to the rate of change of the equation, or slope. Therefore, the correct equation is $w = 45b + 25000$.

19. A: The function can be factored to identify the zeros. First, the term $3x$ is factored out to the front because each term contains $3x$. Then, the quadratic is factored into $(x + 3)(x - 2)$.

20. B: The first step is to use the quadratic formula on the first equation ($x^2 - x - 3 = 0$) to solve for x. In this case, a is 1, b is −1, and c is −3, yielding:

$$x = \frac{-b \pm \sqrt{b^2 - 4ac}}{2a}$$

$$x = \frac{1 \pm \sqrt{1 - 4 \times 1(-3)}}{2}$$

$$x = \frac{1}{2} \pm \frac{\sqrt{13}}{2}$$

Therefore, $x - \frac{1}{2}$, which is in our second equation, equals $\pm \frac{\sqrt{13}}{2}$. We are looking for $\left(x - \frac{1}{2}\right)^2$ though, so we square the $\pm \frac{\sqrt{13}}{2}$. Doing so causes the $\pm$ to cancel and we are left with:

$$\left(x - \frac{1}{2}\right)^2 = \left(\frac{\sqrt{13}}{2}\right)^2 = \frac{13}{4}$$

Reading Comprehension

1. C: Choice C is the correct answer because it most extensively summarizes the entire passage. While Choices A and B are reasonable possibilities, they reference portions of Gulliver's experiences, not the whole. Choice D is incorrect because Gulliver doesn't express repentance or sorrow in this particular passage.

2. C: Choice A is incorrect because there is no indication of stress in Gulliver's tone. Choices B and D aren't the best answer because though Gulliver seems fond of his new acquaintances, he didn't travel there with the intentions of meeting new people, nor does he express a definite love for them in this particular portion of the text.

3. D: Satire is a rhetorical device employed to criticize or mock people, politics, society, or other aspects of human behavior. The passage employs satire to mock the absurd practice of appointing individuals to high offices based on their skill in rope dancing, serving as a commentary on the perceived absurdities of the political system. Since Choice D uses the description of a fictional practice to mock a contemporary political context, it is a strong example of the passage's satirical tone.

4. C: The first-person point of view allows readers to intimately engage with Gulliver's personal experiences, thoughts, and observations. This subjective viewpoint can evoke empathy and understanding as readers relate to Gulliver's reactions and emotions in each distinct society he visits. Choice A is incorrect because the narrator draws readers into the experience rather than creating distance between reader and plot. Choice B is inaccurate because again, the narrative style does not create objectivity or neutrality for readers. Choice D is incorrect because the narration does not present the natives' point of view but Gulliver's.

5. A: Choice D is incorrect because while the passages utilize examples to help explain the concepts discussed, the author doesn't indicate that they are specific court cases. It's also clear that the passages don't open with examples, but instead, they begin by defining the terms addressed in each passage. This eliminates Choice B, and ultimately reveals Choice A to be the correct answer. Choice A accurately outlines the way both passages are structured. Because the passages follow a nearly identical structure, the Choice C can easily be ruled out.

6. C: Choice C is correct because it clearly establishes what both assault and lethal force are and gives the specific way in which the two concepts meet. Choice A is incorrect because lethal force doesn't necessarily result in assault. This is also why Choice B is incorrect. Not all assaults would necessarily be life-threatening to the point where lethal force is needed for self-defense. Choice D is compelling but ultimately incorrect; the statement touches on aspects of the two ideas but fails to present the concrete way in which the two are connected to each other.

7. C: Choices A and B are incorrect because it is clear in both passages that intent is a prevailing theme in both lethal force and assault. Choice D is compelling, but if a person uses lethal force to defend himself or herself, the intent of the defender is also examined in order to help determine if there was excessive force used. Choice C is correct because it states that intent is important for determining both lethal force and assault, and that intent is used to gauge the severity of the issues. Remember, just as lethal force can escalate to excessive use of force, there are different kinds of assault. Intent dictates several different forms of assault.

8. C: The situation of the man who is attacked in an alley by another man with a knife would most merit the use of lethal force. If the man being attacked used lethal force in self-defense, it would not be considered illegal. The presence of a deadly weapon indicates malicious intent, and because the individual is isolated in an alley, lethal force in self-defense may be the only way to preserve his life. Choices A and B can be ruled out because in these situations no one is in danger of immediate death or bodily harm by someone else. Choice D is an assault that does exhibit intent to harm, but this situation isn't severe enough to merit lethal force; there is no intent to kill.

9. D: The text mentions several different times how and why the association has been successful and gives examples to back this fact. Choice A is incorrect because the passage doesn't mention the need for people to take action. Likewise, Choices B and C are not mentioned in the text.

10. A: Rainforests have warm and wet climates. They do not have long dry seasons and tend to have temperate temperatures. The giant water lily is ideal for the rainforest because it can grow large leaves and needs a wet environment to grow in. They grow in the shallow basins of rainforest rivers. Choices B and C need dry environments. Choice D needs a very hot environment, which is not characteristic of rainforests.

11. A: While the reader may disagree with the author's position, all of the statements in the passage indicate the author's position is that piloting is a difficult goal that requires serious consideration on the part of a potential flight student. Choices B and D aren't stated. Choice C can be ruled out because the physical and mental toll on piloting students isn't the main position of the paragraph.

12. D: To conclude a sequence and add a final detail. The concluding sequence is expressed in the phrase "[t]he mother sun-fish, having now built or provided her 'hatchery.'" The final detail is the way in which the sun-fish guards the "enclosure." Choices A, B, and C are incorrect.

13. A: Choice A is supported by the passage's mention of Dr. Buck as a trailblazer in integrating traditional indigenous knowledge with modern astrophysics. The use of the word "trailblazer" implies that Dr. Buck is at the forefront of merging these two realms, suggesting that there has been a historical separation or lack of recognition for indigenous understanding of space in modern science. Choice B is incorrect because the paragraph does not mention a unanimously positive opinion about his work. Choice C is incorrect because only the Opaskwayak Cree Nation is discussed. Choice D is incorrect because the first paragraph does not mention the time period in which Dr. Buck worked; therefore, not enough information is given to support this inference.

14. B: Most of the paragraph focuses on the high-stress elements of wedding planning, from "balancing various responsibilities" to "last-minute adjustments or changes in plans." The passage emphasizes this vocation's need for flexibility, initiation, and stress management. The last sentence, however, explains how satisfaction for wedding planners comes from "crafting memorable events that bring romantic dreams to life," even after all the stress the job can bring. Choice *A* is incorrect because the sentence does not mention compensation. Choice *C* is incorrect; the concluding sentence does not remind readers of the reasons why the job is stressful. Finally, Choice *D* is incorrect because it does not compare wedding planning to other careers.

15. C: Choice *C* is correct because the author's use of "our" and "we" suggests a personal connection to both the Appalachian community and media production. The phrase "our region's diverse cultural fabric" implies personal knowledge of the area, while the phrase "by incorporating authentic narratives, we contribute to…" suggests the author has the power to act to dismantle stereotypes.

16. D: Choices *A*, *B*, and *C* provide further detail about specific elements mentioned in the passage; however, they fail to summarize the entire passage. Choice *D* is the only correct answer, as it mentions the importance of the discovery but explains why it falls short of its overblown historical reputation.

17. D: The passage describes the development of canyons through powerful natural processes. It outlines various factors and events (water flow, weathering, tectonic activity, etc.) and then explains how each of these factors contributes to the gradual creation of canyons. Although time is an implied element of cause-and-effect relationships, Choice *A* is not the best answer. The passage describes various processes, rather than comparing and contrasting them, so Choice *B* is not correct. The passage describes a phenomenon but does not present it as a problem with a needed solution; therefore, Choice *C* is incorrect.

18. C: In the passage, the author presents various appealing aspects of Cape Cod, such as "pristine beaches, charming coastal towns, and vibrant maritime culture." These elements aim to lend objectivity to the claim by highlighting universally attractive features of the destination. However, the author undermines that objectivity by introducing biased personal experiences like the annual tradition with the author's family. While personal anecdotes can enhance the reader's connection to the narrative, they can also introduce subjectivity and limit the claim's broad relevance. This makes Choice *C* the most accurate classification of the author's argument in this context.

19. D: The best answer for the blank is "dubious" because it accurately conveys the doubt felt by people who "questioned the sincerity and feasibility of her proposed policies." The other choices imply a positive response that does not fit the sentence. Choices *A* and *B* suggest a receptive response, while Choice *C* implies enthusiasm and excitement. Each of these options contradicts the more critical tone conveyed by "dubious" in this context.

20. B: In the given sentence, the word "alacrity" is the best choice for the blank because it conveys a sense of initiative and enthusiasm in approaching "challenging circumstances." The meaning of "alacrity" is "promptness in response" or "cheerful readiness"; this definition aligns well with Jaci's willingness to "contribute and make a positive impact on the team." The other options convey opposite meanings and would not accurately capture Jaci's positive and eager attitude.

Writing

1. B: Choice *B* correctly removes the apostrophe from *icon's* since the icon is not possessing anything. Choice *D* is grammatically correct but alters the meaning of the sentence—Frankenstein is one of the icons, not the sole icon.

2. C: Choice C correctly adds a comma after style, successfully joining the introductory phrase and independent clause as a single sentence. Choice A is incorrect because the introductory phrase and independent clause remain unsuccessfully combined without the comma. Choices B and D do nothing to fix this.

3. A: Choice A is correct, as the sentence doesn't require changes. Choice B incorrectly changes the noun *enlightenment* into the verb *enlighten*. Choices C and D alter the original meaning of the sentence.

4. D: Choice D is correct because the addition of finer details helps the reader understand exactly what Prometheus did and his impact: fire came with knowledge and power. Choice A lacks a comma after *fire*. Choice B inserts unnecessary commas since *people* is not part of the list *knowledge and power*. Choice C is a strong revision but could be confusing, hinting that the fire was knowledge and power itself, as opposed to being symbolized by the fire.

5. C: Choice C reverses the order of the section, making the sentence more direct. Choice A lacks a comma after *gods*, and although Choice B adds this, the structure is too different from the first half of the sentence to flow correctly. Choice D is overly complicated and repetitious in its structure even though it doesn't need any punctuation.

6. B: Choice B is the correct answer because it states a general fact about Japanese food and serves as a main idea for the paragraph. Although Choices A, C, and D are true facts about Japanese cuisine, they are details that would further support a main idea about Japanese food.

7. C: Choice C is the correct answer. Sentence 10 should follow Sentence 8. It introduces the town of Hakone and provides the framework for the specific information about the town presented in Sentences 9 through 12.

8. D: Choice D is the correct answer. This sentence is more concise and still incorporates all of the information trying to be conveyed in the original sentence. Choices A, B, and C either mix up the information in the original sentence or give incorrect facts.

9. B: Choice B is the correct answer. In this sentence, the words *or bullet train* serve as an appositive, or extra information provided in the sentence. These words are added to the sentence to define *Shinkansen*. However, the sentence would be correct even if these words hadn't been added, so this phrase should be set apart with commas. A correct version of the sentence would look like this: [8]*People from all over Japan ride the Shinkansen, or bullet train, to Osaka to watch the events.*

10. C: The error is in pronoun-antecedent agreement. *They* is the wrong word to use because the pronoun refers to the singular Japanese dish, Soba. Therefore, Choice A is incorrect. Replacing *they* with *it* correctly revises this sentence, so Choice C is correct. Choice B is incorrect because the pronoun is not changed and *is* is changed to the wrong tense, *was*. Choice D is incorrect because although the pronoun is correct, the verb that follows it is the incorrect tense.

11. C: Choice C is correct. Ensure means to make sure something will happen. The service men and women have made sure the nation is safe, so *ensure* is the correct word to use here. Leaving the word as it is, Choice A, would be incorrect. To insure is to protect against loss or damage by providing compensation, and that is not what service men and women do. Choice B is incorrect because *assure* means *to convince*, which does not fit the context of this sentence. Choice D is also incorrect. Deleting the word *insure* wouldn't make the sentence any better. Saying that the men and women "have worked or still work to the safety of our nation" is grammatically incorrect.

12. A: Choice *A* is the correct answer. The transition phrase, *On this day*, helps to clarify that things are closed for a specific reason versus being closed in general.

13. A: Choice *A* is the correct answer. In Sentence 1, the writer mentions Memorial Day and then Veterans Day in the statement of the main idea. Thus, the supporting sentences in the paragraph should also be in this order.

14. D: Choice *D* is the correct answer. This sentence rewords the writer's original sentence while still including all of the correct information. Choices *A, B,* and *C* either remain too wordy, provide inaccurate information, or fail to clarify the writer's idea.

15. D: The original sentence sounds like Decoration Day was both renamed and declared a national holiday in 1950 until you read the last two words of the sentence. Therefore, Choice *A* is not the correct answer. This detail needs to be made clear and is done so by adding a comma before the independent clause that states when the day became a federal holiday, making Choice *D* correct. Choice *B* is incorrect because it removes the comma after the prepositional phrase at the beginning of the sentence—which isn't necessarily a problem since the comma here is optional—but it places a comma incorrectly between the independent and dependent clauses. Choice *C* in incorrect because it places the comma before the prepositional phrase at the end of the sentence, which is typically not done when a prepositional phrase is at the end of a sentence, and it also makes it sound like the federal holiday was declared in 1950.

16. D: The correct preposition to describe the fact that dogs are the descendants of wolves is *from*, so Choice *D* is correct. *From* is the most precise and accurate choice. The other answer choices do not convey the message properly.

17. B: The error in this sentence is a misplaced modifier, so Choice *A* is incorrect. *Which is also known as artificial selection* seems to refer to the word *traits* rather than *selective breeding*. To make it clear that artificial selection is another term for selective breeding, the best revision is to place it within commas right after *selective breeding*. Therefore, Choice *B* is correct. Choice *C* is incorrect because the misplaced modifier is not corrected and commas are placed around a restrictive modifier, which should not be placed within commas. Choice *D* is incorrect because the misplaced modifier is not corrected and a comma is inappropriately placed before *in which*.

18. D: Sentence 2 lacks the Oxford Comma, which helps clearly separate specific terms. Therefore, Choice *D* is correct and Choice *A* is incorrect. Choice *B* is incorrect because semicolons should only be used if any of the items in the series contain commas. Choice *C* is incorrect because em dashes should be used to set off explanatory information, which is not the case in this sentence.

19. C: Choice *C* is correct because Sentences 8 through 10 describe the process of evolution through adaptation. By changing *escape from* to *adapt to* in Sentence 7, the author explicitly states the focus of the following sentences."

20. B: Choice *B* is correct because it presents the idea in a clear and concise manner. Choice *A* is too repetitive and confusing. Choice *C* uses confusing wording and sentence structure. Choice *D* is incorrect because *dog breeding* is carried out by humans, so the phrase *and with the help of humans* is unnecessary.

21. C: Choice *C* is correct. *Significance* matches the tone of the rest of the words in the series as well as the tone of the passage. Choice *A*, *insufficiency*, strays from the tone. How could something be deep and true, yet insufficient, or inadequate? This isn't a logical choice. Choice *B*, *awesomeness*, keeps with a positive tone, but it is less formal than the rest of the words in the series, so it is not the best choice. Choice *D* is incorrect because *gaiety* suggests a lighthearted tone or subject, but even early in the passage, the reader can see that the subject matter is serious.

282

22. B: Choice *B* is correct. Sentence 5 is a digression because this essay is not an argumentative piece on what makes humans human. The sentence does not add to or support the topic at all, and this argument is not brought up again in the passage. Each of the other answer choice has a place and purpose in the passage and are not digressions.

23. B: Here, a colon is used to introduce an explanation. Colons introduce either explanations or lists. Additionally, the quote ends with the punctuation inside the quotes, unlike Choice *C.*

24. B: Choice *B* is correct because it provides clarity by describing what *myopic* means right after the word itself. Choice *A* is incorrect because the explanation of *myopic* comes before the word; thus, the meaning is skewed. It's possible that Choice *C* makes sense within context. However, it's not the best way to say this because the commas create too many unnecessary phrases. Choice *D* is confusingly worded. Using *myopic focus* is not detrimental to society; however, the way *D* is worded makes it seem that way.

25. C: The passage's second paragraph can be divided into two paragraphs because it is about two separate topics. The paragraph's first main focus is education addressing the mind, body, and soul. This first section, then, could end with the concluding sentence, "The human heart and psyche ..." The next sentence should start a new paragraph with "Education is a basic human right ..." The rest of this paragraph talks about what education is and some of its characteristics.

283

Practice Test #2

Arithmetic

1. How would the number 84,789 be written if rounded to the nearest hundred?
    a. 84,800
    b. 84,700
    c. 84,780
    d. 85,000

2. Shawna buys $2\frac{1}{2}$ gallons of paint. If she uses $\frac{1}{3}$ of it on the first day, how much does she have left?
    a. $1\frac{5}{6}$ gallons

    b. $1\frac{1}{2}$ gallons

    c. $1\frac{2}{3}$ gallons

    d. 2 gallons

3. Chris walks $\frac{4}{7}$ of a mile to school, and Tina walks $\frac{5}{9}$ of a mile. Which student covers more distance on the walk to school?
    a. Chris, because $\frac{4}{7} > \frac{5}{9}$

    b. Chris, because $\frac{4}{7} < \frac{5}{9}$

    c. Tina, because $\frac{5}{9} > \frac{4}{7}$

    d. Tina, because $\frac{5}{9} < \frac{4}{7}$

4. Four people split a bill. The first person pays for $\frac{1}{5}$, the second person pays for $\frac{1}{4}$, and the third person pays for $\frac{1}{3}$. What fraction of the bill does the fourth person pay?
    a. $\frac{13}{60}$

    b. $\frac{47}{60}$

    c. $\frac{1}{4}$

    d. $\frac{4}{15}$

5. When rounding 245.2678 to the nearest thousandth, which place value would be used to decide whether to round up or round down?
    a. Ten-thousandths
    b. Thousandths
    c. Hundredths
    d. Thousands

6. Which value is NOT equivalent to the others?
   a. $18:12$
   b. $\frac{6}{4}$
   c. $4:3$
   d. $\frac{36}{24}$

7. Store-brand coffee beans cost \$1.23 per pound. A local coffee bean roaster charges \$1.98 per $1\frac{1}{2}$ pounds. How much more would 5 pounds from the local roaster cost than 5 pounds of the store brand?
   a. \$0.55
   b. \$1.55
   c. \$1.45
   d. \$0.45

8. The value of 6×12 is the same as:
   a. $2 \times 4 \times 4 \times 2$
   b. $7 \times 4 \times 3$
   c. $6 \times 6 \times 3$
   d. $3 \times 3 \times 4 \times 2$

9. What is 3 out of 8 expressed as a percent?
   a. 37.5%
   b. 37%
   c. 26.7%
   d. 2.67%

10. Multiply and reduce $\frac{15}{23} \times \frac{54}{127}$.
   a. $\frac{810}{2,921}$
   b. $\frac{81}{292}$
   c. $\frac{69}{150}$
   d. $\frac{810}{2929}$

11. In an office, there are 50 workers. A total of 60% of the workers are women. 50% of the women (and none of the other workers) are wearing skirts. How many workers are wearing skirts?
   a. 12
   b. 15
   c. 16
   d. 20

12. Which fractions are equivalent, or would fill the same portion on a number line?
   a. $\frac{2}{4}$ and $\frac{3}{8}$
   b. $\frac{1}{2}$ and $\frac{4}{8}$
   c. $\frac{3}{6}$ and $\frac{3}{5}$
   d. $\frac{2}{4}$ and $\frac{5}{8}$

285

13. Consider a four-year private institution that you would like to attend for college. The tuition per year is $22,000, and it is estimated that room and board will be $5,000 per year and books will cost you $500 per year. If your family is expected to pay for 25% of your total expenses, how much will you have to have in a savings account if you would like to have the total amount available before you even attend?

   a. $82,500
   b. $110,000
   c. $88,000
   d. $27,500

14. What is the solution to $7\frac{5}{8} - 3\frac{1}{5}$?

   a. $4\frac{17}{40}$
   b. $10\frac{33}{40}$
   c. $4\frac{11}{20}$
   d. $6\frac{29}{40}$

15. Subtract $50.888 - 13.091$.

   a. 63.799
   b. 63.979
   c. 37.979
   d. 37.797

16. Find the following sum and round to the nearest hundredths place:

$$4.673 + 2.651$$

   a. 73.24
   b. 7.32
   c. 7.33
   d. 7.324

17. If Amanda can eat two times as many mini cupcakes as Marty, what would the missing values be for the following input-output table?

Input (number of cupcakes eaten by Marty)	Output (number of cupcakes eaten by Amanda)
1	2
3	
5	10
7	
9	18

   a. 6, 10
   b. 3, 11
   c. 6, 14
   d. 4, 12

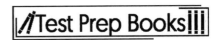

18. A construction company is building a new housing development with the property of each house measuring 30 feet wide. If the length of the street is zoned off at 345 feet, how many houses can be built on the street?
    a. 11
    b. 115
    c. 11.5
    d. 12

19. Bernard can make $80 per day. If he needs to make $300 and only works full days, how many days will this take?
    a. 2
    b. 3
    c. 4
    d. 5

20. Taylor works two jobs. The first pays $20,000 per year. The second pays $10,000 per year. She donates 15% of her income to charity. How much does she donate each year?
    a. $4,500
    b. $5,000
    c. $5,500
    d. $6,000

Quantitative Reasoning, Algebra, and Statistics

1. Which of the following shows the correct result of simplifying the following expression?

$$(7n + 3n^3 + 3) + (8n + 5n^3 + 2n^4)$$

    a. $9n^4 + 15n - 2$
    b. $2n^4 + 5n^3 + 15n - 2$
    c. $9n^4 + 8n^3 + 15n$
    d. $2n^4 + 8n^3 + 15n + 3$

2. Find the equation of the following line:

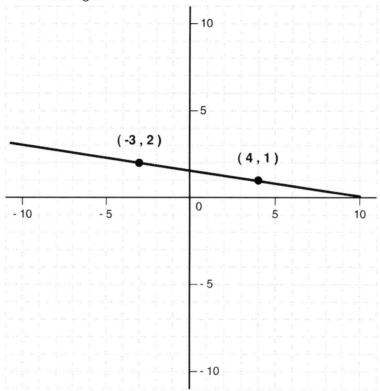

a. $y = -\frac{1}{7}x + \frac{21}{7}$
b. $y = 7x + 29$
c. $y = -\frac{1}{7}x + \frac{11}{7}$
d. $y = \frac{1}{7}x + \frac{11}{7}$

3. Which of the following equations best represents the problem below?

The width of a rectangle is 2 centimeters less than the length. If the perimeter of the rectangle is 44 centimeters, then what are the dimensions of the rectangle?

a. $2l + 2(l - 2) = 44$
b. $(l + 2) + (l + 2) + l = 48$
c. $l \times (l - 2) = 44$
d. $(l + 2) + (l + 2) + l = 44$

4. The variable y is directly proportional to x. If $y = 3$ when $x = 5$, then what is y when $x = 20$?
a. 10
b. 12
c. 14
d. 16

5. If $6t + 4 = 16$, what is t?
   a.   1
   b.   2
   c.   3
   d.   4

6. Before a race of four horses, you make a random guess of which horse will get first place and which will get second place. What is the probability that both your guesses will be correct?
   a. $\frac{1}{4}$

   b. $\frac{1}{2}$

   c. $\frac{1}{16}$

   d. $\frac{1}{12}$

7. An equilateral triangle has a perimeter of 18 feet. The sides of a square have the same length as the triangle's sides. What is the area of the square?
   a.   6 square feet
   b.   36 square feet
   c.   256 square feet
   d.   1,000 square feet

8. Simplify $(5x^2 - 3x + 4) - (2x^2 - 7)$?
   a. x^5
   b. $3x^2 - 3x + 11$
   c. $3x^2 - 3x - 3$
   d. $x - 3$

9. If a car can travel 300 miles in 4 hours, how far can it go in an hour and a half?
   a.   100 miles
   b.   112.5 miles
   c.   135.5 miles
   d.   150 miles

10. If $\sqrt{5 + x} = 5$, what is x?
   a.   10
   b.   15
   c.   20
   d.   25

11. A pair of dice is thrown, and the sum of the two scores is calculated. What's the expected value of the roll?
   a.   5
   b.   6
   c.   7
   d.   8

12. $\frac{5.2 \cdot 10^2}{2.6 \cdot 10^4} =$

    a. 4×10^2

    b. 2×10^{-2}

    c. 2×10^2

    d. 4×10^{-2}

13. What is the perimeter of the figure below? Note that the solid outer line is the perimeter.

    a. 48.565 in

    b. 36.565 in

    c. 39.78 in

    d. 39.565 in

14. How should 0.042 be expressed in scientific notation?

    a. 4.2×10^2

    b. 4.2×10^3

    c. 4.2×10^{-3}

    d. 4.2×10^{-2}

15. What is the equation of a line that passes through the point (2, 3) with a slope of 4?

    a. $y = 4x - 5$

    b. $y = 3x - 8$

    c. $y = \frac{1}{2}x + 3$

    d. $y = \frac{3}{2}x + 4$

16. $-\frac{1}{3}\sqrt{81} =$

    a. -9

    b. -3

    c. 0

    d. 3

17. Ten students take a test. Five students get a 50. Four students get a 70. If the average score is 55, what was the last student's score?

    a. 20

    b. 40

    c. 50

    d. 60

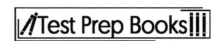

18. A data set is comprised of the following values: 30, 33, 33, 26, 27, 32, 33, 35, 29, 27. Which of the following has the greatest value?
    a. Mean
    b. Median
    c. Mode
    d. Range

19. Mom's car drove 72 miles in 90 minutes. How fast did she drive in feet per second?
    a. 0.8 feet per second
    b. 48.9 feet per second
    c. 0.009 feet per second
    d. 70.4 feet per second

20. Find the equation of a line perpendicular to $y = -8x + 2$ that goes through the point $(-5, 5)$.
    a. $y = \frac{1}{8}x + \frac{45}{8}$
    b. $y = \frac{1}{8}x + 5$
    c. $y = -8x + 40$
    d. $y = -\frac{1}{8}x - \frac{35}{8}$

Advanced Algebra and Functions

1. Solve the equation $\log_{15}(4x - 2) = 3$.
    a. 924.35
    b. 5.52
    c. 1.25
    d. 844.25

2. What is the domain for the function $y = \sqrt{x}$?
    a. All real numbers
    b. $x \geq 0$
    c. $x > 0$
    d. $y \geq 0$

3. Of the given sets of coordinates below, which ones lie on the line that is perpendicular to $y = 2x - 3$ and passes through the point $(0, 5)$? Select all that apply.
    a. $(-6, 10)$
    b. $(-2, 7)$
    c. $(2, 6)$
    d. $(4, 3)$

4. What is the value of $x^2 - 2xy + 2y^2$ when $x = 2, y = 3$?
    a. 8
    b. 10
    c. 12
    d. 14

5. Is the following function even, odd, neither, or both?

$$y = \frac{1}{2}x^4 + 2x^2 - 6$$

    a. Even
    b. Odd
    c. Neither
    d. Both

6. For which of the following are $x = 16$ and $x = -16$ solutions?
    a. $x^2 + 64 = 0$
    b. $x^2 + 8x - 4 = 0$
    c. $x^2 - 4x - 4 = 0$
    d. $x^2 - 64 = 0$

7. A pizza delivery driver charges a flat fee of $5.50 per delivery and then $7.25 per small pizza. A college student has collected $80 from their friends. How many small pizzas can be delivered from this driver?
    a. 7
    b. 11
    c. 10
    d. 8

8. What is an equation for the line passing through the origin and the point $(2,1)$?
    a. $y = 2x$
    b. $y = \frac{1}{2}x$
    c. $y = x - 2$
    d. $2y = x + 1$

9. What are the y-intercept(s) for $y = x^2 + 3x - 4$?
    a. $y = 1$
    b. $y = -4$
    c. $y = 3$
    d. $y = 4$

10. If $\sqrt{1 + x} = 4$, what is x?
    a. 10
    b. 15
    c. 20
    d. 25

11. Suppose $\frac{x+2}{x} = 2$. What is x?
    a. -1
    b. 0
    c. 2
    d. 4

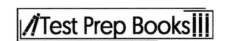

12. If $a \neq b$, solve for x if $\frac{1}{x} + \frac{2}{a} = \frac{2}{b}$
    a. $\frac{a-b}{ab}$

    b. $\frac{ab}{2(a-b)}$

    c. $\frac{2(a-b)}{ab}$

    d. $\frac{a-b}{2ab}$

13. If $\log_{10} x = 2$, then x is
    a. 4
    b. 20
    c. 100
    d. 1,000

14. Find the solutions of $(4x + \sqrt{7})(9x + \sqrt{11}) = 0$.
    a. $-\frac{7}{4}, -\frac{11}{9}$
    b. $-\frac{\sqrt{7}}{4}, -\frac{\sqrt{11}}{9}$
    c. $\frac{\sqrt{7}}{4}, \frac{\sqrt{11}}{9}$
    d. $-\frac{\sqrt{7}}{2}, -\frac{\sqrt{11}}{3}$

15. If $f(x) = (\frac{1}{2})^x$ and $a < b$, then which of the following must be true?
    a. $f(a) < f(b)$
    b. $f(a) > f(b)$
    c. $f(a) + f(b) = 0$
    d. $3f(a) = f(b)$

16. The area of a given rectangle is 24 square centimeters. If the measure of each side is multiplied by 3, what is the area of the new figure?
    a. 48cm
    b. 72cm
    c. 216cm
    d. 13,824cm

17. $x^4 - 16$ can be simplified to which of the following?
    a. $(x^2 - 4)(x^2 + 4)$
    b. $(x^2 + 4)(x^2 + 4)$
    c. $(x^2 - 4)(x^2 - 4)$
    d. $(x^2 - 2)(x^2 + 4)$

18. What is the slope of the line tangent to the graph of $y = x^3 - 4$ at the point where $x = 2$?
    a. $3x^2$
    b. 4
    c. -4
    d. 12

293

19. If the point$(-3, -4)$ is reflected over the x-axis, what new point does it make?
   a. $(-3, -4)$
   b. $(3, -4)$
   c. $(3, 4)$
   d. $(-3, 4)$

20. What are the center and radius of a circle with equation $4x^2 + 4y^2 - 16x - 24y + 51 = 0$?
   a. Center $(3, 2)$ and radius $1/2$
   b. Center $(2, 3)$ and radius $1/2$
   c. Center $(3, 2)$ and radius $1/4$
   d. Center $(2, 3)$ and radius $1/4$

Reading Comprehension

The next four questions pertain to the following excerpt:

"Did you ever come across a protégé of his—one Hyde?" He asked.

"Hyde?" repeated Lanyon. "No. Never heard of him. Since my time."

That was the amount of information that the lawyer carried back with him to the great, dark bed on which he tossed to and fro until the small hours of the morning began to grow large. It was a night of little ease to his toiling mind, toiling in mere darkness and besieged by questions.

Six o'clock struck on the bells of the church that was so conveniently near to Mr. Utterson's dwelling, and still he was digging at the problem. Hitherto it had touched him on the intellectual side alone; but now his imagination also was engaged, or rather enslaved; and as he lay and tossed in the gross darkness of the night in the curtained room, Mr. Enfield's tale went by before his mind in a scroll of lighted pictures. He would be aware of the great field of lamps in a nocturnal city; then of the figure of a man walking swiftly; then of a child running from the doctor's; and then these met, and that human Juggernaut trod the child down and passed on regardless of her screams. Or else he would see a room in a rich house, where his friend lay asleep, dreaming and smiling at his dreams; and then the door of that room would be opened, the curtains of the bed plucked apart, the sleeper recalled, and, lo! There would stand by his side a figure to whom power was given, and even at that dead hour he must rise and do its bidding. The figure in these two phases haunted the lawyer all night; and if at any time he dozed over, it was but to see it glide more stealthily through sleeping houses, or move the more swiftly, and still the more smoothly, even to dizziness, through wider labyrinths of lamplighted city, and at every street corner crush a child and leave her screaming. And still the figure had no face by which he might know it; even in his dreams it had no face, or one that baffled him and melted before his eyes; and thus it was that there sprung up and grew apace in the lawyer's mind a singularly strong, almost an inordinate, curiosity to behold the features of the real Mr. Hyde. If he could but once set eyes on him, he thought the mystery would lighten and perhaps roll altogether away, as was the habit of mysterious things when well examined. He might see a reason for his friend's strange preference or bondage, and even for the startling clauses of the will. And at least it would be a face worth seeing: the face of a man who was without bowels of mercy: a face which had but to show itself to raise up, in the mind of the unimpressionable Enfield, a spirit of enduring hatred.

This excerpt is an adaptation of Robert Louis Stevenson's *The Strange Case of Dr. Jekyll and Mr. Hyde*

1. What is the purpose of the use of repetition in the following passage?

   It was a night of little ease to his toiling mind, toiling in mere darkness and besieged by questions.

   a. It serves as a demonstration of the mental state of Mr. Lanyon.
   b. It is reminiscent of the church bells that are mentioned in the story.
   c. It mimics Mr. Utterson's ambivalence.
   d. It emphasizes Mr. Utterson's anguish in failing to identify Hyde's whereabouts.

2. Words and phrases such as "besieged by questions," "digging," "imagination," and "haunt" in the passage serve to arouse a sense of _____.
   a. intrigue
   b. elation
   c. animosity
   d. rigidity

3. What is the setting of the story in this passage?
   a. In the city
   b. On the countryside
   c. In a jail
   d. In a mental health facility

4. According to the passage, what is Mr. Utterson struggling with as he tosses and turns in bed?
   a. A murderer who is stalking Mr. Utterson since he moved to the city.
   b. The mystery surrounding a dark figure and the terrible crimes he commits.
   c. The cases he is involved in as a detective.
   d. A chronic illness that is causing Mr. Utterson to hallucinate.

The next four questions pertain to the following set of passages:

Passage 1

Wi-Fi, short for Wireless Fidelity, allows devices to connect to the internet and communicate wirelessly within a local area network (LAN). It uses radio frequency signals to transmit data between devices like smartphones, laptops, and routers. The process begins with a router, which acts as a central hub for the network. The router receives data from the internet through a wired connection, often via a broadband modem.

To enable Wi-Fi, the router converts the data into radio waves using a wireless radio signal. These signals operate on the 2.4 GHz and 5 GHz frequency bands and use a protocol called IEEE 802.11. Devices equipped with Wi-Fi capabilities, such as laptops or smartphones, have wireless network adapters that can receive and interpret these radio signals. When a device within the router's range wishes to connect, it sends a request to the router, which then grants access and establishes a two-way communication channel.

Wi-Fi allows for the seamless transfer of data, enabling internet access and local network interactions without the need for physical cables. However, the effectiveness of Wi-Fi can be influenced by factors such as signal interference, distance from the router, and the number of connected devices.

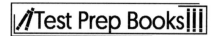

Passage 2

Providing free Wi-Fi in American cities is not just a convenience; it is a vital step towards fostering inclusive communities and catalyzing overall societal progress. Access to the internet has become an essential utility—akin to water and electricity—and it shapes the way we learn, work, and communicate. By offering free Wi-Fi, cities can bridge the digital divide, ensuring that all residents, regardless of economic status, have equal access to the vast number of resources available online.

Education is a primary beneficiary of ubiquitous internet access as students can research, collaborate, and access educational materials from anywhere in the city. Free Wi-Fi also promotes economic development by providing job seekers with a platform to explore opportunities and entrepreneurs with a means to establish and grow their businesses.

Moreover, free citywide Wi-Fi enhances public safety through improved communication and emergency response capabilities. It strengthens the social fabric by enabling community engagement, fostering civic participation, and connecting residents with local services. Ultimately, offering free Wi-Fi is an investment in the collective prosperity of a city. It would empower individuals, promote digital literacy, and create a more connected and dynamic urban environment.

5. Which option provides the most complete summary of the second paragraph of Passage 1?
    a. Radio signals are useful for so much more than morning talk shows and music stations.
    b. A router turns data into radio waves so that devices like laptops or smartphones can interact with the signal by sending and receiving information.
    c. When radio signals sent from a Wi-Fi router are interrupted or slowed down, the quality of Wi-Fi service can be negatively affected.
    d. Wireless network adaptors allow internet-enabled devices to send and receive signals in the form of radio waves.

6. Which of the following best characterizes the point of view and tone of Passage 2?
    a. First-person point of view and formal tone
    b. Third-person point of view and informal tone
    c. First-person point of view and informal tone
    d. Third-person point of view and formal tone

7. Which choice describes the best potential use of both passages?
    a. Passage 1 gives basic informational background about Wi-Fi, and Passage 2 presents a persuasive argument about the availability of Wi-Fi in one particular context.
    b. Passage 1 explains the benefits of Wi-Fi, while Passage 2 explains the drawbacks of it.
    c. Passage 1 explains how Wi-Fi works, and Passage 2 nudges readers to appreciate how it compares to other technologies.
    d. Passage 1 discusses the hardware components of Wi-Fi connectivity, while Passage 2 explains how it supports education.

8. Given the evidence in the passages, with which statement would the authors of both passages most likely agree?
    a. Access to the internet is a basic human right.
    b. Wi-Fi deserves appreciation for its diversity of uses.
    c. Without the internet, society will collapse.
    d. Wi-Fi is the most important technological advancement of the twentieth century.

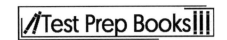
The next question pertains to the following passage:

Insects as a whole are preeminently creatures of the land and the air. This is shown not only by the possession of wings by a vast majority of the class, but by the mode of breathing to which reference has already been made, a system of branching air-tubes carrying atmospheric air with its combustion-supporting oxygen to all the insect's tissues. The air gains access to these tubes through a number of paired air-holes or spiracles, arranged segmentally in series.

It is of great interest to find that, nevertheless, a number of insects spend much of their time under water. This is true of not a few in the perfect winged state, as for example aquatic beetles and water-bugs ('boatmen' and 'scorpions') which have some way of protecting their spiracles when submerged, and, possessing usually the power of flight, can pass on occasion from pond or stream to upper air. But it is advisable in connection with our present subject to dwell especially on some insects that remain continually under water till they are ready to undergo their final moult and attain the winged state, which they pass entirely in the air. The preparatory instars of such insects are aquatic; the adult instar is aerial. All may-flies, dragon-flies, and caddis-flies, many beetles and two-winged flies, and a few moths thus divide their life-story between the water and the air. For the present we confine attention to the Stone-flies, the May-flies, and the Dragon-flies, three well-known orders of insects respectively called by systematists the Plecoptera, the Ephemeroptera, and the Odonata.

In the case of many insects that have aquatic larvae, the latter are provided with some arrangement for enabling them to reach atmospheric air through the surface-film of the water. But the larva of a stone-fly, a dragon-fly, or a may-fly is adapted more completely than these for aquatic life; it can, by means of gills of some kind, breathe the air dissolved in water.

This excerpt is from The Life-Story of Insects *by Geo H. Carpenter*

9. Which statement best details the central idea in this passage?
   a. It introduces certain insects that transition from water to air.
   b. It delves into entomology, especially where gills are concerned.
   c. It defines what constitutes insects' breathing.
   d. It invites readers to have a hand in the preservation of insects.

The next question pertains to the following passage:

When selecting a career path, it's important to explore the various options available. Many students entering college may shy away from a major because they don't know much about it. For example, many students won't opt for a career as an actuary because they aren't exactly sure what it entails. They would be missing out on a career that is very lucrative and in high demand. Actuaries work in the insurance field and assess risks and premiums. The average salary of an actuary is $100,000 per year. Another career option students may avoid, due to lack of knowledge of the field, is a hospitalist. This is a physician that specializes in the care of patients in a hospital, as opposed to those seen in private practices. The average salary of a hospitalist is upwards of $200,000. It pays to do some digging and find out more about these lesser-known career fields.

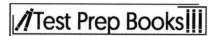

10. What is the central idea of this passage?
   a. The comparison of the salaries of actuaries and hospitalists
   b. Encouragement to research a career as an actuary
   c. Lesser-known careers offer high salaries
   d. Encouragement to research lesser-known careers

The next question pertains to the following passage:

Hard water occurs when rainwater mixes with minerals from rock and soil. Hard water has a high mineral count, including calcium and magnesium. The mineral deposits from hard water can stain hard surfaces in bathrooms and kitchens as well as clog pipes. Hard water can stain dishes, ruin clothes, and reduce the life of any appliances it touches, such as hot water heaters, washing machines, and humidifiers.

One solution is to install a water softener to reduce the mineral content of water, but this can be costly. Running vinegar through pipes and appliances and using vinegar to clean hard surfaces can also help with mineral deposits.

11. From this passage, what can be concluded?
   a. Hard water can cause a lot of problems for homeowners.
   b. Calcium is good for pipes and hard surfaces.
   c. Water softeners are easy to install.
   d. Vinegar is the only solution to hard water problems.

The next question pertains to the following passage:

While scientists aren't entirely certain why tornadoes form, they have some clues into the process. Tornadoes are dangerous funnel clouds that occur during a large thunderstorm. When warm, humid air near the ground meets cold, dry air from above, a column of the warm air can be drawn up into the clouds. Winds at different altitudes blowing at different speeds make the column of air rotate. As the spinning column of air picks up speed, a funnel cloud is formed. This funnel cloud moves rapidly and haphazardly. Rain and hail inside the cloud cause it to touch down, creating a tornado. Tornadoes move in a rapid and unpredictable pattern, making them extremely destructive and dangerous. Scientists continue to study tornadoes to improve radar detection and warning times.

12. Which of the following is the central idea of this passage?
   a. The danger of tornadoes
   b. The formation of tornadoes
   c. A comparison of thunderstorms to tornadoes
   d. What to do in the event of a tornado

The next question pertains to the following passage:

A famous children's author recently published a historical fiction novel under a pseudonym; however, it did not sell as many copies as her children's books. In her earlier years, she had majored in history and earned a graduate degree in Antebellum American History, which is the time frame of her new novel. Critics praised this newest work far more than the children's series that made her famous. In fact, her new novel was nominated for the prestigious Albert J. Beveridge Award but still isn't selling like her children's books, which fly off the shelves because of her name alone.

13. Which one of the following statements might be accurately inferred based on the above passage?
    a. The famous children's author produced an inferior book under her pseudonym.
    b. The famous children's author is the foremost expert on Antebellum America.
    c. The famous children's author did not receive the bump in publicity for her historical novel that it would have received if it were written under her given name.
    d. People generally prefer to read children's series than historical fiction.

The next question pertains to the following passage:

George Washington emerged out of the American Revolution as an unlikely champion of liberty. On June 14, 1775, the Second Continental Congress created the Continental Army, and John Adams, serving in the Congress, nominated Washington to be its first commander. Washington had fought under the British during the French and Indian War, and his experience and prestige proved instrumental to the American war effort. Washington provided invaluable leadership, training, and strategy during the Revolutionary War. He emerged from the war as the embodiment of liberty and freedom from tyranny.

After vanquishing the heavily favored British forces, Washington could have pronounced himself the autocratic leader of the former colonies without any opposition, but he famously refused and returned to his Mount Vernon plantation. His restraint proved his commitment to the fledgling state's republicanism. Washington was later unanimously elected as the first American president. But it is Washington's farewell address that cemented his legacy as a visionary worthy of study.

In 1796, President Washington issued his farewell address by public letter. Washington enlisted his good friend, Alexander Hamilton, in drafting his most famous address. The letter expressed Washington's faith in the Constitution and rule of law. He encouraged his fellow Americans to put aside partisan differences and establish a national union. Washington warned Americans against meddling in foreign affairs and entering military alliances. Additionally, he stated his opposition to national political parties, which he considered partisan and counterproductive.

Americans would be wise to remember Washington's farewell, especially during presidential elections, when politics hit a fever pitch. They might want to question the political institutions that were not planned by the Founding Fathers, such as the nomination process and political parties themselves.

14. What is the purpose of this passage?
    a. To introduce George Washington to readers as a historical figure worthy of study
    b. To note that George Washington was more than a famous military hero
    c. To convince readers that George Washington is a hero of republicanism and liberty
    d. To inform American voters about a Founding Father's sage advice on a contemporary issue and explain its applicability to modern times

The next question pertains to the following passage:

Cloud formation is a complex yet fascinating process that unfolds in predictable stages. In the first step, the Earth's surface warms through solar radiation. As the surface heats up, water molecules from oceans, lakes, and rivers absorb this energy, transforming into water vapor through a process known as evaporation.

299

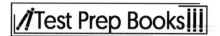

Next, the mass of warm, moist air ascends further into the atmosphere. As it rises, the air cools due to the decrease in atmospheric pressure at higher altitudes. This cooling causes the water vapor to condense into tiny water droplets.

Once these droplets form, they cluster together and create visible water vapor masses that we recognize as clouds. The altitude and appearance of clouds vary depending on factors such as temperature, humidity, and atmospheric stability. Finally, as these droplets condense, larger droplets may eventually fall en masse to the Earth's surface as precipitation.

In essence, cloud formation is a dynamic process tied to the Earth's atmospheric conditions, transitioning from the initial warming and evaporation to the ascent, cooling, condensation, and finally, the culmination in the release of precipitation.

15. Which of the following best describes the organizational structure of the passage?
    a. A sequence of steps in a natural process is described in detail.
    b. Pairs of steps in a natural process are compared and contrasted.
    c. A series of problem-solution pairs are presented.
    d. Each stage is presented as a cause, with the resulting effect described.

The next question pertains to the following passage:

Late one night, I found myself jolted awake by an unfamiliar sound echoing through the stillness. The rhythmic tapping on my window seemed almost deliberate, an ominous beckoning that shattered the serenity of my room. Panic gripped me as my imagination conjured up countless chilling scenarios, each more sinister than the last.

A chilling breeze carried the echoes of that mysterious sound, raising the hair on my arms. I strained my ears in the darkness, desperately trying to decipher its origin. Was it a branch scraping against the window in the wind? Was it an animal hunting its prey? Had I even heard anything at all?

The unknown has a way of breeding fear, and in that moment, I was paralyzed by the uncertainty of what lurked beyond the safety of my walls. The house seemed to creak and groan in mockery, magnifying my trepidation. Every shadow morphed into a potential threat as I struggled to harness my breathing.

I hesitated, caught between the impulse to investigate and the chilling fear that rooted me to my bed. The night held its secrets close, and as I lay there, grappling with the unknown, the echoes of that unsettling sound lingered, leaving me suspended in a horrible limbo between curiosity and fear.

16. What effect does the point of view have on the reader of the passage?
    a. The point of view creates distance between the reader and narrator, making readers doubt the accuracy of the events.
    b. The point of view brings readers into the situation, sparking curiosity and anxiety as they wonder about the origin of the noise.
    c. The point of view presents the plot objectively, preventing the readers from feeling emotionally attached to the outcome.
    d. The point of view makes readers feel confused, as they cannot determine the narrator's relationship to the events.

The next question pertains to the following passage:

Increased funding for the arts in public schools is an essential investment in the holistic development of students. The arts—encompassing visual arts, music, theater, and dance—contribute significantly to fostering creativity, critical thinking, and emotional intelligence.

First, exposure to the arts enhances cognitive abilities and academic performance. Numerous studies have demonstrated a positive correlation between arts education and improved performance in subjects like mathematics and language arts. Students engaged in artistic activities often develop better problem-solving skills and exhibit increased concentration and self-discipline.

Moreover, the arts play a crucial role in nurturing emotional intelligence. Through self-expression and exploration of various artistic media, students develop a deeper understanding of themselves and their peers. This emotional awareness is an invaluable asset in fostering empathy, tolerance, and effective communication—skills that are essential in a diverse and interconnected world.

Arts education not only fosters interpersonal relationships, but it also has the potential to reduce dropout rates and enhance overall school engagement. Critics may argue about budget constraints, but neglecting the arts deprives students of a comprehensive education, limiting their ability to adapt and innovate in an ever-changing society. Thus, increasing funding for the arts in public schools is not a frivolous expense but rather a strategic investment in the future success and well-being of our students.

17. Which sentence strives to prove that the arts help prepare students to be better community members as adults?
   a. "Students engaged in artistic activities often develop better problem-solving skills and exhibit increased concentration and self-discipline."
   b. "Numerous studies have demonstrated a positive correlation between arts education and improved performance in subjects like mathematics and language arts."
   c. "This emotional awareness is an invaluable asset in fostering empathy, tolerance, and effective communication—skills that are essential in a diverse and interconnected world."
   d. "Critics may argue about budget constraints, but neglecting the arts deprives students of a comprehensive education, limiting their ability to adapt and innovate in an ever-changing society."

The next question pertains to the following passage:

Pok-ta-pok, a sacred and ritualistic ball game played by the ancient Maya, holds cultural and historical significance. Dating back to around 1400 BCE, this traditional sport was not merely a physical competition but a symbolic representation of religious beliefs and societal values.

The game was typically played on a large stone court, often adorned with intricate carvings and surrounded by spectators. The objective of pok-ta-pok was to pass a rubber ball through a stone ring (like a smaller basketball hoop, only turned 90 degrees so the ball passed through it horizontally) without players using their hands. Players could touch the ball only with their hips, elbows, and knees. The game required exceptional skill, agility, and teamwork.

Beyond its physical challenges, pok-ta-pok held spiritual importance. The game was seen as a cosmic battle between the forces of light and darkness, symbolizing the journey of the sun across the sky. The ball itself represented celestial bodies, and the act of passing it through the ring mirrored the sun's passage through the underworld and its subsequent rebirth.

In addition to its ritualistic nature, pok-ta-pok also served social and political purposes. It was a means of resolving conflicts, strengthening community bonds, and demonstrating prowess. The victors were not only celebrated for their athletic achievements but also revered for their role in maintaining cosmic balance and spiritual harmony in the Mayan worldview. The game of pok-ta-pok, with its rich symbolism and cultural depth, stands as a testament to the intricate interweaving of sport, spirituality, and society in ancient Mayan civilization.

18. What is the purpose of the information inside parentheses in the second paragraph?
    a. To help readers understand an ancient sport by connecting it to a more familiar, modern sport
    b. To give readers a chance to decide if they prefer pok-ta-pok over basketball
    c. To encourage readers to appreciate the origins of basketball
    d. To compare and contrast the history of two different sports

For the next two questions, choose the best word to fill in the blank in each sentence.

19. Natalia's years of hard work and planning finally came to _____ when she successfully opened her own bakery in the heart of the city.
    a. fruition
    b. closure
    c. interruption
    d. deterioration

20. The neighborhood's _____ was evident in the luxurious mansions, upscale boutiques, and exclusive restaurants that lined the streets.
    a. decrepitude
    b. barrenness
    c. affluence
    d. congeniality

Writing

The next five questions pertain to the following passage:

(1) Fred Hampton desired to see lasting social change for African American people through nonviolent means and community recognition. (2) As a result, he became an African American activist during the American Civil Rights Movement and led the Chicago chapter of the Black Panther Party.

(3) Hampton was born and raised in the Maywood neighborhood of Chicago, Illinois in 1948. (4) Gifted academically and a natural athlete, he became a stellar baseball player in high school. (5) After graduating from Proviso East High School in 1966, he later went on to study law at Triton Junior College. (6) While studying at Triton, Hampton joined and became a leader of the National Association for the Advancement of Colored People (NAACP). (7) As a result of his leadership, the NAACP gained more than 500 members. (8) Hampton worked relentlessly to establish recreational facilities in the Maywood neighborhood and improve the educational resources provided to the impoverished black community.

(9) The Black Panther Party (BPP) was another that formed around the same time as and was similar in function to the NAACP. (10) Hampton was quickly attracted to the Black Panther Party's approach to the fight for equal rights for African Americans. (11) Hampton eventually joined the chapter and relocated to downtown Chicago to be closer to its headquarters.

(12) His charismatic personality, organizational abilities, sheer determination, and rhetorical skills enable him to quickly rise through the chapter's ranks. (13) Hampton soon became the leader of the Chicago chapter of the BPP where he organized rallies, taught political education classes, and established a free medical clinic. (14) He also took part in the community police supervision project and played an instrumental role in the BPP breakfast program for impoverished African American children.

(16) Hampton's greatest achievement as the leader of the BPP may have been his fight against street gang violence in Chicago. (17) In 1969, Hampton held a press conference where he made the gangs agree to a nonaggression pact known as the Rainbow Coalition.

1. Which of the following sentences, if any, should begin a new paragraph?

   Gifted academically and a natural athlete, he became a stellar baseball player in high school. After graduating from Proviso East High School in 1966, he later went on to study law at Triton Junior College. While studying at Triton, Hampton joined and became a leader of the National Association for the Advancement of Colored People (NAACP). As a result of his leadership, the NAACP gained more than 500 members.

   a. NO CHANGE
   b. Gifted academically and a natural athlete, he became a stellar baseball player in high school.
   c. After graduating from Proviso East High School in 1966, he later went on to study law at Triton Junior College.
   d. While studying at Triton, Hampton joined and became a leader of the National Association for the Advancement of Colored People (NAACP).

2. Which of the following would be the best revision for the underlined portion of Sentence 9 (reproduced below)?

   The Black Panther Party (BPP) <u>was another that</u> formed around the same time as and was similar in function to the NAACP.

   a. was another activist group that
   b. had lots of groups that
   c. had a lot of members that
   d. was another school that

3. Which is the best version of the underlined portion of Sentence 10 (reproduced below)?

   Hampton was quickly attracted to the <u>Black Panther Party's approach</u> to the fight for equal rights for African Americans.

   a. NO CHANGE
   b. Black Panther Parties approach
   c. Black Panther Partys' approach
   d. Black Panther Parties' approach

303

4. Which is the best version of the underlined portion of Sentence 12 (reproduced below)?

His charismatic personality, organizational abilities, sheer determination, and rhetorical skills <u>enable him to quickly rise</u> through the chapter's ranks.

a. enable him to quickly rise
b. are enabling him to quickly rise
c. enabled him to quickly rise
d. will enable him to quickly rise

5. The writer wants to add the following sentence to the passage.

As a result of the pact, a multiracial alliance between blacks, Puerto Ricans, and poor youth was developed.

Where should the sentence be placed?
a. After Sentence 8
b. After Sentence 13
c. After Sentence 16
d. After Sentence 17

The next five questions pertain to the following passage:

(1) While the various tales do take on the individual perspectives, Chaucer's internal character retains a unique presence throughout the text. (2) The Canterbury Tales provides the ultimate example of a story about stories also being a story containing multiple stories. (3) Chaucer does these by compiling embedded narratives from multiple sources while delivering them through a single, primary voice. (4) From the beginning, it's clear that Chaucer is the source of the text. (5) Yet, Chaucer is more than just a storyteller; he's an honest storyteller. (6) Chaucer provides bold character descriptions of these individuals, including their faults. (7) This can be seen when Chaucer sheds light on the nature of the Prioress. (8) He describes that, while she's supposed to be a pious nun, she is actually a walking façade. (9) The prioress is noted for counterfeiting courtly behavior so that people think highly of her.

(10) With Chaucer providing such detailed observations, the readers have a more complete picture of what is going on and who the other characters really are. (11) Another example of this is the sarcastic and brutally honest description of the miller: "The millere, that for drunken was al pale." (12) This description of the miller's drunkenness sheds light on why he seems so crazy. (13) It's because he's a drunk. (14) Thus, Chaucer's own narrative gives readers a legit perspective amongst a host of questionable storytellers. (15) He also provides information on the characters that can help the reader grasp their tales more fully.

(16) One of the signature methods of Chaucer's storytelling is that he doesn't just tell a story, his characters do as well. (17) As a writer, Chaucer actually immerses himself into the collective character discussions. (18) In many ways, Chaucer is a vehicle for the characters to tell their individual stories. (19) Chaucer actually takes on the styles and voice of the characters. (20) A good, eloquent tale like the Knight's Tale is written that way because that's how the knight would have told it. (21) Likewise, it's also why several tales are poorly written, have crass delivery, or lack a driven plotline. (22) Chaucer seeks to tell the story in the way his drunken character would have.

6. Where is the most logical location for Sentence 1 (reproduced below)?

> While the various tales do take on the individual perspectives, Chaucer's internal character retains a unique presence throughout the text.

a. NO CHANGE
b. Between sentence 3 and sentence 4
c. Between Sentence 6 and Sentence 7
d. At the end of the last paragraph

7. Which of the following would be the best replacement for the underlined portion of Sentence 3 (reproduced below)?

> <u>Chaucer does these by compiling embedded narratives</u> from multiple sources while delivering them through a single, primary voice.

a. NO CHANGE
b. Chaucer does this, compiling embedded narratives
c. Chaucer does this by compiling embedded narratives
d. Chaucer does these through compiling embedded narratives

8. Which of the following would be the best replacement for the underlined portion of Sentence 21 (reproduced below)?

> <u>Likewise, it's also why several tales are poorly written,</u> have crass delivery, or lack a driven plotline.

a. NO CHANGE
b. Likewise it's also why several tales are poorly written,
c. Likewise it's also why several tales are, poorly written,
d. Likewise, it's also why several tales are, poorly written,

9. Which of the following would be the best replacement for the underlined portion of Sentence 14 (reproduced below)?

> Thus, Chaucer's own narrative gives readers a <u>legit</u> perspective amongst a host of questionable storytellers.

a. NO CHANGE
b. truest
c. reliable
d. doubtful

10. Should the writer add the following sentence after Sentence 21?

> The *Miller's Tale* is rather crazy and crass because he is drunk while telling it.

a. Yes, because it explains why this story was banned in schools.
b. Yes, because it provides a supporting detail for the previous sentence and gives purpose to the last sentence of the passage.
c. No, because the writer is discussing the Knight's Tale, not the Miller's Tale.
d. No, because this sentence implies that Chaucer was drunk when he wrote the story, which is irrelevant and out of place in the passage.

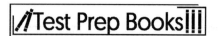

The next five questions pertain to the following passage:

(1) It may sound far fetched, but it's possible to perform surgery on a tree. (2) Tree surgery and other activities promoting the health and safety of trees and plants are just some of the many responsibilities of an arborist. (3) An arborist, sometimes called a "tree doctor," is primarily responsible for keeping trees and other plants alive. (4) Most of their work consists of identifying and treating diseased trees rather than removing them like a landscaper would. (5) If a tree is "sick," arborists must first identify what is wrong with the tree by using the clues available to them. (6) They are able to examine a tree's bark, take soil samples, and look at a tree's branches and leaves in order to pinpoint exactly what is wrong with the tree. (7) Once they identify the tree's specific malady, they get to work treating it as a doctor would treat a sick human being who has come down with an illness. (8) They can perform tree surgery (cutting branches or cutting out infected wood and then dressing the open wound), soil can be treated with chemicals, apply specialized fertilizers and pesticides, and even seal up exposed wood with wound paint (a type of sealant). (9) There are a pathway to becoming an arborist that are available to anyone interested. (10) Most municipalities in the United States do not require a degree in arboriculture in order to become an arborist. (11) However, several certifications and licenses are required in order to become eligible for the job. (12) One of the most in-demand certifications is offered by the Tree Care Industry Association, which offers a program to become a Certified Tree Care Safety Professional. (13) After taking classes and passing a rigorous exam, the prospective arborist is awarded the certification. (14) However, their work is not yet done. (15) Most states require an arborist to hold licensure in order to use most of the chemicals and pesticides that trees are treated with. (16) The process of earning this license usually involves passing an examination on how to properly and safely use and dispose of chemicals and pesticides. (17) For anyone who loves working outdoors and is fascinated by the living and breathing world of plants, becoming one is a solid career choice that is exciting and satisfying.

11. Which phrase works best in place of the underlined word in sentence 17 (reproduced below)?

For anyone who loves working outdoors and is fascinated by the living and breathing world of plants, becoming <u>one</u> is a solid career choice that is exciting and satisfying.

    a.   one with nature
    b.   an arborist
    c.   a tree scientist
    d.   a landscape architect

12. Which is the best decision regarding the underlined portions of sentence 7 (reproduced below)?

Once they identify the tree's specific malady, they get to work treating it as <u>a doctor would treat</u> a sick human being <u>who has come down with an illness.</u>

    a.   Leave them as they are now
    b.   Delete "a doctor would treat"
    c.   Delete "who has come down with an illness"
    d.   Delete both underlined portions

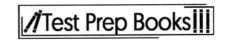

13. Which sentence contains unnecessary information and should be removed?
    a. NO CHANGE
    b. Sentence 16
    c. Sentence 14
    d. Sentence 5

14. Which is the best version of the underlined portion of sentence 8 (reproduced below)?

    They can perform tree surgery (cutting branches or cutting out infected wood and then dressing the open wound), <u>soil can be treated with chemicals</u>, apply specialized fertilizers and pesticides, and even seal up exposed wood with wound paint (a type of sealant).

    a. (as it is now)
    b. treating the soil with chemicals
    c. treat the soil with chemicals
    d. soil chemical treatments

15. Which is the best decision regarding the underlined portion of sentence 9 (reproduced below)?

    There are <u>a pathway</u> to becoming an arborist that are available to anyone interested.

    a. Leave it as it is now
    b. Revise it to "many pathways"
    c. Revise it to "many pathway"
    d. Revise it to "a pathways"

The next five questions pertain to the following passage:

(1) Cesar Chavez was a labor organizer and union boss who is best known for working to improve the lives of American farm workers. (2) Born in 1927 to a Mexican-American family of agricultural workers, Chavez witnessed the hardships that they endured on a daily basis. (3) He left school in order to work on a farm, which inspired his passion to change the poor conditions his family tolerated. (4) Chavez was a veteran who served in the United States Navy. (5) In 1962, Chavez co-founded the United Farm Workers (UFW) union. (6) Before the UFW's crusade against systemic-labor issues, agricultural workers did not have the legal right to unionize, and Chavez aimed to change this unfortunate fact. (7) Chavez, inspired by Mahatma Gandhi, advocated for nonviolent resistance. (8) Chavez and the UFW created and organized a number of boycotts, protests, and strikes in order to raise awareness about agricultural workers' conditions on farms in the United States that were successful. (9) The most notable of these was the Delano grape strike in 1965. (10) The strike was aided by the general public's boycott of non-union grapes and lasted until 1970, when Chavez signed an agreement with major grape growers. (11) Although he was arrested several times and received numerous death threats, Chavez never backed down from the adversity he faced. (12) Eventually, the UFW held its greatest victory of all: the passing of the California Agricultural Labor Relations Act in 1975. (13) A landmark statute, this law granted unionization rights to farm workers for the first time in American history. (14) Besides that, Chavez shifted his focus to controlling the use of harmful pesticides in agriculture. (15) He also embarked on a university speaking tour and became involved in real estate development. (16) Although he passed away in 1993, his legacy has extended beyond his achievements in the area of workers' rights. (17) Chavez's famous slogan, "¡Sí, se puede!" (Yes, we can!) remains a rallying cry for those fighting for workers' rights to this day.

16. Which sentence is inconsistent with the overall style and tone of the passage and should be removed?
    a. Sentence 5
    b. Sentence 4
    c. Sentence 17
    d. Sentence 16

17. Which is the best version of the underlined portion of Sentence 6 (reproduced below)?

    Before the UFW's crusade against <u>systemic-labor issues</u>, agricultural workers did not have the legal right to unionize, and Chavez aimed to change this unfortunate fact.

    a. NO CHANGE
    b. systemic, laborious, issues
    c. systemic labor issues
    d. systemic labor-issues

18. Which is the best version of Sentence 8 (reproduced below)?

    Chavez and the UFW created and organized a number of boycotts, protests, and strikes in order to raise awareness about agricultural workers' conditions on farms in the United States that were successful.

    a. NO CHANGE
    b. Chavez and the UFW created and organized a number of boycotts, protests, and strikes in order to raise successful awareness about agricultural workers' conditions on farms in the United States.
    c. Chavez and the UFW created and organized a number of successful boycotts, protests, and strikes in order to raise awareness about agricultural workers' conditions on farms in the United States.
    d. Chavez and the UFW created and organized a number of boycotts that were successful, protests, and strikes in order to raise awareness about agricultural workers' conditions on farms in the United States.

19. Which is the best version of the underlined portion of Sentence 12 (reproduced below)?

    Eventually, the UFW <u>held</u> its greatest victory of all: the passing of the California Agricultural Labor Relations Act in 1975.

    a. NO CHANGE
    b. secured
    c. proscribed
    d. induced

20. Which version of the underlined portion of Sentence 14 (reproduced below) provides the most effective introduction to the last paragraph?

    <u>Besides that</u>, Chavez shifted his focus to controlling the use of harmful pesticides in agriculture.

    a. NO CHANGE
    b. After he was done with politics
    c. After the UFW disbanded
    d. Later in life

308

The next five questions pertain to the following passage:

(1) Since the first discovery of dinosaur bones, scientists have made strides in the technological development and methodologies used to investigate these extinct animals. (2) We know more about dinosaurs than ever before and are still learning fascinating new things about how they looked and lived. (3) However, there are still many things about dinosaurs that scientists are unsure of and will never know for certain. (4) Can earlier perceptions of dinosaurs inhibit progress towards further understanding of dinosaurs?

(5) All discoveries associated with these animals are based on physical remains. (6) To gauge behavioral characteristics, scientists cross-examine these finds with living animals to explore potential similarities. (7) While this method is effective, these are still deductions. (8) Some ideas about dinosaurs can't be tested and confirmed simply because humans can't replicate a living dinosaur. (9) For example, a Spinosaurus has a large sail, or a finlike structure that grows from its back. (10) Paleontologists know this sail exists and have ideas for the function of the sail. (11) They are uncertain of which idea is the true function. (12) Some scientists believe the sail serves to regulate the Spinosaurus' body temperature, yet others believe it is used to attract mates. (13) Still, other scientists think the sail is used to intimidate other predatory dinosaurs for self-defense. (14) These are all viable explanations, but they are also influenced by what scientists know about modern animals. (15) Yet, it's quite possible that the sail could hold a completely unique function.

(16) While it's plausible, even likely, that dinosaurs share many traits with modern animals, there is the danger of over-attributing these qualities to one unique species. (17) For much of the early nineteenth century, when people first started studying dinosaur bones, the assumption was that they were simply giant lizards. (18) For the longest time this image was the prevailing view on dinosaurs, until evidence indicated that they were more likely warm-blooded. (19) Scientists have since discovered that many dinosaurs had feathers and actually had many other traits that modern birds have.

21. The writer is trying to decide where to use the following sentence in the passage:

The biggest problem with studying dinosaurs is simply that there are no living dinosaurs to observe.

Which of the following would be the most appropriate placement of the sentence?
    a. After Sentence 1
    b. Before Sentence 5
    c. After Sentence 14
    d. The writer should not use the sentence in the passage.

22. Which sentence should be deleted from the passage?
    a. Sentence 4
    b. Sentence 13
    c. Sentence 15
    d. Sentence 18

23. Which of the following would be the best way to combine Sentences 10 and 11 (reproduced below)?

> Paleontologists know this sail exists and have ideas for the function of the sail. They are uncertain of which idea is the true function.

   a. Paleontologists know this sail exists and have ideas for the function of the sail and they are uncertain of which idea is the true function.
   b. Paleontologists know this sail exists and have ideas for the function of the sail however, they are uncertain of which idea is the true function.
   c. Paleontologists know this sail exists and have ideas for the function of the sail however they are, uncertain, of which idea is the true function.
   d. Paleontologists know this sail exists and have ideas for the function of the sail; however, they are uncertain of which idea is the true function.

24. Which of the following would be the best replacement for the underlined portion of Sentence 15 (reproduced below)?

> <u>Yet, it's quite possible</u> that the sail could hold a completely unique function.

   a. NO CHANGE
   b. Yet it's quite possible,
   c. It's quite possible,
   d. Its quite possible

25. Which of the following would be the best replacement for the underlined portion of Sentence 18 (reproduced below)?

> <u>For the longest time this image was the prevailing view on dinosaurs</u>, until evidence indicated that they were more likely warm blooded.

   a. NO CHANGE
   b. For the longest time this was the prevailing view on dinosaurs
   c. For the longest time, this image, was the prevailing view on dinosaurs
   d. This was the prevailing view of dinosaurs

Written Essay

An ongoing debate within college athletics has been whether or not collegiate athletes should receive compensation for their performance. While many athletes receive scholarship money or room and board stipends, some people claim that such compensation is not enough.

Write a response in support or opposition of compensating collegiate athletes. Support your position with examples that further explain your point of view.

Answer Explanations #2

Arithmetic

1. A: The hundreds place value is located three digits to the left of the decimal point (the digit 7). To decide whether to round this digit up or keep it, look at the digit to the right and see if it is 5 or greater. In this case, the digit to the right is 8, so we round up the hundreds place (from 7 to 8). All digits to the right of the hundreds place are replaced with zeros, giving us 84,800.

2. C: If Shawna has used $\frac{1}{3}$ of the paint, she has $\frac{2}{3}$ remaining. $2\frac{1}{2}$ gallons is the same as $\frac{5}{2}$ gallons. The calculation is:

$$\frac{2}{3} \times \frac{5}{2} = \frac{10}{6} = \frac{5}{3} = 1\frac{2}{3} \text{ gallons}$$

3. A: In order to compare the fractions $\frac{4}{7}$ and $\frac{5}{9}$, a common denominator must be used. The least common denominator is 63, which is found by multiplying the two denominators together (7×9). The conversions are as follows:

$$\frac{4}{7} \times \frac{9}{9} = \frac{36}{63}$$
$$\frac{5}{9} \times \frac{7}{7} = \frac{35}{63}$$

Although they walk nearly the same distance, $\frac{4}{7}$ is slightly more than $\frac{5}{9}$ because $\frac{36}{63} > \frac{35}{63}$. Remember, the sign $>$ means "is greater than." Therefore, Chris walks further than Tina, and Choice *A* correctly shows this expression in mathematical terms.

4. A: To find the fraction of the bill that the first three people pay, the fractions need to be added, which means finding the common denominator. The common denominator will be 60.

$$\frac{1}{5} + \frac{1}{4} + \frac{1}{3}$$

$$\frac{12}{60} + \frac{15}{60} + \frac{20}{60} = \frac{47}{60}$$

The remainder of the bill is:

$$1 - \frac{47}{60} = \frac{60}{60} - \frac{47}{60} = \frac{13}{60}$$

5. A: We use the place value to the right of the thousandths place, which would be the ten-thousandths place. The value in the thousandths place is 7. The number in the place value to its right is greater than 4, so the 7 is bumped up to 8. Everything to its right is removed, giving us 245.268.

6. C: A ratio written as $a : b$ has an equivalent fractional form of $\frac{a}{b}$. Therefore, 18 : 12 is equivalent to $\frac{18}{12} = \frac{3}{2} \cdot \frac{6}{4}$ reduces to $\frac{3}{2} \cdot \frac{36}{24}$ reduces to $\frac{3}{2}$ as well. Choice *C* is 4 : 3, which is the same as $\frac{4}{3}$. This option is not equal to the other three values.

7. D: $0.45

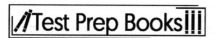
List the givens.

$$\text{Store coffee} = \$1.23/\text{lb}$$

$$\text{Local roaster coffee} = \$1.98/1.5 \text{ lb}$$

Calculate the cost for 5 pounds of store brand.

$$\frac{\$1.23}{1 \text{ lb}} \times 5 \text{ lb} = \$6.15$$

Calculate the cost for 5 pounds of the local roaster.

$$\frac{\$1.98}{1.5 \text{ lb}} \times 5 \text{ lb} = \$6.60$$

Subtract to find the difference in price for 5 pounds.

$$\begin{array}{r} \$6.60 \\ -\$6.15 \\ \hline \$0.45 \end{array}$$

8. D: By rearranging and grouping the factors in Choice *D*, we can notice that $(3 \times 2) \times (4 \times 3) = 6 \times 12$, which is what we were looking for.

9. A: 37.5%

Solve this by setting up the percent formula:

$$\frac{3}{8} = \frac{\%}{100}$$

Multiply 3 by 100 to get 300. Then divide 300 by 8:

$$300 \div 8 = 37.5\%$$

Note that with the percent formula, 37.5 is automatically a percentage and does not need to have any further conversions.

10. A: $\frac{810}{2921}$

Line up the fractions.

$$\frac{15}{23} \times \frac{54}{127}$$

Multiply across the top and across the bottom.

$$\frac{15 \times 54}{23 \times 127} = \frac{810}{2921}$$

11. B: If 60% of 50 workers are women, then there are 30 women working in the office. If half of them are wearing skirts, then that means 15 women wear skirts. Since nobody else wears skirts, this means there are 15 people wearing skirts.

12. B: $\frac{1}{2}$ is the same fraction as $\frac{4}{8}$, and both would fill up the same portion of a number line.

None of the other choices represents a pair of equivalent fractions, as seen below.

A.

C.

D.

13. A: Total tuition for four years is:

$$\$22{,}000 \times 4 = \$88{,}000$$

Total room and board for four years is:

$$\$5{,}000 \times 4 = \$20{,}000$$

Total cost of books for 4 years is $\$500 \times 4 = \$2{,}000$. Therefore, it is estimated that you will spend $\$88{,}000 + \$20{,}000 + \$2{,}000 = \$110{,}000$ on college. Your family is going to pay 25% of this cost, which is:

$$0.25 \times \$110{,}000 = \$27{,}500$$

Therefore, you will be responsible for:

$$\$110{,}000 - \$27{,}500 = \$82{,}500$$

Therefore, to obtain your goal, you will need to have $\$82{,}500$ in your account before college starts.

14. A: Convert the mixed fractions to improper fractions: $\frac{61}{8} - \frac{16}{5}$. Subtract using 40 as a common denominator and rewrite to get rid of the improper fraction:

$$\frac{61}{8} - \frac{16}{5} = \frac{305}{40} - \frac{128}{40} = \frac{177}{40} = 4\frac{17}{40}$$

313

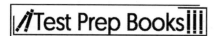
15. D: Set up the problem, larger number on top and numbers lined up at the decimal. Begin subtracting with the far-right column. Borrow 10 from the column to the left, when necessary.

16. B: To add decimals, add them vertically, making sure to align the decimals. First, add the thousandths place: $3 + 1 = 4$. Next, add the hundredths place: $7 + 5 = 12$. The 1 gets carried to the tenths place, so adding the digits in the tenths place results in $1 + 6 + 6 = 13$. The 1 here gets carried to the ones place as well, so the sum of the ones are: $1 + 4 + 2 = 7$. Putting this together results in 7.324. The 2 is in the hundredths place, and the value to the right is 4, which is less than 5. Therefore, this value rounds to 7.32.

17. C: Since Amanda eats twice as many cupcakes as Marty, we multiply the input by 2 to get the output. Filling in for the missing numbers would result in $3 \times 2 = 6$ and $7 \times 2 = 14$.

18. A: To determine the number of houses that can fit on the street, we can divide the length of the street by the width of each house's property: $345 \div 30 = 11.5$. However, the construction company is not going to build half a house, so they will need to build either 11 or 12 houses. Since the width of 12 houses (360 feet) would extend past the length of the street, only 11 houses can be built.

19. C: The number of days can be found by taking the total amount Bernard needs to make and dividing it by the amount he earns per day:

$$\frac{300}{80} = \frac{30}{8} = \frac{15}{4} = 3.75$$

But Bernard is only working full days, so he will need to work 4 days, since 3 days is not enough time.

20. A: Taylor's total income is $20,000 + $10,000 = $30,000. Fifteen percent as a fraction is $\frac{15}{100} = \frac{3}{20}$. So,

$$\frac{3}{20} \times \$30{,}000 = \frac{\$90{,}000}{20}$$

$$\frac{\$9{,}000}{2} = \$4{,}500$$

Quantitative Reasoning, Algebra, and Statistics

1. D: The expression is simplified by collecting like terms. Terms with the same variable and exponent are like terms, and their coefficients can be added.

2. C: To find the equation of the line containing the two points, first find the slope (the change in y over the change in x):

$$m = \frac{2 - 1}{-3 - 4} = -\frac{1}{7}$$

314

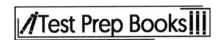
Then, substitute the slope and one point into the point-slope formula: $y - y_1 = m(x - x_1)$:

$$y - 1 = -\frac{1}{7}(x - 4)$$

$$y - 1 = -\frac{1}{7}x + \frac{4}{7}$$

$$y = -\frac{1}{7}x + \frac{4}{7} + \frac{7}{7}$$

The correct answer is $y = -\frac{1}{7}x + \frac{11}{7}$.

3. A: The perimeter of a rectangle is $P = 2l + 2w$. We are told $P = 44$, so $2l + 2w = 44$. We are also told that the width is 2 cm less than the length: $w = l - 2$. Substituting this for w in the perimeter equation, we get $2l + 2(l - 2) = 44$, which is Choice *A*.

Although it's not necessary to answer the test question, we could solve the equation to find the length and width. The equation simplifies to $4l - 4 = 44$, or $l = 12$, and since $w = l - 2$, we find $w = 10$.

4. B: The variable y is directly proportional to x, which means that whenever x is multiplied by a number, y is multiplied by that same number. When x changes from 5 to 20, it is multiplied by 4, so the original y value must also be multiplied by 4. That means $y = 3 \times 4 = 12$.

5. B: First, subtract 4 from each side. This yields $6t = 12$. Now, divide both sides by 6 to obtain $t = 2$.

6. D: The probability of picking the winner of the race is $\frac{1}{4}$, or $\left(\frac{number\ of\ favorable\ outcomes}{number\ of\ total\ outcomes}\right)$. Assuming the winner was picked on the first selection, three horses remain from which to choose the runner-up (these are dependent events). Therefore, the probability of picking the runner-up is $\frac{1}{3}$. To determine the probability that multiple events all happen, multiply the probabilities of the events:

$$\frac{1}{4} \times \frac{1}{3} = \frac{1}{12}$$

7. B: An equilateral triangle has three sides of equal length, so if the total perimeter is 18 feet, each side must be 6 feet long. A square with sides of 6 feet will have an area of $6^2 = 36$ square feet.

8. B: By distributing the implied one in front of the first set of parentheses and the -1 in front of the second set of parentheses, the parentheses can be eliminated:

$$5x^2 - 3x + 4 - 1(2x^2 + 7) = 5x^2 - 3x + 4 - 2x^2 + 7$$

Next, like terms (same variables with same exponents) are combined by adding the coefficients and keeping the variables and their powers the same:

$$3x^2 - 3x + 11$$

9. B: 300 miles in 4 hours is $\frac{300}{4} = 75$ miles per hour. In 1.5 hours, the car will go 1.5×75 miles, or 112.5 miles.

10. C: To solve this equation, square both sides to eliminate the radical, resulting in $x + 5 = 25$. Subtracting 5 from both sides to solve for x gives $x = 20$.

11. C: To find the expected value, take the product of each individual sum and the probability of rolling the sum, then add together the products for each sum. There are 36 possible rolls.

The probability of rolling a 2 is $\frac{1}{36}$.

The probability of rolling a 3 is $\frac{2}{36}$.

The probability of rolling a 4 is $\frac{3}{36}$.

The probability of rolling a 5 is $\frac{4}{36}$.

The probability of rolling a 6 is $\frac{5}{36}$.

The probability of rolling a 7 is $\frac{6}{36}$.

The probability of rolling an 8 is $\frac{5}{36}$.

The probability of rolling a 9 is $\frac{4}{36}$.

The probability of rolling a 10 is $\frac{3}{36}$.

The probability of rolling an 11 is $\frac{2}{36}$.

Finally, the probability of rolling a 12 is $\frac{1}{36}$.

Each possible outcome is multiplied by the probability of it occurring. Like this:

$$2 \times \frac{1}{36} = a$$

$$3 \times \frac{2}{36} = b$$

$$4 \times \frac{3}{36} = c$$

And so forth.

Then, all of those results are added together:

$$a + b + c \ldots = expected\ value$$

In this case, it equals 7.

12. B: First, $\frac{5.2}{2.6} = 2$. Next:

$$\frac{10^2}{10^4} = 10^2 \times 10^{-4} = 10^{-2}$$

So, the answer is 2×10^{-2}.

13. B: The figure is composed of three sides of a square and a semicircle. The sides of the square are simply added:

$$8 \text{ in} + 8 \text{ in} + 8 \text{ in} = 24 \text{ in}$$

The circumference of a circle is found by the equation $C = 2\pi r$. The radius is 4 in, so the circumference of the circle is 25.13 in. Only half of the circle makes up the outer border of the figure (part of the perimeter) so half of 25.13 in is 12.565 in. Therefore, the total perimeter is:

$$24 \text{ in} + 12.565 \text{ in} = 36.565 \text{ in}$$

The other answer choices use the incorrect formula or fail to include all of the necessary sides.

14. D: Scientific notation requires that the non-decimal portion of the number lie between 1 and 10, which requires moving the decimal point to the right 2 places, or multiplying by 10^2, to get 4.2. Therefore, the original number is 4.2×10^{-2} to move the decimal point back to the left 2 places.

15. A: Begin by writing the equation in point-slope form:

$$y - y_0 = m(x - x_0)$$

In this case, this gives the equation:

$$y - 3 = 4(x - 2)$$

Solving for y, the slope-intercept form is the result, $y = 4x - 5$.

16. B: $-\frac{1}{3}\sqrt{81} = -\frac{1}{3}(9) = -3$

17. A: Let the unknown score be x. The average will be:

$$\frac{5 \times 50 + 4 \times 70 + x}{10} = \frac{530 + x}{10} = 55$$

Multiply both sides by 10 to get $530 + x = 550$, or $x = 20$.

18. C: Each value can be calculated so that they can be compared to find which one is the greatest. The mean is equal to:

$$\frac{26 + 27 + 27 + 29 + 30 + 32 + 33 + 33 + 33 + 35}{10} = 30.5$$

The median is equal to:

$$\frac{30 + 32}{2} = 31$$

The mode is equal to 33 because that number occurs 3 times in the data set. The range is equal to:

$$35 - 26 = 9$$

Therefore, the mode is the greatest value of the answer choices.

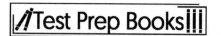

19. D: This problem can be solved by using unit conversion. The initial units are miles per minute. The final units need to be feet per second. Converting miles to feet uses the equivalence statement 1 mi = 5,280 ft. Converting minutes to seconds uses the equivalence statement 1 min = 60 s. Setting up the ratios to convert the units is shown in the following equation:

$$\frac{72 \text{ mi}}{90 \text{ min}} \times \frac{1 \text{ min}}{60 \text{ s}} \times \frac{5{,}280 \text{ ft}}{1 \text{ mi}} = 70.4 \frac{\text{ft}}{\text{s}}$$

The initial units cancel out, and the new units are left.

20. A: The slope of the given line is -8 because it represents m in the form $y = mx + b$. The slope of a line perpendicular to a line has a slope that is equal to the negative reciprocal of the slope of the given line. Therefore, the slope of the line perpendicular to $y = -8x + 2$ is $\frac{1}{8}$. Substitute the slope $m = \frac{1}{8}$ and the point $(-5, 5)$ into the point-slope formula $y - y_1 = m(x - x_1)$ to obtain:

$$y - 5 = \frac{1}{8}(x + 5)$$

$$y - 5 = \frac{1}{8}x + \frac{5}{8}$$

$$y = \frac{1}{8}x + \frac{5}{8} + \frac{40}{8}$$

$$y = \frac{1}{8}x + \frac{45}{8}$$

Advanced Algebra and Functions

1. D: Rewrite the equation in exponential form to obtain $15^3 = 4x - 2$. Then, solve for x. Add 2 to both sides to obtain $3375 + 2 = 4x$. Then, divide both sides by 4 to obtain $x = \frac{3377}{4} = 844.25$.

2. B: The domain is all possible input values, or x-values. For this equation, the domain is every number greater than or equal to zero. There are no negative numbers in the domain because taking the square root of a negative number results in an imaginary number.

3. D: The first step is to find the equation of the line that is perpendicular to $y = 2x - 3$ and passes through the point $(0, 5)$. The slope of a perpendicular line is the negative reciprocal of the original slope, and since our original slope is 2, the new slope is $-\frac{1}{2}$. The y-intercept is the value of y when $x = 0$, and since we know $(0,5)$ is on the new line, our new y-intercept is 5.

The new equation is $y = -\frac{1}{2}x + 5$.

In order to find which points lie on the new line, we can substitute each choice's x and y values into the equation to determine whether they form a true statement.

For the point in A, the equation $10 = -\frac{1}{2}(-6) + 5$ makes the statement $10 = 8$.

This is not a true statement, so the point $(-6, 10)$ does not lie on the line.

For B, the equation $7 = -\frac{1}{2}(-2) + 5$ makes the statement $7 = 6$, which is not a true statement.

318

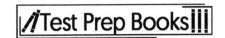

Therefore, Choice *B* is not a point that lies on the line.

For Choice *C*, the equation $6 = -\frac{1}{2}(2) + 5$ is the same as $6 = 4$, so it is similarly false.

For *D*, the equation $3 = -\frac{1}{2}(4) + 5$ makes a true statement, so the point $(4, 3)$ lies on the line.

4. B: Start with the original equation: $x^2 - 2xy + 2y$, then replace each instance of x with a 2, and each instance of y with a 3 to get:

$$2^2 - 2 \times 2 \times 3 + 2 \times 3^2 = 4 - 12 + 18 = 10$$

5. A: The definition of an even function is that $f(-x) = f(x)$. We can plug in $-x$ to our function to see what we get:

$$f(-x) = 1/2(-x)^\wedge 4 + 2(-x)^\wedge 2 - 6$$

Since $(-x)^4 = x^4$ and $(-x)^2 = x^2$, we see that $f(-x)$ is equal to the original function, so our function is even.

The definition of an odd function is that $f(-x) = -f(x)$. We can calculate $-f(x)$:

$$-f(x) = -1\left(\left(\frac{1}{2}\right)x^4 + 2x^2 - 6\right) = \left(-\frac{1}{2}\right)x^4 - 2x^2 + 6$$

This does not equal $f(-x)$ (which, remember, is the same as our original function), so our function is not odd.

6. D: Each value can be substituted into each equation. Choice *A* can be eliminated, since $16^2 + 16 = 80$. Choice *B* can be eliminated, since $16^2 + 8 \times 16 - 4 = 380$. Choice *C* can be eliminated, since $16^2 - 4 \times 16 - 4 = 188$. But, plugging in either value into $x^2 - 64$ gives:

$$(\pm 16)^2 - 64 = 64 - 64 = 0$$

7. C: Let x be equal to the number of pizzas delivered. The flat fee of \$5.50 is equivalent to the *y*-intercept, and the charge per small pizza of \$7.25 is equivalent to the rate of change, or slope, in the linear equation $y = mx + b$. This results in $y = 7.25x + 5.5$. Set this equal to 80 and solve:

$$80 = 7.25x + 5.5$$

$$74.5 = 7.25x$$

$$x \approx 10.28$$

x is approximately equal to 10.28. Therefore, we need to round down to the nearest whole number to account for the total number of pizzas the students can afford. They can purchase 10 pizzas.

8. B: The slope will be given by:

$$m = \frac{y_2 - y_1}{x_2 - x_1}$$

$$m = \frac{1 - 0}{2 - 0} = \frac{1}{2}$$

The y-intercept will be 0, since it passes through the origin, $(0,0)$. Using slope-intercept form, the equation for this line is:

$$y = \frac{1}{2}x$$

9. B: The y-intercept of an equation is found where the x-value is zero. Plugging in zero for x in the equation, we get $0^2 + 3(0) - 4 = -4$.

10. B: Start by squaring both sides to get $1 + x = 16$. Then subtract 1 from both sides to get $x = 15$.

11. C: Multiply both sides by x to get $x + 2 = 2x$. Then, subtract x from both sides to get $2 = x$.

12. B: $\frac{2}{a}$ must be subtracted from both sides, with a result of $\frac{1}{x} = \frac{2}{b} - \frac{2}{a}$. The reciprocal of both sides needs to be taken, but the right-hand side needs to be written as a single fraction in order to do that. Since the two fractions on the right have denominators that are not equal, a common denominator of ab is needed. This leaves $\frac{1}{x} = \frac{2a}{ab} - \frac{2b}{ab} = \frac{2(a-b)}{ab}$. Taking the reciprocals, which can be done since $b - a$ is not zero, with a result of $x = \frac{ab}{2(a-b)}$.

13. C: If $\log_{10} x = 2$, then $10^2 = x$, which equals 100.

14. B: The left-hand side of this polynomial equation is already factored. Therefore, set each factor equal to 0 and solve for x to find the solutions.

$$4x + \sqrt{7} = 0 \qquad 9x + \sqrt{11} = 0$$

$$4x = -\sqrt{7} \qquad 9x = -\sqrt{11}$$

$$x = -\frac{\sqrt{7}}{4} \qquad x = -\frac{\sqrt{11}}{9}$$

The two solutions are $x = -\frac{\sqrt{7}}{4}$ and $x = -\frac{\sqrt{11}}{9}$.

15. B: Here, f is an exponential function whose base is less than 1. In this function, f is always decreasing. This means that when a is less than b, $f(a) > f(b)$.

16. C: The area of a rectangle is $A = lw$. We don't know the length or width of this rectangle, but the area is 24, so we can say that $lw = 24$. Length and width are each multiplied by 3, so the area of our new rectangle is $3l \times 3w$, or $9lw$. Since we know that $lw = 24$, the area of the new rectangle is $9lw = 9 \times 24 = 216 \ cm^2$.

17. A: This has the form $t^2 - y^2$, with $t = x^2$ and $y = 4$. It's also known that $t^2 - y^2 = (t + y)(t - y)$, and substituting the values for t and y into the right-hand side gives $(x^2 - 4)(x^2 + 4)$.

18. D: The first derivative of a function gives the slope of the function's tangent line at any point. This function's first derivative is $y' = 3x^2$. Since $x = 2$, we calculate the slope as $3(2)^2 = 12$.

19. D: When an ordered pair is reflected over an axis, the sign of one of the coordinates must change. When it's reflected over the x-axis, the sign of the y-coordinate must change. The x-value remains the same. Therefore, the new ordered pair is $(-3, 4)$.

20. B: The technique of completing the square must be used to change the equation below into the standard equation of a circle:

$$4x^2 + 4y^2 - 16x - 24y + 51 = 0$$

First, the constant must be moved to the right-hand side of the equals sign and each term must be divided by the coefficient of the x^2-term (which is 4). The x- and y- terms must be grouped together to obtain:

$$x^2 - 4x + y^2 - 6y = -\frac{51}{4}$$

Then, the process of completing the square must be completed for each variable. This gives:

$$(x^2 - 4x + 4) + (y^2 - 6y + 9) = -\frac{51}{4} + 4 + 9$$

The equation can be written as:

$$(x - 2)^2 + (y - 3)^2 = \frac{1}{4}$$

Therefore, the center of the circle is $(2, 3)$ and the radius is:

$$\sqrt{\frac{1}{4}} = \frac{1}{2}$$

Reading Comprehension

1. D: Context clues indicate that Choice *D* is correct because the passage provides great detail of Mr. Utterson's feelings about locating Hyde. Choice *A* does not fit because there is no mention of Mr. Lanyon's mental state. Choice *B* is incorrect; although the text does make mention of bells, Choice *B* is not the *best* answer overall. Choice *C* is incorrect because the passage clearly states that Mr. Utterson was determined, not unsure.

2. A: Although this is fiction and we are seeing the passage through the eyes of a character, the author is in control of word choice and tone. *Intrigue* means to arouse curiosity, so we are confronted with words and phrases such as "besieged by questions," "digging," "imagination," and "haunt." Choice *B*, elation, means joy. Choice *C*, animosity, means strong dislike. Choice *D*, rigidity, means stiff or unyielding.

3. A: The setting is first established as a "nocturnal city," and is described later in the passage as a "lamplighted city," making Choice *A* correct.

4. B: Mr. Utterson is struggling with the mystery surrounding a dark figure and the terrible crimes he commits. As Mr. Utterson tosses and turns in bed in the long paragraph, we see him wanting to discern the figure's face as he imagines him committing the crimes, but Mr. Utterson has no idea who the figure is.

5. B: The second paragraph of this passage explains how routers send and receive data, allowing devices to connect to the internet. Choice *A* is not supported by direct evidence from the paragraph. Choice *C* is supported by the third paragraph but not the second. Choice *D* includes specific details from the second paragraph, but it does not provide a summary of the entire paragraph.

6. D: Passage 2 is presented from an objective point of view; it does not employ "I" or insert the narrator into the text. Phrases like "a vital step towards fostering inclusive communities and catalyzing overall societal progress" and "primary beneficiary of ubiquitous internet access" mark its formal tone. Therefore, Choice *D* is the correct answer.

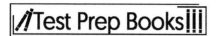

7. A: Passage 1 is factual and objective, while Passage 2 aims to convince readers of the importance of free, accessible Wi-Fi. Choice *B* is incorrect because neither passage focuses solely on benefits or drawbacks. Choice *C* is true for the first half but false for the second half because Passage 2 does not compare and contrast. Choice *D* is incorrect because it provides specific details from the passages without explaining their overall message.

8. B: Passage 1 emphasizes that Wi-Fi interfaces with many types of devices, while Passage 2 expands on its potential uses in public environments. Therefore, both authors would likely agree that people should recognize the potential variety of Wi-Fi applications. Choice *A* is incorrect because the author of Passage 1 does not write about accessibility in terms of human rights. Choice *C* is too sweeping a claim to be supported by either passage. Choice *D* is incorrect because neither author claims that Wi-Fi is the most important invention of modern times.

9. A: Choice *A* is correct because the second and third paragraphs are focused on insects that spend part of their lives in water and part of their lives in the air. Choice *B* is incorrect because gills were not a large focus of the passage, and were only mentioned in the last sentence. Choice *C* is incorrect because although the passage describes the structures that allow insects to breathe, it is not the central idea of the passage. Choice *D* is incorrect because the passage does not invite the reader to do anything.

10. D: Choice *D* is correct. The passage begins by pointing out that it is important to explore various career options and continues with examples of careers that students may shy away from due to lack of knowledge. To support the idea that these careers should be explored, the author provides attractive details, such as high salaries, for these careers. The passage ends by stating that it pays to look into lesser-known careers. Choice *A* is incorrect. Although the salaries of both careers are given, the main idea of the passage is not to compare these two careers but to offer two high-paying career options that may be overlooked due to lack of knowledge of these fields. Choice *B* is incorrect because although the author describes the work and the pay of an actuary, the point is not to encourage a career specifically as an actuary. The purpose is to provide an example of an often-overlooked career, and it's only one out of two examples that are given. Choice *C* is incorrect because the passage does not state that lesser-known careers offer high salaries. In fact, there may be many lesser-known careers that have low salaries and many well-known careers with even higher salaries.

11. A: The passage focuses mainly on the problems of hard water. Choice *B* is incorrect because calcium is not good for pipes and hard surfaces. The passage does not say anything about whether water softeners are easy to install, so Choice *C* is incorrect. Choice *D* is also incorrect because the passage does offer other solutions besides vinegar.

12. B: The central idea of this passage is the formation of tornadoes. Choice *A* is incorrect because although the passage does mention that tornadoes are dangerous, it is not the main focus of the passage. While thunderstorms are mentioned in the passage, they are not compared to tornadoes, so Choice *C* is incorrect. Choice *D* is incorrect because the passage does not discuss what to do in the event of a tornado.

13. C: We are looking for an inference—a conclusion that is reached on the basis of evidence and reasoning—from the passage that will likely explain why the famous children's author did not achieve her usual success with the new genre (despite the book's acclaim). Choice *A* is wrong because the statement is false according to the passage. Choice *B* is wrong because, although the passage says the author has a graduate degree on the subject, it would be an unrealistic leap to infer that she is the foremost expert on Antebellum America. Choice *D* is wrong because there is nothing in the passage to lead us to infer that people generally prefer a children's series to historical fiction. In contrast, Choice *C* can be logically inferred since the passage speaks of the great success of the children's series and the declaration that the fame of the author's name causes the children's books to "fly off the shelves." Thus, we can infer that she did not receive any bump from her name since she published the historical novel under a pseudonym, which makes Choice *C* correct.

14. D: The author finishes the passage by applying Washington's farewell address to modern politics, so the purpose probably includes this application. Choice *A* is incorrect because George Washington is already a well-established

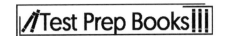
historical figure; furthermore, the passage does not seek to introduce him. Choice *B* is incorrect because the author is not fighting a common perception that Washington was merely a military hero. Choice *C* is incorrect because the author is not convincing readers. Persuasion does not correspond to the passage. Choice *D* states the primary purpose.

15. A: The passage follows a clear and logical sequence, beginning with the warming of the Earth's surface and ending with cloud formation. Words and phrases such as "in the first step," "next," and "finally" serve as evidence of the sequential structure. The passage does not compare and contrast steps or offer the steps as part of a problem-solution relationship, so Choices *B* and *C* are incorrect. Although the passage explains how each step of the process causes an outcome, Choice *D* is not the best answer.

16. B: The best answer is Choice *B*, since the passage is written in the first-person perspective. This allows readers to experience the events through the narrator's senses and emotions. The narrator describes the unsettling experience of being jolted awake by an unfamiliar sound at night, conveying a sense of panic and uncertainty. In this way, the point of view enhances the tone of curiosity and anxiety, drawing readers into the suspenseful atmosphere as they wonder about the origin of the mysterious noise. The narrative style does not create distance between reader and narrator, so Choice *A* is incorrect. The first-person point of view is not objective, so Choice *C* is incorrect. Since the story is told using the pronoun "I," readers know that the narrator is involved in the plot, so Choice *D* is incorrect.

17. C: This sentence specifically addresses the development of emotional intelligence through arts education, emphasizing its importance in fostering empathy, tolerance, and effective communication. It directly connects the skills cultivated in the arts to the broader context of preparing students for active and positive engagement in a diverse and interconnected society. Choice *A* mentions problem-solving skills and self-discipline, while Choice *B* mentions academic performance; these elements are valuable but don't directly relate to community engagement. Choice *D* touches on the broader impact of neglecting arts education but doesn't explicitly focus on the development of skills relevant to community participation.

18. A: The explanation of the orientation and size of a basketball hoop gives readers a familiar anchor point as they learn about an ancient, lesser-known sport. It helps readers understand that a pok-ta-pok hoop was similar to a basketball hoop, only smaller and oriented in a different direction. Choices *B* and *D* are incorrect because the passage does not dwell on basketball; it only mentions basketball as a specific point of reference. Choice *C* is incorrect because the passage does not explain the origins of basketball.

19. A: The best answer for the blank is Choice *A* because it perfectly captures the idea of "Natalia's years of hard work and planning" leading to success. "Fruition" refers to the point at which something is achieved or realized, and in this context, it conveys the successful opening of Natalia's bakery after a period of dedicated effort. Choice *B* is tempting because it suggests an end result; however, "closure" generally refers to the resolution of an emotional situation rather than the realization of a plan or goal. "Interruption" suggests a disruption or hindrance, and "deterioration" implies a decline in quality or condition.

20. C: Choice *C* is best because it accurately describes the wealth, prosperity, and abundance of the neighborhood. "Luxurious mansions, upscale boutiques, and exclusive restaurants" are indicative of a high socioeconomic status. "Affluence" means "having a great deal of wealth," and in this context, it aligns well with the opulent characteristics of the neighborhood. Choice *A* does not fit because "decrepitude" implies a state of decline or deterioration. Choice *B*, "barrenness" implies emptiness or abandonment. "Congeniality" refers to friendliness or compatibility, which is unrelated to the economic status of the neighborhood, so Choice *D* is incorrect.

Writing

1. D: This is a difficult question. The paragraph is incorrect as-is because it is too long and thus loses the reader as it changes focus halfway through. Choice *D* is correct because if the new paragraph began with "While studying at

Triton," we would see a smooth transition from one paragraph to the next. We can also see how the two paragraphs are logically split in two. The first half of the paragraph talks about where he studied. The second half of the paragraph talks about the NAACP and the result of his leadership in the association. If we look at the passage as a whole, we can see that there are two main topics that should be broken into two separate paragraphs.

2. A: The BPP is another activist group. We can figure out this answer by looking at context clues. We know that the BPP is "similar in function" to the NAACP. To find out what the NAACP's function is, we must look at the previous sentences. We know from above that the NAACP is an activist group, so we can assume that the BPP is also an activist group.

3. A: Choice *C* is incorrect because it misplaces the apostrophe. While Choice *D* contains proper construction of a possessive, it changes the name of the organization from the Black Panther Party to the Black Panther Parties. Choice *B* also changes the name of the organization, and it doesn't use a possessive form.

4. C: Choice *C* is correct because the passage is in the past tense and "enabled" is a past tense verb. Choice *A*, "enable," is present tense. Choice *B*, "are enabling," is a present participle, which suggests a continuing action. Choice *D*, "will enable," is future tense.

5. D: The only pact that is mentioned is the nonaggression pact discussed in Sentence 17, so *After Sentence 17*, Choice *D*, is the most logical placement. Choice *A* is incorrect because Sentence 8 talks about recreational facilities and improved educational resources for the black community, so an alliance between blacks, Puerto Ricans, and poor youth would be out of place if discussed after Sentence 8. Choices *B* and *C* are incorrect. The main clue that the sentence should not go after Sentence 13 or Sentence 16 is that there has been no pact mentioned in either of these sentences.

6. B: Sentence 1 does not function well as the introduction to the passage, so Choice *A* is incorrect. Without any introduction to a specific piece of literature, it refers to the various tales. At this point, the reader does not know which tales the writer is referring to. However, the second sentence mentions the Canterbury Tales, and this sentence does function well as an introductory sentence for the passage. Choice *B* is correct because Sentence 1 elaborates on what is said in Sentence 3, and it does not disrupt the flow between Sentence 3 and Sentence 4 because Sentence 4 still makes sense when it follows Sentence 1. Choice *C* is incorrect because the sentence would break the flow between Sentence 6 and Sentence 7 and its content would be out of place in this location. Choice *D* is incorrect because this paragraph is not a conclusion to the overall passage. This passage describes how Chaucer uses various styles and tones to tell the stories from the characters' perspectives. Since Sentence 1 also focuses on the presence of Chaucer's internal character, it would not make a good concluding sentence to this paragraph.

7. C: Choice *C* is the correct answer because *these* is the incorrect pronoun for this particular section of the sentence; instead, the singular pronoun *this* should be used. Therefore, Choice *A* is incorrect. While Choice *B* correctly uses *this*, it also inserts a comma afterwards, which disrupts the flow of the sentence. Choice *D* is incorrect because it uses *these* and incorrectly uses *through* instead of *by*.

8. A: Choice *A* is the correct answer because there are no issues with this section of the sentence. The whole sentence is clear and uses proper punctuation. Choice *B* lacks an introductory comma after *likewise*, which is incorrect. Choices *C* and *D* add unnecessary commas.

9. C: Choice *C* is correct because *reliable* is a more formal way than the word *legit*, which is an informal slang term, to convey that Chaucer provides an honest or genuine view of his characters. The tone of the passage is formal, so the word choices should all be formal. Sentence 14 contrasts Chaucer's narrative with the narratives of "questionable storytellers," which points us in the direction of choosing words such as *reliable* or *true*. Although Choice *B* is a form of *true*, this is not the correct form for this sentence. Choice *D* is incorrect because *doubtful* would not be the appropriate description of the perspective given by Chaucer's narrative since a main idea in the passage is that Chaucer is an honest storyteller.

10. B: Choice *B* is correct because this sentence gives an example of a poorly written and crassly delivered story, adding a supporting detail for the previous sentence. Additionally, without this example, the next sentence, which mentions the drunken character, would have no basis. Choice *A* is incorrect because the passage does not mention schools banning this passage. Choice *C* is incorrect because the writer has moved on from explaining the style in the *Knight's Tale* and is now explaining a contrasting style, using the *Miller's Tale* as an example. Choice *D* is incorrect because the next sentence goes on to explain that Chaucer's purpose is to tell the story the way a drunk character would. It does not say nor does it imply that Chaucer was drunk.

11. B: Choice *B* is best because it relates the concluding sentence back to the subject of the passage. Choice *A* is only tangentially related to the topic of arboriculture, Choice *C* is not specific to the profession being discussed, and Choice *D* contradicts the information found in Sentence 4.

12. C: Choice *C* is best as it removes the portion of the sentence that becomes redundant after the phrase "a sick human being" is used. Choice *A* leaves in the redundancy of "that has come down with an illness," Choice *B* removes all context for the phrase "a sick human being," and Choice *D* makes the sentence read as if an arborist treats trees with the same treatment used on human beings.

13. A: Choice *A* is best as each of these sentences contain necessary information that fits alongside and enhances their surrounding sentences. Choice *B* expands on the information found in Sentence 15, Choice *C* introduces the new topic of discussion in Sentence 15, and Choice *D* introduces the topic of tree diagnosis as found in Sentence 6.

14. C: Choice *C* is best as the structure of this phrase matches the other phrases in the series, which each contain a verb corresponding to "They can" as well as one or more direct objects. Choices *A, B,* and *D* do not match the other phrases in the series as Choice *A* is a clause with its own subject, *soil;* Choice *B* uses the wrong verb tense for the subject *they;* and Choice *D* does not have a verb to describe an action upon the soil at all.

15. B: Choice *B* is best as the plural "many pathways" agrees with both instances of the verb *are* in the sentence. Choice *A* makes *pathway* singular despite *are* being plural, Choice *C* leaves *pathway* singular despite adding the plural modifier *many,* and Choice *D* keeps the modifier, *a,* singular while making *pathways* plural.

16. B: Choice *B* is best because its subject, Chavez's military service, distracts from the passage's overall theme of Cesar Chavez's fight for farm workers' rights. Sentence 5 discusses the union Chavez founded, Sentence 17 discusses Chavez's enduring legacy in farm worker collective bargaining, and Sentence 16 likewise introduces the discussion of Chavez's legacy as found in Sentence 17.

17. C: Choice *C* is best because it removes the unnecessary hyphen separating *systemic* and *labor.* Choice *A* uses an unnecessary hyphen, Choice *B* changes the nature of the issue (labor) into a descriptor for systemic issues, and Choice *D* uses an unnecessary hyphen between *labor* and *issues.*

18. C: Choice *C* is best because it qualifies the nature of the boycotts, protests, and strikes as being successful. Choice *A* places the modifier on "farms in the United States," Choice *B* qualifies the awareness that was raised by the activities as being successful, and Choice *D* places the modifier only on *boycotts* and not on *protests* or *strikes.*

19. B: Choice *B* is best as it most accurately conveys that the UFW received a victory when the bill was passed. Choice *A* implies that the UFW had the victory before the bill was passed, Choice *C* would mean that the UFW forbade its own victory, and Choice *D* implies that the UFW passed the bill themselves.

20. D: Choice *D* is best because it maintains the timeline of the passage. After discussing the UFW's controversial actions and landmark legislative victory, the passage begins to speak about Chavez's later years leading to his passing. Choice A implies that there is a mutual connection between strike-breakers, violence, and pesticides. Choice B implies Chavez walked away from activism. Choice C is incorrect as the passage does not say that the UFW disbanded after 1975.

21. B: Choice B is correct. Placing the sentence at the beginning of the second paragraph introduces the problem of not being able to observe living dinosaurs. This idea is then expanded upon in the rest of the paragraph by explaining that scientists can only compare the remains of dinosaurs to living animals in order to speculate about the functions of various body parts. Choice A is incorrect because the first paragraph begins with an appropriate introductory sentence. The sentence in question would be out of place at the beginning of the first paragraph. Choice C is incorrect because the sentence works better as an introduction rather than a conclusion to this paragraph. Choice D is incorrect. This sentence should be added to the passage because it establishes the point that there are problems with studying animals that can never be observed.

22. A: Choice A is the sentence that should be deleted from the passage. There is no discussion in the passage about knew ideas being inhibited by previous perceptions. Rather, the passage points out that ideas do change as more is learned. Choice B is incorrect because this sentence is important in reinforcing the point that scientists are only going by what they know about modern animals when trying to figure out the purpose of certain characteristics in dinosaurs. Choice C is incorrect because this sentence introduces the topic of this paragraph. Choice D is incorrect because this sentence supports the point being made in this paragraph.

23. D: Choice D correctly applies a semicolon to introduce a new line of thought while remaining in a single sentence. The comma after *however* is also appropriately placed. Choice A is a run-on sentence. Choice B is incorrect because the single comma is not enough to combine the sentences. Choice C adds unnecessary commas around *uncertain* and does not provide the appropriate punctuation around the word *however.*

24. A: Choices B and C add unnecessary commas, while Choice D uses the possessive *its* instead of the contraction *it's.*

25. D: Choice D strengthens the overall sentence structure while condensing the words. This makes the subject of the sentence, and the emphasis of the writer, much clearer to the reader. In Choice A, the language is choppy and over-complicated. Choice B is better, but the use of "For the longest time" is unnecessary. This idea is already implied by saying that "this was the prevailing view on dinosaurs until" certain evidence was found. Choice C introduces unnecessary commas.

ACCUPLACER Practice Tests #3 – #6

To keep the size of this book manageable, save paper, and provide a digital test-taking experience, the 3rd through the 6th practice tests can be found online. Scan the QR code or go to this link to access it:

testprepbooks.com/bonus/accuplacer

The first time you access the tests, you will need to register as a "new user" and verify your email address.

If you have any issues, please email support@testprepbooks.com.

Dear ACCUPLACER Test Taker,

Thank you for purchasing this study guide for your ACCUPLACER exam. We hope that we exceeded your expectations.

Our goal in creating this study guide was to cover all of the topics that you will see on the test. We also strove to make our practice questions as similar as possible to what you will encounter on test day. With that being said, if you found something that you feel was not up to your standards, please send us an email and let us know.

We would also like to let you know about other books in our catalog that may interest you.

TSI

amazon.com/dp/1637754434

SAT

amazon.com/dp/1637753381

ACT

amazon.com/dp/163775583X

We have study guides in a wide variety of fields. If the one you are looking for isn't listed above, then try searching for it on Amazon or send us an email.

Thanks Again and Happy Testing!
Product Development Team
info@studyguideteam.com

FREE Test Taking Tips Video/DVD Offer

To better serve you, we created videos covering test taking tips that we want to give you for FREE. **These videos cover world-class tips that will help you succeed on your test.**

We just ask that you send us feedback about this product. Please let us know what you thought about it—whether good, bad, or indifferent.

To get your **FREE videos**, you can use the QR code below or email freevideos@studyguideteam.com with "Free Videos" in the subject line and the following information in the body of the email:

    a. The title of your product

    b. Your product rating on a scale of 1-5, with 5 being the highest

    c. Your feedback about the product

If you have any questions or concerns, please don't hesitate to contact us at info@studyguideteam.com.

Thank you!

Made in the USA
Las Vegas, NV
10 October 2024

96589402R00188